Comments on "Views On Good News"

Nobody needs to struggle to understand this daily devotional helpful book. It's a pleasure and easy to read. The author gets the reader's attention in the first paragraph by telling a very interesting story or illustration from daily common temporary life. She makes the reader think in the second paragraph by discussing practical, real-life situations that everyone can relate to. Then, she continues by suggesting and presenting a wonderful Christian principle enforced by a Bible verse or two for the reader's spiritual nourishment. Young people and adults alike will enjoy this devotional daily reading and will be blessed if they read it regularly.

Rev. Mgrdich Melkonian, Moderator of the Armenian Evangelical Union of North America and Senior Pastor of First Armenian Presbyterian Church, Fresno, CA.

This book is a real dynamo of spiritual power that will energize and transform your life by enabling you to acquire inspiring ideas and reliable directions from God for each day of the year. The messages of this book will deepen your faith, revive your hope and deliver you from discouragement.

Rev. Kevork (George) Terian, Chairman of the Armenian Evangelical Union of North America Book Publication Committee and Pastor, Armenian Cilicia Evangelical Church, Pasadena, CA.

Jesus used parables to teach His disciples the "Good News!" In her book, *"Views On Good News,"* Asien Surmeian has followed our Lord's teaching model by providing stories and examples from everyday life to illustrate her messages on the Christian faith and lifestyle. This treasury of 365 inspirational meditations is certain to be a blessing to many. At last, we all have ready access to these practical lessons which she has been publishing, as her personal ministry, in the "Armenian Observer" since 1994. Thank you, Asien, for your ongoing faithfulness and commitment to the mission and ministry of sharing the gospel of our Lord and Savior Jesus Christ.

Rev. Ron Tovmassian, Senior Pastor, United Armenian Congregational Church, Los Angeles, CA.

Asien has faithfully walked us through the Bible—using wonderful metaphors to make God's Word come alive. She has captured our hearts as she describes so irresistibly how one may lead a Christ-centered life.

Joyce Philibosian Stein, Indian Wells, CA.

Comments (continued)

Asien Surmeian's weekly essays "Views On Good News" is a most welcomed addition to the "Armenian Observer" and the readers' responses are an excellent testimony to their core meaning. Her thoughts are clearly enunciated based on her experiences and buttressed with apropos quotations from the Good Book, the Bible. There is some history, some psychology, some nationalism and even pragmatism in her essays which make them relative to everyday life. Her topics cover the gamut of everyday life—success, respect, failure stress, enlightenment, marriage, gossip, family relations, and, of course, relationship with God. Her enthusiasm is beyond reproach and her belief in what she writes is very sincere, always giving an optimistic avenue to the right direction. The spirituality sprinkled throughout her essays makes the readers ponder about their own life. Her essays do have a healing power. To quote her: "A careless word may kindle strife; a cruel word may wreck a life. A timely word may lessen strife; a loving word may heal and bless.

Osheen Keshishian, Professor Glendale Community College, Editor & Publisher of the "Armenian Observer," Los Angeles, CA.

In this rich, life-transforming and heart-warming spiritual journey, Asien Surmeian beautifully and movingly shares her living Christian faith by combining Biblical truths with invaluable lessons applied to contemporary life. It is a sheer pleasure to enjoy her weekly columns in the "Armenian Observer," and now, this compilation of her profound and compelling articles offered in a book format, will guide us to direct our collective energies toward what we are for, instead of what we are against, by placing our feet firmly on the right path. What an inspiring and precious gift!

Garbis Der Yeghiayan, Ph.D., President, Mashdots College, Glendale, CA.

Views On Good News

Good News

365 Inspiring Daily Devotionals For Christian Living

By Asien Surmeian

Views On Good News
Copyright © 2003 by Asien Surmeian

Library of Congress Cataloging-in-Publication Data
Surmeian, Asien

Views on Good News: 365 Inspiring Daily Devotionals for Christian Living.

ISBN 0-9742746-0-7
1. Christian growth   2. Devotional

Cover art work: Asien Surmeian

Typesetting: Steve Surmeian
Printing: Windsor Productions
              (windsorpro@mac.com)

Views On Good News
365 Inspiring
Daily Devotionals
For Christian Living

By Asien Surmeian

Armenian Evangelical Union of North America

Book Publication Committee

2003

*A*ffectionately

dedicated to Steve,

my husband and

my best friend.

ACKNOWLEDGEMENTS

*F*irst and foremost, my praise and gratitude is to the Lord for His ever-inspiring divine Word, which is my guide and light for every article I write. May to Him be all the glory!

My thanks and continuous appreciation to my husband Steve for all his word-processing skills in printing and storing all my articles on discs over the years.

My sincere gratitude to Professor Osheen Keshishian, publisher and editor of the weekly newspaper, "The Armenian Observer." I thank Prof. Keshishian for the opportunity and privilege to have a window of ministry since 1994 in his fine publication.

My gratitude also to the Armenian Evangelical Union of North America (AEUNA) for their moral support and their seal of approval. My special thanks to the Rev. Mgrdich Melkonian, Moderator of the AEUNA and Senior Pastor of the First Armenian Presbyterian Church of Fresno, CA, and the Rev. Kevork G. Terian, Chairman of the AEUNA Book Publications Committee and Pastor of the Armenian Cilicia Evangelical Church, Pasadena, CA.

Last but not least, my warm and heartfelt thanks to all those who read my articles through "The Armenian Observer." Their enthusiastic, heartwarming comments to me have been most appreciated and encouraging. I thank them for their vision in suggesting that I compile my articles into a devotional book such as this.

It is my sincere hope that this book will be a blessing to all those who read it. It has certainly been my great joy and blessing to have written these devotionals.

FORWARD

A tourist, while in New York City, decided to visit the Empire State Building at night. He took the elevator, and upon reaching the fiftieth floor, he became disappointed because he saw that the whole city was engulfed in mist and dense fog. The elevator man, who noticed the tourist's disillusionment, said to him, "It's all mist and fog for sixty-six stories up, but after that you will see the star-studded sky."

As we go through life, we encounter many bewildering experiences that leave us dazed and stunned; however, if we cultivate a personal relationship with God, through the regular and systematic study of His immutable Word, the Bible, He will guide us from darkness to light, from doubt to certainty, from fear to a trusting faith, and from confusion to salvation.

The paramount purpose of the Bible-based meditations that Mrs. Surmeian has written is to help us have a closer walk with God Who alone can give us strength, courage and inspiration to surmount obstacles, solve problems and meet the daunting challenge of everyday life in this complicated world. Every page of this book contains a precious nugget of truth that will lead you through the mist and fog of this life to the vast vistas of the spiritual realm. For every day there is a superbly illustrated message that can impart strength to the weak, healing to the depressed, and bring hope to the dying.

One of the astounding values of this book is that it provides a strong antidote for worry which takes the joy out of life and multiplies our misery. Several decades ago, a Chinese Christian, when commenting on the distressing conditions caused by war, said: "It is better to light a candle in the darkness than to curse the darkness." This is exactly what our author does in this book: to dispel the dark and ominous clouds of despair, she lights up the candle of enduring hope because worry cannot set in where hope abides.

We humans have a hunger in our soul that secular reading cannot satisfy, because in every heart there is a vacuum that only God can fill. If you discipline yourself to read one page of this book every day, your focus will shift from temporal priorities to eternal values, your heart will be flooded with unparalleled joy, and your life will be transformed by the grace of Jesus Christ, our exalted Lord and only Savior.

Rev. Kevork (George) Terian,
Chairman, Armenian Evangelical Union of North America Book Publications Committee and Pastor, Armenian Cilicia Evangelical Church, Pasadena, CA

HAPPY NEW YEAR! *January 1*

*E*nthusiastically, the crowd stands every year in the cold of the night by the thousands in Times Square, New York City. Is it a ball game, a rock concert? No! It's just a huge lighted ball that descends from a tall building shortly before midnight. The entire event takes only a minute. It seems hardly worth fighting traffic and subways to experience a few moments of excitement—except that it happens to be New Year's Eve!

This celebration is about passage of time. The old year's problems become a dim memory when we think of getting a fresh start. The words of St. Paul come to mind: "Forgetting those things which are behind and reaching forward to those things which are ahead, I press toward the goal..." (Phil.3: 13). With the single-mindedness of an athlete in training, St. Paul is teaching us to lay aside everything harmful, and to forsake anything that may distract us from being effective Christians.

Entering the New Year provides us with an excellent opportunity to make a fresh start. Remembering God's faithfulness and forgetting past mistakes can make entering the New Year a time of joyous anticipation.

A dear friend whose husband recently suffered a mild heart attack confessed to me that often a life-threatening experience has a way of rearranging one's priorities. "Unfortunately," she added, "It took a heart attack to bring into sharper focus what's really important in life. Now we don't participate in things that are shallow or meaningless in the long run." There is wisdom in their conclusion. Like the author of Psalm 39, they realized that life is too short, and we have less time than we think to waste on things that have no lasting significance or value. Verses 5 and 7 say, "Certainly every man at his best state is but vapor...Surely they busy themselves in vain...And now, Lord, what do I wait for? My hope is in You!"

Life is short no matter how long we live. If there is something important we want to do, we must not put it off for a better day. We must express our love to those for whom we care as often as we can. If there is an undisciplined area in our lives, perhaps we can work at it. And above all, we must continue to be exemplary ambassadors for Christ. King David, the author of Psalm 39, realized that accomplishing worldly tasks would have no value in eternity.

Have we reached the same conclusion? God alone can deliver us from a life of meaningless activities. Let's not wait for a close call with death to be convinced of the importance of making the most out of life. It's <u>how</u> we live that matters—not <u>how long</u>. As we stand with our backs to the past year and our faces directed toward the New Year, we can be confident that we are not afraid to enter the unknown future when we walk with the all-knowing God.

May the Lord bless you all and give you a delightful surprise during each day in the New Year. A joyous and Happy New Year to you all!

A NEW YEARS INVITATION

*W*e are cordially invited to receive God's blessings. In the months ahead, God has a special invitation for each one of us. His Word, the Bible, is our invitation. The dress code? Come as you are. No R.S.V.P. is needed to "Discipleship." Come and see.

Andrew and John were Jesus' first disciples. They heard John the Baptist refer to Jesus as the "Lamb of God," and when they saw Him passing by, they followed Him. They walked right behind him. Turning around, Jesus asked, "What do you seek?" The two replied, "Teacher, where are you staying?" Jesus answered, "Come and see" (John 1: 35 – 39). They went, and that was the most important invitation they had ever received.

By the end of the day, Andrew found his brother, Simon Peter, and told him that they had found the Messiah! Isn't it amazing that so many centuries later, we still seek the same Messiah! We, like millions before us, want to know Him better. It is also amazing that Jesus still extends the same invitation to us today: "Come and see." We are invited to experience Christ's love.

The Bible is God's open invitation to all of us. He invites us to enjoy renewed life in His Kingdom the moment we trust him. What we'll receive we cannot purchase anywhere. Once we have it, no one can take it away from us. It's a gift from God by grace.

In the months ahead, can we truly afford to depend entirely on ourselves and hope for the best, or should we put our hope and trust in God and do our very best as well? Through faith in Him, we can be filled with hope that never fails and life that will never end spiritually. Some individuals might still be looking everywhere but to God for purpose and meaning in their lives. Why wait until all else has failed before trying God? Why save the best for last? In the months ahead, the same invitation still reads: Come as you are. "Come and see!"

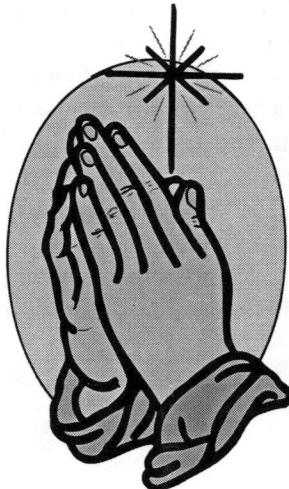

*H*ow would you rate the past year? It was a good year for most of us. Some might even like to stay there for a while longer, but we can't. It is time to put away the old date book. It is time to hang the new calendar on the wall and make a fresh start—a new beginning.

Talking about beginnings, we cannot do better than the Bible. "In the beginning God created the heavens and the earth." Genesis 1: 1 answers the age-old question of the universe's origin. Even more important, that opening verse introduces us to the majestic One Who is behind it all.

As another new year begins, it seems appropriate to turn to the beginnings of the Bible and read the account of how the eternal God spoke the world into existence. God as Creator, is of course, just one of the many descriptions of the Almighty that the Bible reveals to us. Therefore it seems a good idea to use the new year to study His Word and learn more about who He is to each of us personally.

The Bible not only tells us that the world was created by God, it also tells us who God is. It reveals God's deepest desire; to relate and to fellowship with those whom He created. God took the ultimate step toward fellowship with us through His historic entrance to this planet in the person of His Son, Jesus Christ. Yes, we can know our Creator in a very personal way.

God is the only one who can make things new for us. Along with the old calendar and date books, we can cast aside some of our old negative attitudes as well. We can call on God, the "renewal specialist," to help us build new spiritual values into our lives. I like Psalm 5:10 which says, "Create in me a pure heart O God, and renew a steadfast spirit in me." It is a prayer for a pure heart and a steadfast spirit of faithfulness to God and a willing spirit of service.

Ten unforgettable words: "In the beginning God created the heavens and the earth." In this age of sophisticated science, we can be influenced to miss this key point because so much of what we read assumes a godless origin of this world. We know our Creator is the Living God. Just ten words. Let us not forget them. They are the foundation of all the beauty and majesty of the universe.

As the new year moves along, why not make a special effort to know God more intimately? Let us use this year to know God as never before.

*I*n the beginning of a year, many magazines and newspapers often chronicle the best and the worst of the past twelve months, and some even offer predictions for the coming year. If a news magazine were to do a feature on our lives, what would it say about the best and the worst of our past year as children of God? Based on recent actions, what might it predict about our spiritual life in the months ahead?

Our past does not have to be our future. No matter how many times we might have failed, God graciously offers His forgiveness for all the shortcomings and poor choices we may have made when we repent and ask for His forgiveness. It is also true that our past successes do not guarantee future victories. Each new day of the new year will present us opportunities, once again, to choose God's way, or succumb to tests and temptations. But in the new year, we also have the opportunity to wipe the slate clean and make a fresh new start!

The Apostle Paul says in Phil. 3:13 – 14, "…Forgetting those things which are behind and reaching forward to those things which are ahead…" St Paul had reason to forget what was behind. He had approved of and even held the coats of those who stoned St. Stephen, the first Christian martyr. Paul was called Saul then (Acts 7:57, 58).

Most of us perhaps have done a few things of which we may not be proud. But because our hope is in Christ, we can let go of the past, and look forward to what God will help us become. We must not dwell on our past, but only learn from it. And never let our past actions cloud our bright new future.

In the Old Testament the prophet Amos tells us about a vision he saw. The Lord was holding a plumb line next to a wall, which represented Israel (Am.7:8). God had made this nation straight and true, but it no longer measured up to His standards. A plumb line is a cord with a weight tied to one end. Bricklayers use it to ensure that the wall they are building is straight. Another plumb line prophet stands in the New Testament. He is the Plumb Line Itself, and His name is Jesus Christ. Comparing our lives with His shows how far out of line we are from what God requires. God's Word is our plumb line that makes us become aware of our actions. How do we measure up to that?

If our hearts desire that we grow spiritually and have a closer walk with the Lord, we can consider studying God's Word more often, and apply its principles to our daily lives. Realizing that we are forgiven, we can move on to a life of faith and obedience, and look forward to a fuller and more meaningful life. As He convicts and guides us, we will discover that He straightens us little by little, and we become more and more conformed to His image.

During the year ahead, let us make it our goal to get to know God even better. We should also pause and appreciate God's blessings. The key question is: Are we willing to let this Plumb Line—Jesus Christ—measure and remake us each day? Christ is the only builder who can straighten any crooked life!

*W*ho does not like to look at rainbows? The largest and brightest ones I have ever seen were in the islands of Hawaii—just breathtaking! The multicolored arc in the sky, which is caused by reflection of sunlight through droplets of water, is first mentioned in Genesis 9:12 – 16. The rainbow appears as a sign of God's gracious covenant promise with Noah, and His pledge that never again would He destroy all flesh by flood.

The rainbow of God's grace in Genesis 9, however, fades when compared to God's New Testament grace shown at Calvary. At the cross, God demonstrated His love for us through the sacrificial death of His Son, Jesus Christ. At the cross, Christ the sinless lamb alone carried the sins of this world. And at the cross, God's wrath against sin was placed on Jesus Christ, Who became every believer's substitute. When the Light of the world met the storm clouds of judgment at Calvary, a beautiful bow of promise and forgiveness came into view! And the Bible says, one day, all His people will gather around God's throne where a rainbow encircles it (Rev.4: 3).

Christ is the true light of the world. As His followers, we reflect His light to the world around us. Our exemplary lives must point unbelievers to Christ. Perhaps there are a few who may not yet have recognized that light or have somehow distanced themselves from Him. They may feel that their lives are too complex for God to understand. But God created the entire universe, and nothing is impossible for Him. God's love and power are bigger than any problem that we may have.

Although God created the world, the people He created eventually forsook Him. Even His chosen people, who were to be the light to the rest of the world for the coming Messiah, rejected Him, despite the fact that the Old Testament pointed to His coming. Then God sent His only begotten Son. What Jesus taught and did are tied inseparably to Who He is. Jesus is fully human and fully divine. Although He took upon Himself full humanity and lived as a man, He never ceased to be the eternal God Who existed before time began; the Creator and Sustainer of all things, and the source of eternal life. This is the truth about Christ, and the foundation of all truth (Jn.1: 1).

Yes, Christ is the Light of the world. So, the next time we see a rainbow in the sky above, let us remember that Christ, the Light of the world, met the storm clouds of judgment at Calvary where a precious promise of forgiveness was made. It is God's promise of a free gift of eternal life for all those who turn to him by faith. This is God's abundant love, mercy and grace, and His everlasting covenant of forgiveness and peace to all mankind through Christ Jesus.

*I*n biblical times, when a king or emperor was to visit a certain region, the existing bumpy roads were made straight and surfaced to make the monarch's journey smooth. A herald was also sent in advance to prepare the people for the king's arrival. John the Baptist had that task; to prepare the hearts of the people of Israel for their coming king—Christ, the Messiah.

Every life has a purpose, and God chose John for this extraordinary mission. John was the son of a righteous couple, Zacharias the priest and his wife Elizabeth, who were advanced in age and childless. And yet, in God's perfect timing, an angel of the Lord appeared to Zacharias announcing that their long desire for a son would be fulfilled. Elizabeth would bear a son, and his name was to be John. He would be filled with the Holy Spirit even from his mother's womb, and he would prepare people for the coming of the Lord (Lk. 1: 11 – 25).

The Bible describes John's childhood in one sentence: "And the child grew and became strong in the spirit; and he lived in the desert until he appeared publicly to Israel" (Lk. 1:80). He was about age 30 (six months older than Jesus) when he began his ministry. His message was "the baptism of repentance for the remission of sins" (Lk. 3:3). People from all over Judea went to be baptized by him in the Jordan River, confessing their sins. Some asked if he was the long-expected Messiah. John said that there is One coming after him Who is mightier than he. He will baptize you, not with water, but with the Holy Spirit.

John saw Jesus coming toward him and said, "Behold! The Lamb of God Who takes away the sins of the world" (Jn. 1:29). John felt unworthy to baptize Jesus, but Jesus said, "Permit it to be so now, for it is fitting for us to fulfill all righteousness" (Mt. 3:15).

Why did Jesus, Who was completely sinless, ask to be baptized? Jesus didn't need the "baptism of repentance," but He did it to obey the Father, and God showed His approval. When Jesus came out of the water, the heavens were opened to Him, and the Holy Spirit descended like a dove and lighted upon Him. And a voice came from heaven saying, "This is My beloved Son, in Whom I am well pleased" (Mt. 3:16, 17). This was indeed a theophany—the manifestation of God.

This occasion marked the beginning of Christ's Messianic ministry. Through the baptism He was consecrated to God with His divine approval. Although Jesus was filled with the Holy Spirit from birth, this was a unique divine anointing that was bestowed upon Him as Christ the Savior! From this point on, miracles accompanied His teaching with God's spirit upon Him.

John the Baptist knew his purpose in life. He was part of God's plan from the moment he was conceived. He prepared the people's hearts for the coming of the Lord! He felt unworthy to even loosen Jesus' sandals, the lowliest slave's task. He says in Jn. 3:30, "He must increase, but I must decrease." God has a purpose for all of us. We can trust Him to guide us. God can use each one of us in His service. As His ambassadors on earth, have we made ourselves available?

𝒫eople often feel that one has to be deprived of fun in life to please God. That is perhaps the idea many have about Christian life; a series of joyless tasks, rather than having the freedom to do what they please. True freedom, however, is not doing what we want; on the contrary, true freedom comes from choosing to do that which is right.

Over a year ago, I had an experience that focused on my freedom as a driver and the law. Driving out of a parking lot, I was waiting for an opportunity to make a left turn into a busy two-way street. Suddenly I realized that out of several exits I could have taken, I chose the one that was leading me to cross over a double-double yellow line. I was upset with myself for not thinking clearly, because I knew this street well. I considered backing up, but several cars behind me were already waiting for me impatiently. I had no place to go but complete my turn. Well, I did, and so did all the cars behind me!

For the next mile or so, I was miserable. I kept looking in my rear-view mirror to see if a police car with flashing lights was following me. I was lucky. Was this really freedom? I had put myself into a kind of bondage for a short time. The lesson I was reminded of once again, was that true freedom is doing what is right. Some of us perhaps long for the freedom to do whatever we please. Paradoxically, freedom is not found in release from restraint, but in submission to the way of life given to us for our protection.

In 1 Peter 2: 16 we read, "Live as free men, but do not use your freedom as cover-up for evil; live as servants of God. Show proper respect to everyone....fear God." We are taught to be good citizens of the earthly government under which we live, and be law abiding, obedient, and to promote the good name of Christians and Armenians as well. Obedience gives us peace of mind and heart with the freedom to be ourselves.

In the same way, God's Word is not a yoke of bondage and joyless life. Rather, it is one of true freedom and joy, knowing that our all-loving Heavenly Father is with us always. Let us not take advantage of all the freedoms available to us. We can do what we please, if what we do pleases God. True freedom is doing what is right.

"*L*ove your neighbor as yourself" did not make much sense while I was growing up. How far from my home could I consider as my neighborhood? Was it five houses across the street from where I lived, and five houses opposite to that? What about the people down the street, or the next block? I was to love my neighbor as myself, but who was my neighbor?

In the gospel of Luke Chapter 10, Jesus uses a most meaningful parable to illustrate that. During Christ's ministry, an expert in the law, wishing to test Jesus, said, "Teacher, what must I do to inherit eternal life?" Jesus answered with a question, "What is written in the law?" The man answered with the two commandments he was taught: "Love the Lord your God with all your heart and with all your soul and with all your strength and with all your mind; and love your neighbor as yourself." "You have answered correctly," Jesus said. "Do this and you will live." This man, however, wanted to justify himself, so he said to Jesus, "Who is my neighbor?" Jesus answered by telling the parable of the Good Samaritan. This parable is perhaps one of the most superb classics on the subject of human kindness in all literature; well known to all.

A certain traveler was robbed, beaten and left on the road half dead. Two Jews, a priest and a Levite, walked by, saw him, but each ignored him and passed on the other side of the road. A Samaritan traveler, however, had pity on him and stopped to help. After caring for his immediate needs, he took him to the nearest inn. He paid two days' wages to the innkeeper for the injured man's care, with the assurance of paying more upon his return. Applying this to today's language, he was better than dialing 911!

Jesus asks now, "Which of these three do you think was the neighbor to the man who fell into the hands of robbers?" The expert in the law replied, "The one who had mercy on him." Jesus said, "Go and do likewise."

There was such open hostility between Jews and Samaritans in those days that the teacher of the law couldn't even bear to say "Samaritan" in answer to Jesus' question. By this parable Jesus asserted that love knows no national boundaries. Our neighbor is any one of any race, creed, or social background who is in need. Love means acting to meet a person's need.

As we examine the two greatest commandments, we see a God-centered life. Love for God is our vertical relationship with our Creator. Love for neighbor is for every one we come in contact with. That is our horizontal relationship with our fellow man. The two form the sign of a cross! Without a vertical line, a cross becomes a minus sign. It is incomplete. The two are the greatest commandments of all! They were essential then, and they remain essential for us today. The closer we come to our Creator, the easier it becomes to love our fellow man. Through His love we realize that neighborhoods have no boundaries. Through His love we can even love the unlovable. God's love daily sensitizes our hearts, minds and attitudes, and prepares us to love our neighbor. By God's grace our growth and maturity will continue throughout our lifetime. We are indeed all Christians under construction.

*T*he following amusing prayer was given to me by a friend. Most of us would identify with the request if we wish to be honest before the Lord. Here it is:

"Dear Lord, so far today, I have done all right. I haven't gossiped, haven't lost my temper, haven't been greedy, grumpy, nasty, selfish or overindulgent. I am thankful for that. But in a few minutes, God, I am going to get out of bed, and from then on, I will probably need a lot more help. Amen."

If we think we can get through the day without the Lord, we are mistaken. We need His divine guidance, wisdom and discernment in every area of our lives. If we are willing to ask for it, we can trust that God will always meet our needs. The alarm has already gone off. We are out of bed. We brush away our mental cobwebs and think of the day ahead. We ask ourselves, "What shall I wear today?" The Lord cares about what we wear, but He is more concerned about what we "put on" spiritually.

The Apostle Paul offers a strategy to help us know what to "put on." The dress code is in Gal. 5:22: "But the Fruit of the Spirit is love, joy, peace, patience, kindness, goodness, faithfulness, gentleness and self-control." St. Paul uses the metaphor of "fruit" we are to produce to describe the conduct of the faithful.

Love refers not to an emotional affection or physical attraction, but to respect and devotion that willingly leads to self-sacrificial service for our love for God. Joy is a delight based on unchanging divine promises and eternal spiritual realities. Joy is not the result of favorable circumstances. It is present in the believer's heart, even when the circumstances are most painful. Joy is a gift from God, and as such, believers are to rejoice in the blessing. Peace is the inner calm that results from the confidence in one's relationship with Christ. Patience refers to the ability to endure irritating situations, and the power to wait calmly.

Kindness is a tender concern for others, reflected in a desire to treat others gently, just as the Lord treats all faithful. Goodness is the moral and spiritual excellence manifested in active kindness. Faithfulness is the loyalty and trustworthiness taught in God's Word. Gentleness is a humble attitude which has no desire for revenge or retaliation. And self-control is the discipline to restrain one's impulses and the strength to resist temptation.

What a divinely designed wardrobe St. Paul has for us! It is the indwelling of the Holy Spirit that produces these virtues in all those who walk depending on the Lord. This is why the person was praying in bed, seeking God's help. If we want the Fruit of the Spirit to grow in us, we must join our lives to Christ daily; know Him, Love Him, imitate Him.

How has our day been so far? Living righteously in today's world is not easy. But dressed with the Fruit of the Spirit daily is never out of style! Here we have nine divinely designed accessories to dress for success!

*L*ife presents us with the privilege of choices and possibilities. Some are bad, others are good, and a few the very best. Each of us must decide and choose; what are our first priorities in life? What is our purpose for living? We have only one life. We can live it any way we wish, but we can live it only once!

Christ Himself gave us the uppermost priority when He said in Matthew 6:33, "But seek first the Kingdom of God and His righteousness, and all these things shall be added to you." Meaning, above and beyond everything else, we must pursue this first. Many people in the world today, however, are not receptive to the Word of God. And yet, "seek first" means a strong-minded pursuit with persistence and determination. As Christians, we must always determine and do what is right. Can success in any field be achieved without commitment, courage and determination?

In a world of instant everything, "seek first" is not a popular belief. But if we really want to follow our dreams, such as a God-given idea, a plan, or a goal that leads to God-honoring results, we must develop and exercise courage and vision. Vision is the ability to see above and beyond the majority. For Christians, vision is knowing how to include God's power into our circumstances and remain focused in spite of obstacles. When we have a God-given dream, we will also receive God-given drive as well. We can be certain of that!

The events in Numbers chapters 13 and 14 are fascinating. Caleb and Joshua were among the 12 spies sent by Moses to investigate Canaan, the Promised Land. Forty days later, the group returned with a divided report. Ten were panicked and negative about everything they saw, but Caleb and Joshua were enthusiastic. Two had vision and courage to stand against the ten and expressed their dreams. The other ten did not.

What an illustration of life! Unfortunately, those who lack vision and courage, and refuse to dream are always in the majority. They always outnumber those who "walk by faith and not by sight" (2 Cor. 5:7). The ten focused on the negative; two focused on what could easily be accomplished by the power of God. Ten were intimidated by the size of the Canaanite men and their power; two were confident in the power of their great God. Ten saw problems; two saw solutions. Isn't it sad when we focus on obstacles rather than seek answers?

What is our "Canaan" today? What is our challenge? What "giants" in our lives make us feel like "grasshoppers"? How does the future look for us today – at school, in business or at home? Caleb and Joshua came back having seen exactly the same obstacles the other ten spies saw, but they had a different attitude. They enthusiastically said, we can do it. And so can we! Although we live in a negative world where the majority says we can't, we know we can when we trust God. Our heavenly Father is watching over us. He is loving—He cares. That can make all the difference in the world for us Christians.

ALWAYS ON TARGET

*A*n acquaintance of mine recently was practicing to improve his archery skills. Seeing him, I remembered a story I was told some time ago.

A traveler was crossing the country by car. Driving through a small town, he noticed several target boards on trees and walls with the arrows always shot exactly into the center of the bull's-eye. Curious, he stopped at the town's diner for lunch. Interested to meet this skillful archer, he asked the waiter if he knew that person. It happened that the archer also was having lunch at the same diner, and they met. After complimenting the man for his talent and skill in archery, the traveler asked him if he had a special trick that he could share. "Certainly," said the archer, "it's very simple. I first shoot the arrows, then I draw the circles around them!"

In a similar way, some people try to twist Scripture to justify their actions. Again and again, we hear about individuals who take God's Word and give it their own personal interpretation that supports their agenda. In their desire to conform to the world's shifting values, they compromise and twist the words of God to suit their life style. The Bible is a powerful book, "inspired by God" (2 Tim. 3:16), one that can change lives and influence the world for good.

Therefore, St. Peter warns us about individuals who do not approach God's Word with honest motives, respect its authority, and who distort its message. He says in 2 Peter 3:17, "...Be on your guard so that you may not be carried away by the error of lawless men and fall from your secure position. But grow in the grace and knowledge of Christ."

The Word of God is like an archer's arrow, and it never fails to hit the intended mark. If God's Words often strike us in our hearts, we should delight in them. They may at times hit us where it hurts, but they will also meet our deepest needs. God's Word is always on target!

*T*he story is told about an atheist who embraced Christianity. The new convert went to his pastor and said, "Before I became a Christian I stole a rope from my neighbor's barn. After reading about Zacchaeus in the Bible, I decide to return it. But my neighbor still won't reconcile with me." The pastor questioned him a little further. "Are you sure that's all you took from the barn?" Embarrassed, the man replied, "Well, to be perfectly honest, I didn't return what was attached to the rope—my neighbor's prize calf!"

Zacchaeus was a chief tax collector (Luke 19:1 – 10). Rome imposed heavy taxes on all nations under their control. Tax collectors were Jews by birth who chose to work for Rome. They overcharged their fellow man, keeping the extra money for themselves, and were considered traitors. Zacchaeus, as chief tax collector, certainly was wealthy.

It was at this time that Jesus entered Jericho. Zacchaeus wanted to see Jesus. Because of the crowd and being small in stature, the Bible says he climbed a tree for a better view. Jesus saw him and called him by name. "Zacchaeus, make haste and come down, for today I must stay at your house." It is the only place in the gospels where Jesus invited Himself to be someone's guest. Zacchaeus welcomed Jesus joyfully. The people murmured that He was visiting a sinner! Despite this, Jesus loved him.

Once in the house, Zacchaeus had a genuine change of heart. Christ's visit and love moved him. He stood up and said, "Lord, I give half my possessions to the poor, and if I have cheated anyone out of anything, I will pay back four times the amount." What had happened to this man, this traitor? Jesus hadn't even had an opportunity to minister to him! This event took place toward the end of Christ's three years' ministry. Zacchaeus must have heard of Jesus' teachings. Matthew, one of Christ's disciples, also a tax collector, had left a comfortable life to follow Jesus (Matt. 9:9 –13). Zacchaeus undoubtedly knew Matthew as a colleague. Zacchaeus had begun to reevaluate his life, and didn't like what he saw.

When Jesus entered his house, Zacchaeus knew what to do. He demonstrated inward change by outward action. He proved his faith by a complete change of heart and behavior. Jesus forgave him and said that He had come to seek and to save that which was lost. Jesus knocks on the doors of our hearts as well, and still loves to bring as many as possible into His Kingdom, no matter what our background or previous way of life. Only when we allow Him to become the Lord of our lives, can we experience His abundant blessings.

The new convert in the above story soothed his conscience by taking back only the "rope." He finally realized that by taking back the "calf" also would demonstrate his true regret and remorse. Honest restitution is a mark of genuine repentance. It has been said: God formed us, sin deformed us, but Christ can transform us!

*I*t has been said that success often rises out of the ashes of failure. When we are hit the hardest and things seem at their worst, we must still try our hardest and never quit. The following individuals did just that.

What would one think of an inventor who fails hundreds of times in his experiments? That was Thomas Edison, one of the greatest inventors in history. After countless failures he discovered a filament that would stay lit in his incandescent light bulb. He did not quit—he persevered.

Victor Hugo, a well-known French novelist, was quite popular in the early days of his career. He would not bow his knee to Napoleon III, and he fought bitterly against him with his pen. Hugo was soon banished out of France for 19 years. While in exile he wrote his greatest works. Hugo said later, "Why was I not exiled sooner?" Difficulties opened his heart and soul to the problems of humankind and gave him vision to create his most brilliant works.

In 1944, James Michener served in the U.S. Navy on a remote Pacific island. His war experiences provided the material for a book. Although he realized that short stories were not popular, the book was published nevertheless. Reviews said it had a few possibilities but it would never win a Pulitzer Prize. This work received the 1947 Pulitzer Prize for fiction and was the source of the musical play "South Pacific."

St. Paul is the best example of someone who persevered despite apparent failures. His list of seeming failures and suffering would have led most of us to quit. He was imprisoned numerous times, shipwrecked, stoned several times, and experienced beatings, hunger and thirst (2 Cor. 11:23 – 27). By these and many more persecutions, we could easily see him utterly defeated. Yet, St. Paul's ministry is well known, studied and accepted as an unmistakable, glorious success! Except for Jesus Christ Himself, no one did more to shape the history of Christianity than Apostle Paul. Rather than give up, St. Paul concentrated on using the inner strength received from the Holy Spirit.

It is easy to be discouraged and wish to quit. We all face problems in our relationships, at work, or at school, that cause us to want to walk away. Our difficulties should not diminish our faith or disillusion us. Perhaps there is a purpose in our suffering. Problems and human limitations often have their benefits. As Christians, not only do difficulties bring us closer to God, but also give God the opportunity to demonstrate His power in our lives.

Why not then look beyond our failures and afflictions. Because of God's mercy we must never be discouraged, but seek His strength through His spirit. Success can rise from the ashes of failure when we seek God and persevere through His guidance.

*I*t is amazing how much press and notoriety a person can receive nowadays, even for unfavorable reasons. Journalists and TV cameras pop up everywhere, and overnight every state in the nation, if not the world, knows what happened and who were involved. Therefore, we must be even more careful whom we admire.

Often we get the impression that our society, and especially the youth, has a difficult time finding heroes. We all need someone to admire, someone to respect and even to model our lives after. Too often, however, we look in the wrong places when we are searching for role models. We look for celebrities; perhaps a good athlete, a TV personality, a singer, or someone who commands respect because of leadership skills. But before we make our choices, we need to know who that person truly is. Often that is not easy because of the image which the media has created.

There is a big difference between celebrities and heroes, and as we all know, celebrities often receive more attention. Celebrities are those who make the news, but heroes are those who make history. Time is a good indicator or a good "scale" that proves who true heroes really are, but causes celebrities to fade away.

In Psalm 112 we see a clear set of guidelines for what makes a man and a woman good and worthy of honor. "Blessed is the man who fears the Lord, who delights greatly in His commandments. His children will be mighty on the land; the generation of the upright will be blessed. Wealth and riches will be in his house, and his righteousness endures forever."

Those faithful to God will be honored. They will be blessed and will enjoy security and freedom from fear. We all want to live without fear. Our heroes are fearless people who face challenges and overcome them. The psalmist teaches us that fear of God can lead to a fearless life. To fear God means to respect and revere Him as the Almighty God. When we trust God completely, we will discover that all other fears will subside.

Are we looking for a godly hero? In a society where so many are anything but godly, how can we set the right example? How can we be the heroes our Lord wants us to be for His glory? We can read Psalm 112. It's a pattern all Christian men and women need to follow if we want to make a difference in our world.

When we think about people to admire, let's not choose a short-term celebrity, but choose a man or woman of God whose deeds are honorable and whose service will survive the test of time! Celebrities make news—Heroes make history!

*R*onnie, a young man from Illinois, often heard his mother say to him, "Something good is going to happen to you one day, and when it does, you will remember the bad thing that caused the good thing to happen."

After graduating high school, Ronnie looked for a job. Being outgoing and at ease with people, he walked into a Montgomery Ward store in his home town and applied for a job. Although it was only a stepping stone job, he thought that it would eventually set him on a long career in retail. But he was turned down. Disappointed, he decided to pursue a career in another direction. He got a job broadcasting minor league baseball games. After five years of that, he left broadcasting, but remained in the entertainment business. Ronnie eventually moved to California to begin an acting career. One break led to another, and he soon was a well-known actor! Well, you can probably guess by now who Ronnie is.

Using his fame, Ronnie moved into politics, becoming governor of California, and eventually President of the United States, serving from 1981 to 1989. For Ronald Reagan, the disappointment of not getting the retail job was the "bad thing" that led to the good things that would come later in his life. His mother was right indeed!

We all face disappointments in life at one time or another that look like gigantic roadblocks. Yet, we should never be discouraged because these disappointments are temporary tests. Yes, tests. They are not dead ends, but detours that often lead to something better. God has a purpose, and He allows certain things to occur for good reasons. Although we don't know what they are at the time, eventually all things work together for good to those who love God (Rom. 8: 28). In fact, St. James advises us, "…count it all joy when you fall into various trials, knowing that the testing of your faith produces patience" (Js. 1:2, 3). Count it all joy? It must be true, because the Apostle Paul also says, "…we glory in tribulation, knowing that tribulation produces perseverance, and perseverance, character, and character, hope. And hope does not disappoint, because the love of God has been poured out in our hearts by the Holy Spirit Who was given to us" (Rom. 5:3 – 5).

Both these great godly men agree that we will have trials – not if, but when. Rejoice in our suffering, not because of it, but while in it. These saints are not in favor of a morbid view of life, but a joyous and triumphant one. A Christian, they believe, can rejoice in suffering because it is not meaningless. Part of God's purpose is to produce character in His children. Although not easy to do, we can view our hardships as times of learning. Perhaps, for example, some of our youth didn't get into the colleges they wanted to attend, or didn't make the team they wanted to play for. Perhaps some of us didn't get the promotion we may have hoped for, or some other tough situation. We can keep in mind what Ronnie's mom told him.

So, let's cheer up and remember that tough times never last very long, but tough people do!

℞ecently I was drawn to read the book of Ecclesiastes again. Solomon spoke of his insights and experiences of life almost 3,000 years ago, yet the applications of his message remain amazingly relevant today.

Solomon takes us on a mental journey through his life, explaining how everything he tried, tested and tasted was meaningless, useless and empty. Do these thoughts come from a man who "had it all"; a king with tremendous intellect, power and wealth? The 12 chapters of Ecclesiastes are an analysis of Solomon's life experiences and a personal, critical essay about its meaning. After his autobiographical journey, he makes this triumphant conclusion: "...Fear God and keep His commandments, for this is the whole duty of man. For God will bring every deed into judgment, including every hidden thing, whether it is good or evil" (Eccl. 12:13, 14).

When Solomon became king, he asked God for wisdom, above all. God granted him his request. He became the wisest man of his time. He studied, taught, judged and wrote (his father, King David, had fought all the wars before him). Kings and leaders came to learn from him, but with all his practical insight of life, Solomon failed to follow his own advice, which led to his downfall.

Near the end of his life, he finally took inventory of the world in which he lived and experienced. Hoping to spare his fellow man the same fall, he concluded that everything apart from God is hollow and meaningless. "Vanity of vanities...all is vanity" (12:8). He is not discouraging us, but rather, wishes to direct our hopes to the ONE who can fulfill them. Solomon affirmed the value of knowledge, relationships, work and pleasure, but only in their proper place. All temporary things in life, he said, must be seen in light of eternity

What Solomon wrote almost 3,000 years ago is as fresh as if it were written yesterday. Love God, he said, serve, honor, obey, and get to know Him better. His words in Ecclesiastes challenge us to find true and lasting meaning in God alone. As Solomon did, let us also take stock of our lives. God is asking each one of us to question our purpose and direction in life. He has a plan for each of us. Let's trust Him and make ourselves available to Him for His glory.

Enjoy life, Solomon said. Do that which is good, and receive all that is good as gifts from God. Isn't it overwhelming to know that people spend their lives striving for the very enjoyment that God gives freely as a gift!

*S*erious problems often begin with a little compromise. On a recent trip to Lebanon and Syria, my husband and I and another couple, dear friends of ours, were to take a trip by taxi from Aleppo, Syria to Beirut, Lebanon. We had separated from a larger group for a few days and did our own sight-seeing. Neither of us had been in this part of the world before. We didn't speak Arabic and discovered that most people in Aleppo didn't speak English. Amazingly, once out of the hotel, our Armenian language was our best means of communication.

Through a previous Armenian taxi driver, we met Nubar (not his real name), who agreed to take us from Aleppo to Beirut's beautiful airport. We were on the last leg of our 15 day trip. Nubar was age 32, spoke no English, but fluent Armenian. He picked us up at 9:00 a.m. at the hotel, and we were ready to go. But as he loaded our luggage into his car's trunk, we noticed a package. He explained it was frozen lamb's meat with the tail included, precious to some people in Beirut. Someone had asked him to deliver it as a favor. We took his word for it.

We passed the border with the usual lengthy checking. Our passports and visas were in order, and we expected to be on our way soon. But Nubar was still talking to several people in Arabic, "tipping" them right and left. When my husband asked why he was doing that, he said, "Oh, that's for the meat. It's illegal to pass meat across the border!" I couldn't believe my ears and said, "Why did you take it then?" He raised both shoulders, and with one hand in the air, said, "Eh."

We delayed longer with additional "tipping" all around. But Nubar still lingered. It turned out they had taken the meat for inspection. Finally, it passed the exam and we left. In Beirut, he delivered the meat to someone's refrigerator after our six hours drive. When he returned to the car he said that the electricity was out, and the generator wasn't working either, but that was not his problem.

"What if?" was now the big question in our minds. What if there was more than just meat in that package? Not only could Nubar have been thrown in prison, but we as well as his accomplices! We were four innocent people who knew nothing of the laws of that land. We had been at the mercy of Nubar's poor judgment. Nubar "tipped" many people for that meat who pretended they never saw it, and let it pass the border. Praise God for that!

Yes, serious problems often begin with a little compromise. That is what Jesus said when He warned His disciples to be aware and to avoid the "yeast" of the Pharisees and the "yeast" of Herod (Mark 8:15). Jesus used a common ingredient for bread as a metaphor. He pointed out that what seems like an innocent component can be explosive. Just like a small amount of yeast can cause an entire lump of dough to rise, a little compromise also opens the door to unlawful, wrongful acts with destructive consequences. Our driver Nubar did just that. Although he knew better, he opened the door to a seemingly harmless act which could have turned into a disaster for four innocent people. The lesson for all of us Christians is: Never compromise under any circumstances. I still praise God for a fortunate ending!

*E*arly last spring, I noticed unusual activity in our patio. Sparrows were flying in and out, happily conveying some message amongst themselves. If this was a sign of nest building, my husband and I agreed that we should discourage it. By the end of the day I became aware that the nest was already built, and a happy pair of sparrows was sitting in it. It was evident that we would be having some guests for a while.

This incident reminded me of a similar story. Some city workers were assigned to trim rows of trees along several streets. A tree marked to be trimmed, however, had a nest with baby sparrows in it. Not having the heart to disturb the nest, they went to other trees until the young birds had grown and abandoned their nest. Later when the workers came back to finish the job, the birds were gone. They examined the nest and discovered in the bottom of it a little scrap of paper. The sparrows had used it along with dried twigs to build their nest. On the paper were these words: "We trust in the Lord always."

We don't know if these workers saw the amazing significance of those words, but their concern and care for the tiny sparrows was God's way of caring for His creatures. In the same manner, our Heavenly Father takes special care to protect us also from dangers we can't foresee. Often we are not even aware of His guarding hand. At other times His care is clearly evident in most unusual ways! In the Gospel of Luke 12:7 we read, "Do not be afraid; you are of more value than many sparrows."

Our loving God, who takes note of sparrows and all the creatures in the universe, will most certainly protect and provide for His own children. An unknown author has written:

> I don't know, and I cannot see
> What God's kind hand prepares for me,
> But I do know that over all
> Rules He Who notes the sparrow's fall.

Our patio's nest has now three tiny sparrows in it. When they abandon their nest, I'll be looking forward to examining the bottom of their nest.

*N*ot long ago, several law students were seated around a table discussing ethics. A federal judge warned the students saying, "I can assure you that at some time or another, you will all be asked to do something dishonest. Your future and your integrity lie in that moment. Whatever your particular situation, including your children and a big mortgage, there is only one answer for you: No!"

With the complexity of today's social and educational issues, more and more people seem to have trouble knowing what is right. We may all face some crucial and decisive moment more than once during the course of our lives. But as Christians we have an advantage. We know what is right because God has spelled it out for us in His textbook, the Bible. The principles of God's Word are there to guide us. If we study the Bible and seek His will in prayer, we will have the discerning spirit to know right from wrong. Then by our actions, our family members and those with whom we interact will also know what is right, and respect our integrity.

We read in Proverbs 22:1, "A good name is more desirable than great riches." Also, "Lying lips are an abomination to the Lord. But those who deal truthfully are His delight" (Prov. 12:22). Those who lie have no joy because of the risks and dangers in their plan. But the righteous, truthful individuals who are guided by God's principles fear nothing, and therefore, they have peace and joy.

Samuel, a man of God and a prophet, who ruled Israel at the end of the period of the Judges, and anointed Israel's two kings; first Saul, and later David; was about to retire. This is what he said in his farewell speech: " 'I am old and gray haired, and look, my sons are with you. I have walked before you from my childhood to this day. Here I am. Witness against me before the Lord and before His anointed: Whose ox have I taken, or whose donkey have I taken, or whom have I cheated? Whom have I oppressed, or from whose hand have I received any bribe?' And they said, 'You have not cheated us or oppressed us, nor have you taken anything from any man's hand' "(1 Sam. 12:2 – 4).

Although the language may sound somewhat amusing to us today, Samuel challenged the people to testify against any covenant stipulation he may have violated. He knew he had nothing to hide—nothing to fear! What a man! What a record! In a society that often treats honesty like an artifact from an ancient world, how important it is for us Christians to be an example of truthfulness and honesty.

It takes a lifetime to build a reputation, and a moment to lose it. As ambassadors of Christ, Our behavior must be above reproach. And if anyone suggests anything dishonest, we will have one and only one answer: No! As in the verse of the above Proverb, we will be "dealing truthfully"—a sure way to bring "delight" to our Heavenly Father.

The recent missions to space reminded me of the Apollo XV mission to the moon several years ago, with Col. James Irwin aboard. It was at the National Religious Broadcasters Convention in Washington, D.C., not long ago, where one of the main speakers was Col. James Irwin; the former astronaut who was part of the crew that made the successful moon walk. Irwin spoke of the excitement connected with leaving this planet and thinking how privileged he was to be part of this unique crew. He also spoke of the impact the experience had on his spiritual life. He said that while on the lunar surface, he sensed both the glory of God and the condition of earth-bound men.

When he returned to earth, he realized he could not content himself with being merely a celebrity. He would have to be a servant, telling his fellow men of a better way to live. Irwin concluded by saying that if we think it a great event to go to the moon, how much greater is the wonder that God came to earth in the person of Jesus Christ!

Perhaps never before have we taken the time to consider that God's one major goal in the lives of all His people is to conform us to the image of His Son. What exactly is that "image of His Son"? Briefly stated, a servant's heart and a giving spirit! There is nothing more invigorating than a servant's heart and a giving spirit, especially when we see them demonstrated in a person who may be considered a celebrity or hero of some sort.

Jesus said, "For even the Son of Man did not come to be served, but to serve…" (Mark 10:45). Jesus is the supreme example of servant/leader. Being a servant is not a sign of inner weakness, but incredible strength! The gentle and humble lifestyle of Jesus is nowhere more evident than in the account of John13, where he washed the feet of His disciples! He did not do this just to get them to be nice to each other. His far greater goal was to extend His mission on earth after He was gone. These men were to move into the world, serving God, serving each other, and serving all people to whom they took the message of Christ. He consciously and voluntarily chose to be one who served – one who gave. So then, if we are to become increasingly more like Christ, then we too are to give and to serve.

Because men walked on the moon, science and technology have made tremendous advances. But because God walked on earth, we know both our origin and our destiny. We can know our Creator personally, and we can live in His light; graciously, cheerfully like Christ, Who was gentle and humble at heart.

Our faith affects others. As Christians, our words, actions and love can be an example to those around us. In Mark chapter 2 we read that Jesus was in Capernaum. A large crowd gathered at the house where He was teaching. Eager to hear Him, people filled the house and even stood outside.

In biblical times, houses were built of mud bricks and stone, and had flat roofs accessible by means of an outside staircase. The roofs were covered with slabs of dry clay mixed with straw, supported by mats of tree branches placed across wooden beams. Flat roofs were used for sleeping on hot nights, drying fruit, grain, or a quiet place to pray. Jesus was in such a house teaching. Suddenly four men came carrying a paralytic on a stretcher. This helpless man's need moved his faithful friends to action, and they brought him to Jesus. Being impossible to get in through the door, they took the paralytic up to the roof. They removed several slabs, made an opening and lowered the man on his stretcher into Christ's presence. Jesus saw their bold persistent action; visible evidence of their faith and their trust in His ability to heal. Jesus said to the paralytic, "Son, your sins are forgiven."

Many Jews in those days believed that all diseases and afflictions were a result of one's sins. This paralytic may have believed that as well. Therefore, Jesus dismissed that thought and freed him from that guilt. The Jewish leaders however, accused Jesus of blasphemy—claiming to be God or to do what only God can do. In Jewish law, blasphemy was punishable by death (Lev. 24:16). This clearly showed that they did not believe that Jesus is God, and He has God's power to heal both body and soul.

Jesus then said to the paralytic, "I say to you, arise, take up your bed, and go home." Immediately he rose and did so in the presence of all, praising God. Those present were amazed and glorified God saying, "We never saw anything like this!" Christ met the man's deepest needs, healing him in both body and soul. His ability to heal totally and immediately was indisputable proof of His deity.

When we recognize someone's need, do we act? What a blessing to have faithful, devoted and creative friends. Opening up the roof was a blessed window of opportunity for a friend. Although we may not physically identify with the paralytic, yet some of us might need to bring our attitudes, our hearts and thoughts into the presence of Christ in prayer, and ask for His healing. Wrong thoughts, unfounded fears, unforgiving attitudes and anger can affect us physically. If this is the case, whether it is for us personally or for a friend, we know that Christ holds the cure for our deepest needs. Human need moved these four faithful creative men to an unselfish act. May it also move us to compassionate action when needed. Christ healed the paralytic and sent him on his way—not only with legs that walked, but with a heart that was forgiven. He is the Alpha and the Omega, the First and the Last. He is the great Physician Who can make us whole and pure within!

*I*t was first at a department store that I became aware of it, many years ago. Two young saleswomen were talking. One had just come to work and could hardly wait till closing time. The other said that she was leaving soon, and was relieved by that thought. I was a few feet away shopping, amazed by their conversation. Why were these young women hired? But more important, why were they still on the job with such an attitude? Though many years have passed since then, I continue to witness similar attitudes, by both male and female employees.

It is obvious that we seek employment for earnings. Since each dollar earned has the full value of one dollar, why should we give less than our best to our employer? We must try our best in whatever we do.

It is true, we are often surrounded by mediocrity, but that is no reason for us to be mediocre. This should never be true of a Christian, especially of an Armenian! I read of a survey that was taken recently. One hundred business executives were asked what qualities would they like to see in their employees. The following five characteristics headed the list: (1) Be on time with a pleasant attitude; (2) Don't tell off-color jokes or make inappropriate remarks; (3) Listen more than talk; (4) Don't criticize another employee openly; and (5) Avoid gossip.

It is interesting that four out of five qualities suggest that we should be careful in communicating with others. God's Word teaches us much the same things. "Do not let unwholesome talk come out of your mouth..." (Eph. 4:29) "Do you see a man who speaks in haste? There is more hope for a fool than him." (Prov. 29:20) "A man who lacks judgment criticizes his neighbor, but a man of understanding holds his tongue." (Prov. 11:12) "Do not go about spreading slander among your people." (Lev. 19:16)

Clearly, the survey reveals more than helpful tips for holding a job. These "tips" are inspired guidelines for a God-pleasing life as well. As children of God, we owe it to ourselves and to our Armenian heritage to try to excel and take pride in all that we do. We simply cannot let ourselves be satisfied with plain mediocrity. That is never good enough for a servant of God, and it is never good enough for an Armenian!

*T*he story is told that on a stormy, rainy night, an elderly couple entered the lobby of a small hotel and asked for a room. The young clerk informed them there was no vacancy. The hotel was filled, as were all other hotels in the area because of a traveling circus in town. But the young clerk, not wishing to send this fine elderly couple out in the rain, offered his small, modest room in the back of the hotel. The elderly couple hesitated, but the young man insisted, and had his room prepared for them. The next morning, when the man paid his bill and thanked the young clerk, he said, "You are the kind of man who should be managing the best hotel in the United States. Some day I'll build you one." The clerk smiled politely.

A few years later the young clerk received a letter from the elderly man, recalling the stormy, rainy night at the hotel, with an invitation to come to New York. A round trip ticket was enclosed in the letter. When the clerk arrived, his host took him to the corner of 50th and Park Avenue and showed him a magnificent new building. "This is the hotel I built for you to manage," the man explained. The elderly man was William Waldorf Astor, and that hotel was the original Waldorf Astoria. The young clerk was George C. Boldt, who became its first manager!

Generosity and selflessness produce an abundant life of joy and rich rewards. According to the Scriptures, if we give freely to others, we will receive abundant blessings. In Proverbs 11:25 we read, "The generous soul will be made rich, and he who waters will also be watered himself." What a beautiful picture this verse paints!

God blesses us when we give freely of our treasures, time, talent and energy. We also realize and recognize that whatever we have is truly the result of God's blessings given to us, to be used not only for ourselves, but for the joy of helping others as well.

We should never underestimate the importance of what we are doing in God's service. He knows and sees it all. God asks for our faithfulness, and rewards with fruitfulness. When we give freely of ourselves, we are always the recipient. And most often, when we least expect it, as the young clerk experienced.

God blesses the bountiful soul and repays what is cheerfully given. When we consider others' interest more important than our own, we are linked with Christ. He is our true example of humanity and humility. An unknown author has written:

> "Service is working and giving,
> And not regretting the cost;
> It's knowing and understanding
> That no good deed will be lost."

*W*e live in a frantic, noisy world, yet it seems that some people fear quietness and silence. In my morning walks I pass by some people on the streets wearing earphones with the volume set so high that I can identify the song on the tape they are listening to. How can they stand the volume so high? And what does all that noise do to their eardrums? At the gym, some people do the same. I'm amazed, not only for the noisy world they are creating for themselves, but it is also antisocial. When I see an acquaintance, I just wave my hand to them. Communication among some people is a lost art.

For some of us, on the other hand, the radio gets us out of bed in the morning at a set time. Even before we get into the shower another radio or TV is on, and we listen to the news that developed while we slept. When we jump into the car, we turn on our favorite radio station. I have even seen drivers wearing earphones as they go to work. Perhaps it's a lecture or a book they might be listening to on tape, which can be dangerous for blocking out all other traffic sounds.

Doesn't it seem that we fear the quiet? All these sounds and noise may be lethal to our spiritual well-being and an attack on our physical lives. Surprisingly, it is not a new problem. Three thousand years ago, an unknown psalmist wrote of the One Who is the Source of all calm: "Be still, and know that I am God" (Ps. 46:10). In this frantic and noisy world, how proper it is for us to take time off to be still. We must truly be concerned for our well-being, because we all desperately need to slow down, so that each day we can take some time for quiet moments of solitude, meditation, prayer and soul-searching. If we do that, out agitation will begin to fade, how insignificant and petty our differences will seem, how great God Almighty will appear, and how small our troubles will become. As a result, peace, security and confidence will move right into our souls.

When we look at the devotional life of Jesus, we'll see that He often set aside time to pray. As His ministry grew, causing more people to come to Him, He often withdrew off by Himself and prayed. More is accomplished by prayer than has ever been, or will be accomplished by human endeavor. Prayer is everyone's privilege, and all of us must call upon the power of our Almighty God.

Daily communication with our Creator is beneficial to everyone's physical and mental well-being. Let's not wait until there is a personal crisis to call on "Help@God.com." Prayer makes E-mail look as old fashioned as a quill pen. We have direct access to God Himself, our Creator. No interceding computer, no need for uplinks, satellites, modems or anything. Just us and God – person to person, heart to heart. Prayer is an available tool to all; a "P-mail" to share our thoughts with God and pray for guidance and wisdom. Cheerleading for God is spelled P-R-A-I-S-E! This should be our song!

The current songs, information and entertainment that we claim to enjoy steal precious quiet moments we truly crave. Like the psalmist says, we need to "Be still and know that He is God." Let's not be afraid of the quiet, but enjoy it!

*M*ost of us agree that our parents and grandparents are great storytellers. Their well-chosen fables always pointed to a moral principle with a lesson in life. The following story deals with the problem of boastfulness and pride.

A frog, wishing to escape the cold winter climate, expressed his desire to migrate with some geese. The wild geese agreed to take him with them, but there was one problem; frogs can't fly. "Leave that to me. I've got a splendid idea," said the frog. He asked two geese to help him by picking up a strong reed, each holding one end. The frog planned to grasp the reed with his mouth. The geese and the frog started on their journey. Passing over a town, villagers came out to see the unusual sight. Someone cried out, "Who came up with such a clever idea?" That made the frog so puffed up with a sense of importance that he exclaimed, "I did!" His pride was his downfall, for the moment he opened his mouth, he lost his grip and fell to his death.

We read in Prov. 16:18, "Pride goes before destruction, and a haughty spirit before a fall." The Lord always crowns humility with His blessings. Even Jesus' disciples struggled with it. When Jesus learned that they had been arguing among themselves as to who would be the greatest in God's Kingdom, He responded, "If anyone desires to be first, he shall be last of all and servant of all" (Mk. 9:35).

John the Baptist said he was not even worthy to be Christ's servant, to perform the humble task of loosening the straps of His sandals (Jn. 1:27). But according to Lk. 7:28, Jesus said that John was the greatest of all prophets! If such a great person felt inadequate to even be Christ's servant, how much more should we lay aside our pride to serve Christ! The Word of God, in both the Old and New Testaments, says plenty about pride and humility.

"I was wrong" or "I need advice" are difficult phrases to utter because they require humility. Pride is an ingredient in every quarrel. It stirs up conflict and divides people. Humility, by contrast, heals. Pride can destroy individuals as well as nations. It makes us think we can take care of ourselves without God's help. Even serving God and others can result in boastful pride, if we aren't careful.

It is believed that Benjamin Franklin made a list of character qualities he wanted to develop. When he mastered one virtue, he would go on to the next. He did pretty well, he said, until he got to humility. Every time he thought he was making significant progress, he would be so pleased with himself that he became proud.

Proud people seldom realize that pride is their problem, although everyone around them is well aware of it. When we become filled with self, we have no room for wisdom or for God. But if we would study His Word and praise Him, not only would we be wiser, but would have no time to talk about ourselves. A Christ-centered life cannot be a self-centered one. At times, our pride could be our worst enemy. Therefore, let us defeat it before it brings us down. As we humble ourselves under the mighty hand of God, He will exalt us in due time! Humility can be sought, but never celebrated.

One of the expressions my grandmother often used as I was growing up was: "Don't make hasty, unjust judgments on people, for the yardstick we use on others may someday be used as a measure for us." Then she would tell the following story.

A village baker bought his butter from a local farmer. One day the baker felt that the farmer had been reducing the amount of butter in the packages, but charging the same. So he weighed the butter, saw that he was right, and the baker accused the farmer of fraud. In court, the judge asked the farmer if he had measuring weights. "No sir," replied the farmer. "How then, do you weigh the butter that you sell?" asked the judge. The farmer answered, "When the baker began buying his butter from me, I thought I would get my bread from him. I have been using his one pound loaf as the weight for the butter I sell. If the weight of the butter is wrong, he has only himself to blame!"

The faults we see in others may often be the reflection of our own acts. Jesus says in Mt. 7: 1, 2: "Judge not, that you be not judged. For what judgment you judge, you will be judged; and with the measure you use, it will be measured back to you." Jesus tells us to examine our own motives and conduct instead of being judgmental. The traits that bother us in others are often those we see in ourselves. Do we find it easy to magnify the faults of others while excusing our own? Jesus teaches us that if we are ready to criticize someone, we must check to see if we deserve the same criticism. Also, we should not be too hard on the person who might have done wrong, but lovingly forgive, and see if we can help them.

The Pharisees of Jesus' day seemed to be especially active in fault-finding. They would try to elevate themselves by tearing down and slandering peoples' character. Not only is this a sign of pride and self-glorification, but it is certain that we will be judged in a similar manner. Jesus' statement, "Judge not" is against that kind of hypocritical attitude that tears others down in order to build one's self up. It isn't a blanket statement against all critical thinking. He doesn't mean we should ignore wrong doing. But He teaches us to exercise a discerning spirit. This warning had special relevance for the Pharisees, who were inclined to look down on Gentiles because of their lack of knowledge of God's revelation in the Old Testament.

Yes, it is tempting to judge others, even our own fellow Christians. But we must also remember that only God knows a person's heart, and He is the only One with the right to judge. When we judge someone, we invariably consider ourselves better—and that is arrogant. A Christian must not judge hypocritically or self-righteously.

Do we build people up or tear them down? If we are looking for faults to correct, we must look first into the mirror of God's Word, and ask Him to help us see our own faults clearly. Only gentle and humble criticism that first recognizes one's own faults can help. If not, we might be like the baker in the above story. Jesus knew human nature well when He said, "Judge not, and you shall not be judged." What is the measure we have been using lately?

*T*he human perspective of impossibility was an occasion for God to demonstrate His unfailing love and power.

While Moses led several hundred thousand Israelites on foot in the wilderness, he was faced with yet another challenge. Tired of manna, the people wanted meat. God promised Moses that He would provide it to them for a whole month. Moses had witnessed God's power in spectacular miracles in the past, yet at this time he questioned God's ability to feed this immense number of people. Then God answered Moses, "Is the Lord's arm too short? You will now see whether or not what I say will come true for you" (Numbers 11: 18 – 23).

If even Moses doubted God's power, how much easier it would be for us to do the same. Depending on God completely is essential, regardless of our level of spiritual maturity. When we face challenges, we often forget God's faithfulness. We only see our present state of difficulties. But if we were to look back, then we also would see our joys and victories, and the presence of the ONE Who never left us nor forsook us. After all, "Is the Lord's arm too short?"

It is interesting to see God's answer, often given in the form of a question. God intended to prove to Moses and to all future generations, including us, that nothing is impossible with Him. Yes, we can find release from anxiety or worries when we remember that we are always under God's watchful eye and protection. There is nothing quite like the peace that comes through a deep and abiding trust in Him.

Why be reluctant then, to trust an unknown future when we can trust an all-knowing God? We can be assured that the ONE Who brought us this far will certainly continue to direct us in the present, future and always. "Is the Lord's arm too short?"

*A*ctor and comedian George Burns had appeared on a television comedy show a few years before his death. Sitting in an armchair with a newspaper in his hand, he was asked by someone on the show about the news of the day. "Well," said Burns, "bad news depresses me, therefore I cut out all of the bad news to see what's left." Then he held up the first page. There were no articles left, but a shredded newspaper. Seriously though, isn't that about right?

There is really nothing new about such stories, however. They are simply modern versions of what people have been doing since Adam and Eve first disobeyed God. So, what is real news? It isn't the kind of conduct that comes naturally to most people. Honorable behavior takes more courage and strength than we alone are capable of. Only through divine guidance and power are we led to be examples of what God considers good. When someone acts ethically, lovingly, and for the good of humanity, that is good news! That is very good news!

Prime time television has its problems also. Nightly, our living rooms are the site of murders, bad language, violence, and some shows even make fun of our Christian faith. Those same shows also try to convince us that immorality is a joking matter, and that violence is entertaining. Unfortunately, the moral content of television has been on the decline for years. But that does not mean we have to go down with it. The psalmist who knew nothing about TV said, "Turn away my eyes from looking at worthless things" (Ps. 119:37). That's a good verse to post over our TV sets.

Those who put together TV programs we watch are conditioning us to think the way they want us to think. That's really a frightening thought when we consider which programs are the top-rated ones these days. The key is to realize that the networks are not committed to Christian values. So if we are committed to follow the Word of God, we'll find ourselves receiving conflicting signals from television.

"Blessed is the man who walks not in the counsel of the ungodly, nor stands in the path of sinners…" (Ps. 1:1). Here we see the joys of obeying God and refusing to listen to those who discredit or ridicule Him. Although many may think of laws, instructions, and commandments as limiting and restricting, the law of God paradoxically frees us. It frees us from wrongful acts and gives us peace of heart and mind. Modern society longs for peace of mind. Yet, it's so simple to achieve. If we love God, our Creator, and obey His Word, we will have peace. We must always trust God Who alone stands above all circumstances and pressures of daily life.

The Bible reports that kind of uplifting news. It tells us that when we repent, we can be forgiven, no matter what our past might have been, because Christ died on the cross for us. When we put our trust in Him, God sends His Holy Spirit to enable us to become His disciples, do good and become examples of His good news.

For the most part, the entertainment world is not going to cast off any restraints on their shows. Therefore, let us honor God with our viewing habits. Let's not just watch the screen, but screen what we watch. We can sure use self-control with our remote control.

*J*ust as the sun can be overshadowed by dark clouds, so can moods of pessimism and doubt plunge us into an attitude of darkness. At times our situation may seem so hopeless that we think we'll never see the joy of sunshine again. We have the tendency to indulge in self pity, thinking no one has problems like ours! Well, let's see what a lieutenant, a U.S. Navy pilot who spent 6? years as a prisoner of war in North Vietnam, has to say. The experience of those pitch-dark days has given him an appreciation of ordinary privileges that most of us take for granted. Today, nearly three decades after his release the lieutenant said: "There is no such thing as a bad day when there is a doorknob on the inside of the door!" Then he adds that after so many days in a locked cell, he considers the privilege of walking outside whenever he wishes to be one of his life's greatest luxuries!

A prisoner for some 2,370 days! We may not be able to choose our circumstances, but we can certainly choose our attitude toward them. The Apostle Paul, who was also in prison several times, tells us of his experiences. He says, "I have learned in whatever state I am, to be content...I can do all things through Christ Who strengthens me" (Phil. 4:11 – 13). Whatever our circumstance may be, we can learn to draw on the power of Christ for strength. St. Paul chose an attitude of hope, and I'm sure the lieutenant did as well. Otherwise he would have died in his cell. We always have a choice, and that choice will make a difference.

It is also helpful to consider what others endured. We are not alone. The most effective cure for the blues is to remember that God allows suffering so that our experience can prepare us to enter into other peoples' afflictions and help them. "We've been there!" Clouds of testing can bring showers of blessings. One of the great ironies of trouble is that it can bring us closer to God. We often don't do that willingly. A life of ease teaches less than a life of pain. Life's challenges are designed, not to break us, but to bend us toward God. We need to learn that God is trying to teach us through our struggles.

For a Christian, no suffering is without purpose. We should bring our problems, heavy or light, to the One Who is the great burden bearer. No burden is too heavy for God's almighty arms. Is our back straining under a mounting load of burdens? We can turn them over to the Lord. St. Peter instructs us to cast all our cares upon God, because He cares for us (1 Pet. 5:7). We read the same in Ps. 55: 22: "Cast your burdens on the Lord, and He shall sustain you." Do we? Often we continue to bear them ourselves, even when we say we trust God. Or we turn them over to Him in prayer, and then take them all back.

When our days continue to be dark, we must cling to the truth of God's goodness and faithfulness. Let's dare to give our heartaches a challenging name, such as "growing pains." We are growing spiritually day by day, by the hand of our Heavenly Father. He is not finished with us just yet. Let's praise God in spite of our trials, trust Him, and our burdens will turn into blessings.

On a recent cruise, my husband and I had the opportunity to get acquainted with the ship's officers, who were all Greek, beginning with the captain. Since I speak the language, we were treated as special guests. As I was chatting with the captain one day, he invited us to meet him on the ship's bridge. The following day arrangements were made, and we were escorted there. The panoramic view from the bridge was incredible! Visibility was excellent, and the weather conditions great! It was the best spot on the entire cruise ship.

As the many panels, controls, etc., were explained to us, one thing became clear. When one sails on the high seas, one needs to know three important facts; one's location, destination and course. By referring to the map and compass, one can reach the desired destination. With all the modern instruments and technology, it sounded so simple.

As I thought of the events of that day, the following question came to mind. How does a follower of Christ stay on course and avoid spiritual "shipwreck"? St. Paul wrote in 1 Tim. 1:19, "…having faith and a good conscience, which some had rejected, concerning the faith have suffered shipwreck…" As Christians, how do we hold onto a "good conscience"? As God's children, we must treasure our faith in Christ more than anything else, and do what we know is right.

A "good conscience" serves as the rudder that steers the Christian through the rocks and reefs of error. Those who ignore the truth of their conscience, as a result, suffer shipwreck of their Christian faith, which is spiritual catastrophe. God created man with a conscience as his self-judging faculty. Because God wrote His law on man's heart (Rom. 2:15), man knows the basic standards of right and wrong. When we violate those standards, our conscience produces guilt, which acts as the mind's security system and generates fear, shame and doubt as a warning to the soul's well-being. On the other hand, when we do God's will, we enjoy the affirmation, assurance, peace and joy of a "good conscience."

In order to work as God designed it, the conscience must be informed and cultivated to the highest moral and spiritual level. That means submitting it to the Holy Spirit for guidance, and through the study of God's Word. St. Paul's fully enlightened conscience exonerated him completely. But ultimately, only God can accurately judge man's motives.

There is evidence of God's moral law in every society and culture. For example, all cultures prohibit murder, and yet in all societies that law is broken. We know what is right, but we insist on doing what is wrong. It is not enough to know what is right, we must also do it. No one must ever violate their own conscience – their warning system – when it is activated. Repeatedly ignoring the conscience's warning desensitizes it, and eventually silences it. That is what St. Paul refers to as "spiritual shipwreck."

How are we doing? Are we on course? As we live in faith and act on those inner tugs, which are the divine guidance of the Holy Spirit, what we do will be right. To stay on course, we must trust the unfailing compass of God's Word.

$\mathcal{M}$any people get their exercise on the treadmill. When the odometer says that the individual has walked or run a mile, we know that the person actually has gone nowhere.

Life without God is like being on a treadmill. Ecclesiastes 1:4 – 7 summarizes by saying that generations come and generations go, the sun rises and sets day after day, year after year, the wind blows repetitively, rivers flow into the sea that never fills. And like these natural phenomena, life is always moving, but never arriving—always encountering changes, but never finding anything really new. Then, at some point, comes death for all of us. People without God are without hope and soon are forgotten. What a dreary, empty and depressing prospect.

The solution for emptiness is to center our focus on God our Creator. His love can fill the emptiness of our soul. Our fear, respect and awe for God will fill our lives along with serving Him and others, rather than with selfish pleasures. For generations people are searching, yet the more they try to obtain from the world, the more they realize how little they really have. No pleasure or joy is possible without God our Creator. Without Him search for satisfaction is fruitless. Our quest for fulfillment will cease only when we strive to know and love God. He is the source of all wisdom, knowledge and joy!

Because life is short, we need divine wisdom that is greater than anything this world can offer. We need the precious Word of God. His wisdom spares us the bitterness of futile human experience and gives us a hope that goes beyond death.

Jesus says in Mark 8: 36 – 37, "For what will it profit a man if he gains the whole world, and loses his own soul? Or what will a man give in exchange for his soul?" Christ asks submission of self and self-centeredness. He wants us to stop trying to control our own destiny, and to let Him direct us. Many people spend all their energy seeking pleasure. Jesus says, however, that a world centered on possessions, position, or power is ultimately worthless. Whatever we have on earth is only temporary – it cannot be exchanged for our soul. If we work hard at getting what we want, we might eventually have a pleasurable life, but in the end we will find it hollow and empty, and with no eternal value.

Are we willing to make the pursuit of God more important than the selfish pursuit of pleasure? Why not follow Jesus and know what it means to live abundantly now, and to have eternal life as well.

How different life is for those who already know God! Yes, they too sometimes experience routine, monotony and difficulties, but instead of being on a "treadmill," they are on a meaningful journey. Anyone can have that hope that so many children of God already know and experience. To have all that the world has to offer, yet to not have Christ, is to be spiritually and eternally bankrupt. All the world's goods will not compensate for losing one's soul. True satisfaction and fulfillment cannot be found outside of a relationship without out Maker and Sustainer. Life without Christ is a hopeless end. Life with Christ is endless hope!

*W*hat comes to mind when we hear the words "Doubting Thomas"? The disciple of Jesus Christ, of course; the one who has gone down in history as the doubter and skeptic for disbelief in the resurrection of Jesus Christ. He missed the appearance of Christ to the other disciples and said that he needed visual and factual proof of the risen Lord. In fact, he declared that unless he saw the scars and was invited to place his finger where the nails were driven, and place his hand into Jesus' side, he would not believe (Jn. 20:24 – 29). Thomas represents the prototype for all who dismiss the reality of Jesus Christ on the basis of rational argument. But let us look at him in a different light, more as a prototype of all of us who might be afflicted by doubts.

Thomas was one of Jesus' twelve disciples, also called "Didymus," meaning "twin" in Greek. It isn't known whose twin he was. His name appears in each of the apostolic lists (Mt. 10:3). Although he receives little mention in the synoptic gospels, Thomas became important in the latter portion of John's gospel. He alone appears as a tower of strength, encouraging the disciples to accompany Jesus into a hostile Judea, even if it meant death. He suggests, "Let us also go, that we may die with Him." He didn't hesitate to follow Jesus (Jn. 11:16).

We don't know why Thomas was absent the first time Jesus appeared to the disciples after the resurrection. But a week later, Christ appeared again to the eleven disciples, and He offered Thomas the opportunity to test the reality of His body. Jesus didn't rebuke Thomas for his failure, but instead compassionately offered him proof of His resurrection. Jesus lovingly met him at the point of his weakness.

"My Lord and my God!" With these words, Thomas declared his firm belief in the resurrection, and therefore, the deity of Jesus, the Messiah and Son of God. This is the greatest confession one can make! Thomas' confession functions as the fitting capstone of St. John's purpose in writing. If it weren't for Thomas, we wouldn't have had this powerful confession of faith recorded in history.

Jesus said to Thomas, "Because you have seen Me, you have believed; blessed are those who have not seen and yet have believed" (Jn. 20:29). Thomas' response stands as a paradigm for all Christians who are called to believe in Christ without having seen Him, or granted tangible proof of His existence. Thomas' response is the same for all who later believe; "My Lord and my God!"

Jesus foresaw the time when the tangible evidence which Thomas received would not be available. When Christ permanently ascended to the Father, all those who believe would do so without the benefit of seeing the resurrected Lord. Therefore Jesus pronounced a special blessing on all those who believe without having Thomas' privilege.

Thomas wanted Jesus' presence. But God's plan is wiser. He has not limited Himself to one physical body. He wants to be present with us at all times. Even now, He is with us through His Holy Spirit. We can talk to Him, and we can find His words to us in the pages of the Bible. Today, 2,000 years later, He can be as real to us as He was to Thomas.

*D*isregard for God's standards and lack of Godly fear are not just modern phenomena. Much, much worse conditions prevailed several thousand years ago, in the days of Noah. The Bible says, "The Lord was sorry that He had made man on earth, and He was grieved in His heart. I will destroy man, whom I have created, from the face of the earth" (Gen. 6:6, 7).

But there was one exception. Noah found favor in the eyes of the Lord. One man, his wife, his three sons and their families were not influenced by their environment. They were righteous, blameless, and walked with God. The story of Noah and the ark is known to us all. Noah believed God's warnings about a flood that would destroy the world, and did as he was instructed by faith.

He took his entire family, and all species of earth's creatures in pairs into the ark. The floods came and destroyed all upon the earth except those in the ark. Eventually the ark came to rest on Mount Ararat. Noah, his family and all creatures went forth from the ark. The rainbow, which was first seen after the flood, symbolizes God's promise to never again flood the earth. As God commanded, Noah's family multiplied and replenished the earth. But many generations later, people stopped walking with the Lord, and without God, once again they became corrupt.

Many centuries later we see a new ark for mankind in the shape of a cross. This cross was made for one person only; the son of God, Jesus Christ, who loved us, and by His death on the cross, cleansed us and rescued us from darkness. Noah's ark had accomplished its purpose. The crucifixion of Jesus Christ, His love for us, and the enduring offer of hope is and will be with us forever.

The cross is our new ark for mankind. It is never too late to get on board—its dimensions are limitless. This invitation is not for one person or one family. There is room for all who love and accept Christ by faith.

This is God's wonderful plan that ends with rainbows of new hope! Those who put their trust in Him and walk with Him receive the gift of abundant life. Jesus said, "I have come that they have life, and that they may have it more abundantly" (John 10:10).

A friend confessed to me recently that every year at about this time, she experiences feelings of melancholy, knowing that she will soon face another birthday. My response to her was that although none of us past the age of 21 is thrilled about another birthday, I find it rather comforting to know this "aging process" happens to everyone—God is fair! Yet, we all handle it differently. It all depends on our perspective.

Whether we like it or not, aging is natural. But what is old age? One hundred years ago, most people in their forties were thought of as being old. Today, people that age are considered young. Yes, time passes quickly as the writer of Psalm 90 points out so bluntly. Because of that we need the kind of attitude poet Robert Browning displayed when he wrote, "Grow old with me, the best is yet to be!" It is interesting to note that some of the most creative people in history were still creating at age 70, 80 and older. The following individuals are examples of only a few.

Between the ages of seventy and eighty three, Commodore Vanderbilt added about 100 million dollars to his fortune. Tintoretto, at seventy four, painted the "Paradise," a canvas 74 by 30 feet. Verdi, at seventy four, produced his masterpiece "Othello"; at eighty he composed "Falstaff"; and at eighty five, his famous "Ave Maria." Cato at eighty began the study of Greek. Stradivari made his first violin at the age of sixty, and some of his best at eighty. At the age of ninety, Julia Ward Howe said, "All the sugar was in the bottom of the cup." And Grandma Moses was seventy eight before her paintings were discovered, and at age ninety two her autobiography was published.

We all know that what we will be tomorrow depends on the choices we make today. Realizing that life is precious helps us use the time we have more wisely and for eternal good. We all want our lives to be effective, productive and purposeful. To use our years productively, we must develop a positive outlook on the passage of time. As Christians, a correct view of life includes a search for wisdom and guidance in God's Word, trust in His goodness and love, and a continuous walk with Him. We may not be able to choose our circumstances, but we can choose our attitude toward them.

The Apostle Paul writes in Phil. 4:13, "I can do all things through Christ Who strengthens me." Whatever our circumstances we can draw on the power of Christ for strength, and have a productive, purposeful life at any age. We always have a choice—and that choice will always make a difference. As we maintain this perspective, we will enjoy the passage of time. And yes, all the sugar may still be in the bottom of the cup!

One machine I know how to handle well is my sewing machine. Having the need to use it, I began to thread it, but soon discovered that it was completely dead. I tried everything I knew with no results. When I finally looked behind its cabinet I saw that the plug was disconnected. Relieved, I plugged it back in and was able to complete the job.

I looked at this experience in a new light. Here I was using an elaborate, beautiful piece of machinery that did more things than I have use for, and yet, without power it did absolutely nothing.

This could often be the case with each one of us as Christians. We look like we have it all together, but until we are daily connected to the power of God, the source of Divine Power, we can be as unproductive as any unplugged piece of electrical machinery. We cannot be truly spiritually alive until we are connected by faith into the true Source of Power; God's Power that brings divine illumination into our existence. How wonderful is God's love for us that His everlasting power and light are available to each one of us by faith!

In the Gospel of John, Jesus says, "I am the light of the world. Whoever follows Me will never walk in darkness but will have the light of life." (8:12) As followers of Christ, we receive the knowledge of his teachings and are not in darkness any more. His Light brightens our path so we won't stumble, as He gives us the discerning spirit to live the illuminating productive life of a Christian.

When we neglect our daily walk with our Lord, we feel that void and miss the power that comes only from a healthy relationship with Christ. That is when it feels like there is a loose cord or loose connection somewhere. We don't feel spiritually quite "with it."

To walk in His Light we need to stay "plugged in," connected through prayer, reflecting on His Word and in complete reliance of His Power—not our own. There is never any power failure in His presence. Christ is the Light of the world! For He is the emissary of God, who is Light, and who calls each one of us out of any darkness we might be experiencing into His wonderful Light!

*W*e had an early start. It was exciting to be in Rapid City, South Dakota. This was the day we were going to visit Mount Rushmore and see the well-known works of sculptor Gutzon Borglum. At an elevation of 5,725 feet, the 60 foot high granite heads of four U.S. presidents, George Washington, Thomas Jefferson, Abraham Lincoln and Theodore Roosevelt, were now only a few miles away. I could hardly wait!

Even though we were somewhat delayed at breakfast, we arrived at the famous site at 10:00 A.M. We looked up and could see nothing. A persistent fog had blanketed the entire peak! What a disappointment! How could we possibly accept this? To have finally come to the base of this breathtaking wonder and never get a glimpse of it? We were not going to give up.

Sometimes when we read the Bible, we may find our spiritual eyesight "in a fog" as well. We struggle and strain, but we cannot see the timeless truths that lie within its passages. Our spiritual eyesight and understanding can be blanketed by a persistent fog. We feel discouraged and often ready to give up. That is why the Apostle Paul prayed for the Ephesian faithful when he said, "....may God give you the spirit of wisdom and of revelation in the knowledge of Him, having the eyes of your hearts enlightened...." (Eph 1:17, 18) Yes, our spiritual vision can at times get clouded. But as we seek the guidance of the Holy Spirit, we receive spiritual discernment that clears away the "fog" so we can see the marvelous truths in His Word.

Did we get to see Mount Rushmore? Did the fog lift? Yes, indeed! We were assured at the information desk that if we would return in two hours, it will all be clear. We went sight-seeing elsewhere, and came back. Mount Rushmore was as overwhelming as it was described to us, and more! The impressive likenesses of the heads of the four U.S. presidents remind visitors of our nation's heritage and history.

In the same manner, let us never get discouraged when having difficulties understanding scripture completely. We must always remember that we need the illuminating and enlightening help of God's Spirit to clear out our "fogged up" spiritual eyesight. Only through His Word can we walk in the Light -- His illuminating Light.

*T*he very first words that Jesus said to Simon Peter were, "Come, follow Me...." (Mk. 1:17). And the last words that Jesus said to him were, "You follow Me" (Jn. 21:22). Through every step between those challenges, Peter never failed to follow Jesus—even though he stumbled at times.

Peter, originally named Simon, became one of Jesus' twelve disciples. After Jesus became part of Peter's life, this simple Galilean fisherman became a new person, but not a perfect one. We often assume that Jesus' disciples were great men of faith from the first day. No! They had to grow in their faith, as all believers do. Peter often spoke and acted in haste. And yet, Peter emerges as a leader among the disciples during Jesus' ministry. His name always occurs first in the lists of the disciples, and along with James and John, he is singled out for special revelations of Jesus' divinity (Mt. 17:1, 2).

Jesus saw in Simon, not who he was, but who he would become, and greeted him with a new name; Peter—in Greek meaning "rock" (*petra*). Impulsive Peter certainly didn't act like a rock some of the time. When Jesus chose His disciples, He wasn't looking for perfect men – He was looking for real people who could change through His love. Jesus bestowed the name "Rock" on Simon as a sign of his future role as upholder of the Christian traditions established by Jesus.

As Peter followed Jesus, his life changed completely. From a simple fisherman he became a "fisher of men" (Mt. 4:19). Peter's possessions were always at Christ's disposal. He often stayed at Peter's house in Capernaum, and used Peter's boat as a platform to speak to the crowds. Jesus accepted Peter just as he was, and in spite of his failures, Peter went on to do great things for God.

When Jesus was about to be arrested, trying to protect Him, Peter pulled a sword and struck the high priest's servant, cutting off his ear. But Jesus told Peter to put away his sword and allow God's plan to unfold. If Peter would have had his way, Jesus would not have gone to the cross, and God's plan of redemption would have been hindered. Later Peter hastily promised that he would lay down his life for Jesus; only to be answered with Jesus' prophesy that he would in fact deny being one of His disciples.

Yes, Peter later denied Jesus three times, and remembering Jesus' prophesy, he went outside and wept bitterly (Mt. 26:75). Later the risen Christ removed the cloud of guilt from Peter's heart when He asked him three times if he loved Him. Peter answered three times, "Yes, Lord." Then Jesus told him to feed His sheep, asking Peter to commit his life to Him. Peter is not presented as rock solid through the gospels, but he became a solid rock in the days of the early Church, as we see in Acts, Ch. 2 – 4.

The Apostle Peter's life provides a remarkable example of a man who was given a second chance. In the final chapter of John's gospel, Jesus restores Peter completely! What Christ did for Simon Peter, He can and will do for each of us when we follow Him!

*D*uring the month of February, Armenians in the United States and around the world commemorate the memory of St. Vartan Mamigonian and the Battle of Avarair in 451 A.D. As Christians, we are very much aware of the supreme sacrifice that St. Vartan and his brave men made. They carried not only the cross of Christianity, but the cross of suffering as well.

The Battle of Avarair was not a battle for land, but for religious freedom. These heroic warriors sacrificed their lives in the battle against the pagan Persians. These great men of faith, however, did not fight and die in vain. They died so that we, and all future generations, would live as Christian Armenians. Because of that, it was a victory! Our faith has remained strong. Over the years we have bent with the winds of change, but our Christian faith has never been broken. In the years that followed the battle, Armenians continued to fight for their faith, until the Treaty of Nuvarsag was signed in 484 A.D. They had at last regained the freedom to exercise their Christian faith.

This courageous act of Katchen Vartan and his brave men brings the following verse to mind from the Apostle Paul's epistle to the Corinthian believers: "My dear brothers, stand firm. Let nothing move you. Always give yourselves fully to the work of the Lord, because you know that your labor in the Lord is not in vain" (1 Cor. 15: 58).

The commemoration of Vartanantz each year is truly a time of spiritual renewal for all Armenians. The example of Katchen Vartan's courageous stand is honored annually in our churches, schools and various organizations. The Battle of Avarair, its patriotism, self-sacrifice, courage and faith has been an inspiration to poets, song writers, historians, clergy, soldiers and students of all generations ever since.

Today our people in Armenia confront another kind of Avarair. The independent Republic of Armenia faces numerous challenges. But there is a positive awakening of religious and national freedom. Let us pray that God will guide their leaders, grant them wisdom and strengthen their faith as they work united toward a stronger Armenia.

We are fortunate and blessed to be living in the United States of America. We have no religious battles to fight, as those in the past, and no persecutions. St. Vartan and his men, and more recently our forefathers, suffered all that. We can learn and benefit from the past. As Christian Armenians, let us continue to live honorable and exemplary lives, make every effort to perpetuate the faith, culture, and principles of our forefathers, and pass that torch on to our coming generations. Then and only then will Vartanantz remain a truly victorious celebration for all Armenians.

$\mathcal{M}$ost people view lighthouses favorably. We see beautiful lighthouses on postcards, birthday cards, needlepoint pillows, and even printed on T-shirts. Artists have been painting seascapes for generations, often including the lighthouse in their composition. A few days ago I came across a magazine that had a brief history of 27 lighthouses around the country that one can visit, go for a picnic, watch for whales, or even spend the night in those converted to "Bread & Breakfast" inns.

Why do people favor lighthouses? In addition to being close to picturesque coastal scenes, lighthouses are favored for the protection they provide. Their rotating high powered beacons safeguard ships in coastal waters. Their purpose is to project light into darkness.

I often wondered what the disciples thought when Jesus told them, "You are the light of the world." (Matt. 5:14) Perhaps they thought, as we probably would; "Who me? How can I be the light of the world? I am not qualified." Yet Christ, knowing the disciples, did not say, "You are *like* a light." He said, "You *are* the light." In the Gospel of John 8:12, Jesus also says, "I am the light of the world. Whoever follows me will never walk in darkness but will have the light of life."

As Christians we identify with Christ, and as His followers we reflect His light. We also then, are the light of the world. An incredible statement, and yet so simple. We don't even have to become one—we are already. Light dispels darkness. Even the smallest candle in a pitch dark room brings light. As Christians, our manner of life should be the light in darkness. What part of our daily environment is in darkness? It could be a place of employment, neighborhood, classroom or while visiting someone in a hospital. Whether we bring light to thousands, or touch only a few, we are called to be the light. We are not all asked to be a giant searchlight or a 1000-bulb chandelier, or even a lighthouse. We are simply told to let our light shine in our environment so that others may see our good works, our Christian character and principles.

Light is silent. There is no noise, no music, no banners or trumpets. Even a lighthouse along a rugged shoreline, merrily shines as its beacon turns. Often with hardly a word being said, a child of God who is being watched sends off a very distinct message. As Christians, we draw strength from God's Word. We are the light of the world. Let us walk in the light and just shine!

*I*sn't it amazing that the "Titanic", the "unsinkable" luxury liner, constructed by experts, sunk during its maiden voyage in 1912. But Noah's ark, made by a layperson thousands of years earlier did not!

Recently I noticed that the old version of "Titanic" was on TV. Although I had no time to watch it, I was reminded of the latest version, which I saw. One of the saddest parts of the tragedy in that film was the way third class passengers were prevented from getting to the lifeboats. It did not matter, it seems, that some of them were children; the first class passengers were boarded first.

I understand that class distinctions were observed even after some of the bodies of the "Titanic" passengers were found and transported to Nova Scotia. The history of the "Titanic" revealed that the remains of first class passengers were placed in coffins, while third class passengers were put in body bags. Is this a reality in the world today? Perhaps so!

Our Heavenly Father, however, does not put a distinction on any of His children. He does not call us on the basis of our station or level in life. The Apostle Paul says in his epistle to the Galatians in 3:28, "There is neither Jew nor Greek, slave nor free, male nor female, for you are all one in Christ Jesus." Unity in Christ transcends ethnic, social and sexual distinctions. Christ broke all man-made barriers that separate people, and offered His love freely to anyone who would call on Him – the One true God. We need not see a tragedy such as the "Titanic" to open our eyes. We need only to look to Calvary. There, Christ gave His life for people of every language, race and nation.

This reminds me of an experience I had in the Holy Land a few years ago. While in Jerusalem with my husband and some 50 faithful, we visited a location believed to be the site of the Upper Room where the Last Supper took place. While in the room, I was overwhelmed by the spiritual significance of this very place. Suddenly I noticed a young couple come up the stairs. They seemed to be from some part of Africa, colorfully dressed, with scarves wrapped around their heads. As they walked around, they began to sing a familiar hymn; "Nearer My God to Thee." We all joined singing the same hymn. They sang in their language, some of us sang in Armenian, some in English, and still others in their language.

It was a spiritually moving moment of titanic proportions. I had tears in my eyes; I could hardly sing. Somehow I felt connected to these people I had never seen before. When the hymn ended, they said "Amen, Jesus, Amen." They didn't have to say more. We had communicated as fellow Christians. That day, like never before, I experienced the powerful meaning of the words of St. Paul in Eph. 2:19, "We are no longer strangers and foreigners, but fellow citizens and members of the household of God." God's spirit calls us to look beyond barriers, to the unity we are all called to enjoy as Christians. We are one in Christ!

*T*he "60 Minutes" program on TV was about Alcatraz; a small island four miles off the coast of San Francisco. The island once was a Federal prison for dangerous prisoners until 1963. It is now uninhabited, open to the public for daily tours. The host of the "60 Minutes" program was accompanied by an elderly man who at one time was himself a prisoner at Alcatraz. As a free man, he was describing what life was like when he was there. At one point they walked into a large empty room which he described as their dining room. There used to be long wooden tables, row after row, where the inmates ate all their meals. Then with a smile, he talked about the fights he witnessed there.

A day wouldn't pass, he added, without a big fight. Someone would start it, and before they even knew what it was all about, the tables would be kicked and turned over with food flying all around. Then he mentioned one prisoner who really liked dessert. The moment he set down for his meal, this man would eat his dessert first. He would secure that pleasure before anything else, because he didn't know what would happen the next moment. Recently, my husband and I took the tour of Alcatraz and couldn't help but remember that inmate when we walked into that same dining room.

The above story also reminds me of a T-shirt I saw that read, "Life is Uncertain, Eat Dessert First"! True, life is uncertain, therefore Jesus told the parable of a rich greedy man who planned to build bigger barns to store his earthly goods so that he could live many years of pleasure and ease. But God unexpectedly announced, "Fool! This night your soul will be required of you" (Luke 12:20).

This rich "fool," as Jesus calls him, had made his money honestly through the productivity of his land. And there is nothing wrong with that; the Bible does not condemn wealth. Nevertheless, in God's eyes he was a fool because of his selfishness. He responded to his abundance with pride and self-congratulations, according to the parable, with no concern for the needs of others. And God was totally absent from his plans. He was an egotistic rich man in this world; a pauper for eternity.

Jesus challenges us to think beyond earthly goods, and use part of what God has given us for His Kingdom. Faith, service and obedience to His Word are ways to become rich in God's eyes. The rich man in Jesus' parable died before he could begin to use what was stored in his big barns. If we accumulate wealth with no concern for helping others, we will enter eternity empty handed.

Great fortunes can be made and lost overnight, and no amount of money can provide health, happiness or eternal life. How much better it is to let God be our Master. Through Him we can have peace of mind, joy and security, both now and for eternity. Yes, life is uncertain, but as children of God, His joy can be our divine "sweet dessert" now and forever!

*C*elebrity figures are often elevated to such fame that their names and faces are well recognized the world over. Frank Sinatra was one of America's most celebrated and popular entertainers for several decades. He was perhaps best known for his song titled "My Way." Why was this song so favored by many? Was it because it struck a chord of independence to his fans, a chord of arrogance and self-will? It is a dominant desire of human beings to do things their own way. And that is exactly how the song ends: "I did it my way." Good, bad, or questionable; most of us want to do things our own way.

In the ordinary things of life, self-determination may be commendable. But in our relationship with God, our way is never right if it isn't in accord with His will. Just before Christ's arrest, Jesus submissively knelt down in the Garden of Gethsemane and prayed saying, "Father, if it is Your will, take this cup away from Me; nevertheless not My will, but Yours be done" (Lk. 22:42).

It is never wrong to express our true feelings to God. Jesus exposed His dread of the coming trials, but He also reaffirmed His commitment to do what God wanted. The cup He spoke of meant the terrible agony He knew He would endure – His temporary separation and alienation from the Father, and the horror of crucifixion He would experience in order to die on the cross for the world's sins. God's answer to Jesus' prayers did not allow His Son to avoid suffering. However, God provided angelic help for Jesus to face what was to come. Sometimes God answers prayers by eliminating trials; and sometimes He answers by strengthening us in the midst of them.

Regardless of how painful the surrender of our will may seem, obedience to God brings us blessings in this world and in the world to come. The right choices often require hard work and self-sacrifice. Let's not be enticed by apparent shortcuts that seem right to us, but end in spiritual death. The right choices usually leave us with peace in our heart and mind.

When God doesn't come first in our lives, everything else loses its meaning. Life becomes a tiresome process of doing "our thing in our own way," and just getting through the day, only to do the same again the following day. But when God has first priority in our lives, life becomes an exciting, meaningful adventure. Even our routine projects take on meaning and hold a greater purpose. If any of us have had enough with "our own way" and bored with life, perhaps we can reexamine our relationship with God. Our boredom could be a signal that we are slipping away from Him.

Trustful obedience to God's way brings blessings both now and for eternity. When we feel like saying, "I want to do it my way," let us remember that Jesus did it His Father's way!

*R*ecently, my husband Steve and I went on a two week cruise. Before our departure, Steve informed me that all the ship's officers were Greek. I didn't give it much thought, but from the moment we stepped aboard, I realized it was a delightful advantage. I enjoyed watching the officers' surprised expressions when I spoke to them in Greek (although Armenian, I was born and raised in Greece). One day, upon entering our cabin, we were surprised to find a lovely basket of fruit and a bottle of champagne, which we shared that evening with others at our table.

What we didn't realize was that this cruise would be a blessing to us beyond measure. One evening after the midnight buffet, Steve and I had a fascinating conversation with the ship's hotel manager. Next to the captain, he was in charge of everything. A brilliant man, well-traveled, he knew seven languages. He spoke lovingly of his parents, his humble beginnings in Athens. We talked until 1:30 a.m.

Next morning I took my Bible and went to the top lounge to read. Steve was to meet me there and take me to lunch. He came a little early and sat with me. Suddenly, the hotel manager came, pulled up a chair and sat with us. "Oh, we have the same Bible," he said, and immediately began to recite the Beatitudes in ancient Greek: "Blessed are the poor in spirit, for theirs is the kingdom of heaven, ...etc." (Matt. 5:3 – 10). He continued from the Psalms, then he chanted beautiful *sharagans* from Greek liturgy. I was amazed.

He said, "You know, I'm 47 years old, never been married. I traveled, saw a lot and enjoyed life, but nothing fills that void or brings more joy to my heart than the Word of God!" And he put his hand on my open Bible and quoted the words of Christ from John 14:6, "I am the Way, the Truth and the Life..." I was moved almost to tears. This man spoke of his faith from his heart for the next hour and a half!

The most delightful moments in life seem to catch us by surprise. Our previous conversations didn't indicate that he was a devoted Christian. We let him do most of the talking, and what a testimony it was! After lunch I had an idea. I had with me that week's Armenian Observer. I went to their office and had a copy made of my article, included a note, and sent it to the hotel manager. That evening was a formal attire night. We were invited to dine at the Captain's Table. They seated me between Steve and the manager, with the captain directly across from me. The manager said he liked my article and found it uplifting. He gave me his card and asked if I could mail him a few more of my articles. I did so upon our return. The remaining days of our trip were unforgettable! The captain was also a warm, friendly young man. In fact, I was introduced to him by the manager as one from "the old school, like them."

We must never underestimate the impact we can have for Christ. At work, neighborhood or school, people observe our behavior. By displaying our Christian values and principles in our daily lives, others will know who we are. In my case, being on vacation, all I did was study my Bible in a public place, and people would come to me. This sent forth a quiet, and perhaps, a more convincing message than a long sermon. It was truly a blessed vacation!

*W*hile on driving vacations around the country, I take particular pleasure in reading any signs that catch my attention. A large sign painted on the side of a "fix-it" shop read: "We Can Mend Everything but a Broken Heart." I admired and was intrigued with that clever bit of advertising, which raised a vital question; is there anyone who can mend a broken heart?

When the broken pieces of our lives seem beyond hope of repair, when our backs are straining under a heavy burden, or sadness overwhelms us, where can we find comfort and help? Can human wisdom, the love of family, friends or business associates provide the healing we need? As helpful and comforting as their support may be, we soon discover that the pain, the inner ache of our souls, is still there.

We know ONE, however, Who can mend broken hearts. He is the ONE known as "the Father of mercies and God of all comfort." (2 Cor. 1:3) If any of us is struggling beneath a crushing weight of sorrow and distress, scripture teaches us to "cast our burdens on the Lord and He shall sustain us." (Ps. 55:22) We can be certain that in our times of anguish and sorrow, God is watching over us. He alone can giver relief to our aching souls. He sees each of us as if we were His only child in the whole world, and He will offer relief or the strength to endure.

In His own time, and according to His own wisdom, He will uphold and sustain us, and mend our broken hearts. Are we encountering any burdens today? Let us bring them all to the ONE Who can mend anything, and continue to praise Him for the help and peace that only He can deliver!

*A*n advertisement reads, "Say it with flowers." That is one way we tell our special someone of our love, along with a well-chosen card. It is true that February 14 is the biggest day of the year for flowers and candy. But not long ago, I was amazed to read the following statement from an expert: "Three businesses make money off Valentine's Day—retail stores, the flower industry and detectives," says a Miami private investigator. Then he adds, "To us it's like Christmas!" Why detectives? Because of the request from some people who suspect that the one they love may be spending Valentine's Day in someone else's arms. If they suspect unfaithfulness, they know it will reveal itself on that day. "And it usually does," says the investigator!

When it comes to our relationship with God, the Bible says we all have a "heart problem." We have been investigated, and not only have we fallen short of our love for God, but have also been found unfaithful. We have put other things ahead of out Heavenly Father. We read in Jer. 17:9, "The heart is deceitful above all things and beyond cure. Who can understand it?" God makes it perfectly clear that it's a matter of the heart. Our hearts have a tendency toward wrongful acts from the time we were born. It's easy to fall into the routine of forgetting and forsaking God. The second commandment of the ten that God gave to Moses on Mount Sinai commands that we are not to worship other Gods. "...For I, the Lord your God, am a jealous God..." (Ex. 20:5). Anything and everything that takes priority before our Heavenly Father becomes an idol.

If we are to know God intimately then, and walk with Him faithfully, something must happen deep inside us, at the very core of our being. Our hearts must be made right with Him. King David says in Ps. 139:23 – 24, "Search me, Oh God, and know my heart; test me and know my anxious thoughts. See if there is any offensive way in me, and lead me in the way everlasting." It's not a light matter to be examined by God. This is like taking X-rays of an individual, and performing exploratory surgery for sin! God teaches and guides us through His Word. Then He shows us how we can turn to Him in repentance, show remorse, turn our lives around and be forgiven.

God measures love by obedience and faithfulness. Jesus teaches us that those who follow Him demonstrate their love to God and to one another by obedience to His commands. Love and obedience are closely connected. Love is not only a noun; it's to be an active verb.

But the supreme expression of God's love for us was Christ's death on the cross for our sins. Through Jesus' death and resurrection, God demonstrated His boundless love, even to the extent of sacrificing His Son so that we might have new life—eternal life. This is God's love for us. Are we ready to be examined and investigated by God?

A Happy Valentine's Day to you all!

*A*bout a decade ago, one of the popular songs heard on the radio and hummed by many went something like this: "What the world needs now is love, sweet love; it's the only thing that there's just too little of…etc." Is love all we need? Is that the answer? If we all just loved each other a little more, would that be enough to solve all the problems in the world? That could work perhaps, only if the love was pure, with no false motivations or hidden agendas. But who has a love that big?

There is only One Who can demonstrate love that perfect and that immense. We read in 1 John 4:7 – 8, "Beloved, let us love one another, for love is of God; and everyone who loves is born of God and knows God." We all believe that love is important, but love is usually thought of as a feeling. In reality, love is a choice and an action.

God is the source of our love. How much has God loved us? So much that He sacrificed His only Son for us. Jesus is our example of what it means to love. Everything He did in life and death was supremely loving. Our love should be like His. How well do we display our love for God in the choices we make and the actions we take?

St. John further says, "God is love." It is a simple truth taught to the youngest of children. Our world, however, with its shallow and selfish views of love, has contaminated our understanding of love. The world thinks that love is what makes a person feel good, and that it is all right to sacrifice moral principles in order to obtain such "love." But that is not real love. It is the exact opposite – selfishness. Real love is like God's love, which is holy, just, pure and perfect. If we truly know God, we will love as He does.

It is easy to say that we love God when that love costs us nothing. But the real test of our love for God is how we treat the people near us; our family members and fellow faithful. We cannot truly love God while neglecting to love those who are created in His image. As Christians, we are part of God's family, with fellow believers as our brothers and sisters. God's love is the source of all human love. In loving us as His children, God kindles a flame in our hearts. His Holy Spirit gives us the power to love, while perfecting us day by day in His ways. God has not yet finished His work in us.

Love! It is the theme of most of the songs that are written, and thousands of books that are published each year. Is love all we need? Yes! All we need is love – the perfect love of God.

One of the things I noticed when I first came to this country many years ago, was that almost every household item we bought came with instructions. A "how-to-assemble" pamphlet in the box explained how things are assembled or installed with helpful illustrations. I was amazed and appreciated the efficiency. If we would follow the instructions, the results would turn out as desired. If we chose to ignore them, failure was almost certain—and no one wishes that.

Our Christian life comes with instructions as well. They are all found in the Word of God, and are available to all for wisdom, Christian maturity and guidance in every situation. These truths of the Bible are not only to be read, but applied. "Do not merely listen to the Word ... do what it says," we read in James 1:22.

Several years ago I read a story in the "Dear Abby" column I never forgot. A young man from a wealthy family was about to graduate from high school. It was the custom for the parents to give the graduate an automobile. "Bill" and his father had spent months looking at cars, and the week before graduation, they found the perfect car. On the eve of his graduation, Bill's father handed him a gift wrapped Bible. Bill was so angry that he threw the Bible down and stormed out of the house. He and his father never saw each other again. It was the news of his father's death that brought Bill back home again. As he sat one night going through his father's possessions that he was to inherit, he came across the Bible his father had given him. He brushed away the dust and opened it to find a cashier's check made out to the exact amount of the car they had chosen together!

I hope Bill read the Bible cover to cover, for it contained much that he needed to learn: "A foolish son is a grief to his father, and bitterness to her who bore him" (Prov. 17:25). God's Word must be part of every Christian's life as a moral and ethical guide, obeyed out of love for God, and by the power that His Spirit provides. In 2 Tim. 3:16 – 17 we read, "All scripture is given by inspiration of God, and is profitable for doctrine, for reproof, for correction, for instruction in righteousness, that the man of God may be complete, thoroughly equipped for every good work."

The Bible covers all aspects of life. It is the code book God has given us for every need. But it won't be helpful if we don't read it and follow what it says and teaches. The law of God reveals the problem of sin, but the answer is found in Jesus Christ. When we put our faith in Him as our personal Lord, He forgives us and enables us to live by His strength in ways that please Him—victoriously. Jesus says in John 14:15, "If you love Me, you will keep My commandments."

Many people store the Bible on the shelf instead of in their hearts. The principles and commands of the Bible are priceless gifts from God. These principles have endured for 3,500 years, and they are never going to change; one more reason why we must follow God's "instruction book"—His "manual." When we keep our eyes on the Lord, we won't lose sight of life's purpose. God's law pinpoints our problems, but God's grace provides the solution. And that is The Good News!

*A*re we sometimes discouraged, thinking that we have so little to offer to God? Some of us might be thinking, "If only I was more talented or was very wealthy, I would do so much more for the Lord—give thousands of dollars to worthy Christian causes, the church, etc." But that could be an excuse for doing nothing. Instead of thinking what we could do if we had millions, we should check and see if we are doing the best we can with what we have right now. If we don't do our best with the gifts we possess, given to us by our Creator, we would probably do no better if we had more.

In the parable of the minas (Luke 19:12 – 27), Jesus laid down the principle that faithfulness "in a very little" opens the door to greater opportunities. Also, in the story of the widow in 1 Kings 17:8 – 16, a woman believed God's promise through Elijah and shared with him the little she had. Because of this, she became God's instrument for feeding the prophet and her own household during three difficult years of drought.

The word "widow" was practically synonymous with "poor," because in Biblical times widows were largely unprotected by the law, and were easily exploited. In a nation that required by law to care for its prophets, it is ironic that God directed Elijah to a widow to care for him. When the widow of Zarephath met Elijah, she thought she was preparing her last meal. Elijah asked her to make some kind of "cake" with the bit of flour and oil she had left. He presented her with a test of faith demanding complete commitment. Despite the scarcity of food, she was to feed God's prophet before she took care of herself and her son! But a simple act of faith produced a miracle. She trusted Elijah and gave all she had to him.

Miracles often seem so out of reach for our feeble faith. But every miracle, large or small, begins with an act of obedience. We may not see the solution until we take that first step of faith. The blessings of life and prosperity that came to this gentile widow is a stark contrast to the starvation that Israel faced. The widow showed enough faith to feed Elijah and referred to his God as Lord!

God's help often appears where we least expect it. He provides for us in ways that go beyond our narrow definitions or expectations. No matter how bitter our trials or how seemingly hopeless our situation, we should look for God's caring touch with faith. We may find His providence in some strange places. When we are faithful "in a very little" He may give us greater opportunities and enlarge our capacities in all directions. Why not leave that in God's hands and do what we can today with what we have with our time, talents and resources! Let's not squander or waste our talents. God will reward us abundantly, and His blessings will never cease, not only throughout our own lives, but through the lives of our loved ones as well!

*L*et's just imagine this for a moment. It is dark and cold. Two men are thrown into prison, not knowing when they'll be out or when they'll have a meal. What do they do? They sing! These two were the Apostle Paul and his faithful associate Silas. How could they sing under these terrible circumstances? They were imprisoned in Philippi, a city far from home. Their backs were raw from beatings, yet they sang hymns of praise (Acts 16:20 – 40).

They had risked their lives to proclaim Christ to people who resented them and strongly opposed their message. They were falsely accused by men with selfish motives who lied about their message and demanded their arrest. The town officials ordered that they be beaten and placed in stocks in the inner cell. Stocks were made of two wooden boards joined with iron clamps, leaving holes big enough for their ankles. The prisoner's legs were placed across the lower board, and the upper board was locked over them.

Paul and Silas, who were peaceful men and had committed no crimes, were put into stocks designed for holding the most dangerous prisoners in absolute security. Despite their wounds and the gloomy situation, they praised God, praying and singing as the other prisoners listened.

The Apostle Paul's and Silas' attitude teaches us an important lesson: Our inner attitude does not have to reflect our outward circumstances. Both were joyful, knowing that no matter what happened to them, Christ was with them. And what a testimony that was to the other prisoners! The Apostle Paul was imprisoned several times throughout his ministry, yet in his letters to the new churches he urges them to be joyful. Isn't it amazing that a prisoner would be telling the churches to rejoice!

It is easy to get discouraged about unpleasant circumstances, or take events of less importance too seriously. If we haven't been joyful lately, we may not be looking at life from the right perspective. Ultimate joy and peace come from Christ dwelling within us. True peace comes from knowing that God is in control. Jesus says in John 14:27, "Peace I leave with you, My peace I give to you; not as the world gives do I give to you. Let not your heart be troubled, neither let it be afraid."

No matter what afflictions or crises we may face, we too can choose how we will respond, with the help of the Holy Spirit. God will supply all our needs, but in a way that He knows is best for us. We must remember the difference between wants and needs. We may not get all that we want, but by trusting in God our attitudes can change. By accepting His provision and power, we can have His peace and joy, singing under all circumstances.

*W*alking through a public building, I heard a popular radio talk show program. I recognized the host's voice, who was talking to a celebrity guest, asking him the following question. "Name the richest person you know, who knows you by name." Interested to hear the answer, I sat on the nearest bench and waited. There was a long, very long silence on the part of the guest. Then they both laughed rather uneasily, and finally the host changed the subject completely—still laughing. I was amused by the guest's reaction to the question. He was caught completely off guard. As I entered the elevator, I could still hear them chatting.

Who is the richest person we know, who knows us by name? For a Christian, the answer is very simple; Jesus Christ, of course. He is the richest person we know, full of mercy and grace. Not only does God know each of us by name (Jn. 10:3), but even the number of hairs on our head is controlled by His sovereign will (Mt. 10:30). These are Jesus' words; a powerful affirmation indeed of God's sovereignty. Jesus is teaching us that divine providence governs and controls the timing of even the smallest and most insignificant matters of our lives. We are very valuable to God, so much so that He sent His only begotten Son to die in the cross for us, so that whoever believes in Him shall not perish but have eternal life (Jn. 3:16).

It is possible, of course, to have influential friends, and to associate with the rich and famous. There is nothing wrong with that. But not to know Christ? How tragic it is for any of us to be acquainted with leaders in government and commerce, and to miss having a vital relationship with God through faith in His Son Jesus Christ. No matter whom we know, we'll remain spiritually outcasts if we don't know Christ. That's why Jesus says, "For what will it profit a man if he gains the whole world, and loses his own soul?" (Mk. 8:36)

As Christians, our first and foremost bond is our precious relationship with our Creator. Therefore, if we know Him, we know the most important person of all! Though human leaders have much to offer, we must keep our eyes focused on Christ first, our ultimate leader. Unlike any human leader, He will never change. He is the same yesterday, today and forever. In a changing world, we can always trust our unchanging Lord. He is our strong anchor, even through suffering and uncertainty.

A world centered on position, power or possessions is ultimately worthless. Whatever we own on earth is only temporary; it cannot be exchanged for our soul. Are we willing to make the pursuit of God more important than anything else? Only as followers of Christ will we know what it means to live abundantly now, and have eternal life as well. Some of us, perhaps, are not acquainted at all with the rich and famous. Well, if we know Christ personally, we know the richest and most important person of all! He is a friend who will never fail us or forsake us (Heb. 13:5). He is the richest One to know! As Christians, it's Who we know that counts. The benefits of this relationship are out of this world!

$\mathcal{T}$he story is told that at a remote corner of a cemetery there was an unmarked tombstone with a single word written on it—"Forgiven." Nothing more—simply "Forgiven." One cannot help but wonder, who was forgiven, for what, when and by whom? What caused someone to leave that message forever engraved upon that tombstone?

The mysterious secret of that grave has been long buried. But one thing remains certain by the living; that the need for forgiveness still exists. Someone remarked, "Everyone should have a cemetery plot in which to bury faults." What is more serious, however, is that we all behave below God's standards at one time or another. No one is able to perfectly keep all God's commandments. The Bible says, "For all have sinned, and fall short of the glory of God" (Rom. 3:23).

Some wrong actions are worse that others, and their consequences are more serious. Regardless of how great or small the wrongful acts, they separate us from our Creator. Therefore, we are in need of God's divine forgiveness. God provided us a Savior! He sent His one and only Son to this earth, born of a virgin, to become a man, and to ultimately give His life on the cross for our redemption. Because of that we know we have forgiveness by God's grace.

There are countless verses in the Bible on forgiveness. In Matt. 18:21 – 35, Peter asks Jesus how many times shall we forgive when someone sins against us; up to seven times? Jesus answered, "Seventy times seven." The issue is not what others have done to us, but what Christ has done for us. If we were to take the Lord's Prayer, which Christ taught His disciples as a model prayer, we say, "And forgive us our debts as we forgive our debtors." This is both a prayer and a confession. For the person who prays for forgiveness, admits at the same time that he or she is guilty.

Only when God has given us the grace to forgive others can we utter a true prayer for forgiveness. This was looked upon by Christ as of such importance that He emphasized it several times in the Gospels. No, we don't need a cemetery plot in which to bury our wrongful acts. We only need to turn to God in prayer and repent. Only then can we truly grow and mature spiritually.

God can change our lives from darkness to light, from weakness to strength, from anger to love, from tribulation to peace, from sadness to joy, from defeat to victory, from fear to faith, from "I can't" to "I can"! Forgiveness rests on the atoning work of Christ. It is an act of sheer grace. And yes, Lord, forgive our debts as we forgive our debtors!

I have received nothing but glowing reports from my dentist in recent years. Wishing to take some of the credit, I explained during my last visit that I had faithfully followed her time consuming tooth care routine, including flossing. At this point, my dentist took the opportunity to give me her version of "natural law." With a twinkle in her eyes she said, "Oh you don't have to floss every tooth, only floss the ones you want to keep." We laughed and agreed that natural laws do exist in our world. We just don't like to admit that nature is unforgiving and will always punish those who neglect or refuse to obey the rules.

Spiritual laws also exist in our world, whether we acknowledge them or not. God's laws, like natural laws, are inflexible. We simply cannot ignore or neglect them without facing the consequences. In his epistle to the Galatians, Apostle Paul said, "Do not be deceived: God cannot be mocked. A man reaps what he sows. The one who sows to please his sinful nature, from that nature will reap destruction; the one who sows to please the Lord, from the Lord will reap eternal life. Let us not become weary in doing good, for at the proper time we will reap a harvest if we do not give up" (Galatians 6:7 – 9).

We reap what we sow. This principle applies not only negatively, but also positively. This is an unfailing and unchangeable law. Everything in nature reproduces after its own kind. And every one of us will reap what we sow and be responsible for our own destiny. It would certainly be surprising if we planted corn and onions came up. Every action has results. If we are unkind to friends, we will lose their friendship. If we plan to please God, we'll reap joy and everlasting life.

It is discouraging to continue to do right and receive no tangible results. But St. Paul challenges us to keep on doing good and trust God for results. In due time, we will reap a harvest of blessings.

Let us not forget our spiritual laws and its principles. Like the "natural law" for tooth care, if ignored, can eventually bring deterioration. The law of Cause and Effect simply means that whatever we think or do in life will come back to us in due course. We will undoubtedly reap whatever we sow.

*I*t is exciting to be promoted. When we work hard, eventually we are rewarded. But what if one is an assistant manager of a department store and is "promoted" to be a delivery boy. That doesn't sound right, does it? For us, promotion means elevation of status and better pay. But not according to what God considers promotion in His service.

In Acts chapter 6, we see that the early Church in Jerusalem had some problems. A dispute had developed between the Hellenists (Jewish Christians from the Diaspora whose first language was Greek) and the Hebrews (Palestinian Jewish Christians who spoke Aramaic, a Semitic language). The Hellenists complained to the apostles that their widows were neglected in the daily distribution of food. Jews who had accepted the Christian faith were usually cut off from their families. Therefore, the sharing of food and resources was a necessary mark of the early Church. To correct the situation, the twelve apostles selected seven Hellenists and put them in charge of the food distribution program. One of these men was Stephen.

This task was not taken lightly. The requirements were: "Men of good reputation, full of the Holy Spirit and wisdom." Were these seven appointed as teachers or pastors? No! They were appointed to wait on tables! That is God's idea of promotion – serving. Striving for excellence in small assignments prepares one for greater responsibilities.

Stephen's name is Greek, *Stephanos*, which means "crown" or "wreath," laurels given to champion athletes at the earliest Olympic games. Stephen was a layman who emerged as a leader in that gifted group of seven. The Bible says he "did great wonders and miraculous signs among the people." God used Stephen in that serving capacity in a most amazing way. He proved to be an outstanding administrator, leader, teacher and debater. But with power came opposition.

When Stephen was arrested and brought before the council, his opponents testified falsely against him. They distorted his words, depicting them as a direct attack against their Mosaic Law and God. But God's Spirit was powerfully with Stephen. His face shone with God's empowering presence. His words centered on Christ Who had made such a difference in his life. Stephen's message to the council angered his audience. He was dragged by a furious mob and stoned outside the city. As the stones battered his body, he fell to his knees in prayer. His words echoed Jesus' last words on the cross: "Lord, do not hold this sin against them" (Acts 7:60).

Around the world, the gospel has most often taken root in places prepared by the blood of martyrs. One way God trains His servants is to place them in insignificant positions. Although St. Stephen appears in only one episode in Acts, striking consequences resulted from his death. The persecution of Christ's disciples which followed (Acts 8) led to a more widespread preaching of the gospel. In a short time the Word of God spread like ripples in a pond, where from a single point, each wave leads to the next, spreading wider and further. God's idea of promotion is serving Him and others, often in the simplest ways. And that is a privilege!

*S*everal years ago on a winter evening, the electrical power in our entire neighborhood went out. Every member of our family was home—we had just finished dinner. We lit several candles, but soon learned the outage might last a while. Nothing functioned in the house since we had no power, and it was getting chilly. I suggested we go to the living room and start a fire in the fireplace. We all sat around the fire reclining on comfortable cushions, drinking Armenian coffee and hot chocolate that I made in the fireplace. Not only did we make the best of an unexpected situation, but it also turned out to be an intimate fun evening with blessed results.

My sons and daughter began to ask me questions about my childhood in Greece, and about their great grandparents. They asked about the Armenians there, and our relatives who all went to Armenia in 1947. And how only by God's plan and grace were we prevented from going, and eventually we came to the United States. They asked about our spiritual life, our church, Armenian schools and education, our traditions, holidays, etc. The discussions were often lively, and at times very emotional for me. We did not realize we had talked for several hours. Even when the electricity was back, we continued talking. When we let the fire die and went to bed, we all agreed that we wouldn't mind doing this a few times a year, even if we had to lose power to accomplish it. The unexpected event became a blessing to us.

It is a joy to see our adult children interested in their roots. And how would they know if we don't pass this valuable information and personal lessons from our lives to them? The book of Joshua and the Israelites crossing the Jordan River comes to mind. Joshua was Moses' successor. After 40 years of wandering in the wilderness, this new generation was eager to enter the Promised Land, but first they had to cross that river. God had parted the Red Sea to let them come out of Egypt (Ex. 14), and here He parted the Jordan River to let them enter Canaan (Josh. 3:16).

After crossing safely, God directed them to first build a memorial from 12 big stones taken from the river bed by 12 men; one from each tribe (Josh. 4:6, 7). This may seem like an insignificant step, but God didn't want them to plunge into their task unprepared. They were to focus on Him first and remember Who was guiding them. This monument of 12 big stones was to be a constant reminder of their crossing the Jordan River on dry ground. Their children would see the stones, hear the story, and learn about God's goodness and mighty power!

We all have family traditions or momentos to help our children learn about God's work in our lives. We must take the time to tell them what God has done for us; His blessings, our answered prayers, and even the unanswered ones that turned out to be a blessing in the long run. Retelling our stories or building additional insights in their hearts and minds will continue to keep memories of God's goodness alive in our families. Although we are all busy, let's set aside quiet moments, time to build our own "memorials" to God's faithfulness. The wonderful works of God that occurred in our lives will affect those who hear about them as powerfully as those who experienced them!

*S*everal stories with the same point were being told as I was growing up. The following was a popular one.

Mr. Z was gravely ill. He had not seen his former best friend, Mr. J, for years because of their broken relationship. Wishing to make things right between them, he sent word for J to come and see him. When J came, Z told him that his condition was serious and he didn't want to die with such hurtful feelings between them. Then, by carefully chosen words and difficulty, Z apologized for hurtful things he had said and done. He also told J he forgave him for his offenses. All appeared well until J stood up to leave. As he walked out of the room, Z called out after him saying, "Remember, if I get well, this apology doesn't count!"

Does this story sound somewhat familiar? What a picture of the way we sometimes treat one another! The forgiveness we offer is often superficial, lacking depth, and is given with a selfish motive. We say we forgive, but when the first little friction arises, how quickly we resurrect the past. We do "bury the hatchet," but with the handle sticking out. That way we can conveniently pick it up again and use it to our advantage.

The Apostle Paul says in Ephesians 4:32, "Be kind to one another, even as God in Christ forgave you." This is Christ's law of forgiveness as taught in the Gospels. We also see it in the Lord's Prayer, "Forgive us our debts as we forgive our debtors." Do we? God does not forgive us because we forgive others, but solely because of His great mercy.

It is easy to ask God's forgiveness, but difficult to grant it to others. Whenever we ask God to forgive us, we should ask ourselves, have I forgiven those who have wronged me? Those who are unwilling to forgive have not understood Christ who forgave even those who crucified Him (Luke 23:34). The key to forgiving others is to remember how much God has forgiven us. Is it so difficult for us to forgive someone who has wronged us a little, when God has forgiven us for so much? Realizing God's infinite love and forgiveness can help us love and forgive others. Forgiveness is the glue that restores our broken relationships.

If God is willing to forgive us with all our faults, how can we not do the same to those who have wronged us? True Christ-like forgiveness means to bury the hatchet, including the handle, once and for all, deeply and completely.

*N*ot long ago I locked myself out of my car. Ready to go out, I drove the car out of the garage into the driveway. While the engine was running, I ran into the house to get my sunglasses. When I closed the door, all the doors locked automatically. Luckily, I still held onto my purse where I had an extra key. It was a lesson I won't forget.

As I drove away I thought how sad it would be for all those who might some-day be "locked out" of God's eternal Kingdom for not knowing Christ. Jesus tells the parable of the ten bridesmaids in Matthew 25:1 – 13. This parable is about a wedding. As I researched Jewish weddings of biblical times, I noted that there are two distinct parts to this kind of wedding. First, the bridegroom with family, relatives and friends, dressed in their best, would walk to the bride's house with gifts and music to claim his bride and observe certain religious ceremonies. Then, a procession would follow as the bridegroom takes his bride and her people to his house to complete the wedding festivities that would often last a full week. For a night wedding, lamps or torches were needed for the procession.

In this parable Jesus tells of ten bridesmaids who were also waiting for the bridegroom. But while the groom was delayed, and the time of his coming was not known, the ten fell asleep! At midnight it was announced with excitement, "Behold, the bridegroom is coming; go out to meet him." Now, of the ten maidens, five were wise and five were foolish. The wise were prepared with oil in their vessels and lamps, but the foolish, unprepared as they were, soon ran out of oil. They asked the wise if they could borrow some oil. But the wise refused because there was not enough for both of them. While the foolish maidens quickly ran out to buy more oil, the bridegroom suddenly came! Those who were ready followed the groom to the wedding banquet, and the door was shut! When the five foolish maidens returned, they came to the door saying, " 'Lord, Lord, open to us!' But He answered and said, 'Assuredly I say to you, I do not know you.' "

Jesus is warning His listeners, "Watch therefore, for you know neither the day nor the hour in which the Son of Man is coming." In this parable Christ clarifies what it means to be ready for His return, even though the time is not known. He stresses that every person is responsible for his or her spiritual condition of readiness. Christ also teaches us that spiritual preparation cannot be bought or borrowed at the last minute. Our relationship with God must be personal. In this parable, an earthly story with an heavenly meaning, Jesus underscores the importance of being ready in any event – even if He delays longer than expected.

Our groom is Christ, the Messiah! His bride is the Church, and the people in the wedding procession are the faithful who follow Him. We are all invited to RSVP to His wedding banquet! Let us continue to be wise and keep our spiritual lamps ready, full of His "oil," and be watchful. Let us have the Light of His Holy Spirit shine in and through us and work diligently in His service to be worthy of entering the "wedding banquet" of His Kingdom.

*W*e were on one of our driving vacations, exploring places we had not seen before. My husband Steve and I flew to Utah, rented a car, and planned to drive through several states, such as Colorado, Wyoming, Idaho, Montana and South Dakota. After spending a few days sight-seeing in Utah, we had an early start driving out of Salt Lake City.

We had just exited the interstate to have breakfast in a small town nearby. I had my Bible open on my lap as usual, giving a devotional to an audience of one—Steve. Suddenly I noticed he looked in his rear view mirror and said that flashing red and blue lights of a police car were behind us. He pulled to the side, while I thought that it couldn't possibly be for us!

The officer came to the window and asked for Steve's driver's license. "Californians—are you on vacation?" he asked. Then he politely pointed out that the speed limit drops considerably on the streets of this town compared to the interstate, and that we should be more careful. Steve admitted that he had not slowed down sufficiently after leaving the highway, and that we were actually on our way to have some breakfast.

At this point I thought I must add a few words myself, and told the officer that perhaps it was my fault, distracting the driver by talking non-stop with my devotional on this beautiful Sunday morning. He looked at both of us, my Bible still open on my lap, handed us only a WARNING ticket, and told us to be more cautious. He then gave us directions to a coffee shop! We thanked him, and needless to say, we were more careful with local speed limits.

Similarly, when we violate God's laws we may not always have to pay a severe penalty. Sometimes He gives us a warning. Our spirit has to be open and sensitive to His voice. God's guidance may come to us through our conscience, or it could come through the gentle advice of a friend or family member. We might hear it in a sermon or while reading the Bible. It is important that we listen to the Lord's warnings. They are given in grace by a patient, all-knowing God. If we don't, the consequences of our actions might be a lot worse than a policeman's warning.

God is omnipresent, and because of this, we can never be isolated from His Spirit. This is indeed very good news to all those who know and love God, because no matter what we do or where we go, we will never be far from God's comforting presence (Rom. 8:35). That's God's grace for us!

I like sweets. When we go to banquets, as soon as we take our assigned seats I take the program, turn to the page where it says "Menu," and I only read the bottom line. I first want to know what are we having for dessert. My husband tells me I have given a new meaning to the expression "Bottom Line."

This phase, "Bottom Line," comes from the world of business and finance. It usually appears as the final line of the last page of a financial report, and it refers to an individual's or a company's asset balance. This "bottom line" tells how one stands on the most important aspect of the report—how much money one made or lost.

This principle appears in other aspects of society as well. For an olympic athlete, after years of training, the bottom line is winning that all-important medal! A coach, for example, may tell his players that the bottom line for their team is not for individual athletic performance to impress the crowd, but for their team to win!

So what is the bottom line for the followers of Christ? The author of Ecclesiastes clearly gives us a hard, unblinking look at life with his bottom line words: "…Fear God and keep His commandments, for this is the whole duty of man. For God will bring every deed into judgment, including every hidden thing, whether it is good or evil" (Ecc. 12:13 – 14).

Reverence for God and His Word is absolutely essential in Christian life. No matter what the apparent circumstances or contradictions of life are, we must work for the single purpose of knowing God. In Ecclesiastes Solomon shows us that we should enjoy life, but this does not exempt us from obeying God's commandments. We should search for purpose and meaning in life, but they cannot be found in human endeavors. We should acknowledge the evils and injustices of life, yet maintain a pure, positive attitude with strong faith and trust in God.

The Bible teaches us that all people will stand before God. We will not be able to use life's inconsistencies as an excuse for failing to live God-honoring lives. To live properly, we need to recognize that human effort apart from God is futile and vain. We must put God first, then receive every thing good as gifts from God, and realize that God will judge both evil and good. How strange that people spend their lives striving for the very enjoyment that God gives freely as a gift!

Obedience is the measure of our love for God. When we trust God and make Him the center of our existence, then the "bottom line" of our lives will not be loss, but will be the gain of God's approval. That is our "bottom line."

*W*hile driving, I was listening to Dennis Prager's radio program. A young man called with a personal story. He said he had graduated from a prestigious university and its graduate business school. As a student he was led to believe that in a few years, with the education he had received, he could be a successful top executive or president of some big corporation. The young man confessed he was doing OK, but was frustrated for not being one of the "big boys" yet.

He was unhappy, "kicking himself," as he put it, for not reaching the potential he thought he had. One day while driving around in an exclusive neighborhood, he recognized a young man and stopped. They talked, and it turned out that they had graduated together. Seeing him living in such a big house, his envy and frustration grew even more.

A few months later, while in line at a large discount department store, he looked at the cashier's name tag and recognized her. It turned out she had also graduated with him. The caller exclaimed, "Dennis, God was teaching me a lesson! God delivered me from my pride! I am a much happier man today, and I am doing well." The host thanked him for a great story and went on to local news.

God is teaching us lessons more often than we think. I was amazed by the young man's insight. There is absolutely nothing wrong with being a cashier. But our pride often may be our worst enemy. Now that the young man's frustrations were over, he was relaxed and perhaps may do even much better.

Comparing ourselves with others constructively with a goal is good. But being frustrated, envious and impatient can be dangerous. Fortunately, the young man didn't turn to dishonest means. We read in Proverbs 13:11, "Wealth gained by dishonesty will be diminished, but he who gathers by labor will be increased." And St. Paul says in Gal. 6:4, "Each one should test his own actions. Then he can take pride in himself, without comparing himself to somebody else..."

When we do our very best, we feel good about the results. People make comparisons for many reasons. Some point out others' flaws in order to feel better about themselves. Others simply want reassurance that they are doing well. When we are tempted to compare, we must examine ourselves as individuals before God, rather than in comparison with others. His loving acceptance will comfort us even when we fall short of our expectations.

There is no formula or shortcut for success. But self discipline is a character trait of all successful people. When we are motivated by a spirit of foresight and diligence and avoid procrastination, we will discover that we will have no fear for the future. Although most of us focus on the human side of success, and there are many verses in Proverbs speaking about achieving financial security, there are even more verses that underscore the importance of a commitment to the Lord. Following God is the primary quality of one who is successful in God's eyes. Prov. 16:3 confirms: "Commit to the Lord whatever you do, and your plans will succeed." Now that is a "win-win" formula!

*A*long with hundreds of tourists, I have walked with reverence through countless impressive cathedrals in several cities and capitals of the world, including ours in Washington, DC. Most of these ancient cathedrals stand as examples of fine artistry and craftsmanship. It is amazing what can be done when people combine their skills for a common goal. Architects, masons, stained glass artists, sculptors, metal smiths and others, work cooperatively, doing what they do best; building a church.

In Old Testament times something similar happened when a magnificent temple was built under the watchful eyes of King Solomon. Highly skilled workmen combined their God-given abilities to produce an impressive structure suitable for worship.

Then, God began a new building program by forming the New Testament Church. Amazingly, He used countless devoted Christians, men and women, with their unique skills to build it. God's new church was not constructed of stone and mortar, but was made entirely out of people. That building program has been going on for nearly 2,000 years, and its dynamic growth continues to this day.

The Apostle Paul writes in Ephesians 2:20 – 22 that all Christians are being built together to become a dwelling in which God lives by His Spirit, with Christ Himself as the precious, life-giving "Chief Cornerstone." He uses the metaphor of the building. Believers certainly are not literally pieces of rock, but dedicated men and women who derive their life and vitality from Christ, the original living "Cornerstone."

Every follower of Christ has been given special skills and talents in building God's church for His glory. We often call a church building "God's House." In reality, God's household is not a building, but a group of dedicated, devoted Christians. God lives in us and shows Himself to a watching world through us. By this, people can see that God is love and Christ is our Lord when we live in harmony with each other. Every child of God is a church builder. As Christian men and women, we are all gifted craftsmen, building the greatest masterpiece in the world—God's Church!

*T*his amazing story passed across my desk. According to syndicated columnist L. M. Boyd, an out of work, penniless man was strolling along a San Francisco beach in 1949. This man, Jack Wurm, found a bottle on the sand with a note inside that read, "To avoid confusion, I leave my entire estate to the lucky person who finds this bottle, and to my attorney, Barry Cohen. Share and share alike." The courts accepted the document as the last will of Daisy Singer Alexander, heiress of the Singer sewing machine fortune. She had thrown it into the Thames River in London twelve years earlier. It somehow made its way across the oceans and was washed ashore in California where Jack Wurm went from poverty to wealth.

The Bible also speaks of a great wealth, reserved in heaven (1 Peter 1:4). It speaks of a imperishable inheritance available to all those who acknowledge their spiritual poverty, to become heirs to that wealth by trusting in Christ as Savior and Lord. The Apostle Paul writes in Eph. 1:13, 14: "Having believed, you were sealed with the Holy Spirit of promise, Who is the guarantee of our inheritance until the redemption of the purchased possession."

The Holy Spirit is not only a fulfillment of God's promise to indwell in the hearts of His people, but also is an assurance that He will bring us to our final inheritance—as a down payment or first installment on our full redemption. St. Paul used the word "seal" as a metaphor for the Holy Spirit's supernatural work in a believer's life; a seal-like impression made by a king's signet ring, with the Holy Spirit as an inward mark of God's ownership of His people. It is a sign that we are validated as members of God's family. The Holy Spirit is the promise of God. Jesus says in Luke 24:49, "I am going to send you what the Father has promised."

Remarkably, this promise is extended to every person under the sun on the basis of their faith and trust in Christ. In His infinite love, God has adopted us as His own children with all the rights and privileges, but also with all its responsibilities. Through Christ's sacrificial death on the cross, resurrection and ascension, He brought us into His family and made us heirs. As Christians, we are the Master's children. What a privilege!

Daisy Singer Alexander put her wealth in a bottle because she couldn't take it with her. Jack Wurm, who inherited it, couldn't take it with him either. But praise God, we are heirs of a wonderful, imperishable inheritance that begins in this life and will be fully realized throughout all eternity. We are stockholders of the divine treasures of heaven. What is our assurance? It is the Holy Spirit who already lives in all those who have received Christ into their hearts!

*I*t has been said, imitation is the best form of flattery. Apostle Paul uses this thought in the following manner. St. Paul instructs the Corinthian believers: "Be imitators of me, as I am of Christ" (1 Cor. 11:1). He describes how he tried to model his life after Christ, conducting himself with holiness and righteousness. The Apostle was not being arrogant or proud when he drew attention to himself, or thought himself as perfect. He said this because, at that time, the Corinthian faithful did not know much about the life, ministry and teachings of Christ. He could not tell them to imitate Jesus because the gospels had not yet been written. The best way to teach these new Christians about Christ was to point them to a mature, Godly man whom they trusted. The Apostle Paul had been in Corinth for almost two years and had built a relationship of trust with many of these new followers. He believed Christian growth is best achieved through imitating an example. A Godly mentor was crucial to his discipleship ministry.

The natural question then comes to mind. Who is our spiritual example? Whom do we imitate? Often people, and especially the youth, look to their environment, searching for role models. And most of us are tempted to look in the spotlights to find our heroes. We fail to see that most Godly men and women are not to be found in the spotlights. They are graciously and humbly, quietly and faithfully serving their families, their community and God.

How can we learn more and set the right example for others? God's book, the Bible, "The Breath of God," (as we Armenians so appropriately call it) is the only book with countless heroes, with Christ being highest above all. He is the Head of His Church. By reading the Bible, meditating on it, and putting it into practice, we will know Whom to imitate. By doing so, we will begin to truly know Christ Himself.

*T*he following story was related to me by my grandmother when I was a child. There was a king who had a silver bell placed in a high tower of his palace, early in his reign. He announced to his people that he would ring the bell whenever he was happy so that his subjects would know of his joy. The people anticipated the sound of that silver bell to ring, but it remained silent. Months and years passed, but no sound of the bell was heard. The monarch grew old and gray, and eventually he lay on his death bed. As some of his weeping citizens gathered around him, he discovered that he had truly been loved by his people all through the years. At last the king was happy. Just before he died, he reached up and pulled the rope that rang the silver bell! Imagine, a lifetime of unhappiness for not knowing that he was warmly loved and accepted by his loyal subjects.

The human spirit rings with hope at the sound of an encouraging word! Therefore, St. Paul says in 1 Thes. 5:11, "Comfort each other and edify one another…" Just as the Apostle Paul gives the churches uplifting messages of hope, we too can serve Christ and bring joy to others by our encouraging words. One of the greatest ministries we can have is to lift the spirits of our fellow man.

Let's look around us and be sensitive to others' needs and offer support. Let's give someone a pat on the back when they deserve it, or compliment a child who does something well. Commend young parents who attend church with their children. Encourage the person who keeps helping others even though he or she may receive little appreciation from them.

We can also have a wonderful ministry as card senders. Even those who appear to "have it all together" may need a lift. On the surface, a person may seem fine – especially at church. But beneath that "doing great" exterior may be a spirit that is ready to give up hope. A card with uplifting words can help. All of us need a word of encouragement from time to time, especially when facing a major new challenge; the loss of a job, an illness, or loss of a loved one.

We also need words of appreciation as we carry out our daily responsibilities, whether at home, work or church. Let's determine to encourage, not flatter, at least one person every day. Prov. 17:22 says, "A merry heart does good like medicine, but a broken spirit dries the bones." We could be that pain relieving medicine! We could give someone a joy transfusion!

One of the best evidences of our Christian faith is our kindness to others. Like that monarch, many lonely soles live out their days without the joy of knowing they are loved and appreciated by others. Kindness is the oil that takes the friction out of life's difficulties. Let's not wait until it's too late to be kind. It takes only a moment to be kind, but the results could last a lifetime!

*I*t is early morning and we ask ourselves that all-important question: What should I wear today? What we wear is important to most of us. We want to dress appropriately, be in style, and look our best. Our schedule usually determines the kind of clothes we wear each day. Many feel that clothes do make a lasting impression. Also, when we feel we look good, we go through the day with more energy and confidence.

Perhaps our Lord is concerned with what we wear physically, but He is far more interested in what we "put on" spiritually. St. Paul lists in Colossians 3:12 – 15 some of the precious qualities we should wear throughout the day: Compassion, kindness, humility, thankfulness, gentleness, patience, forgiveness and love. It teaches us to imitate Christ's compassionate, forgiving attitude, let His peace rule in our hearts, always be thankful, let His love guide our lives and live as Christ's representative.

Is it difficult for some of us to forgive others who have wronged us? Yet God has forgiven so much about us! The key to forgiving others is to remember how God dealt with us – with patience and much gentleness. All the virtues that St. Paul encourages us to develop are perfectly bound together by love. As we clothe ourselves with these virtues daily, the last garment we are to "put on" is love, which holds all the rest in place.

As Christians we should live in peace. To live in peace does not mean that suddenly all differences of opinion disappear. But it does require that loving Christians work together despite differences. Such love is not a feeling, but a decision to meet others' needs. To live in love leads to peace between individuals and among the members of the body of believers.

If problems in our relationships result in conflict, it may be just a matter of "clothing." We should check St. Paul's list to see which of the above-mentioned spiritual garments we have neglected to wear that day. Then we'll know what to wear every morning of each day!

*I*t has been said that one of the best things about the future is that it comes one day at a time. This expression is often used because some of us, at times, worry about the future. Admittedly, life for even the most dedicated of God's people can sometimes be difficult. Circumstances may be hard, and thoughts of the future may become heavy and uncertain. But the Lord wants us to bring our cares to Him. His words to us are, "I say unto you, do not worry about your life." (Matt 6:25)

A simple statement such as this is always a puzzle to most of us. How can we be so carefree when we think of our future? Christ further says, "But seek first the Kingdom of God and His righteousness, and all these things shall be added to you" (Matt. 6:33). "Seek," means an earnest, serious pursuit. We are told in effect, before we go any further, above all and beyond everything else, this should be our first priority. Christ stresses the words, "But seek first..." We should actively choose to give Him first place in every area of our lives.

Common sense and our circumstances, however, strongly suggest that we must consider the future. Yet Christ knows our circumstances better than we do, and wishes that we put our relationship with Him first. Worry not only consumes our thoughts, it also reduces our ability to trust God. Worry immobilizes us, but concern moves us to action. Planning for tomorrow with prayer is time well spent, while worrying about it is time and energy wasted. When done well, planning can alleviate worry.

If we want to overcome our worries, we must accept each day with thanksgiving as a new and precious gift from God, and live it to the fullest. We can then plan carefully for the future by seeking His wisdom and guidance through prayer. Then we will start thinking of the future, one day at a time.

When we start each day with prayer, we will be able to say with the psalmist, "This is the day the Lord has made; we will rejoice and be glad in it" (Ps 118:24). Yes, let us rejoice and praise God each day!

*N*ehemiah was commissioned by Artaxerxes, King of Persia, to rebuild the walls of Jerusalem which were in ruin, and the city was defenseless. When Nehemiah arrived in Jerusalem around 445 BC, he faced opposition. He and his crew were mocked by their enemies who did not want to see the walls built. Nehemiah paid no attention to his critics. He was convinced that God was with them. He prayed, left the matter in God's hands and went back to work. The project was completed in 52 days despite opposition. Nehemiah, writing in the first person, said, "When all our enemies heard about this, all the surrounding nations were afraid and lost their self-confidence, because they realized this work had been done with the help of our God" (Neh. 6: 16).

In more recent times, the builders of the Panama Canal faced enormous obstacles of geography, climate, and disease. After the French gave up, the commission was reorganized, and in 1907, President Theodore Roosevelt put the construction work under the direction of the United States Army Corps of Engineers. Colonel George Washington Goethals was chosen to head the project. The colonel had to endure severe criticism from many back home who predicted that he would never complete the "impossible task."

The great engineer, however, pressed steadily forward in his work without responding to those who opposed him. A subordinate asked him one day if he was going to answer his critics. Goethals replied that he would in time. When asked how and when he intended to do that, he said, "With the completed canal!" His answer became reality on August 15, 1914, when the canal opened to traffic for the first time. The construction of this canal ranks as one of the greatest engineering works of all time. It was estimated that it would be completed in ten years, but the canal was in operation three years sooner than expected!

If we try to respond to all our critics as we serve the Lord, nothing worthwhile would be accomplished. But if we are confident we are doing God's will, we can first pray, then close our ears to criticism, and press on with the work. God judges us by our obedience, faithfulness and devotion—not by what others think or say. Completing the task is the best way to silence critics.

*W*e have created instant lifestyles for ourselves. One hour photo processing, same day dry cleaning, drive-through meals, etc. If things don't happen instantly, we get impatient. As Christians, we often direct our impatience toward God, especially when we undergo trials. We want God to act instantly and rescue us. But God is never in a hurry. Look how long He delayed before He sent Christ into the world. Yet, "When the fullness of the time had come, God sent forth His Son..." (Gal. 4:4). There is a right time for us as well, according to God's will; the right time to bring us to maturity and strong faith, because trials result in spiritual growth.

We can't know the depth of our character until we see how we react under pressure. God wants to make us perfect and complete, but not keep us from all pain.

The story is told of an impatient student who asked a Christian college president, "Can I take a shorter course of studies than the one in the college catalog? I would like to graduate sooner." "Oh, yes," replied the president. "It all depends on what you want to be. When God wants to make a giant oak, He takes a hundred years. But when He wants to make a squash, He takes six months."

The oak tree is a good example for this country. Last summer, however, when my husband and I were in the Middle East, we saw the mighty cedars of Lebanon that were symbols of majesty and strength in biblical imagery in the Old Testament. They are now reduced to a small number and are protected in a mountaintop park. Cedar wood is highly esteemed for its durability and was used for building King David's palace (2 Sam. 5:11), Solomon's temple (1 Kings 5: 6 – 10), and later, the new temple built after the Babylonian exile (Ezra 3:7). Full grown cedars may attain a height of 40 meters, and don't produce seeds until after 40 years! Yes, when God wants to make a giant cedar, He takes hundreds of years!

We read in 2 Peter 3:18: "Grow in the grace and knowledge of our Lord and Savior Jesus Christ". St. Peter urges his readers to grow spiritually and get to know God better. No matter where we are in our spiritual journey and faith, our ungodly world will always challenge our faith. Difficulties usually help us grow. Trials can be considered joy, not because we like pain or deny its existence, but because we know that God uses life's difficulties to build our character. They are tests of faith given in order to develop our perseverance and patience. We all find our patience tested daily. We can thank God for those opportunities to grow and deal with them with His strength.

God Who began a good work in us will continue it through our lifetime. His work in us began when we first accepted Christ in our hearts. His Holy Spirit now lives in us, enabling us to be the kind of Christians He wants us to become. God will help us grow in grace, one day at a time.

Who wants to be a squash? When our patience is being stretched, we are given the opportunity to expand. And a lot of expansion is needed. God is not finished with us yet!

WHAT ABOUT HONESTY?

*A*s though things were not puzzling enough in today's society, some people feel that honesty is fast disappearing from our daily lives. There was an ongoing conversation between three people seated in front of me on an airplane. "You are guilty only if you are caught," said one of them. I wondered if the expression "Honesty is the best policy" was truly out of date. Often, however, when our environment appears discouraging, something positive happens to restore our faith in today's society and people.

I was at a small clothing store not long ago which had its own parking lot. A young woman suddenly walked in asking who owned a certain car. She asked me to follow her, explaining that she had hit my car while pulling out of her parking space. I was shocked to see the big ugly dent on my car! She apologized. I certainly appreciated her honesty. It all ended well— my car was repaired.

A few months later while at the gym, I heard my car's license plate number paged. I went to the front desk. This time, another young woman was telling me almost the same story! My car was hit so badly that one door wouldn't even open. It seemed unbelievable. Twice in one year! Again my car was repaired beautifully. My husband jokes about knowing a good auto body repair shop by now.

How refreshing it is to meet people with integrity who live by God's standards! The exemplary behavior and honorable character of these two women will remain with me forever, despite the inconveniences of car repair. In a society that often treats honesty like an artifact from an ancient world, we need to demonstrate the validity of King Solomon's wise words, "The Lord detests lying lips, but He delights in those who are truthful." (Prov. 12:22)

As Christians we are ambassadors of Christ, and living by God's standards is a delight to our Heavenly Father. Yes, it is refreshing and comforting to know that honesty is still the best policy and not out of date.

One of the most endearing pictures I know is Jesus portrayed as a shepherd. After rescuing a lamb, He carries it to the safety of His fold. There are many references to sheep and shepherds throughout the Bible. Many important figures in the Old Testament were shepherds, including Abraham, Isaac, Jacob, Jacob's sons, Moses and David. The occupation first appears in Genesis 4:2, when Abel, a "keeper of sheep," comes into conflict with Cain.

The inspiration of this Biblical imagery, Christ as our shepherd, is taken, no doubt, from the gospels of Luke 15 and John 10: 11 – 14. Jesus says, "I am the Good Shepherd. The Good Shepherd gives His life for His sheep…I know My sheep, and My sheep know Me." Christ declares Himself to be the Shepherd of mankind; that is, of as many of them as will accept Him as their Shepherd. People of all nations, as one flock, can be led by one Shepherd. It is a beautiful metaphor, ever cherished by Christians, of Jesus' tender and devoted care for His people.

As one journeys through Israel, it is common to see flocks of sheep and goats. Most of them are owned by Bedouins, nomadic people who live in tents on hillsides of Judea and Samaria.

In Psalm 23, David identified himself with sheep. "The Lord is my shepherd." He wrote out of his own experience because he had spent his early years caring for sheep. As the Lord is our Shepherd, so are we His sheep. The focus is on the discipleship qualities of those who follow.

As our Good Shepherd, Christ says again in Luke 15: 4 – 7, "What man among you, if he had a hundred sheep and has lost one of them, does not leave the 99 in open pasture and go after the one which is lost until he finds it? And when he has found it, he lays it on his shoulders, rejoicing." God's love for each individual is so great that He seeks each one out, and rejoices when he or she is "found." We each are so precious in His sight. Our Good Shepherd, Christ, gave His life for His sheep and became the Door to God's fold. Then He rose from the grave to care and guide His flock through His Spirit.

As the Good Shepherd, He knows each of us intimately. As we get to know His voice and follow Him, we will have everything we need to grow and flourish spiritually. Sheep without a shepherd are like those who wander away from God. Do we see ourselves as part of God's flock? Can we say as David said, "The Lord is my Shepherd."

A mid-western college had financial needs. The buildings were old, the dorms needed renovation, and staff salaries were meager. A stranger visited the campus and asked a man who was washing windows where he could find the college president. "I think you can see him at his office at noon," replied the man. The visitor met the president at his office. Surprised, he recognized the same man who was washing windows, now dressed in different clothes.

That same week, a letter came with a gift of $50,000.00 for the college. The humble spirit of service on the part of the president had made such a positive impression on the visitor that he was moved to help. The benefactor saw a man who was not too proud to help where needed, and was led to contribute generously.

God rewards those who take a lowly place. Christ says in the gospel of Luke 14:11, "For whoever exalts himself will be humbled, and he who humbles himself will be exalted." How can we humble ourselves? Humility does not mean putting ourselves down. Truly humble people compare themselves only to Christ. They recognize their gifts and strengths, and use them.

Jesus is teaching the principle of humility throughout the gospels. The disciples came to Him one day early in their training and asked, "Who is the greatest in the Kingdom of Heaven?" (Matt. 18:4) Jesus called a little child and had him stand among them and said, "I tell you the truth, unless you change and become like little children, you will never enter the Kingdom of Heaven. Therefore, whoever humbles himself like this child is the greatest in the Kingdom of Heaven." Jesus used the child as an example. We are not to be childish, but rather child-like with humble and sincere hearts. Service also keeps us aware of others' needs, and takes the focus from ourselves. Jesus truly challenged society's norms.

I have personally seen an individual who, on a Sunday, dressed in a suit, repaired one of the church's toilets. I know for sure he is not a plumber. It was something that needed attention and he did it. And this was not the first time. I have also seen a pastor helping the church custodian setting up some long tables in the social hall. Manpower was needed, and he happened to be the only man on the premises. A real leader has a servant's heart. Servant-leaders appreciate others' worth and realize that they are not above any job. As disciples of Christ, when we see the need, we must take the initiative and help like a faithful servant.

Jesus' mission was to serve others and to sacrifice His life. He says in Matt. 20:28, "The Son of Man did not come to be served, but to serve, and to give His life a ransom for many." Christ did not come as a conquering king. He came as a servant. By giving His life on the cross for us, did the ultimate act of sacrifice.

Real greatness in Christ's Kingdom is shown by service and sacrifice, and not out of selfish ambition or vain conceit. "Whoever exalts himself will be humbled, and he who humbles himself will be exalted." That's humility's reward!

A man and his wife were considering buying a piano and donating it to their church. Wishing to know and appreciate the various steps of its construction, they made arrangements to visit a piano manufacturing plant.

The guide took them first to a large workroom where the workers were cutting and shaping wood and steel. Nothing there suggested the resemblance to a piano. Then they were escorted to several workrooms where parts were being smoothed, painted, polished and assembled, but still there were no strings or keys—no music.

Finally, the guide took the guests to the showroom, where someone skillfully was playing music of the masters on a beautiful piano. The visitors, now more informed of the various steps involved in the development of this marvelous musical instrument, were able to see the finished product and fully appreciate its beauty.

The Word of God comes to us through St. John, "Beloved, we are children of God, and it has not yet been revealed what we shall be." (I John 3:2) If our spiritual progress or maturity seems slow at times, let us not be discouraged. "God, who began a good work in us, will bring it to completion..." (Phil. 1:6) The scriptures portray Christian life as a process of growth in which we advance from one stage to the next; from spiritual infancy to maturity, from being rooted in faith to being firmly established. When we sincerely open our hearts and minds to God, and wish to know Him more intimately, He brings us to wondrous maturity one step at a time.

When one day His work will be completed in us, the results in His showroom will be worth all the time spent being formed, shaped and polished in His workroom! God is at work, and He is not finished with us yet!

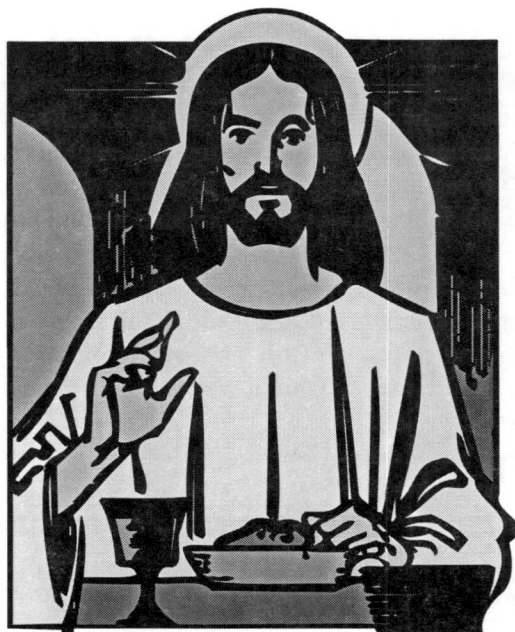

*W*hen it comes to how tall we stand, inherited genetic factors establish a certain boundary that limits our height. Regardless of good diet and exercise, physical growth ceases at a certain point. No matter how hard we may try, when that limit is reached, we can't grow any taller.

Our potential for spiritual advancement and growth, however, is limitless. How "tall" we become in the knowledge of God depends on our own desire and thirst that we have for Him, and how much we draw on His Word. We are not held back by genes we inherited from our earthly parents. The sky is the limit!

Christian maturity doesn't just happen, however. Our "diet" has to be right and we must "exercise" our spiritual muscles regularly. Unless we feast on God's precious Word, there will be no progress. And unless we obey it, we will never realize our full potential for further growth.

In the epistle to the Hebrews we see that these faithful had been notably zealous in the Word of God in former times. But now they had forgotten even the first principles of the gospel. In his letter, written sometime before 70 A.D., the author tells them, "For though by this time you ought to be teachers... you have come to need milk and not solid food" (Heb. 5:12). Strong words! They were like infants, lacking spiritual maturity and fruitfulness. They were urged to put away childish things and grow up! It seems clear that the recipients of this epistle had not even applied the basics of the Word that they once knew into their own lives.

Knowledge without obedience, not only does not advance us, but allows us to fall back. These once faithful people had been exposed to scriptures long enough to have been able to teach it to others by now, but like little children, they needed to be instructed over again in the first principles of the gospel of Christ. When our cup runneth over with the knowledge of the true Word of God, it will reach and touch others.

How "tall" do we stand in God's sight? How much have we developed during this past year? Whatever our answer, we can stand even taller. Let us not become spiritually anemic in God's sight. St. Peter writes, "...Be on your guard so that you may not be carried away by the error of lawless men and fall from your secure position. But grow in the grace and knowledge of our Lord and Savior Jesus Christ" (2 Pet. 3:17 – 18).

No matter where we are in our in our spiritual journey, no matter how mature we are in our faith, no matter how "tall" we stand in the sight of God, the sinful world around us will challenge our faith. We still have much room for growth. If every day we find some way to draw closer to Christ, we will be prepared to stand for truth in any and all circumstances.

*I*t has been reported that the average person's feet travel more than four times the earth's circumference in a lifetime. That is a lot of walking! But where are our feet taking us and why?

In Romans 10:15 – 17, the Apostle Paul writes, "How beautiful are the feet of those who preach the Gospel of peace, who bring glad tidings of good things!" St. Paul quotes Scripture from Isaiah 52:7, which refers to those who bring the exiled Jews the good news of their imminent release from captivity in Babylon. In the New Testament, Paul applies the same verse that brings the good news of Christ's deliverance from sin's captivity. It is wonderful to have feet that our Lord calls "beautiful"! And it does not pertain to aesthetics.

It is a privilege to share the Word of God with others; His news of redemption and peace. Unfortunately, not all who hear God's Word welcome it, writes the Apostle. Yet, "Faith comes by hearing, and hearing by the Word of God" (Rom. 10:17). He states that unless someone goes and tells others about God's Word, how will they hear it? How will they know?

Although the early Christians had access to the Old Testament and used it, they did not have the New Testament yet. The letters from the Apostles were read and reread by the faithful for spiritual nourishment and instruction. The teachings of Christ were memorized and passed on from person to person. Sometimes the teachings were set to music, and so psalms and hymns became an important part of Christian worship and education.

As Christians today, where are our feet taking us and why? With St. Paul's written word in mind, we can walk with a purpose; to carry our Christian faith wherever we go. Whether we walk in high heels or low, whether we walk wearing a cast or lean on a cane, whether we use a walker, or even a wheelchair, we can carry God's Word to others. Our Lord does not mind how we walk, as long as we walk with Him, and for Him. Our lives can truly be a blessing and shining example to others of the power and truth of the Gospel. Then we can also have, as Scripture says, "beautiful" feet!

*W*e all recognize Michelangelo's name. It is often thought that his name was Michael Angelo, but actually Michelangelo was his first name, and Buenarotti his last. He was not only a brilliant painter, but also an architect, poet and sculptor.

It is said that Michelangelo believed that every block of stone he set out to carve contained in it a fully formed statue waiting to be released. All he had to do was chip away everything that wasn't part of the statue, and there it would be revealed—the beautiful statue of a male or female, an angel, or a soldier, a horse, etc. It sounds easy, but for most of us it's not. Michelangelo's creative vision allowed him to see the masterpiece that was in it. Many looking at the same cold block of marble might have seen nothing and walked away. But Michelangelo saw the beauty of what could be, and patiently chipped off piece after piece, and smoothed off the rough edges to create the masterpiece he envisioned.

That is similar to what God has patiently doing with us as His children. God who has begun a good work in us will complete it throughout our lifetime (Phil. 1:6). His work in us began when we first believed in Him, when His Holy Spirit took residence in our hearts. St. Paul describes this to the Philippian faithful as a process of Christian growth and maturity.

God takes us just as we are, like blocks of marble. But because of His great love for us, He does not want to leave us the way He found us. He sees through our surface to "what we could be," and gently chisels away all the rough edges for the transformation of our character. He lovingly polishes all of the rough surfaces until He sees the beauty of His own re-creation as a vital part of our Christian maturity.

God wants to make us complete, and yet correction is painful for us. As His obedient children, we must not complain of the transformations He makes in us, but see our struggles as opportunities for growth. Clouds of testing can bring us showers of blessings. God is the source of all love, and He is deeply concerned about our development. As our Heavenly Father, He corrects us to bring us closer to Himself. Every Christian is in a continuing education program. The more we know of Christ and His teachings, the more we are being transformed closer to His image. This is a life long process. It is difficult for us to see the transformation in ourselves until we look back at the situation. It takes patience and trust to let go of our will and let God do the polishing.

In Proverbs 3:5, 6 we read, "Trust in the Lord with all your heart, and lean not on your own understanding; in all your ways acknowledge Him, and He shall direct your paths." Knowing that God loves us and delights in us, we must welcome His corrections. As we trust in his wisdom, He will direct our lives. About 1,000 years later, Jesus emphasized this same truth in Mt. 6:33: "Seek first the kingdom of God and His righteousness, and all these things shall be added to you."

God is our center of safety. He chisels away anything that stands in the way of the masterpiece He is creating in us. If God considers us His work of art, we dare not treat ourselves or others with disrespect. He is, after all, the Sculptor, and we are His works in progress!

*W*hen we are young we tend to think that old age is far, very far away. In fact we live and think as though we will never die. And yet, we read in Psalm 90:12 that we should learn "to number our days, that we may gain a heart of wisdom." That is, whatever our age, we should evaluate the use of our time in light of the briefness of life. The best way then, to number our days, evaluate or organize them, is to make sure that our life is patterned each day after the teachings of Christ. Only then can we be assured that our life will not be lived in vain.

Realizing that life is short helps us to use the little time we have more wisely and for eternal good. We should take time to ask: What do I want to see happen in my life before it is too late? What steps could I take toward that end? Because time is short we want our life and work to count, to be effective and productive. We must therefore apply ourselves to loving and serving God.

What legacy will we leave when our days attending school are over? What legacy will we leave if we were to change jobs or move to another neighborhood or city? How will people remember us? Will our friends look across the years and recall our dedication to God, our kindness? Will they have respect for our standards? Our integrity? Will they look fondly at our contributions that we left behind? Or will they remember us for things we know we should have done, said or allowed to happen? We must never downplay the importance of good deeds. Christ tells us, "Let your light so shine before men, that they may see your good works and glorify your Father in heaven" (Matt. 5:16).

Of the thousands of verbs in the English language, by which one are we likely to be remembered? He encouraged. She praised. He supported. She cared. He served. She prayed. None of these will cost us a red cent. What if dishonoring verbs are linked to our name? He cheated. She complained, etc. It is not too late to repent and trade those in for Christ-honoring ones. Then pray and trust God to build them into our character. Someone is always watching as we build a legacy. Someone will remember us for what we are doing, even today.

Our Heavenly Father calls on us to make a difference in what we say, how we live, how we show love, how we demonstrate our faith, and how we maintain our purity. Let us make sure that we leave a legacy of ongoing Godly values. That's the best way to number our days. That's the best way to let our light shine and bring glory to God.

A woman named Kiki was perfectly healthy, but in deep despair. She tried to commit suicide by jumping from her apartment window, but instead she became paralyzed from her waist down. In the hospital, completely frustrated, she sensed that Christ was speaking to her heart saying, "Kiki, you had a healthy body, but a disabled soul. From now on you will have a disabled body, but a healthy soul." As she prayed, cried and prayed again, and thought long and hard over the experience, she surrendered her life to Christ.

When she was finally allowed to go home, she prayed again for a way to share God's grace with others. Suddenly the idea of a newspaper ad occurred to her. Kiki put this ad in her neighborhood church paper: "If you are lonely or have a problem, call me. I am in a wheelchair and don't get out much. We can share our problems with each other. Just call—I'd love to talk." The response to that ad was tremendous—some 30 calls every week.

What motivated this young woman to reach out from her wheelchair to help others in need? Her new purpose in life! One of the great ironies of affliction is that it can bring us closer to God. A life of ease teaches us less than a life of trouble and pain. We need to learn what God is trying to teach us through our struggles. Our losses may be part of God's plan for us. What appears to be human tragedy is often the seed of divine triumph. Rather than feel sorry for herself again, Kiki reached out to make a difference for others.

Every child of God can do something for those in need. Limited as we may be by sickness, disability or old age, we can still call, pray with others on the phone, or write. When we yield to God's will, not only can we live victoriously, but can be a blessing to others as well. We may often be discouraged or question our humble position or talents. But our limited ability accents God's unlimited power.

Jesus said, "I am the vine, and My Father is the vine dresser" (Jn. 15:1). No vine can be fully fruitful without pruning. The richest, most productive lives are those that have been strengthened through the painful process of affliction. What we see as tragedies may be only blessings in disguise, and opportunities through which God chooses to exhibit His love and grace. Although it is hard to see any good purpose at the time of trials, but over the years we often can see it more clearly.

Perhaps some of us are being "pruned" today; dreams lost, loved ones in life are taken away from us. If we could only see the purpose of those trials from the perspective of God's wisdom; if we could only interpret these sufferings in their relationship to life's blessings; we would be able to dry our tears and praise the Lord for them all.

God is committed to the task of helping us to grow spiritually so that the character traits of His Son Jesus Christ begin to take shape in us. Even in our most painful situations, we can trust God to do what is best.

*T*he story is told that a few boys were discussing what they wanted to be when they grew up. When it was J's turn to comment, he did not name any of the professions one would expect, such as doctor, lawyer, engineer, policeman, fireman, etc. What he wanted to be was a philanthropist. When asked why he said, "Because they are the ones who have all the money."

According to Webster's Dictionary, a philanthropist is one who "loves to benefit mankind." Having a lot of money then, does not make one a philanthropist. In fact, even a person with a moderate income who seeks to benefit mankind and gives from his or her limited income is more of a philanthropist than a person of great wealth who gives very little proportionately. So young J was only partially correct.

The Apostle Paul called for compassion and generosity, and exhorted the Corinthian Christians to be cheerful givers. In 2 Cor. 9:6 – 14 he says, "He who sows sparingly will also reap sparingly, and he who sows bountifully will also reap bountifully. So let each one give as he proposes in his heart, not grudgingly or of necessity; for God loves a cheerful giver." St. Paul uses the illustration of sowing seed to explain that the resources God gives us are not to be kept. Instead, they should be cultivated in order to produce more "crops." When we invest what God has given us in His work, He will provide us with even more to give in His service.

St. Paul repeated in some way what Christ had said in Luke 6:38; "Give, and it will be given to you: good measure, pressed down, shaken together, and running over will be put into your bosom. For with the same measure, it will be measured back to you." The imagery is of a container of grain filled to the brim and running over the edge! Don't you love that illustration!

Our attitude is more important than the amount we give. God will supply all the needs of the generous giver. In addition, Apostle Paul also emphasizes the spiritual rewards for those who give generously to God's work. We should not expect to become wealthy through giving. Those who receive our gifts will be helped, will praise God, and will pray for us. As we bless others, we will be blessed.

We are most fortunate to have a good number of philanthropists among our Armenian people. They give generously with willing hands and loving hearts at both national and international levels. God will certainly continue to bless them, multiply their energy and wisdom, and grant them a discerning spirit to continue their good works.

When we have experienced the matchless grace of God, our hearts should be filled with compassion for our brothers and sisters in Christ. By extending to them a helping hand in whatever way possible, regardless of income or vocation, we too can be philanthropists!

Our actions speak louder than words. Let us assume the following scenario. Someone has a bumper sticker that reads "KKLA 99.5 FM Christian Radio," but all we hear from his car stereo is loud Rap or Rock music. A businessman has chosen a checkbook with the "fish" sign on it, displaying his Christian faith, but is known to be dishonest in his profession.

What kind of message are these people sending? Which are we going to trust; what they display or what they do? Which speaks louder; the bumper sticker or the radio? The fish sign or a person's dishonest business ethics? Our actions send loud messages; messages that drown out what we say.

In the Book of Acts we see a very interesting example. We read that "The disciples were first called Christians at Antioch" (Acts 11:26). Antioch then became the birthplace of the name "Christian." But why Antioch? After the stoning of St. Stephen, the followers of Christ were scattered away from Jerusalem. Many of them went to Antioch of Syria, the third largest city of the Roman Empire, now modern Antakiya, Turkey. It was located 300 miles north of Jerusalem and was called "Queen of the East." Antioch was embellished with everything that Roman wealth, Greek aestheticism and Oriental luxury could produce. Although an idolatrous city, multitudes of its inhabitants accepted Christ, and it became the center of organized efforts to Christianize the world.

This young church at Antioch was a curious combination of Jews and a mixture of Gentiles who spoke Greek or Aramaic. It is significant that this is the first place where the believers were called "Christians", named after Christ. All these faithful had in common was Christ—not race, not culture, or even language. Christ can cross all boundaries and unify all people. The very first Christians, however, were Jews as were the 12 disciples.

We don't know who first named the faithful "Christians." It is believed that it was likely first labeled by non-Christians as a term of derision or ridicule. They saw Christ in the works and lives of the believers and named them "Christians" after Christ. What a compliment! But whether adopted by believers or invented by enemies, "Christian" is a term that was increasingly applied to Christ's followers in the late first and early second centuries. Eventually the disciples liked the name, and it has remained as the appropriate one for followers of Christ—the highest name human beings can bear upon this earth!

It is easier to talk about Christianity than to live it. Even though it's a start, it doesn't take much courage to put a fish sign somewhere to be seen. What takes courage is living in a way that others can see Christ in us. We are called and equipped by the Holy Spirit to reflect Christ's character and bring honor to His name. Yes, what we do speaks louder than what we say or display.

*T*here is a verse in the Bible which has been translated into more than 1,100 languages. It tells of One Who loved us with an everlasting love. The verse is found in John 3:16. "For God so loved the world that He gave His only begotten Son, that whoever believes in Him should not perish but have everlasting life."

I have seen this well-known verse translated and recorded into 27 of the important world languages which are understood by three quarters of the earth's population. It is truly an exciting experience to open the Bible, and right there, in its first few pages, to see all 27 languages of John 3:16 alphabetically listed, including Armenian! It begins with Afrikaans, Arabic, Armenian, and so on. The list ends with Vietnamese. It is found in the Gideon Bible, King James version, in the drawer of almost every hotel room in the United States. I discovered this many years ago, and made it my habit to always look. It is the first thing I do as soon as I enter a hotel room. If Armenian is not included, that means it is an older Bible. The newer ones all have it. The name "Gideon" is taken from the Old Testament, the book of Judges, chapters 6 through 8.

Why John 3:16? It is unquestionably a most meaningful verse. "For God so loved the world ..." The word "so" emphasizes the intensity or greatness of God's love for us. It summarizes the heart of the Gospel and God's plan for eternal life. The entire Gospel comes into focus in this verse. God's love reaches out to us. Here God sets the pattern of true love, the basis of all love relationships. When we love someone dearly, we are willing to give freely to the point of self-sacrifice. That's what God did with the life of His Son. Through Christ we can have new life – life everlasting. Our love toward others should be sacrificial as well. Genuine, self-sacrificing love for one another is a mark of our identity in Christ.

No other country in the world, to my knowledge, has allowed Bibles in their hotel rooms; certainly none of the countries I have visited. I have looked. There may be a few, however. May God continue to bless America!!! Over the years, those Bibles in the hotel rooms have brought such hope and blessing to so many who despondently turned to the Bible for help in time of desperate need.

The truths of the Bible never need updating. Its teachings never need revision. Scripture only needs to be gratefully embraced as God's abiding truth, and then obediently put into practice. The Word of God is the truest source of wisdom and understanding known to man.

*W*e hear a distant call in the sky: "Honk! Honk!" We look up and see a V-shaped formation of geese passing overhead going south. The geese fly in this formation because they can travel farther and more efficiently that way. Also each goose can see the other and follow the leader; usually a wise gander which knows the way perfectly, day or night.

We can learn great truths by observing the order and harmony in creation. As with the geese, Christians likewise who work together with a plan are usually more effective in their work and accomplish more than the ones who go solo.

Another lesson we can learn is shared leadership. When the bird in the front of the flying "V" gets tired from facing the wind, it moves back and lets another takes its place. Similarly, how much more could we accomplish in our churches and other worthy organizations if we would share responsibilities. Sometimes the ones who have been staying in the background need to be willing to accept a position of leadership.

Still another lesson we can learn from the geese is encouragement. While in formation, and particularly at night or in clouds and fog, geese honk, helping to keep the flock together. Christians too should encourage and exhort one another to strengthen their oneness in Christ. Psalm 104:24 comes to mind: "Oh Lord, how manifold are Your works! In wisdom You have made them all." The longer one lives to see the vast riches of God's creation, the more one realizes the truth of this statement.

Creation is filled with amazing variety, revealing the rich creativity, goodness and wisdom of our loving God. As we observe our natural surroundings, we must praise and thank God even more for His wisdom and sovereignty over all creation. God has supreme, unlimited power over the entire universe. He creates, He preserves, He governs.

Why not take a fresh look at the people around us and see each one of God's unique creations. See each one with his or her special talents, abilities and gifts, and praise God for them. All creation is like a majestic symphony or a great choir composed of many harmonious parts that together offer up songs of praise. This is a picture of how we as Christians should praise God, individually yet as part of the great choir of faithfuls worldwide. Are we singing our part well in the worldwide choir of praise?

"Laugh Your Way to Good Health" was the title of an article I read a few years ago in a well-known monthly magazine. The author, Nick Gallo, stated that new research indicates that humor is good medicine for good health. He pointed out that when a person laughs heartily, several physical benefits occur. There is a temporary lowering of blood pressure, a reduction of muscle tension, and most individuals feel a relaxed afterglow. He concluded that a sense of humor, combined with faith and optimism, is a potent force for better health.

Mr. Gallo made an observation that echoes what Solomon wrote thousands of years ago. "A merry heart does good, like medicine, but a broken spirit dries the bones" (Prov. 17:22). Christians, above all others, should benefit from laughter because we have the greatest reason to be joyful. Our faith is firmly planted in God, and our optimistic attitude is based on the assurance that we are under God's wise care.

Yet many of us occasionally meet individuals with pessimistic attitudes who only see that roses have thorns, yet others rejoice that thorns have roses. Rather than seeing the thorns on roses, why not be thankful for the roses among the thorns? The Apostle Paul writes in Philippians Ch. 4, "Rejoice in the Lord always. Again I will say rejoice!" Isn't it remarkable that Paul's letter to the faithful in Philippi was written while he was imprisoned in Rome. Yet joy is the prominent note of this epistle. A man, who for thirty years was mobbed, beaten, stoned and cuffed, is amazingly overflowing with joy! St. Paul's attitude teaches us an important lesson: Our inner attitudes do not have to reflect our outward circumstances. He was joyful because he knew that in all circumstances, Christ was with him.

He further advises people to meditate on what is true, noble, just, pure, lovely, of good report, virtuous and praiseworthy. We can discipline ourselves to contemplate good thoughts. What we put into our minds determines what comes out in our words and actions. Reading uplifting Bible verses, or listing God's attributes can get us on the right track. Paul did not tell them to deny their worries, but to give them to God in prayer.

We all need to become avid "rose gardeners," hunting for "buds of beauty" within our thorny circumstances. It is a sure cure for the blues. We also know that ultimate joy comes from God's spirit dwelling within us. Why not rejoice in the Lord always! And enjoy a good laugh when we can. A merry heart is good medicine.

The recent rains brought to mind the history of the umbrella in England. Some 200 years ago an Englishman and great humanitarian named Jonas Hanway was the first to introduce the umbrella to the English people. As Hanway traveled in foreign countries, he discovered this device with fabric-covered frame used for protection against rain and sun. He saw the usefulness of what was then the little known umbrella.

Hanway decided to bring it to England, confident it would be readily accepted. To his surprise, however, people endlessly made fun of him. Yet Hanway paid no attention to this and faithfully continued to improve the umbrella. The ridicule and harassment through amusing and insulting cartoons went on for nearly 30 years, and he was know as the "peculiar umbrella man." Eventually after his death, people recognized its usefulness, and today no one would want to be in England without one.

A more solemn spiritual parallel to this story is found in the perseverance and faithfulness of St. Paul. The "ambassador in chains" was kept in Roman dungeons enduring terrible persecution. Yet he confidently declared, "None of these things move me; nor do I count my life dear to myself, so that I may finish my race with joy..." (Acts 20:24). In spite of all opposition, he defended the truth of the gospel which the Lord had commissioned him to proclaim to the world.

The Apostle Paul considered everything he had accomplished in his life, before knowing Christ, to be all "loss" when compared to the greatness of serving Christ. This is a profound statement about values! Single-mindedness is a quality needed by anyone who wishes to do great and honorable works. St. Paul was a single-minded person, and the most important goal of his life was to tell others about Christ.

He was transformed by Christ from a persecutor of Christians to a preacher for Christ. He preached throughout the Roman Empire on three missionary journeys. He wrote encouraging letters of faith to various churches that he established. These letters became part of the New Testament. He was never afraid to face any issue head on and deal with it. And above all, he was always obedient to God's guidance and direction.

We often feel that life is a failure unless we are getting recognition, fame or success at some level. But the Apostle Paul considered life worth nothing unless he used it in God's service. Great endurance is essential to great achievement. When we know we are right according to God's Word, we must not let anything discourage us. Like St. Paul, we can finish our course with joy, remain faithful and refuse to let anyone or anything deter us. To know Christ personally should be our ultimate goal. Serving Christ even in the smallest way is the biggest job we can do on earth.

*T*he potter's clay has provided Biblical writers with many symbolic illustrations instructional to us. Perhaps best known is the account of creation in Gen. 2:7, which depicts God as a potter, creating man from clay. The theme of God as the Master Potter, molding people and nations, is a common one.

We also read of the prophet Jeremiah, sent by God to watch a potter in his workshop intently shaping clay on his wheel. All seemed to be going well until the potter saw a flaw in what he was making. But instead of throwing the clay away, he reworked it until he had produced a perfect vessel. Then the Word of the Lord came to Jeremiah saying, "Look, as the clay is in the potter's hand, so are you in My hand." (Jeremiah 18:6) With this illustration the prophet was to go and preach to the people of his time.

The potter has power over the clay. He can permit defects to remain or he can reshape the vessel. God does something similar with the faithful as well. He has the power to reshape, to conform us to His purpose. His goal is to improve and to mold our character to become more Christ-like. Our reaction should not be to become mindless and passive—one aspect of clay—but to be willing, pliable and receptive to God's impact on us. As we yield to God, He begins to reshape us into useful, valuable vessels!

As the potter controls what he does with clay, so is the Lord sovereign over us. This continues until the "clay" takes on the shape the Potter (God) intends. It is slow work—so slow that it takes a lifetime to make a man and a woman after His own purpose.

By God's grace, some faithful seem to go through life without major reshaping experiences because they have not faced great difficulties. But with others, in His infinite wisdom, God seems to take special measures. As a result, these individuals develop a higher level of spiritual maturity than others because of the trials they faced and conquered.

If any of us is going through an unusual difficulty, disappointment or pain, let us not despair. The Potter is at work in our lives. Although we may not understand it now, perhaps one day we'll see that our Potter's loving hands carefully and tenderly molded and fashioned us until He had created the perfect vessel for His purpose.

*A*most beautiful azalea bush was growing in our back yard. I admired its beauty and vivid color. We never had an azalea before, and this one had grown completely on its own. The only problem with this azalea was its location. It chose to grow in the most remote corner of our yard.

This flower is too attractive to be growing in such a spot, I thought. So, I carefully removed it one spring and planted it in our front yard. The soil, after all, was richer with plenty of afternoon sunshine, and a location where we could all enjoy its beauty. I thought I had a green thumb, but it wasn't long before this free-spirited, beautiful azalea died. It was a lesson I will not forget.

We frequently see a parallel to this in our lives as Christians. Often we are unhappy because of the circumstances into which our sovereign God has placed us to serve Him. It is so easy to fall into an attitude of, "Life would have been much better if only..." We often fail to realize that God is guiding us to use our talents in circumstances of His choosing. Some may be difficult, but they will bring us to a new degree of spiritual beauty. Discontentment can uproot us and stop our spiritual growth. In contrast with this is the person who finds purpose and satisfaction right where he/she is placed—who has joy and meaning in the present. Contentment comes when we accept what God is doing in our lives and are grateful for the opportunity to serve Him.

God knows everything about us and what is best for us. When we seek His guidance, He'll give us direction, and even a new attitude. The "soil" and "spot" where He has planted us is perhaps just what we need. So why not trust Him and allow Him to bring us to new levels of maturity.

By trusting Him, we will find new dimensions to life that will help us; not only to get on with purposeful living, but even blossom right where we are planted, like the beautiful azalea. One of our Heavenly Father's promises is, "Never will I leave you, never will I forsake you." (Heb. 13:5) Now that is enough to allow us to bloom anywhere!

*I*n God We Trust" sounds familiar. We have seen it so often that it may have lost its meaning to some of us. It is boldly printed on the back of United States currency and some coins. Webster's Dictionary defines the word "trust" as "reliance or faith in the honesty and integrity of another person or thing."

When the founding fathers of this nation put their names on the Declaration of Independence, they believed that God was the only firm foundation upon which to build a nation that would endure. George Washington stated it simply: "It is impossible to rightly govern the world without God and the Bible." Reliance upon God was deeply rooted in this country's important documents and institutions from the beginning. When the leaders of this nation assembled to write the Constitution, Benjamin Franklin proposed that each session be opened with prayer. He said, "I have lived a long time, and the longer I live the more convincing proof I see of this truth—that God governs the affairs of man."

The United States of America is great because it was founded upon God's Word and prayer. But today many have the mistaken notion that our private and national affairs can be run without God. Confidence in God and His Word is no longer the foundation of society. In our homes we nightly view events in the news on TV that were unthinkable or unimaginable only a decade ago. It is time that we return to the values of God's Word.

There is only one way out, and that is to look up. Answers will be found only when we call upon God as individuals and as families. Abraham Lincoln said, "I believe the Bible is the best gift God has given to man. All the good from the Savior of the world is communicated to us through this book." There is a truly beautiful verse that comes to mind from 2 Chronicles 7:14. "If my people who are called by My name will humble themselves, and pray and seek My face, and turn from their wicked ways, then I will hear from heaven and will forgive their sin and heal their land." True repentance is changed behavior.

It is a glorious thing to be a Christian; the most exalted privilege of mankind. To accept Christ as Lord and Master, and to strive sincerely to follow the life which He taught is certainly, and by far, the most satisfying way of life. It means peace of mind, contentment of heart, forgiveness, joy, hope, life here and now, life abundant, life that shall never end spiritually. Blessed are those who enjoy that privilege.

*T*he famous masterpiece "The Last Supper" is the creation of the gifted, well-known artist Leonardo da Vinci. It is said that after he composed the drawing on canvas, he had an unpleasant argument with his neighbor. Angry at this man, the artist decided to paint Judas' face resembling his neighbor. Portraying him as the betrayer of Jesus, he would have made his face despicable to all those who would view the painting. This would have been his revenge.

Pleased with this clever thought, he began painting energetically. He chose to paint Judas' face first, and in no time, he completed it to his satisfaction. His hostile, angry feelings toward his neighbor were portrayed perfectly on Judas' face. Delighted with the results, he thought that all his friends now would easily recognize Judas as the face of his neighbor with whom he had argued.

But when Leonardo began to paint the face of Jesus, he could make no progress. Something seemed to hinder his best efforts. His gifted abilities seemed to have vanished. Frustrated, he finally came to the conclusion that the hindrance he was experiencing was due to the continuing anger and resentment he felt toward his neighbor. According to the story, Leonardo wasted no time. He went immediately to his neighbor and restored their friendship. With peace in his heart he returned to his studio and painted out the face of Judas. He began once again painting the face of Christ, this time with the success that the ages have come to acclaim and appreciate. The point of the story is clear. As long as we deal with feelings of resentment and anger, as long as we paint with colors of hatred in our hearts and thoughts, the Holy Spirit cannot paint the lovely, peaceful features of Christ in our lives.

In the gospel of Matthew 18:21, the Apostle Peter asked Jesus, "Lord, how many times shall I forgive my brother when he sins against me? Up to seven times?" Peter thought he was being especially generous when he said this, because three times was what the teachers of the law had taught. But Peter's generosity faded when compared to Jesus' instruction when He answered, "Not seven times, but up to seventy times seven." Our Lord meant that we should not even keep count, but forgive those who truly repent.

True forgiveness brings peace, joy, freedom and blessings into our lives. When forgiveness is withheld, our fellowship with God is broken, and our hearts grow hard and cold. It can become destructive to our personal lives, transforming us into our own worst enemy. Some of us might feel that we can do only so much. It takes two to quarrel, and two to reconcile. Yes, but if we do our part and the problem remains, there is still a plan to follow. Let us not harbor resentment, but overcome resentment with good. Let God work out any injustices. It's been said that the best way to conquer an enemy is with the weapon of love.

How many times has our heavenly Father forgiven us? He is our example. His loving kindness never fails. We are each a masterpiece in our Creator's eyes. He has created us in His own image (Gen. 1:27). Let us follow His example, and not only forgive others, but through the freedom of forgiveness, forgive ourselves.

*T*he story is told of a faithful, dedicated Christian man who was bedridden many of his later years with a chronic illness. A friend stopped by to visit him, and when he saw him weak in bed, he said, "I suppose you still believe it's a wonderful day." Turning toward a window, luminous with warm sunlight, the sick man said, "I do! I will never let a tray of medicine bottles block my horizon!"

The Apostle Paul had a similar outlook. He lived with a "thorn in the flesh." He didn't name his "thorn." Some think that on the basis of Gal. 6:11, it was an eye condition. Although the "thorn in the flesh" seems to suggest a physical problem, we cannot be sure. We know, however, that the ailment was chronic. In any case, the Apostle Paul says that he pleaded with the Lord three times that it might depart from him. But the Lord said to him, "My grace is sufficient for you, for My strength is made perfect in weakness." (2 Cor. 12:8, 9) St. Paul's request was not granted. Instead, God revealed to him that divine strength is made perfect in human weakness!

That settled it for the Apostle. We don't read that he ever complained or indulged in self-pity. He never used his physical weakness as an excuse. Rather, he regarded this "thorn" as a heavenly advantage. When he was weak in himself, he was strong through the Lord.

When we are strong in abilities or resources, we are tempted to do God's work, trusting only in ourselves. That could often lead to pride. When we are weak, however, and allow God to fill us with His power, we become stronger than we could ever be on our own. God does not intend for us to seek to be weak, passive or ineffective. Life provides enough hindrances and setbacks without us creating them. But when those obstacles come, we must depend on God. Only through His power can we be effective, to do His work that has lasting value.

The fact that God's power is available, especially in our weakness, should give us courage. Our weakness not only helps develop Christian character, it also deepens our faith and worship time with our Creator. By admitting our shortcomings, we affirm God's strength.

What a lesson for us! A self-centered attitude in sickness, or any other time of adversity, clouds our vision. But faith and optimism open the door to God's grace and power. Deliverance may not be granted, our "thorn" may not be removed, but we can have the same strength of spirit expressed by St. Paul. In God's strength we can say, "A tray of medicine bottles cannot block our horizon."

*O*ften God delights in astonishing us by the wonder of His ways! We see in 1 Kings Ch. 17 that the prophet Elijah was experiencing some very trying times. King Ahab was persecuting him because of drought and famine in the land. God told the prophet to rise, go to Zarephath and dwell there, for He had commanded a widow to provide for him.

We can imagine Elijah's surprise when he discovered that the widow who was to provide for him was extremely poor. When the widow met Elijah, she believed that she was preparing her last meal. In fact, she fully expected that she and her son would soon die of starvation. But the prophet promised that her "jar of flour will not be used up, and the jug of oil will not run dry, until the day the Lord gives rain on the land" (1 Kings 17:14).

A simple act of faith produced a miracle. She trusted this man of God and shared all she and her son had, and ate with Elijah. Miracles often seem so out of reach for most of us, and yet every miracle, large or small, begins with an act of obedience and faith. We may not see the solution until we take that first step of faith. Even when God has done a miracle in our lives, our difficulties may not be over. God's provision is never given in order to let us rest upon it. We need to depend on Him as each new challenge faces us.

Our limited understanding of God's ways often resembles a tiny bird that rests on one of the great pillars of St. Paul's Cathedral in London, or of St. Peter's of Rome. What does that tiny bird know about the architect's magnificent design? It sees only the little space of stone on which it stands. The beautiful carvings, ornamental work and graceful colonnade seem like towering mountains that only hinder and obscure the view.

As Christians, we often see only our immediate circumstances and perceive only a glimmer of God's marvelous purpose. The obstacles that block our vision and get in the way of our plans are actually part of the beautiful designs of divine grace.

Our Heavenly Father knows exactly what He is doing. Although His ways may seem beyond our comprehension, He assures us that all will work out for good if we trust Him (Rom. 8:28). God's ways are never without a purpose.

Growing up, I remember the following old story often repeated by adults. A father and his son were walking along a village road with their donkey. Soon they met a man who told them how foolish they were to walk when they had a donkey that they could ride. So the father and son hopped on. They hadn't gone very far when another man criticized them for both riding on the donkey. They were too heavy for the poor animal and were being inhumane. So the boy got off.

It wasn't long before a third traveler accused the father for being heartless to make his son walk while he rode. So they switched places. Soon they met another person who charged the son for not being thoughtful of his father who was, after all, so much older than he. When last seen, the two were struggling down the road carrying the donkey!

This story was told, of course, in a light hearted spirit, but we all understand the point. If we are overly sensitive to everyone's opinion, nothing worthwhile would be accomplished. This may also result in carrying needless weights of guilt and frustration. Although we all appreciate the approval of others, and we try to avoid offending people, our ultimate accountability is not to them, but to the Lord.

The Apostle Paul wrote, "…We are not trying to please men but God, Who tests our hearts" (1 Thes. 2:4). Ultimately what really matters is to please God. Criticism is often difficult to accept, but if we receive it with humility and a desire to improve ourselves, it can be very helpful.

Many years ago I read an article on this subject that made an impression on me. The article stated that when we are criticized, we first ought to ask ourselves whether the criticism contains any truth. If it does, we should learn from it, even when it isn't given in the right spirit. The article then offered the following four suggestions: 1) As Christians we must bring the matter to God, asking Him to remove all our resentment and teach us the needed lesson; 2) We must keep in mind that we could be wrong, and that the one who criticized us may not know the worst about us; 3) If we have made a mistake, we can humbly and honestly admit it to ourselves and to anyone we may have injured; and finally 4) We must be willing to learn, once again, that we aren't infallible, and that we need God's grace and wisdom to keep us on the straight path.

When we are criticized, let's accept what is true and act upon it. As a result we will become stronger Christians. Let's never fear criticism when we are right, and never ignore it when we are wrong. Those who benefit from rebuke are wise.

*W*hat we call the youth culture nowadays is not really new. Through the ages, youths have made significant contributions to society. Consider the accomplishments of these "kids."

Alexander the Great rose to the throne at 20 and conquered the known world at age 33. George Washington was appointed Adjutant General of the army at the age of 19, ambassador at 21, and won his first battle at 22. Later he became the first president of the United States. Pascal was a genius in calculus before he was 16 years old. He became the founder of the mathematical principle of the cone, and later founded the science of hydrodynamics. The Declaration of Independence and many state papers were written by young men about age 30. They formed the United States of America! Quite a testimony for some who might have said to these men, "Step aside, you are too young."

The Bible also gives us examples of how young people of faith were used to bring glory to God. A young life dedicated to Christ can be the beginning of God-honoring service. An unnamed boy shared his lunch of five barley loaves and two small fish, and became the occasion for Jesus to show His miraculous power by feeding the 5000 (John 6:1 – 13). Daniel showed great courage in the den of lions, and became an unforgettable demonstration of God's protection (Daniel 1).

The boy Samuel listened to God obediently and became an important prophet in His service. Samuel ruled Israel at the end of the period of Judges, and by God's guidance, anointed the first two kings; Saul and David (1 Sam. 3). Young David, a shepherd boy in his teens, fought a giant with only a slingshot, and later became king of Israel (1 Sam. 17:41 – 51).

From what the Apostle Paul wrote to Timothy, we know that the "youth factor" bothered some people, even back in the first century. Although he had been trained by St. Paul and sent as the Apostle's official representative, Timothy had to work hard to earn the respect of the faithful. St. Paul told him, "Let no one despise your youth, but be an example to the believers in word, in conduct, in love, in spirit, in faith, in purity" (1 Tim. 4:12). It is believed that Timothy was about 30 years old at the time. Such an influential position was not usually held by a man so young. He had to earn the respect of his elders by setting an example with his conduct.

That is a challenge we all need to accept, whatever our age. God knows our true potential, and regardless of our age, He can use us for His glory. Being young does not mean we should be discouraged or ignored. Nor does it excuse us from serving the Lord. David was only a shepherd boy when he fought Goliath, but God saw in him a future king! When God looks at us, what does He see?

*P*residential libraries are fascinating to visit. I find the hours spent on their premises most enlightening and informative. Also, I never lose the opportunity to take an out-of-town guest with me. It is an experience they'll always remember.

All presidential libraries I visited have replicas of the Oval Office, just as it was during the years of their administration. On my first visit to President Reagan's library in Simi Valley, I noticed a small sign on his desk that said: "THERE IS NO LIMIT TO WHAT A MAN CAN DO OR WHERE HE CAN GO IF HE DOESN'T MIND WHO GETS THE CREDIT." That statement expresses the spirit that should characterize all Christians. Our Heavenly Father has given at least one gift to each one of us. We must recognize that gift and use it fully for His glory. No one should say I have no gift. That is an insult to our Creator. Not only do we all have at least one gift, but God also equips us with whatever is necessary to use it successfully. We must put our gifts to work and not even think of who gets the credit. It has been said, "Not earning recognition while deserving the credit is better than receiving credit without earning it."

Let us not allow our desire for recognition get in the way of our service. God's gift to us must not be squandered, but must be fully used. Apostle Paul uses the concept of the human body to teach us how Christians should live and work together. He says in Romans 12:4, "For as we have many members in one body, but all the members do not have the same function, so we, being many, are one body in Christ, and individually of one another."

Our churches are composed of people from a variety of interesting backgrounds and with a multitude of gifts and abilities. Despite differences, all believers have one thing in common—faith in Christ. On this essential truth, the church finds unity. Talents, like muscles, improve when we exercise them. Failing to use them causes them to waste away from lack of practice and nourishment.

What gifts and abilities has God given us? Let us use them regularly in serving God and others. We cannot find our richest personal fulfillment until we sacrifice our time, talents, energy and resources in God's service. This is true living! Let us use our God-given gifts for His glory and for the blessing of others. Even if others won't recognize it, God will!

*W*e have all seen them curled up asleep on park benches, others resting under shady trees, or at times pushing a cart, walking in and out of alleys. They are the homeless. They exist in all cities; restless souls, often in poor health.

Homelessness illustrates, to some extent, the human condition without God. To deny God, as some people often do, is to be homeless in a world God created for His glory. To depart from His moral law is to drift aimlessly. To deny Him and to refuse His love is to sink into the coldness of despair and hopelessness.

The logical answer to this human predicament is to believe in Jesus Christ. To trust Him is to come into the warm and loving family of God. Jesus says, "I am the Way, the Truth and the Life. No one comes to the Father except through Me" (John 14:6). This verse, as we Christians know, is one of the most basic and important passages in Scripture.

As the Way, Jesus is the path to the Father. As the Truth, He is the reality of all that God promised since creation. As Life, He joins His divine life to ours, both now and eternally. Jesus is the visible, tangible image of the invisible God. Therefore, He says again, "Come to Me, all you who labor and are heavy laden, and I will give you rest" (Matt. 11:28).

These are the dearest, sweetest words ever heard by human ears; an invitation to all mankind. Christ frees people from all burdens. The "rest" that He promises is love, healing and peace with God. Not the end of all labor, but a relationship with Him that changes meaningless, wearisome toil into spiritual productivity and purpose.

Christ can change each one of us from the inside out – rearranging our attitudes, desires and motives. We are no longer strangers or foreigners, but fellow citizens of God's Kingdom. Through Him we become spiritually alive and members of God's family. This fresh start in life is available to all who seek Christ, believe and put their faith and trust in Him.

Is there someone who perhaps is feeling spiritually homeless? Come home to God. We are all homeless until Christ is at home in our hearts!

*M*ost of us would not drive to an unfamiliar destination without first locating the address on the map. Additional glances at that map assure us that we are headed in the right direction.

For us Christians, the Bible and the guidance of God's Holy Spirit are like a map and compass. The Apostle Paul assured Timothy that Scripture lays out the route of sound doctrine and righteousness. Because Timothy carefully followed Paul's spirited example, he didn't lose his way. St. Paul writes in 2 Tim. 3:16, "All Scripture is given by inspiration of God, and is profitable for doctrine, for reproof, for correction, for instruction in righteousness, that the man of God may be complete, thoroughly equipped for every good work."

The Bible was not written by natural inspiration or an act of human will. Holy men of God wrote by divine revelation as they were moved by the Holy Spirit. Man was the instrument used by God's Spirit to write the Bible, word by word. Therefore, the Bible is the infallible Word of God.

The oneness or unity of the Bible is a miracle. It is a library of 66 books, written by over 35 different authors in a period of approximately 1,500 years. The authors are a cross section of humanity; educated and uneducated, and includes kings, fishermen, public officials, farmers, teachers and a physician. The subjects include religion, history, law, science, poetry, biography and prophesy. Yet its various parts are as harmoniously united as the parts of the human body. Although the authors used their own minds, talents, language and style, they were moved to write as God instructed them. All Scripture is "God-breathed," as we Armenians appropriately call it.

The Bible is the most important book anyone can study. Its facts never need updating. Its teachings never need revision. It is the truest source of wisdom and understanding known to man. It has been said: Study the Bible to be wise; believe it to be safe; practice it to be holy.

Perhaps for some of us, Bible reading, prayer and Sunday worship were once very much part of our lives. Yet now, we might be wondering how did we somehow drift away? Why not look to that "map and compass" again. With God's Word as our map and His Spirit as our compass, we are sure to be back on course again!

A woman came to the gym the other day, someone I had not seen for a long time. When she saw me, she came closer and asked with a smile, "Do you remember me?" I said, "Yes, you are Jane, aren't you? Where have you been? You used to work out regularly." She said that she was busy driving across the country for a few years. Then she told me her story.

"Here I was," she confessed, "a woman in my forties, living alone with no responsibilities, and with a desire to do something new and adventuresome. So I became a truck driver—driving those great big 18-wheelers, transporting goods across the U.S.A.!" I was amazed!

At first glance Jane is of average height and size, with nothing particularly impressive about her. She is a rather quiet, sweet young lady. She said that she had to study and pass special driving tests. I asked her if she was afraid of being alone on the road, often driving at night. "Afraid? I have a big German shepherd next to me that is trained to protect me, and a gun under my seat. But most of all, I say my prayers every time I get behind the wheel, and off I go," she added. Imagine!

Now I knew that this young woman was neither an average nor ordinary "plain Jane"! This Jane was prepared, ready and meant business! She was in town for a short break, and was soon to go on the road again. I was equally impressed that although she was prepared with her dog and a gun, she knew in her heart from where her true power and protection came. This Jane knew the Lord!

As children of God, we too venture into unfamiliar territories – often in business or in our personal lives. At times, it may get pretty scary and discouraging. But even failures can be nothing more than temporary tests to prepare us for permanent and lasting triumphs. So why not take some risks in our service for God? Why not venture out into the unknown, even if it feels scary? "The Lord is near to all who call upon Him, to all who call upon Him in truth (Ps. 145:18).

It's a joy and a delight to be used by God. Is there anything more rewarding, more fulfilling? Perhaps not, but there is something more basic, which is to know God more intimately! Even Jane, the truck driver, as prepared as she was, knew to Whom to turn every time she sat behind the wheel!

God is in control. When God is involved, anything and everything is possible. The One Who directed that stone to fly between Goliath's eyes, the One Who split the Red Sea in the middle, the One Who leveled the walls around Jericho, and the One Who brought His Son, Jesus Christ, resurrected out of the tomb, takes delight in working in our lives, to bring glory to His name.

So whatever we do, let's not lose heart and never quit. Extraordinary times require extraordinary wisdom, vision, boldness, flexibility, dedication, and a willingness to adapt with renewed commitment to unchanging biblical principles. The secret is, of course, adapting to our times without altering God's truth.

*A*s Christians we often have our own identification marks. We may, for example, wear a cross. I make sure I wear one when I travel, especially when going abroad. I feel that if anything happens to me (not a pleasant thought), those who find me must know that I am a Christian. Others might be wearing a T-shirt with a Christian camp name on it. I have a few of those as well, and I like them.

Now all that is fine. But the Bible tells us that the one true undeniable sign of Christianity is the love we daily demonstrate for each other. Jesus said, "Love one another. As I have loved you...By this all men will know that you are My disciples..." (John 13:34, 35). This is the principle teaching of Christianity, an example of an eternal expression of Christ's divine love for each one of us. It is by this kind of unselfish, sacrificial love that disciples of Christ were to be known in the world.

As Christ's followers, His standards of love become ours. This is the distinguishing mark of identity for all Christians. We are to love others based on Christ's love for us. True love demonstrates action. As His ambassadors we must look upon the word "love" as a verb. Christ is a living example of God's love, just as we are to be living examples of Christ's love.

The question we could ask ourselves is: How would anyone watching us know that we are true Christians? In what ways do we demonstrate it? Anyone can wear a cross. But genuine, unselfish love for one another should be the mark of our Christian identity.

Jesus says that our sacrificial love will show that we are His disciples. How can we love others as Jesus loves us? By helping when it is not convenient, by giving when it hurts, by devoting energy to others' welfare rather than our own. This kind of love is hard, very hard. That is why others will notice and know that we are empowered by a divine source. "Love as I have loved you" is one of the most powerful ways to show our faith to a skeptical world.

DON'T TARNISH THE PRESENT

*T*he story is told of a certain man whose one great desire was to go to heaven. When he died, an angel took him by the hand and showed him the beautiful sights; breathtaking mountains, lovely flowers, majestic sunsets, children playing in the streets. Seeing all these, the man exclaimed, "Isn't heaven wonderful?" The angel said, "This is not heaven. This is the world in which you lived and never saw." It could be a great tragedy if we were to miss the great splendor of this world that God put us in, and not enjoy it.

Time is valuable. It is to be handled wisely and not squandered. As we travel through life, are we concerned about what really matters, or are we simply fussing with earthbound goals? Time wasted is not lived, but lost. Instead of enjoying the beauty of this present world, some people go through life looking into the rear view mirror. They yearn for the "good old days" when life seemed better, people were happier—or so they think.

The ancient Hebrews of the Old Testament were masters of glorifying their oppressed past. As slaves in Egypt, their lives were unbearable. Yet, after Moses led them out of the bondage of slavery, they were soon idealizing the "good old days." Many of them even wished they were back in Egypt with their necks under the yoke of Pharaoh's whip. Except for Joshua and Caleb, it's no wonder that God never saw that generation worthy of entering the Promised Land. So they murmured, complained and wandered in the wilderness for forty years (Exodus).

As Christians, we should avoid the trap of looking back, unless it's to recall a lesson learned, or to glorify God for what He has accomplished in our lives. We should concentrate instead on the truly good life of enjoying what God has given us today and now. We should live the good life in a relationship with God, and do our best in His service and for His glory.

Planning and enjoying our present life on earth is wise. God wants His children to be happy and do well. But if we live only to enrich ourselves with no concern for helping others, we will enter eternity empty handed. Nothing in this world will last forever. Are we devoting our time to things that have eternal value?

When we live in the past, we tarnish the present and ignore the future. Our daily blessings are reminders of God's goodness. A lifetime devoted to God yields eternal rewards. That's a worthwhile investment. As Christians, we should enjoy the here and now, and remember that the best is yet to come!

*W*e all like to make plans for the future. The Bible encourages wise planning. The book of Proverbs contains many statements that counsel this. "Commit to the Lord whatever you do, and your plans will succeed" (16:3).

Careful planning is wise. Including God in our plans and seeking His will is even wiser. This kind of planning brings forth blessings. St. James warns that the sovereign God will eventually prove He has the final say in all matters of our lives. He brings forth the actual and simple realities of life. We read in James 4:13 – 15, "Come now, you who say, today or tomorrow we will go to such and such a city, spend a year there, buy and sell, and make a profit, whereas you do not know what will happen tomorrow. For what is your life? It is even a vapor that appears for a little time and then vanishes away. Instead you ought to say, if the Lord wills, we shall live and do this or that."

St. James is pointing out that by including God in our plans, we acknowledge Him in our preparation for the future. He does not condemn wise business planning, but rather, planning that leaves out God. Often people live their lives and make plans as if God did not exist. Such conduct is inconsistent with genuine faith, which submits to God. We must make a conscious submission to God's authority as sovereign ruler of the universe. A truly humble person will give allegiance to God, obey His commandments, and follow His leadership. God alone knows the future. "For what is your life?" He asks. Life is like a mist, uncertain, temporary.

St. James mocks self-delusion. He points out that we cannot secure even tomorrow, much less next year. Our lives literally are not in our own control. If we live by God's measure, we would recognize the total dependency of our existence and projects. For only by the will of God can we live or do anything at all. Therefore, "If the Lord wills," or "God willing" should always be part of our attitude. It is not to be used as a cliché, but as a sober reflection of a heart's attitude of dependence on God's will. Despite what we decide to do, God has the final word. He is in control.

It is commendable and wise to set goals. But goals will disappoint us if God is not included in our plans. When we make God's will the center of our plans, we will never be disappointed. We are, after all, included in God's plans—why not include God in ours. That is wise planning.

*W*hile at a drug store I noticed an attractive display of fragrances and stopped to take a look. Since the entire stock seemed to be at hand, I had the opportunity to see and read the various unusual names given to some of the fragrances. Poison, Opium, Ambush, Unruly, My Sin, Obsession, Gossip, etc. I was amazed! And this was only the women's section. I had no time to look at the display set for men. Perhaps a department store had even a wider selection with additional amazing names. But why these strange names?

I have nothing against pleasant fragrances. Perhaps these perfumes or colognes have a very pleasant scent that pleases many. It's their names that amazed me. Is this supposed to be clever advertising? Perhaps the naughtier the name, the more attractive it is, and will tempt us to test it. I don't know. It is the scent inside the attractive bottle that counts. That's what we want to buy and use.

Most of us can think of someone, perhaps a relative or friend, who is known for a particular perfume she wears. This applies to men as well with aftershave or cologne. Even without seeing them, we know they are nearby. In fact, the pleasant fragrance welcomes us or invites us into their presence. Who doesn't like a sweet smelling scent?

Every Christian should also be known for wearing a special "fragrance"— the fragrance of Christ. But this fragrance cannot be bought at a cosmetic counter. It cannot even be bottled and sold by the church. This mysterious fragrance rises always and only out of our inner communion with Christ—with a subtle yet noticeable influence upon others.

In his letter to the Corinthian faithful, St. Paul describes the type of influence we should have on those around us. Our lives are to be a sweet fragrance to our environment. "We are to God the fragrance of Christ ..." (2 Cor. 2:15). As the Gospel's "aroma" is released in the world through Christian teaching, it is always sweet smelling, even though it may be received differently. Christians, with their exemplary lives, also are the fragrance of Christ to the world. A Christian's service is also a sweet fragrance to the Lord; fragrance of the knowledge of Christ. A faithful service in Christ's ministry speaks more eloquently than words. That is something to keep in mind as we evaluate how our lives are being viewed by others. Do they sense the sweet fragrance of Christ? Even when we are not in their company, do they still sense the sweet scent we have left behind?

*I*n all athletic races a good start is important, but the finish is even more crucial. Often a front runner will lose strength and fade to the middle of the pack. Also, a brilliant beginner often sets the pace for a time, but does not finish. He quits the race, burned out, exhausted or injured.

The life of the Apostle Paul had a most dramatic beginning and a victorious, triumphant ending! As for his ministry, it is well known, studied and accepted as an unmistakable, glorious success! Apart from Christ Himself, no one person shaped the history of Christianity more than the Apostle Paul. He was the most effective missionary of early Christianity. More than one fourth of the New Testament writings are attributed to him. Despite unbelievable trials and suffering, rather than quit, he concentrated on using the inner strength received from the Holy Spirit. We see no hint of doubt or regret that he had given his life to the service of Christ and the Church.

St. Paul makes use of the Greek athletic games to illustrate the spiritual race of the faithful. In Philippians 3:13, 14, he says, "Forgetting those things which are behind and reaching forward to those things which are ahead, I press toward the goal for the prize of the upward call of God in Christ Jesus." In Greek athletic games, a victor was awarded a crown; a wreath made of olive branches, the most desired prize in ancient times. While the Greek athletes were in the race to obtain a perishable crown, we as Christians, says the Apostle, are in the race for the "imperishable crown."

Christian life can be compared to an athletic event. Disciplined life is the training ground for Christian maturity. The essential disciplines of prayer, study of God's Word, and worship with fellow Christians, equip us to be able to run with vigor and stamina. When we are empowered with the Holy Spirit, we don't just observe from the grandstands as spiritual spectators, but enter the race with joy.

All through Apostle Paul's teachings, we clearly see the determination of a disciplined spiritual champion! Expecting his imminent departure to be with Christ, the Apostle declared, "I have fought the good fight, I have finished the race, I have kept the faith" (2 Tim. 4:7). He had completed the work that God had entrusted him with, and as a reward he anticipated the "crown of righteousness."

In all competitive races, only one wins the top prize; only one is crowned. In our spiritual race, the good news is that all men, all women, people of all nations can be winners through faith in Christ. We can all be victorious and worthy of the imperishable crown of life! Are we ready to enter the race?

One of the favorite activities youngsters enjoy is to build sand castles on the beach. On hot summer days they can play for hours, often planning elaborate dwellings on the sand. What happens most of the time, however? A series of big waves come crashing onto the shore, and washes all the work away!

In a similar way, some people are not much different. They often choose to build their lives—or aspects of them—on a foundation as unreliable as beach sand. Therefore, Jesus talked about the importance of building our lives on solid foundations. He said in Matthew 7:24 and Luke 6:48 that whoever comes to Him, hears His words and puts them into practice, is like a person building a house by digging deep, and laying the foundation on the rock. When floods and torrents strike, the house will not shake because it is well built. But those who hear His words and don't put them into practice, are like foolish people who build their houses on sand. When rain, floods and winds blow and beat on the house, it will fall.

Are we building our lives on perishable pursuits and shallow principles, or on the solid foundation of Christ's code of obedience through His Word? When life is calm, our foundations may not seem to matter. But when crises come, our foundations are tested. We may feel secure as long as things are calm and the sun is shining. When the storms of disappointment, illness or heartache come, however, and hit us with hurricane-like force, we feel the need of a solid foundation to anchor our souls.

Christ is life's only solid foundation; our unshakable Rock of yesterday, today and forever. His unconditional love should form the foundation of our trust in Christ. Let us build our lives on Him. What is built on Christ lasts forever!

*S*ome things never change. The traffic in Rome is unbelievable! From the airport to downtown Rome, cars were rushing from every direction at almost every intersection. Each driver was forcing his way forward. Horns blared, passions flared, and no one paid any attention to the law or the signals. The traffic lights were considered only as suggestions or decorations. If anyone would stop at a red light, the other drivers would be furious. No police were anywhere in sight to bring order to the chaos. What confusion!

In the book of Judges, we see something very similar to that. The Bible says, "In those days there was no king in Israel; everyone did what was right in his own eyes." (Jdg. 17:6) And what a bitter price they paid for such freedom. The result was the spiritual, moral and political decline of the nation. Although, we fortunately live in a world of law and order, there are still certain principles that we must be aware of. Our lives could also fall into decline, decay and confusion, unless we live by God's principles.

The Scriptures also have "red lights" that point to the "way" in which we should live as Christians. They are prohibitions against pride, envy, hatred, irreverence, selfishness, etc. When God's Spirit alerts us to their presence, we should immediately "hit the brakes." Similarly, as we move into the heavy traffic of daily living, we must quickly respond by obeying the "green lights" of kindness, humility, patience, love, thoughtfulness and purity of spirit.

Society and our environment often have many rewards for those who might compromise their faith. When God gives us a mission, it must not be polluted by a desire for society's approval. We can expect decay if we value anything more highly than God. Why not keep our eyes on Christ, our Teacher and Deliverer. He will help us remain blameless and pure children of God in the midst of any environment and in any generation.

God's stops and starts are to be obeyed. They are designed to help us bring order into our lives. The signals of Scripture are meant for our protection, correction and direction. When we take God's Word seriously and live by it, we show society and the world that yes, as Christians, we do what is right in the eyes of God.

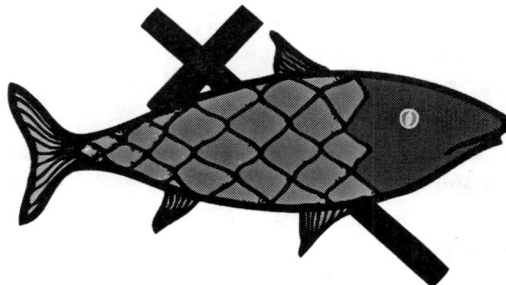

*W*hich of our accomplishments would we be most remembered and valued for, at least for a few years after we are gone? Mary of Bethany, the sister of Martha and Lazarus, the man whom Jesus raised from the dead, is a prime example for us all (Jn.12:1 – 3). Mary perhaps never imagined that her act of love and devotion for Jesus would be remembered by all generations to come. She surprised those who were dining with Jesus by her extravagant generosity. Mary took an alabaster flask of very costly fragrant oil, broke the vase and poured it on Jesus' head and feet as He sat at the table (Mt. 26:6 – 13; Mk. 14:3 – 9). She alone understood Jesus' reference to His impending death, and she anointed Him with her costly perfume that was worth more than a year's wages!

Those at the table said, "Why this waste?" and expressed their concern for the poor. Judas, who would betray Jesus just a few days later, was among them. Her loveless critics called Mary's extravagant act of anointing Jesus "waste." But Jesus quickly vindicated Mary by acknowledging her thoughtfulness. He said, "Assuredly I say to you, wherever this gospel is preached in the whole world, what this woman has done will also be told as a memorial to her" (Mk. 14:9). Had these same people been attending Jesus' funeral rather than a dinner with Him, they would have reacted differently. Yet Mary demonstrated her love and devotion to Jesus while He was still alive—while He was still with them!

After Christ's death and resurrection, early in the morning, several women, disciples of Jesus, came to the tomb bringing spices and fragrant oils to anoint Jesus' body in accordance with Jewish burial customs. Were they able to do that? Of course not! Why? Because Christ was resurrected! The tomb was empty! The huge round stone was rolled away. This was done so that everyone may see, go in and believe! Christ could have been resurrected, whether the stone was rolled away or not. As the women stood there perplexed about all this, they were suddenly in the presence of two angels who said to them, "Why do you seek the living among the dead? He is not here, but is risen!" (Lk. 24:5, 6)

A life lived for God leaves a lasting legacy. And, as we all know, for 2,000 years (since the death and resurrection of Jesus), Mary is still remembered wherever the gospels are preached as a memorial to her and what she did for her Lord.

We can learn a valuable lesson from Mary's devotion. We need to give our best for the Lord. We need to break our best "perfume vases" for the living while there is still time—while they are still with us. Yet all too often, we wait until someone dies to express our praises in a eulogy to show the appreciation that we were reluctant to express in that person's lifetime.

If there are such people who come to mind; family members, friends, or special individuals who would be encouraged or honored by the expression of our love and appreciation; then let us express it while they are still alive—while they are still near—for when they are gone, our loudest praises they will not hear.

*M*ost people like parades. Some are fun, like the Rose Parade in Pasadena on New Year's Day. Other parades are focused on celebrations of great achievements and individuals, such as war heroes, astronauts, olympic gold medal winners, Superbowl winning teams, etc. These events are usually enthusiastically celebrated with cheering crowds lining the streets of major cities, tossing confetti, as bands and celebrities pass in review.

The greatest parade of all time was quite different, however. It happened in Jerusalem 2,000 years ago. The Triumphant Entry of Jesus riding into Jerusalem on a donkey colt (Matthew 21:1 – 11) was predicted more than 500 years before it happened. This shows how Jesus' actions fulfilled the prophet's words, giving us another indication that Jesus was indeed the Messiah. As Jesus entered Jerusalem, the people cheerfully praised God, waving palm branches and spreading their cloaks and palm branches in front of the colt as it passed before them.

Spreading one's garments on the street was an ancient act reserved for high royalty. The Pharisees were offended by people offering Jesus such worshipful praise. The Bible says the multitudes cried out, "Hosanna to the Son of David! Blessed is He Who comes in the Name of the Lord! Hosanna in the highest!" Their shouts were equivalent to "Long live the King!"

The people who were praising God for giving them a king had the wrong idea about Jesus. They expected Him to be a national leader who would free them from under the yoke of the Roman Empire. They expected Jesus to restore their nation to its former glory. They were deaf to the words of their prophets, and blind to Jesus' real mission on earth. When it became apparent that Jesus was not going to fulfill their hopes, many would turn against Him. Their adoration was short-lived, and their commitment shallow, for in a few days they would do nothing to stop His crucifixion. But despite the Triumphant Entry into Jerusalem, Jesus came not as a warrior king on a horse or in a chariot, but as a gentle, peaceable, humble King on a donkey colt.

After Christ's death, resurrection and ascension, the disciples understood for the first time many of the prophesies that they had missed during Christ's three years of ministry. Jesus' words and actions took on a new meaning for them. In retrospect, the disciples saw how Jesus had led them into a deeper and better understanding of His truth. We can also stop and think about events in our lives leading up to where we now are. How has God led us to this point? As the years pass, we will look back and see God's mighty hand more clearly in our lives than we do now.

The mega-parades of remarkable heroes in more recent years took careful planning, but nothing like the preparation for Jesus' Triumphant Entry into Jerusalem. It had been recorded long before it happened. In Zech. 9:9 and Is. 53:5, the prophets described the events that would unfold more than 500 years later! When Jesus rode the donkey into Jerusalem, fulfilling prophesy as He went, He gave us one more reason to shout, "Hosanna!" He indeed was, and is, the promised Messiah!

*P*ride robs us of two blessings—the joy of giving of ourselves to others and the joy of receiving from others. The Apostle Peter had to battle with his pride. The principle is illustrated in John 13, where Jesus washed the disciples' feet. By doing so, He left us some timeless principles regarding humility and servanthood.

In Jesus' day, people walked everywhere. The dusty conditions of the region necessitated foot washing. People removed their sandals and washed their feet upon entering indoors. Jesus was with the disciples in the upper room for their Passover meal. Although the disciples, most likely, would have been happy to wash Jesus' feet, they could not conceive of the idea of washing each others' feet. This task was reserved for the lowliest of servants. Since there was no servant, in this instance, none of the disciples volunteered for that humble task. With their sandals left at the door, they entered the house with proud hearts and dusty feet. It is even more interesting that in Mark 9:33 – 35, we see these same disciples arguing amongst themselves as to who should be considered the greatest in God's Kingdom. They were willing to fight for a throne, but not for the water basin and towel.

As supper ended, Jesus knew that His time was not long—that He would depart from this world to the Father. He rose, laid aside His outer garment, took a towel, poured water into a basin and began to wash the disciples' feet and dry them with a towel. His act shocked the disciples. This dramatic scene demonstrates Christ's humility, and highlights His coming to serve.

While others remained silent, Peter spoke up in indignation that Jesus would perform such a menial task. It was not fitting for the role of the Messiah he had in mind. Peter failed to see beyond humble service itself, to the symbolism of spiritual cleansing. Jesus' action was not upon arrival as was customary, but was deliberately done later to emphasize a point. Peter needed to learn that the Messiah came to serve, not to be served; a model of Christian humility and service that was supremely exemplified by His death on the cross.

Christ took upon Himself the role of a servant, but His greater goal was to extend His mission on earth after He left it. These dedicated men were to move into the world, serving God, serving each other, and serving all people by spreading the message of Christ so courageously until their deaths. They were glad to die for a resurrected living Christ. They had the infallible proofs.

All who identify with Christ should have a servant's attitude. Jesus says in John 13:14, "If then the Lord and the Teacher, washed your feet, you also ought to wash one anothers' feet." Let us not allow pride to rob us of the double joy of serving and being served. Being a servant includes receiving graciously as well as giving graciously.

Our speech reveals plenty about us. For those of us who came to the U.S.A. from another country, our accent often indicates the country or region from which we came. Our words reveal education or refinement, or the lack of it.

The Apostle Peter, on the night Jesus was arrested, sat in the courtyard worrying about what would happen to his beloved Lord. As he spoke, bystanders recognized his accent, and a servant girl said, "You also were with Jesus of Galilee." But he denied it. Again, someone else stated, "This fellow was also with Jesus of Nazareth." Peter again denied it. A little later others came up and said to Peter, "Surely you also are one of them, for your speech betrays you." And once again Peter said for the third time, "I do not know the man!" (Mt. 26:69 – 75).

Peter's Galilean accent differed from the Judean, and was conspicuous in Jerusalem. His three denials are recorded in all four gospels. His promise that he would "never disown his Lord" is also recorded in the gospels (Mt. 26:35). It is a testimony, both to human weakness and the greatness of God's love, mercy and grace! After Peter's denials, immediately a rooster crowed, and Peter remembered the words of Jesus Who had said to him, "Before the rooster crows, you will deny Me three times." So Peter went outside and wept bitterly. Why did Peter weep? Because at that moment he suddenly felt the weight of his own failure. Though he had earlier wanted to fight, and even die for Jesus, now his courage had melted into confusion. The crowing rooster brought things back into perspective with the shocking realization – he had betrayed the One he loved, just as Jesus had foretold!

There is a little of Peter in all of us. Confronted with the truth, Peter "choked" when recognized. Yet it was that same Peter who, after deeply regretting his choice, became a spiritual giant, and devoted the rest of his life in bold witness for Christ and His Church! Oh, how much Jesus loved Peter. He sought him out, forgave him, restored him, and used him in the service of His Church!

In Greek, the word "petra" means "stone" or "rock." Peter declared that Jesus was the Son of the living God. On that confession, Jesus said to Peter, "On this rock I will build My Church" (Mt. 16:18). Its interpretation is a play on words. The "rock" on which Jesus would build His Church is Christ Himself; His work of salvation by dying on the cross for us. Peter was the first great leader in the Jerusalem church. Later St. Peter reminds Christians that they are the Church, built on the foundation of the apostles and prophets, with Christ as the precious chief cornerstone (1 Pet. 2:6, 7). St. Peter will always be known and remembered as an unshakable martyr for Christ and His Church. He was also the first to confess the deity of Christ as the Son of the living God (Mt. 16:16).

What does our speech say about us? Our conversations reveal our eternal destination. A few words out of our mouths speak volumes about our heart and faith. If we ever become a victim of the "choke" factor, Christ will forgive and restore us when we show remorse and admit our failures. We may fail Jesus, but He will never fail us!

*O*nly once in my life did I ever give blood, which was over ten years ago. It was an extended-family emergency for surgery, and blood was needed. A few days before the scheduled surgery, several members of my family went to UCLA to donate blood. The nurse took a drop of blood from my finger, and after running a test, she told me that I could not give blood; I barely had enough for myself. That wasn't news to me. I've been that way all my life. I tried to make her aware of the need. She silently looked at me and walked away. When she returned, I said, "I'm not going to die by giving some blood." She informed me that there was still another test she could run to determine if I could or could not.

The second test revealed that I was on the borderline of yes or no. I said, "Let's make it yes." As I lay on the padded bed, they gave me a card to read while a pint of blood was drawn from my vein. When I was done, she suggested that I stop by the refreshment table and have some orange juice and cookies. While there, I looked again at the card I was given. I learned what percentage of the population had each of the eight blood types. A statement at the bottom of the card caught my attention: "The rarest blood type is the one that's not there when you need it." How true! This made me think of another supply of blood; one that's always available to those who call upon Him. It's the blood of Christ. We read in 1 Jn. 1:7, "The blood of Jesus, His Son, purifies us from all sin." How does Christ's blood cleanse us?

In Old Testament times, an animal had to be sacrificed (Lev. 4) to pay the penalty of sin—a life had to be given, blood had to be shed. Symbolically, the sacrificed animal carried the sin (Ex. 29:38 – 42). The animal died in place of the sinners and allowed them to continue living in God's favor. In the New Testament, God chose to provide the sacrifice Himself, with the blood of His Son Jesus Christ, "The Lamb of God Who takes away the sin of the world" (Jn. 1:29). Jesus didn't die for His own sin; He had none. He died for the sins of the world – our sins. Because of God's love and mercy for us, Christ became the perfect sacrifice. For as one man's disobedience (Adam), many were made sinners. So also through one Man's obedience (Jesus), many will be made righteous before God (Rom. 5:19).

When we commit our lives to Christ and receive forgiveness by confessing our sins, His blood purifies us. And just as Christ rose from the grave, we rise to a new life of fellowship with Him (Rom. 6:4). That's how Christ's blood cleanses us.

Yes, Christ gave His life for us. But the cross that He hung on was not softly padded. He was not lying down. He was hanging by nails hammered through His hands and feet. He didn't hear soft music in the background. He heard only mocking remarks of the crowd, a few sobs, and then silence. Why such pain, humiliation, and even death? He was obedient to His Father's will! We read in Heb. 9:22, "Without the shedding of blood there is no forgiveness." He died so that we may have forgiveness, abundant life and the gift of eternal life. We are free—redeemed through Christ! The rarest blood may not be there when needed, but Christ's blood is always there for each one of us.

*A*cts of treachery are often referred to as "Judas' kiss." This betrayal shows to what extent even a disciple of Jesus Christ can fall; a man who for three years lived in the presence of Jesus and His ministry.

Judas Iscariot was one of the twelve disciples called by Jesus. His name always appears last on the list, usually with the stigma as the one who betrayed Jesus (Mt. 10:4). Judas was from Judea, the only non-Galilean of the disciples. We don't know the exact motivation behind his betrayal. Clearly, he had no spiritual interest in Jesus. It is believed that he expected Jesus to become a powerful religious and political leader and overthrow Rome. He saw political potential for power, wealth, and prestige through his association with Jesus. As treasurer, Judas assumed that he would be given an important position in Jesus' government.

In time, Judas realized that Jesus' kingdom was neither physical nor political, but spiritual. With his worldly hopes crushed, he also realized that his desire for money and status could never be fulfilled if he stayed with Jesus. So he planned to betray Him in exchange for money, and to gain favor with the Jewish religious leaders of the time who opposed Jesus' teachings – 30 silver coins, the price of a slave. But Jesus knew what Judas was like from the beginning, and that is why He chose him as one of the twelve. Judas was the one who would betray Him, so that scripture and God's plan of salvation would be fulfilled. The fact that Judas' betrayal was part of God's plan doesn't free Judas from the guilt of a crime he entered into willingly. He never had a genuine relationship with the Lord Jesus. His highest title for Christ was "Rabbi" (teacher), never "Lord" (Mt. 26:25). He is presented in scripture as an awful warning to the uncommitted followers of Christ who are in His company, but don't share His Spirit. He chose betrayal, and God confirmed him in that dreadful choice.

After the Passover meal in the "upper room," Jesus and the disciples went to the Garden of Gethsemane. That evening Jesus prayed for strength to face the suffering ahead. Judas waited for an opportunity to deliver Jesus to His enemies. While Jesus was in prayer, armed soldiers came, led by Judas. The sign of identification was the last touch of irony. Judas said, "Whomever I kiss, He is the One..." (Mk. 14:44). And with that, the traitor's work was completed.

Upon reflection over his evil deed, Judas tried to return the money, but it was too late. God's plan had been set into motion. Remorseful over his evil deed, Judas committed suicide by hanging himself. How sad that Judas ended his life in despair without ever experiencing the gift of reconciliation. He never repented; never came to seek forgiveness from Christ, Who would have given it, even to His betrayer!

Are we true disciples and followers of Christ, or uncommitted followers? Jesus' death on the cross seals a new covenant between God and mankind. Now all of us can come to God through faith in Christ any time, about anything, knowing that He will accept us and grant us forgiveness and eternal life. Jesus says in Jn. 14:6, "I am the way, the truth and the life. No one comes to the Father except through Me."

*D*uring Holy Week, and especially on Good Friday, millions of Christians around the world rejoice for what God fulfilled through His Son, Jesus Christ, nearly 2,000 years ago. Why do we call this Friday "Good"? Wasn't this one of the darkest days in the history of believers of Christ's time? A sinless Christ who ministered love, healed the sick, brought hope to the lives of so may, was nailed to a cross. Where was the "good" in that?

When the disciples recognized the awful truth of Christ's death, their hopes and dreams were crushed as well. They had believed that Christ, their beloved Teacher, was sent by God, and yet, His body lay in the tomb. In the gospel of John we read, "For God so loved the world that He gave His only begotten Son, that whoever believes in Him should not perish but have everlasting life." (3:16) That little word "so" in the above verse is most expressive. It illustrates the magnitude of God's love. Could we ask for greater evidence of love? It can only be fully known by faith.

Miraculously and by divine plan, Christ was resurrected in a glorified body. Hope was revived, as disciples and fellow believers realized that their Teacher became the risen Lord! He was alive! He had risen!

The gospels would be incomplete without Christ's triumphant victory over death through resurrection. The crucifixion of Christ on Good Friday is the atoning sacrificial act for the remission of all our sins. "I am the resurrection and the life. He who believes in Me, though he may die, shall live." (John 11:25) Christ's resurrection is the basis, the essence and the cornerstone of our Christian faith.

Through faith in Christ we receive forgiveness for all our sins, and the assurance of everlasting life – a new triumphant life. This is the promise of Christ's resurrection, and that is what makes the Holy Week's Friday "Good." Christ endured darkness so that we may live in light—His Light!

A police officer was patrolling on night duty in a town in England when he heard a trembling cry. Turning toward the direction it came from, he saw a little boy in the shadows sitting on the pavement. Fearful, tired and with tears streaming down his cheeks, the child said, "I am lost, please take me home."

The boy could not remember his address, so the policeman began naming street after street, trying to help the boy remember where he lived. When that failed, he named shops and hotels in the area, but all without success. Then the officer remembered that in the center of town there was a church with a large white cross towering high above the surrounding landscape. He pointed to it and asked if he lives anywhere near that church. The boy's face immediately lit up and said, "Yes, take me to the cross, and I can find my way home from there."

The cross is God's compass, pointing the way to Christ. The cross directs confused, lost souls in search of Christ. When we look upon the form of a cross, do we ever think of it as the arms of Christ outstretched to us, saying, "Come to Me, all you who labor and heavy laden, and I will give you rest" (Matt. 11:28). He means here and now, not just eternal rest after death.

Christ frees us from all burdens. He promises love, healing and peace with God; not the end of labor. Through His death on Calvary's cross, Christ became the mediator between God and man. His death and resurrection made our redemption possible. By accepting His offer of forgiveness by faith in His name, we can be certain that He will lead us home.

During this spring season, the love of our Christ reaches out once again and brings springtime renewal for all mankind. The most wonderful thing in Christian faith is God's marvelous power for forgiveness. He is willing to forgive our errors, our sins, our past, no matter what that past has been. If we want to gain happy, healthy lives, we must turn once again to Him, trust Him and renew our faith. Why not devote some time each day to God. Read His textbook, the Bible, pray, be regular in church attendance, and leave all worries and fears to Him, for He cares for us.

Let us take Jesus Christ at His word, "Come to Me..." Yes, the cross is God's compass. The only way home is to come to the cross. Christ says in John 14:6, "I am the Way, the Truth and the Life. No one comes to the Father except through Me."

*T*he story is told of a young boy who stood outside an art gallery looking at a painting of Jesus on the cross. A man next to him asked, "Do you know who that is?" The boy said, "Yes sir, that is Jesus who died on the cross for us. Those around Him are the soldiers who killed Him. And the woman who is crying is His mother." The man patted the boy's head and walked away. He had not gone far when he felt a pull on his sleeve. The same boy who spoke moments earlier added, "Sir, I forgot to tell you that Jesus is not on the cross any more. He rose, He is alive and in Heaven today."

The young fellow sure knew the truth of the gospel. Life for the believer does not end at death, but continues eternally as an endless life of fellowship with God. Therefore, Christ says, "I am the resurrection and the life; he who believes in Me, though he may die, yet shall he live…" and "Because I live, you shall live also" (John 11:25, 14:19). The risen Christ has gone before us. He holds our future securely in His nail-scarred hands. If His body had remained in the tomb, we would have no hope beyond the grave. But Christ has conquered death. Now death is no longer the end, but the door to everlasting life.

The resurrection of Christ is the cornerstone of our Christian faith. Therefore, it is important to recognize that our belief in Christ's resurrection is based on historical fact with solid evidence to support it. The climax of the gospel is the resurrection. Every sermon preached by the apostles included the good news that Jesus is not dead. No matter how eloquent a sermon might be, if it leaves Jesus on the cross or in the tomb, it is not the gospel. *The good news is not that Jesus lived and died, but that He died and He lives!*

The resurrection of Christ was attested to by hundreds of New Testament witnesses who saw Jesus Christ, talked with Him, ate with Him, walked with Him, and declared Him as their Lord and Savior. What was it that transformed the first disciples into a band of champions of their crucified Lord? It could never have been a dead leader. It was a living, conquering Christ.

What gave the great army of Christian martyrs and missionaries the love and power to face death, penetrate jungles, cross deserts, and go to the ends of the earth in their zeal to win disciples to Christ? It was the eternal fact of the resurrection, the truth of Christ's conquest of death. By the miracle of His rising from the dead, Jesus placed the seal of assurance upon the forgiveness of our sins; He cleansed us.

The open tomb becomes the promise of God that if we are believers in Christ, we are going to live forever spiritually. Christ says in Rev. 1:17, 18: "I am the First and the Last. I am the Living One; I was dead, and behold I am alive forever and ever!"

A Blessed and Happy Easter to You All!

*M*any of us have seen impressive burial grounds, far more magnificent than the grave where the lifeless body of Christ was laid to rest 2,000 years ago. We know that the pyramids of Giza are the tombs of the great pharaohs who were once buried in luxury. The tomb of King David in Jerusalem is quite impressive. It is set indoors, and is covered with a crimson velvet cloth, embroidered and embellished with silver and gold threads. The Taj Mahal in India (I've only seen pictures of it) is perhaps the most overwhelming of all, as tombs go.

Although the exact location of Christ's grave is not known for certain, the rock-hewn Garden Tomb in Jerusalem gives a clear picture of what the place of Christ's burial must have looked like.

Every tomb I've seen communicates death, but the grave of Christ offers life, hope and blessings. Today we read again what the two angels said to the women who came to the tomb bringing spices: "Why do you seek the living among the dead? He is not here, but is risen!" (Luke 24:5, 6) To us Christians the resurrection of Christ is the basis, essence and heart of our faith. Christ is not among the dead – He lives! He reigns in the hearts of all believers, and He is the Head of His Church.

What transformed the first disciples into a united group of spiritual champions for their crucified Lord? Certainly, not a dead teacher. He was and He is a living, conquering Christ. What gave the great number of Christian martyrs, apostles and missionaries the love, determination and power to go to the ends of the earth, and even face death in their desire to win disciples for Christ? It was the eternal truth of the resurrection, the everlasting fact of the Savior's conquest of death.

With the great stone rolled away, the open tomb is God's promise that we, who believe in Christ, will have eternal life. The risen Christ offers new life and renewal to all who will receive Him by faith. Through the power of the resurrection, may God's Spirit bring into our hearts the assurance that we have the gift of eternal life. And because of our faith in Christ we can say, He is risen, He lives, therefore, we shall also live!

*T*hree days after the crucifixion of Christ, two of His disciples were walking from Jerusalem to the village of Emmaus. Discouraged because of their Lord's death, they talked of the sad events that occurred in the last few days. Suddenly, Jesus Himself drew near and asked why they were sad. The Bible says, "Their eyes were restrained, so that they did not know Him" (Lk. 24:16).

The news of Jesus' crucifixion had spread throughout Jerusalem. Being Passover week, Jewish pilgrims visiting the city from all over the Roman Empire knew about His death. The disciples from Emmaus, and Jews in general, were counting on Jesus to redeem Israel and rescue the nation from Roman bondage. Most Jews believed that the Old Testament prophesies pointed to a military and political Messiah. They didn't realize that the Messiah had come to redeem people from the slavery of sin. When Jesus died, they lost all hope. They didn't understand that Jesus' death offered the greatest hope possible!

As Jesus continued walking with the two men, one whose name was Cleopas said to Him, "Are You the only stranger in Jerusalem, and have You not known the things which happened there in these days?" (Lk. 24:18) "What things?" asked Jesus. They told Him about the death of the One they thought was the Messiah.

When they arrived home they asked the stranger to come in and eat with them. As Jesus sat at the table with them, He took bread, gave thanks and broke it, and gave it to them; actions that only a host would perform at a meal (Lk. 22:19). Suddenly the two recognized that He was Jesus their Lord! The Bible says, "Their eyes were opened and they knew Him" (Lk.24:31). What did these two disciples see to identify Jesus? Perhaps His nail-pierced hands, as He broke the bread. After that He vanished from their sight. God intervened to keep them from recognizing Him until this point. His resurrected body, though real and tangible, and even capable of ingesting earthly food, nonetheless possessed certain properties that indicate it was glorified, altered in a mysterious way (Lk. 24:42, 43).

Christ could appear and disappear bodily as seen in this text. His body could pass through solid objects – such as the grave clothes (Lk. 24:12), or when He came to His disciples through locked doors (Lk. 24:36; Jn. 20:19 – 26).

The repeated appearance of Jesus after His death brought great joy to His disciples. But on the fortieth day after His resurrection, He gave His disciples these final instructions: "All authority has been given to Me in heaven and on earth. Go therefore and make disciples of all nations…in the name of the Father and of the Son and of the Holy Spirit…and Lo, I am with you always even to the end of the age" (Mt. 28:18 – 20). At this point Jesus blessed His disciples and was carried up into heaven (Lk. 24:51).

Jesus' ascension marked the beginning of a new era. In His glorified body, Christ entered heaven exalted and at the right hand of God, and sent the promised Holy Spirit shortly after that (Jn. 14:16 – 18; Acts 2:33). He now permeates the entire universe with His spiritual presence and power. His Holy Spirit is with every believer and will continue "to the end of the age."

OUR PRECIOUS TOOL BOX

*A*ccording to an old fable, the devil decided to sell some of his well-worn tools. On display were some deceitful instruments, including hatred, jealousy, lying, judging and pride. Set apart from the rest on a prominent spot was a harmless looking device with a very high price tag. "What is this?" someone asked. "That's discouragement," Satan replied. "It is my favorite and most effective tool. With it I can open the hearts of God's most faithful servants and bring upon them discouragement and depression." Some of the most godly people have struggled with these feelings. That tool certainly worked on the following men of God.

Moses, the great leader and faithful servant of God, was discouraged when his first efforts to lead the Israelites out of Egypt and free them from bondage failed. He had obeyed God and yet, Pharaoh had rejected him, and his fellow countrymen turned against him. Discouraged, he turned to God in prayer, "Oh Lord, why have You brought trouble on these people? Why is it you have sent me?" (Exodus 5:22) Does this sound like Moses, the great emancipator?

The tool of discouragement worked on Elijah as well. In I Kings 19, we see prophet Elijah, acting on the authority of God, opposing the evil Queen Jezebel and her pagan deities. When he learned of Jezebel's vow to kill him, he fled for his life. In despair he prayed that he might die. "I had enough, Lord, take my life."

David also was down when he wrote Psalm 6. He felt weak, forsaken, weary and just plain discouraged. "Have mercy on me, Oh Lord, for I am faint, heal me..." Is this the young brave David we know who a few years earlier had delivered the single smooth stone with his sling into Goliath's forehead, and slew him? Is this the same David who often played the harp for King Saul to lift his melancholy spirit? But David knew what to do. He looked up and trusted God, like Moses and Elijah.

That tool of discouragement works in all of us. That does not mean God has abandoned us. His presence and unconditional love is always with us. If even these faithful godly men had struggled with discouragement, that evil tool can easily work on us. These men of faith found comfort and success by seeking God and saw beyond temporary setbacks. God took steps to restore them, gave them a new vision of His power and used them in a mighty way. God can do the same for us when we seek Him in prayer. Only when we realize our own powerlessness can we become strong through His power.

Prayer is still God's mighty force in solving problems even today. Prayer and action go hand in hand. We must recognize that there are no triumphs without setbacks. With prayer, the devil's tools become totally ineffective. Then when difficulties arise, we will turn to God instinctively.

God's guidance for daily living is found in His Word. That is our precious "tool box." In it we have the wisdom to meet all challenges of life. As we grow spiritually, we clothe ourselves with His armor and become seasoned fighters prepared for any battle. Through Him we have the power to take on any opponent and win. "I can do all things through Christ who strengthens me." (Phil. 4:13). Great verse! Let us reach for our "tool box" and get better acquainted with our tools!

On April 24th, Armenians throughout the world pay tribute to the 1.5 million of our people who were massacred in 1915 and the several years following, by orders of the Turkish government.

Spring is a beautiful season, yet it has memories of sorrow and sadness for us Armenians. We are the children and grandchildren of the survivors who were dispersed to all corners of this earth. We are living, we are prospering, we are citizens of many nations now, and yes, proud of it. But we cannot forget the past. Time does not heal these kinds of wounds. It is one thing to suffer a tragedy of this magnitude. It is quite another to be told that nothing occurred, using World War I as a pretext and cover for such a despicable act.

Our martyrs, however, did not die in vain. We continue to maintain the faith for which they died. Our progress, success and accomplishments as individuals and as a thriving Armenian community are perhaps the best retaliation against our painful past. A Christ-centered triumphant life is the best medicine for our still-painful wounds.

Our churches, Armenian schools, community and our press continue to play a central role in the observance of this day annually. In doing so, the precious memory of our people and their spiritual values will continue to remain alive and be sustained, not only in us, but in our younger generations as well.

The Apostle Paul's words to the Philippian believers come to mind; "Finally, brothers, whatever is true, whatever is noble, whatever is right, whatever is pure, whatever is lovely, whatever is admirable, if anything is excellent or praiseworthy, think about such things." (4:8) With this in mind, let us continue to play a central role in this annual observance, so that the precious memory of our people will forever remain alive within us. It is our duty as Armenians.

*H*annah, mother of Samuel, represents the ideal mother of the Old Testament. Her touching story is told in the first two chapters of 1 Samuel.

Hannah was married to Elkanah, but was childless. Elkanah was also married to Peninnah and had several children with her. Peninnah, jealous of Hannah for being the favorite wife, ridiculed her barrenness constantly. Childless women in Biblical times felt dishonored and an embarrassment to their husbands. Elkanah, seeing Hannah weeping, would often say, "Don't I mean more to you than ten sons?" Hannah, however, was a woman of faith and prayer, and God moved ahead with His plan for her motherhood.

While Hannah and her family attended the annual feasts at the tabernacle to worship, offer sacrifices and praise God for all blessings, her sorrow was even more poignant. She once again entered the tabernacle crying bitterly as she prayed. She made a vow saying, "Oh Lord Almighty, if You will only look upon Your servant's misery and remember me, and not forget Your servant, but give her a son, then I will give him to the Lord for all the days of his life…"

Hannah received new strength in prayer and left her problem with God, trusting in His will. Eli, the chief priest, gave his blessing to her as well. In the course of time, Hannah conceived and gave birth to a son, and named him Samuel. Hannah kept her vow. She lovingly tended Samuel in his formative years as she prepared him to serve God. When the child was old enough, Hannah dressed Samuel for his first trip to the tabernacle, where she was to leave him. Hannah gave up what she wanted to keep most – her son! She bravely did what she promised God. Before she left Samuel with Eli, she prayed to God a triumphant prayer of praise and thanksgiving (1 Sam. 2:1 – 10). She had been delivered from disgrace to a position of honor and strength!

Hannah was a woman who prayed in good times and bad, in joy and affliction. It was a true sacrifice for her to part from her son. Elkanah and Hannah returned home, leaving Samuel to serve the Lord under Eli, the high priest. Hannah didn't forget her beloved son. She visited him regularly, and each year she brought him a new priestly robe that she had made herself.

God honored Hannah's faithfulness. We never hear about Peninnah or her children again, but God used Samuel mightily. He was called to fill many roles; priest, judge, prophet, counselor and God's faithful servant at the turning point in Israel's history. God continued to be gracious to Hannah, who conceived and had five more children.

Each one of us may face times of barrenness when nothing comes to fruition. It may be at work, in relationships, etc. Some of us might be in the midst of difficult circumstances. Let us remember to thank God in spite of everything. Healing begins when we name our blessings. Hannah discovered that prayer opens communication with our Creator. We must learn to leave our petitions to His divine will and His timing. And let us be faithful with our promises in prayer. God hears our prayers and will be faithful to us.

*D*elightful moments often leave us with lasting memories that we cherish for years. Such an experience occurred to me a few years ago. I entered a bank and stood at the end of a long line. To avoid boredom, I took some reading material and a pen from my purse. After reading two paragraphs, I summarized the content by writing in the margin, "God sees everything."

The publication I was reading was in English, but instinctively, I wrote the sentence in Armenian. I had barely started reading again when a young man behind me said in perfect English, "You are right, God sees everything." Surprised, I looked at him and smiled. He said that the sentence I wrote gave it away that I was Armenian. I said I was pleased he read Armenian and delighted he agreed with what I wrote. The teller soon called me. "God bless you," I said, and went to the teller. When I completed my business the young man was gone.

By this delightful experience I realized once again that no matter where we are, or what we do, in whatever language, we are constantly watched by others. Suddenly lessons from my childhood came alive, and my mother's voice echoed in my ears. "Be aware, the world is watching every move you make!" Perhaps every mother of every generation said something similar to her child at one time or another.

In Matthew 10:13 Jesus says, "You are the salt of the earth. But if the salt loses its saltiness, how can it be made salty again? It is no longer good for anything, except to be thrown out and trampled by men." Salt was both a seasoning and a preservative. As salt of the earth, we as Christians must add flavor to our environment. Our exemplary lives must affect others positively, just as seasoning brings flavor to food. We are to preserve, protect and perpetuate our faith. We are also given the task to make others thirst for God's Word as the eternal water of life.

In Biblical times salt was either mined in chunks along the Dead Sea, or obtained by means of evaporation. As salt was removed from sediment, the bottom layers were mixed with sand and soil that made salt impure and lose its saltiness, polluted with foreign materials. This mixture was thrown into the streets and onto the temple steps during winter to prevent people from slipping in wet or icy weather. It was literally trampled by men. What a remarkable verse and vivid illustration!

As Christians how do we lose our saltiness? By allowing the worldly environment to influence our lives and our better judgment. Jesus instructs us to remain pure and add flavor to our world. The message of the verse was clear to Jesus' audience then, and it is clear to us now. We have an awesome responsibility to make a difference. As we know, an ounce of example is worth more than a ton of advice.

As I recall the brief experience at the bank, I'm still amazed. Yes, the world is watching every move we make. Therefore, let us live by the lessons with which we have been raised and instructed by Christ. As Christians let us be worthy of that honor and continue to be the salt of the earth!

*M*any years ago while I was a student at a local university, I met a sweet, dear lady who was also a student in one of my classes. It was unusual, especially at the time, to see this tall, slender and very frail woman sitting among her younger classmates, skillfully taking notes in shorthand. We became friends. She told me that she was 81 years of age and had been a character actress all her life. When I asked her why she was taking this philosophy class, she said that it was to learn what she had neglected in her youth. Her husband would drop her off just for that one class, and she appeared to be having the time of her life. I admired her attitude and hunger for knowledge.

On the last week of instruction, my friend seemed a little sad. She showed me a bracelet with many charms attached. Each charm was given to her at a celebration party after completion of a film. She talked of her younger years. For the first time since I met her, she talked about life's vanities. She asked me about my Christian faith, and if my husband was also a Christian. She was concerned about her dear husband, stating that they only had each other.

I shared my Christian faith with this sweet lady, who was much older than my own mom. She was very receptive. I reached into my purse and gave her a Christian booklet that I had only partially read. I suggested that she share it with her husband. He picked her up after class, and I never saw her again. She was happy when we parted. Many years have passed since then, yet I often think of her.

Willingness to learn at any age is a mark of growth and wisdom. But nothing is more important than to increase our knowledge of God's Word. And this is best achieved by attending Bible study. Proverbs 1:5 states, "A wise man will hear and increase in learning, and a man of understanding will acquire wise counsel." People who desire wisdom welcome God's Word and are open to His truths. We never grow too old to learn new spiritual lessons in God's classroom of life. We will never arrive spiritually in this life—there is always a higher plateau to be reached.

*W*hile visiting a friend, a framed needlepoint embroidery on the wall caught my attention. It read: "WHEN LIFE GIVES YOU SCRAPS MAKE QUILTS!" I smiled, knowing that my friend's hobby is quilting. As I pondered on it, however, I concluded that it applies to all of us. We have all been thrown "scraps" in life at one time or another, not only for one quilt, but for several. But how do we turn those "scraps" into quilts?

The thread of living one day at a time is woven throughout the fabric of scripture. Jesus teaches us in the "Lord's Prayer" to ask for our "daily bread" and to refuse to worry about tomorrow. It is a lesson we seem to learn with difficulty, but one that holds the key to life and peace. Jesus says in Mt. 6:24-34, not to worry about anything because our Heavenly Father already knows all our needs. He talks of the birds of the air and the lilies of the field, and how God cares for them. Are we not worth much more than they? Then He adds, "Who of you by being worried can add a single hour to his life?"

Regardless of how things may look today, the Lord is not far from us. He may be giving us an opportunity to trust Him and wait for His help rather than relying on our own resources. Jesus also teaches us not to worry because of its ill effects on us. Worry, for example, may damage our health, consume our thoughts, disrupt our productivity, negatively affect the way we treat others and reduce our ability to trust God. Some of us may already suffer the effects of worry.

There is a difference between worry and genuine concern that we must consider. Worry immobilizes us, but concern moves us into action. Sometimes it's difficult to tell the difference. Carefully planning ahead, calmly considering our goals step by step, and trusting in God's guidance is productive. Worrying, by contrast, can consume us by fear and cloud our spiritual insight. Spiritual vision is our capacity to see clearly what God wants us to do and to see the world from His point of view. Self-serving desires and goals can block that vision. Serving God is the best way to restore it. A discerning eye is one that is fixed on God and His Word.

When Jesus said, "No one can serve two masters," He contrasted eternal values with earthly ones. Our first loyalty should be to those things that don't fade, can't be stolen or used up, and can never wear out. If we allow ourselves to be fascinated with material possessions, they will eventually possess us. Jesus is calling us to choose what is eternal and lasting.

So, what "scraps" has life presented to us this day? We must remember that we are neither alone nor the first. We must recognize that others have faced similar situations as we. True security is in God. His love for us no pen can express—no mouth can confess. The believer in Christ puts his faith in the God of the past, present and future; the First and the Last, the Alpha and the Omega (Rev. 1:8). God's words of comfort remind us of His daily bread, daily light, daily strength. When tomorrow seems too long to endure, God reminds us to trust Him one day at a time. That is today! We lose the joy of living in the present when we worry about the "scraps" of the future.

*M*oses was holding a plain wooden staff. "What is that in your hand?" God asked him in Exodus 4:2. The answer to the question seemed obvious at first. Moses would learn, however, that this ordinary shepherd's rod would soon become a symbol of power and authority to deliver the Israelites from Egyptian bondage.

A shepherd's rod was commonly a three to six foot wooden staff, sometimes with a curved hook at the top. The shepherd used it for walking, guiding his sheep, killing snakes, and many other tasks. Still, it was just a stick. But God used the simple shepherd's rod Moses carried as a sign to teach him an important lesson. God sometimes takes pleasure in using ordinary things for extraordinary purposes.

Today He asks the same question of each of us: "What is that in your hand?" We all have God-given gifts, talents and possessions that He wants us to use to accomplish His will. The primary motivation, of course, is our love for Him and our gratitude for His many blessings we often take for granted. At times we are reluctant, build up events in our minds, and panic over what might go wrong. God does not ask us to do or go where He has not provided the means to help. He will equip us to go wherever He leads. We only need to trust Him to supply courage, confidence and resources at the right moment.

What is that in our hands that we hold on to so tightly? Could it be our voice, a musical instrument, a hammer, a computer keyboard? For some, God's calling might be to show hospitality, help in the church nursery, sing in the choir, tutor a child, serve on the boards, drive the church van, or visit shut-ins. Whatever the gift or tool, we must never consider that talent small or insignificant. While it is easy to assume God can only use special skills, we must never hinder His use of the little, everyday contributions we can make. God uses ordinary people to accomplish extraordinary works. Little did Moses imagine the power his simple rod would wield when it became the rod of God. Even a little is enough for our Creator when it is offered with joy. God often uses small matches to light great torches! "What is that in <u>YOUR</u> hand?"

*T*here are those who believe that our handwriting reveals certain elements about our personality. We have seen graphologists at some parties and restaurants analyzing handwriting as a form of entertainment. Perhaps these individuals offer their services elsewhere as well. Those in the field of graphology observe how the letters slant, the way upper and lower case letters are formed, where and how the "t" is crossed and the "i" is dotted. On the basis of these distinctions, they arrive at conclusions about our personality; whether we are outgoing or reserved, creative or conforming, etc.

Although the reliability of these conclusions may be questioned by many, the words of the Apostle Paul and what he wrote to the Corinthian faithful come to mind. "You are our epistle written in our hearts, known and read by all men; clearly you are an epistle of Christ, ministered by us, written not with ink but by the Spirit of the living God..." (2 Cor. 3:2, 3)

What a remarkable statement! The way we compose the "letters" of our daily conduct indicates the kind of Christians we truly are. Our behavior is known and read by everyone! The Apostle uses powerful imagery. Ink fades and may easily be deleted or blocked out, since it is a temporary fluid. But the Spirit of the living God is Himself Life, and therefore, life-giving. The work of God's Spirit in the transformed lives of the Corinthian faithful was sufficient proof of St. Paul's ministry. People had clearly seen, by the conduct of the faithful, their remarkable transformation brought about by the work of God's Spirit.

How important it is for us to be aware of the handwriting of our lives! Our conduct reveals each day who we truly are. By our exemplary lives we are writing a book, perhaps a chapter each day. By the deeds that we do, by the words that we speak, those around us read the handwriting of our lives!

Our adequacy is from God. He has implanted His Spirit into our hearts, giving us new power and energy to serve Him, and write chapters by our conduct. By this, the handwriting of our lives, we will tell others who we are, to Whom we belong, and Who we serve.

*P*eople often feel that to be a Christian and have a close personal relationship with Christ, means to have an entirely changed demeanor. This perception is simply not true. When God wishes to use us in His service, He calls us to come to Him just as we are. He then takes our traits and talents that may have been used negatively and turns them to positive actions for His glory. An amazing Biblical example is the life and works of the Apostle Paul.

Except for Jesus Christ Himself, no one did more to shape the history of Christianity than the Apostle Paul. His name was Saul, and even before he became a believer, his behavior and actions were significant. He had the finest education available, and was extremely zealous in his faith. He sincerely believed that this new Christian movement was dangerous to his Judaic religion. Saul hated the Christian faith and persecuted Christians without mercy.

He was the worst enemy the gospel ever had. He stood at Stephen's stoning, "giving approval to his death" (Acts 8:1). He was the one who was "breathing out murderous threats against the Lord's disciples" (Acts 9:1). He was, in fact, on his way to Damascus to arrest Christians and bring them in chains to Jerusalem. But as he approached Damascus, he discovered that God had other plans for him. Christ appeared to him in person, struck him down and transformed his life. "Saul, Saul, why are you persecuting Me?" (Acts 9:4). For three days Saul was blind and did not eat or drink anything. After his sight was restored, his life was never the same again.

God did not change Saul's personality—He only changed his name. He was now Paul, a zealous Apostle for Christ! God did not change the intensity of Paul's character, He only changed the mission for which He prepared him—the most effective Christian missionary the world has ever known! God did not waste any part of Paul's talents, training, his Roman citizenship, his brilliant mind, his energy and enthusiasm. Paul was transformed from a persecutor of Christians to a preacher for Christ who led three missionary journeys throughout the Roman Empire. His letters to the various churches are a major part of the New Testament. Paul is often called the "Apostle to the Gentiles."

God chose Christianity's chief opponent and transformed him into its primary proponent! God could have used anyone, but He chose Saul as a prime example of what grace could do! Our walk with God may not resemble Saul's, but we know God loves us, calls us and relates to us wherever we are.

*W*e all like beautiful stories, especially those with a happy ending. Therefore, I was not surprised to see several huge posters of the Cinderella story in a mall. Is there anyone who doesn't know the story of Cinderella? No matter what part of the world we came from, or how many languages we speak, we have all been told this story. And although we all know it's a fairy tale, it is still one of the most favorite ones, and we happily pass it on to the next generation. Oh yes, the handsome young prince with the glass slipper anxiously searched his entire kingdom to find the beautiful girl he had danced with. He finally found Cinderella whose slipper fit perfectly. They married and lived happily ever after in his kingdom.

It's a great story with a beautiful ending. But why did we like this tale so much? Is it perhaps that as children we all dreamed to be part of a royal family, a child of a king, and live like a princess or prince?

The Bible, the Word of God, promises every Christian of any age a real heavenly life in God's Kingdom; a life far better than any mythical story such as Cinderella. The Bible clearly says, "For God so loved the world that He gave His only begotten Son, that whoever believes in Him should not perish but have everlasting life" (John 3:16).

The Word of God promises that whoever believes in Christ will become a child of the King of the universe. That is because at just the right time in history, "when the fullness of time had come" (Gal. 4:4), God sent His Son to earth – the One Who was born of the Virgin Mary. He is the One Who made it possible for us to be born into God's family and become royal heirs of His Kingdom. We are promised a new life, not of this world, but one of quality with spiritual riches.

The Bible is a book with a universal message for all people. Its simple, life related principles can work in any country, crossing barriers of culture and race, to bring love, peace, joy and forgiveness to all faithful. Only the Bible can transform a rebel into a saint and turn anyone from life's rags to spiritual riches. God's love promises a beautiful ending to anyone's personal story, now and always.

From the beginning of history, the human race wandered away from God. The Bible reveals God's love and desire to bring us all back to Him. His plan became possible through His Son Jesus Christ. As Christians we are all heirs of His heavenly Kingdom. And anyone who has not yet turned to Him can do so. This is the Good News of the Bible. The best news ever for all humanity!

X-rays reveal everything! I had the opportunity recently to review a series of x-rays taken through a cast. Although this might seem very ordinary to many, it is still amazing to be able to examine bones in minute detail through something so solid.

We live in a time of tremendous advances in technology. The United States, for some years now, has orbiting satellites with highly sophisticated equipment that make it possible to continually scan the world. Some of these satellites note all suspicious or unfriendly activity for protection of this country.

Another kind of world surveillance has been going on since creation. Second Chronicles 16:9 says, "The eyes of the Lord run to and fro throughout the whole world." Knowing that our Heavenly Father, Who sees everything we do, should motivate us to live a life that pleases Him. And what a comfort that is to us, for our God, to Whom all is revealed, still cares for His own.

As His own then, do any of us feel neglected, forgotten, alone? Do we feel any nagging attitudes that might clutter our hearts? Why not turn it over to Him. God gives His very best to all those who totally surrender to Him. Because of His unconditional love, we are never out of His sight.

Psalms 139 is a precious prayer written by David. The following are the first three verses: "O Lord, You have searched me and You know me. You know when I sit and when I rise; You perceive my thoughts from afar. You discern my going out and my lying down; You are familiar with all my ways."

Sometimes we don't let people know us completely, fearing that they may discover something about us they will not like. But God knows every minute detail about us, even the number of hairs on our head (Matt 10:30), and still accepts and loves us.

God's love is unconditional! We are never out of His sight. There is never a time of day, be it on earth or sea, that God's eyes go dim, when He is unaware of you and me.

*W*e often wonder how could King David, with all his shortcomings, be listed in the Hall of Faith in Hebrews 11. It is also surprising that he is described more than once, as a man after God's own heart (1 Sam. 13:14 and Acts 13:22). The Bible is filled with examples of how God changed failures, even forgiven mega-sins, by turning them into triumphs.

King David experienced the heights of victory and depths of failure. As a shepherd boy and a "rookie" soldier, he killed the giant Goliath with a sling and a single stone. As King Saul's personal harp player, he held a position of favor in the court. As a captain in the army, he won the people's hearts, and defeated formidable enemies. David eventually became king; the most prominent person in Israel. Nothing could stop him now—nothing but sin (2 Sam. 11:1 – 27).

David fell victim to the beauty of a soldier's wife, Bathsheba. Involved in adultery, he had her husband killed in the line of duty to cover his actions. This great psalmist, soldier, musician and monarch had fallen to the level of a murderer. Despite this and other failures, David stands out as one of the Bible's great men of God. How could that be? It is because David faced God and humbly asked for His forgiveness. He took complete responsibility for his actions and repented.

Turning to God, he wrote with faith and humility in Psalm 32: "When I kept silent about my sin, my body wasted away... For day and night Your hand was heavy on me..." And in Psalm 51:1 – 10: "Cleanse me from my sin...wash me, and I shall be whiter than snow... Create in me a clean heart, O God..."

Even in the worst possible situations, God forgives when people truly turn to Him in repentance. No one is immune from the pull of fallible human nature, no matter how small the fall might be. But God knows all that, and He still loves us. That is our merciful God. His love and grace is everlasting.

We can thank God for His complete forgiveness, but nothing can erase the painful consequences of wrong actions. David and his family experienced overwhelming consequences of his wrongful acts until the end of his life. Despite all, David repented, trusted God and relied on His mercy. That is why he is recorded as a "man after God's own heart."

Several editors polled a number of successful authors and assembled a list of some 80 books everyone should read. Which book would you say was No. 1? The Bible! Yes, the Word of God ranked at the top of the list; the oldest best seller in the world! Have the years been kind to the Bible? You bet! Even after thousands of years, the Bible still has the power to change lives. Its refreshing wisdom is relevant to a world struggling with the effects of violence and immorality.

The Bible's long life is impressive. Its poetry continues to inspire readers. But the ability to retain vitality throughout the centuries to all generations is supernatural. The Bible is just as precious and infinite today as when it was written. Critics have tried to bury the Bible for generations. They characterized it as irrelevant, outmoded, a relic of a long past culture. But they were wrong. The Bible continues to be the living Word of God.

The Scriptures are not simply a collection of words from God, a vehicle for communicating ideas. It is a living, life-changing dynamic force as it speaks to us and works in us. Many books inform, but the Bible *transforms*. God's Word reveals who we are, and what we are not. It penetrates the core of our moral and spiritual life. It discerns what is within us, both good and bad. The demands of God's Word require decisions. We must not only read and listen to the Word, but we must also let its truths shape our lives. We read in 2 Timothy 3:16, "All Scripture is given by inspiration of God, and is profitable for doctrine, reproof, for correction, for instruction in righteousness, that the man (and woman) of God may be complete, thoroughly equipped for every good work."

The Bible did not come from the creative works of the prophets' own inventions and interpretations. God inspired the writers, therefore, their messages are authentic and reliable. God used the talents, education, and cultural background of each writer to ensure that the message He intended was faithfully communicated in every word they wrote. It is the Breath of God, as we call it in Armenian.

Although the Bible is the most outstanding piece of literature ever produced, many otherwise educated people know little of what it says. It is admirable that so many writers in the above poll recognized the Bible as the No. 1 book everyone should read. Those who only sample the Bible never acquire a taste for it. When we read God's Word straight through, we will begin to see the unfolding plan of God's redeeming grace for us.

Even only 40 years on earth can do a number on the human body. But the Word of God still stands as an ageless instrument of the Holy Spirit that brings life and encouragement to those who read it and believe. The Bible is the standard for measuring all other books. Let us make it the No. 1 book in our lives.

*I*t sounded like a joke. But someone actually placed this ad in a Kansas newspaper: "I will listen to you talk for 30 minutes with no interruption or comment for $5.00." Did anyone call? Yes!! It wasn't long before this individual was receiving 15 to 20 calls a day. The pain of loneliness was so deep that some people were willing to try anything for half an hour of companionship.

People are created with a two fold need; fellowship with God and companionship with other humans. If we are to realize the full purpose of God's creation, there can be no substitute. Jesus teaches us the two greatest commandments in Matt. 22:37 – 40: "Love the Lord your God with all your heart, soul and mind, and love your neighbor as yourself." It is about our vertical and horizontal relationships. The two form a cross. Our love for mankind is a natural and logical outgrowth of love for God.

The social instinct is deep within all of us, and when this need remains unfulfilled, seeds of loneliness grow and flourish. Spiritual loneliness is even more fundamental to the condition. For this isolation carries feelings of alienation from God, Who alone can fill the vacuum in the human heart. Remedies that don't take this factor into account will provide little more than superficial and temporary relief, such as that newspaper ad. Therefore, a lonely person's greatest need is to ensure a right relationship with God, the Great Physician. He has a cure for every human heart, whether it be spiritual or social.

Resources available to the lonely are more abundant than one realizes. This loneliness could perhaps be the starting point of a new journey toward social and spiritual maturity. If the lonely would abandon the search for someone to keep them company, and instead set themselves to care for others, they would be amazed to discover that their loneliness was quite bearable. It might even entirely vanish.

As Christians, whether we realize it or not, we have God's presence in us. God knows and He does care. He understands, and He longs to deliver us. Christ Himself experienced the maximum impact of loneliness on the cross. Most of His followers had fled. One had betrayed Him. Could it have gotten any worse?

When we are lonely, we need an understanding friend. Christ is the One Who is closer than any friend. He suffered so that we would never have to experience eternal separation from God. To live effectively, we need to lift our attention away from ourselves or the circumstances surrounding us, and keep our eyes on Christ. If we do that, the whole experience can have a positive result. In the final analysis, the determining factor in the battle against loneliness is our attitude towards it. Yes, we might all feel lonely at times, but as Christians, we are never alone!

*A*n English lady friend of mine related the following interesting story. Friends were gathered at an English estate. The day nearly turned into a tragedy when one of the children strayed into the deep end of the swimming pool. The gardener heard the cries for help, plunged in, and rescued the drowning child. That youngster's name was Winston Churchill. His grateful parents later asked the gardener what they could do to reward him. He hesitated at first, then said, "I wish my son could go to college some day and become a doctor." "We'll see to it," Churchill's parents promised.

Years passed. Then while Sir Winston Churchill was prime minister of England, he was stricken with pneumonia. The country's best physician was called. His name was Dr. Alexander Fleming, the man who discovered and developed penicillin. He was also the son of that gardener who had saved young Winston from drowning! Later Sir Winston remarked, "Rarely has one man owed his life twice to the same person."

The prime minister's experience reminds us as Christians of the double gratitude we owe to God. First, we have the precious gift of physical life from our Heavenly Father. Then, through His Son, the Great Physician, He has given us the priceless gift of eternal life. Therefore, the Apostle Paul says in Romans 12:1 – 2, "I urge you, brothers, in view of God's mercy, to offer your bodies as living sacrifices, holy and pleasing to God—this is your spiritual act of worship."

Becoming a "living sacrifice" means dedicating our lives to God. It does not mean endless suffering. In the Old Testament, God accepted animal sacrifices for forgiveness of sins. But in the New Testament, because of Christ's ultimate sacrifice on the cross, we are given the precious gift of eternal life. The Apostle urges the faithful of Rome, and us as well, to respond in grateful obedience. St. Paul further says, "And do not be conformed to this world, but be transformed by the renewing of your mind, that you may prove what is the good and acceptable perfect will of God."

God has good, acceptable and perfect plans for His children. Only when the Holy Spirit renews and redirects our minds are we truly spiritually transformed people, with renewed minds and hearts, living to honor and obey Him. God has graciously given us so much. And through Christ we have received the precious gift of eternal life. To Him we owe double gratitude for life!

*A*n artist wanted to paint a painting of the prodigal son. When he saw an unkempt beggar on the street, he asked him if he would come to his studio and pose. The man agreed, but when he appeared a few hours later, he was neatly shaved and clean. When the artist saw him, he exclaimed, "Oh no, I can't use you now!"

God asks us to come to Him just as we are. We often ask someone to come to church, and they feel they ought to "clean up" their life before they enter a sanctuary. I heard a few amazing answers when I extended an invitation for church. One person said, "Oh, I have to get rid of some of my bad habits first." Another said, "I must clean up my act before anything else." And still another said jokingly, "A light fixture might fall on my head as a punishment from God—I'm a sinner." But Jesus says, "I have not come to call the righteous, but sinners, to repentance" (Luke 5:32).

Jesus was in Capernaum and saw a tax collector named Levi (Matthew's name prior to his conversion) sitting at the tax collector's office. He said to him, "Follow Me." Matthew left everything, rose, and followed Jesus. Matthew even gave a feast in his own house to honor Jesus, and a great number of tax collectors came. When the scribes and Pharisees saw it, they criticized Jesus and the disciples for associating with sinners. But Jesus said, "Those who are well have no need of a physician, but those who are sick" (Luke 5:27 – 32).

Matthew left a lucrative, though probably dishonest tax collecting business, to follow Jesus. He left behind a material future in order to gain a spiritual one, and was proud to be associated with Jesus. Tax collectors were among the most despised persons in that society. They were disloyal Israelites hired by Romans. The money they collected was often partly extorted for personal gain, and partly a taxation for Rome, which made them not only thieves, but also traitors to their own people. They became symbols of the worst kind of people. And Matthew had been one of them.

Matthew also knew the cost to follow Jesus, yet he did not hesitate for a moment. When he left his booth, he declared himself unemployed. For some of the disciples, there was always fishing to return to, but for Matthew, there was no turning back. Jesus gave him a new life. He now belonged to the Son of God. Jesus also gave Matthew a new purpose for his skill. When he followed Jesus, the only tool he carried with him from his past job was his pen. Matthew was a keen observer. The Gospel that bears his name was the result!

St. Matthew's experience points out that each of us is one of God's "works in progress." He trusts us with the skills and abilities He has given us. God has a purpose for each one of us. "Follow Me," Christ says even today. Come as you are. The Holy Spirit will do the "cleaning up"!

I have an artificial red apple hanging in my car almost the size of a real one. Written on it in white letters are the following words: "Only God can count the apples in one seed!" How true! When I look at this apple, another wonder in God's creation comes to mind—the watermelon.

Isn't this amazing. Just one tiny seed is planted in the ground. With rain and warm sunshine it sprouts, and in a few months grows ... how many times its size and weight? And what about the countless seeds spread inside that watermelon, each one capable of doing the same thing all over again!

As we think of God's marvelous creation, we are amazed and bear witness to the infinite wisdom and power of God, the Creator. The words of Psalm 104:24 come to mind: "Oh Lord, how manifold are your works! In wisdom you have made them all." As Christians we see the mighty works of God everywhere in the universe.

If we were to step outside, what would we see? A breathtaking sunrise, a tranquil sunset, fantastic thunderclouds, snow capped picture-perfect mountains along the horizon, graceful birds flying across the sky, at night a sky lit up with twinkling stars, wind gently blowing through the trees? It puts us in awe of God's creations. It makes us thank God, the Creator.

All creation is like a majestic symphony or a great choir composed of many harmonious parts that together offer songs of praise. This is a picture of how we the faithful should praise God—individually, and as a part of the great choir of believers world wide.

In Romans 1:20 the Apostle Paul says, "For since the creation of the world, God's invisible attributes are clearly seen, being understood by the things that are made, even His eternal power and Godhead, so that men are without excuse."

Creation is filled with a stunning variety, revealing the rich creativity, goodness, and wisdom of our loving God. As we take a fresh look at people, we also see each one as God's unique creation, each with his or her own special abilities and gifts. God gave human beings tremendous authority to be in charge of the earth. But with great authority comes great responsibility. How do we treat God's creations? Do we use our resources wisely? God holds each one of us accountable for our stewardship of His gifts.

Let us take a nature walk with a friend today and see God by observing His creations!

A few days ago I saw a bumper sticker that read, "Have I Told You About My Grandchildren?" If that grandmother was like me, it would take hours!

By the grace of God, having become a grandmother for the first time recently, I am experiencing the same joy that several of my friends who are already grandmothers have been talking about. Both my daughters-in-law gave birth within three months, therefore the bumper sticker was even more meaningful to me, because of our family's double blessing!

For a few years now, I have been seeing plenty of baby pictures that my grandmother friends have been passing around. I had told them that I want to see each picture they wished to share, but with one condition; that one day when I become a grandmother myself, I wanted the same time and attention from them for my photos. We all laughed at the time, but now they will have to put up with mine.

We all talk most about what or who is important to us, don't we? The story is told of a little boy who was asked by his mother how his Sunday School class was that morning. The boy said that he had a new teacher who was Jesus' grandmother. The mother, amused, wanted to know, what made him think so. The boy answered that all she did through the entire period was to show pictures of Jesus Christ and tell stories about Him!

The youngster must have had loving grandparents. He saw that Jesus was important to his teacher, therefore he concluded, she must be His grandmother. His conclusion wasn't correct, but his response makes a strong point. We talk most about what or who is important to us.

In the Gospel of Luke we see how children were brought to Christ so He would touch them and pray. When the disciples rebuked them, Jesus said, "Let the little children come to Me, and do not forbid them; for such is the Kingdom of God. Assuredly, I say to you, whoever does not receive the Kingdom of God as a little child will by no means enter it." (Luke 18:16, 17)

Jesus wants children to come to Him because He loves them and because they have the kind of attitude needed to approach God. He did not mean that heaven is only for children, but that people need a child-like attitude of trust in God. It is important that we introduce our children and grandchildren to Christ, and that we ourselves approach Him with the same kind of trust and faith.

*A*s Mother's Day approaches, our attention is directed to Mothers and Motherhood. But let us place our focus for a moment on the most blessed of all mothers. Young Mary of Nazareth had the unique privilege of being mother to the very Son of God. Mary experienced the joys of giving birth to Jesus, and she also witnessed His death. She saw Him arrive as her baby son, and she watched Him die as her Savior!

In His last hours on the cross, even in the midst of His agony, Jesus was concerned about His beloved mother. He looked down from the cross and saw her standing nearby with the other women and John. He then said to His mother affectionately, "Dear woman, here is your son." And to John, "Here is your mother" (John 19:26, 27). And we read that from that time on, this disciple took her into his home. (Her husband Joseph had died by this time.)

Jesus entrusted His precious mother to John, His closest and most devoted disciple, who stayed with Him until the very end at the cross. After Jesus' death and resurrection, we read about Mary one more time. She is in the Upper Room with the disciples and other faithful praying before the day of Pentecost (Acts 1:14).

How important it is that our loved ones are in good hands. As Christian mothers, our children are God's gifts to us. They are placed in our arms to be raised in God's ways, as our own precious mothers did for us.

When I was a student at the university many years ago, young moms, fellow students, would often ask me on Mondays what I did on Sunday. My answer would be, "We went to church as a family, with the children in Sunday School." Their response was typical of the seventy's: "My husband and I have agreed to let our children choose their faith when they become adults." How sad! A fine way to avoid responsibility! How sad for the poor children! Should we wonder why we have so many problems in our world?

"Train a child in the way he should go, and when he is old he will not depart from it" (Prov. 22:6). The verse implies that parents should discern the special strengths God has given each child, and develop the abilities of each one with divine wisdom available to all of us in God's Word. Christian moms are good at this. Even with all our efforts, we still can't be certain of the future. But we must faithfully try as our Godly moms did for us. And above all, we must continue to pray, and pray again for their future. Abraham Lincoln is believed to have said, "No man is poor who has had a Godly mother!"

The story is told that there were three pastors in the family of Rev. Dr. Morgan. At a family reunion a friend asked, "Which Morgan is the greatest preacher?" One son looked at his father, then replied, "Mother!"

A final thought to all mothers: No matter how much education we may receive, degrees, titles or accomplishments in life, none compare to our role as mothers! May God guide all mothers through His Holy Spirit to be the best we can be, for our children and for His glory.

The story is told that a sociologist was planning to write a book on difficulties of growing up in a large family, so he interviewed a mother of fourteen children. After a few questions, he asked, "Do you think all children deserve the full, impartial love and attention of a mother?" "Of course," said the mother. "Well, which of your children do you love the most?" asked the man quickly, hoping to catch her in a contradiction. The wise mother answered, "The one who is sick, until he or she gets well, and the one who is away, until he or she gets home."

The response of this mother reminds me of the parable Jesus tells of the loving shepherd who left 99 sheep in the pasture to seek the one that was lost (Lk.15:4 – 7). Also the parable of the prodigal son, when the loving father threw a party when his lost son returned home (Lk. 15:11 – 31). Jesus teaches us of God's love, and how valuable we all are to Him. He diligently searches for each of us who may have wandered away, and He rejoices when he or she is "found." Besides, those who are "well" and are not "away" experience the Father's love as fully as those to whom He gives special attention. "It is not the healthy who need a doctor, but the sick," says Jesus in Mt. 9:12.

The wise mother's response to the sociologist is the answer of a devoted Christian mom. Next to God's love, nothing is so wonderful as a mother's love. Webster's dictionary defines a mother as a "female parent." Isn't that the understatement of all time? A mother today is a walking encyclopedia. Her small children expect her to know where the sun goes at night, where the rain comes from, how planes can fly, where kittens come from, etc. A mother is also a master mechanic who can free her children's clothes from a bicycle chain, and repair anything broken with glue, tape, a hairpin, a wire twister, or whatever else works at the moment. She is a practical nurse who can remove splinters, stop a fever in the middle of the night, and comfort her child when he or she has nightmares, and so much more.

If this sounds like a big order, it is! Therefore, a wise mom prays regularly, knowing that God has placed the lives and future of her children in her loving hands. A mother's prayers can build a fortress around her children! She hopes that one day her children will bear the imprint of her unselfish, unconditional love in their lives by discerning the value of right from wrong. But God has not left a Christian mom to raise her children alone, whatever her life circumstances may be. He has provided a guide. The Bible, His Word, is God's divine instruction book, where not only mothers, but anyone can find guidelines for wise living.

A thousand men may build a city, but it takes a mother to make a home. A Godly mother provides in her family an atmosphere where each child can find love, acceptance, security and understanding. She is there for every need. Such mothers deserve to be honored, not only one day of the year, but daily. That recognition should involve not only words, but ought to be shown in respect, thoughtfulness, and loving deeds. Someone has said, "Of all the earthly things God gives, there is one above all others: It is the precious, priceless gift of loving Christian mothers."

Happy Mother's Day to all mothers!

*W*e often think that our limited abilities, experiences or education make us unlikely candidates to be used by God. But who are we to question God's choices? He can use us in any small or significant way He pleases for His glory if we trust Him.

God's chosen—a humble, godly servant from Nazareth was a long way from Jerusalem, the center of Jewish life of worship. Yet, the Bible says that the angel Gabriel was sent by God to a virgin betrothed to a man named Joseph, of the house of David. The virgin's name was Mary (Lk. 1:26 – 28).

Mary was "troubled." She had just heard the words, "Rejoice highly favored one, the Lord is with you; blessed are you among women!" Comforting words, it would seem, but startling, because they were spoken by an angel. But the angel told her not to be afraid. She had found favor with God, and will conceive, and bring forth a Son, and shall call His name Jesus. Mary exclaimed, "How can this be, since I do not know a man?" (Lk. 1:34). The angel answered Mary saying that the Holy Spirit will come upon her, and the power of the Highest will overshadow her, therefore, the child will be called the Son of God (Lk. 1:35). After listening to the angel, Mary called herself "the maidservant of the Lord," and said, "Let it be to me according to Your Word." She was a humble, obedient servant with a desire to do God's will. We see delight and praise in Mary's heart in her eloquent prayer, known as the "Magnificat," which means "glorifies."

God's favor, however, does not automatically bring joy. His blessings on Mary, the honor of being the mother of the Messiah, our Savior, would lead to much pain. Her Son would be rejected and die on the cross. But through Him would come the world's only hope, and this is why Mary has been praised by all generations. She gave birth to Jesus Christ, the Son of God, the Savior of mankind. Her submission was part of God's plan to bring about our eternal life with Him!

Mary soon went to visit her relative Elizabeth, wife of Zechariah the priest. Although advanced in years, Elizabeth had been with child for six months, the child who would be known as John the Baptist. As soon as Mary spoke, the baby in Elizabeth's womb leaped for joy. Apparently the Holy Spirit had informed her that Mary's child was the Messiah. Elizabeth called her young relative Mary, "the mother of my Lord," and rejoiced in Mary's blessed condition! (Lk. 1:43 – 45).

This was a profound expression of Elizabeth's confidence that Mary's child would be the long hoped-for and expected Messiah—the One the Old Testament refers to. "The virgin will be with child and will give birth to a Son, and they will call Him Immanuel—which means, God with us" (Is. 7:14). Elizabeth seemed to comprehend the immense importance of the child Who Mary carried. All of this is attributed to the illuminating work of the Holy Spirit.

The qualities that shine most clearly in Mary's character are her deep sense of humility, obedience and unshakable trust in God. We can all learn from Mary to adopt these fine qualities in all circumstances. Mary was and will always be most honored of all women, Queen of Mothers! We admire her, we honor her, because she is the mother of our Savior Jesus Christ!

*A*s amazing as it may seem, grandparents are great bridge-builders between generations. I received that benefit from both my grandmothers. I never knew my grandfathers, but I had two godly grandmothers who played most important roles in my life.

It may appear strange that grandparents can have such a deep influence on the grandchildren. Although there is a generation gap between them of some 50 years or more, yet grandparents have that special ability to bridge that gap, and often do it better than the parents. Parents, as we know, are very busy taking care of family needs.

Story telling was a special talent that both my grandmothers possessed. One, being a school teacher in Adapazar, Turkey, had a long selection of short stories with strong moral messages. I never tired of listening to her. My other grandmother, also originally from Adapazar, had the gift of vivid Bible story telling. I didn't know the stories were Biblical until I attended school. Some of my favorites were Noah and his ark, Moses, Joseph, Job, Daniel, Jonah, the Prodigal Son, and the rich man and Lazarus.

The most amazing thing, however, was that there wasn't one Bible, not only in our home, but not even in the entire Armenian community! Yet this godly woman was able to pass these treasures to me before I even attended school.

The Apostle Paul in his epistle to young Timothy tells him of the strong faith in Christ which Timothy's grandmother Lois and mother Eunice possessed. Because of this, Paul is persuaded that such faith lives in Timothy also. (2 Tim. 1:5) Yes, grandparents have that special ability and bond to influence their grandchildren.

Although grandparents today are busier than their predecessors, they are precious and have that unique opportunity to pass to the youngsters these rich treasures they possess. Not only can they pass the rich heritage of our Armenian Christian faith, but history and tradition as well. We know that the youngsters will love it, and what fun that can be! By doing this, the faith of our fathers will become the faith of our grandchildren. That is the richest and most valuable inheritance of all!

*W*hile at Zuma Beach recently, I asked a lifeguard the following question: "How could you tell if a person is truly in need of your help when there is so much activity and noise in and out of the water?" He simply replied, "No matter what is going on, I can always tell when someone is in real trouble or if there is an actual emergency." And while he was talking to me, his watchful eyes continued to search the water, watching the swimmers. I admired his dedication and commitment to his job.

As he walked away, I thought how much more our Heavenly Father watches over us. In all the confusion here below, He never fails to see or hear any soul that cries out to Him for help in the midst of life's storms. We read in Psalms 55:22, "Cast your burdens on the Lord, and He shall sustain you." Yet knowing this, and after giving them to the Lord in prayer, we soon take our burdens back, holding them tightly and continuing to bear the load ourselves.

Is our heart heavy under a mounting load of burdens? We are advised to give them to the Lord; He cares for us like no one else! Perhaps the burdens and difficulties we experience at the moment have been allowed by God so that we may learn to cast them all on Him. When we carry our worries, stress, and daily struggles by ourselves, that shows that we have not fully trusted God. It takes humility to recognize that God really cares, and to admit our need for Him. Letting God handle our anxieties calls for action, not passivity. Why let circumstances control us? Instead, submit them to the Lord, the ONE Who controls circumstances.

God loves each one of us just the way we are, imperfections and all. He loves us even though we often struggle with our mistakes. He forgave us when we accepted Christ in our hearts. If any of us is faced with life's difficulties, we must remember that God loves us, and He wants to use the tests and trials we experience to make us better people. If we keep this truth in mind, we can be sure that in our times of anguish and distress, God watches over us. He sees us as if we were His only child in the whole world, and He offers relief or the strength to endure. If a lifeguard can see every emergency, God certainly heeds our every need.

*S*everal years ago, the speech research department of a college conducted a test in cooperation with the U.S. Navy. The intent was to discover how the tone quality of one's voice affected sailors when they were given orders. The experiment revealed that the way a person was addressed determined the kind of response that individual would make. When a person, for instance, was spoken to in a soft voice, he would answer in a similar manner. But when a person was loud and shouted in an impatient manner, the answer came back in the same sharp tone. This proved to be true whether the communication was given face to face, over the intercom or by phone.

The above study reminds me of Proverbs 15:1; "A gentle answer turns away wrath, but a harsh word stirs up anger." We all know that it is not only what we say, but how we say it that makes a big difference. Our tone of voice truly sets the "climate" of our communication with people. We would avoid numerous tense situations if we only practice the above verse.

We are created by God with the ability to speak words that nourish others. The Apostle Paul writes in Ephesians 4:29, "Do not let any unwholesome talk come out of your mouths, but only what is helpful for building others up according to their needs, that it may benefit those who listen." St. Paul tells us that as Christians, not only must we stop using unwholesome words, but we must also express thoughts that will help, edify and encourage others. How necessary it is for God's people to eliminate from our conversation all thoughtless words and harsh tones of speech.

Are we grieving or pleasing God with a quarrelsome attitude and harsh tone of voice? Our words have the power to build up or to tear down our fellow man. If anyone speaks to us in a harsh or angry tone, why not intentionally reverse the response by expressing quietness of spirit and loving concern. What a difference our soft response can make! And how puzzling and surprising it will be to all!

*W*hile visiting our nation's capital, Washington, D.C., a few years ago, we took the various tours that were available to the public. Walking through one of the Federal buildings, our guide pointed out a piece of furniture that looked like a large chest with an opening at the top resembling a mail box. She referred to it as the "Conscience Fund." She further explained that there was a steady flow of money coming in from individuals around the country who had cheated the U.S. Government on their taxes or had committed some act of fraud at one time or another. This was their way of paying their debt in cash anonymously. This fund, which began in 1811, received an average of $45,000.00 annually, and so far had taken in a total of more than $3,500,000.00. Amazing!

She spoke of some of the more unique ways citizens responded to guilt and regret. The power of regret, for example, had moved an ex-GI just a few years ago to send a note to the government with a $20.00 bill for some blankets he had stolen during World War II. The note read, "My mind could not rest. Sorry I am late. Now I can get some peace of mind at last." His money was placed in the Conscience Fund.

Regret is a powerful emotion. At times we all have wished we could erase some actions that burden our minds; unkind words, or an immature act that we are not proud of, and certainly don't wish to repeat. These people who paid their debts had probably found great relief from their nagging heavy burden of guilt. But these actions by themselves cannot bring complete peace with God. Only when we personally put our trust in Christ and confess in repentance can we experience God's complete forgiveness for our wrong-doings.

Even Apostle Paul, years after he became a child of God, regretted that he persecuted Christians. In I Timothy 1:13, 14, we read, "Even though I was once a persecutor and a violent man, I was shown mercy because I acted in ignorance and unbelief. The grace of our Lord was poured out on me abundantly along with the faith and love that are in Christ Jesus." St. Paul couldn't undo the past. He did, however, devote himself to God's will, and the Lord used him in a mighty way. This assures us that past mistakes should not ruin our lives even when we can't do anything to undo them. Our Heavenly Father's promises of forgiveness are incomparable to any "Conscience Fund." However, we should never take our wrong-doings lightly. We must turn to the Lord, acknowledge our guilt with true repentance, knowing that God is ready to forgive us because of Christ's death on the cross for our sins. And when God forgives, He also forgets!

Let us therefore be assured that in all situations God is watching over us and sees each of us as if we were His only child. By His love he paves our paths straight, offers relief, or gives strength to endure. Broken things become blessed things when we let Christ do the mending. He removes every trace of our guilty past, and the seal of His unconditional love becomes ours forever. As believers then, let us continue to trust God in all areas of our lives. By true repentance and acceptance of God's grace and forgiveness, the Conscience Fund is paid in full!

*F*rench diplomat and engineer Ferdinand Marie de Lesseps was assistant vice-consul in Egypt from 1832 to 1837. The story is told that while he was traveling on the Mediterranean Sea in 1832, a fellow passenger became seriously ill with a contagious disease. The ship was quarantined. Disappointed and frustrated by the isolation, de Lesseps began to read the memoirs of Charles le Pere, who had studied the possibility of building a canal from the Red Sea to the Mediterranean. To help pass the time, de Lesseps began to plan a detailed project for the construction of a canal across the Isthmus of Suez.

The Viceroy of Egypt granted de Lesseps a concession for the proposed canal. With the backing of the French government, work began in 1859, and the canal was formally opened in 1869. De Lesseps was awarded many honors for his remarkable engineering and executive abilities. The quarantine which had occurred 37 years earlier proved to be most valuable to de Lesseps—and to the world!

Christians also go through a "spiritual quarantine" at times as God prepares them for future invaluable usefulness in His service. This could come in the form of an illness, an injury, unemployment, etc. Although we too may feel terribly frustrated, as de Lesseps did, in every situation we must keep in mind that God does not forsake His own, but draws them aside so that we can get to know Him and understand His purposes better.

What then can we do in periods such as these? We read in Psalms 37:7; "Rest in the Lord, and wait patiently for Him; do not fret." Anger, anxiety and worry are very destructive emotions. They reveal our lack of faith in God's love. When we dwell on our problems, we become anxious, angry and frustrated. But if we concentrate on God and his goodness, we will find peace. "Rest...Wait...Do not Fret." Are we willing to wait patiently for Him to work out what is best for us? Today's frustrating experience may result in a triumphant victory for us in the future. Even when we are too distressed to read the Bible, we can always pray and abide in God's love. This is not, by any means, easy for most of us. Yet we are advised to wait patiently in quiet meditation, which is the proper, calm attitude expected of a child of God.

Just as the writer of the above psalm chose to focus on God and His goodness, our confidence should be in the Lord as well. Although the reasons behind life's difficulties often remain a mystery, the psalmist by faith declares that God would not abandon His people, but prepare them for further usefulness in His service and for His glory!

*W*hen God gives us direction through His Word, are we obedient, or do we sometimes run, claiming He is asking too much of us?

Jonah was an unwilling prophet given a mission he disliked. The Bible says he disobeyed God when he was told to go to the idolatrous city of Nineveh, Assyria's capital, to preach God's message of judgment. Assyria, a great empire, was Israel's most dreaded enemy at the time. So when Jonah heard God telling him to go to Nineveh and call the people to repentance, he ran in the opposite direction. Was Jonah successful in hiding from the Lord? God had to send His own "vessel" to pick Jonah up. He had to send a storm and great big fish to make the runaway prophet change his mind and his direction.

The book of Jonah is more than a story of a man and a big fish. It is a profound illustration of God's mercy and grace. The Ninevites deserved punishment. Jonah knew this. He also knew that if they would repent and worship God, they would be forgiven and spared judgment. But Jonah hated the Assyrians, and he wanted vengeance. He hoped and expected that God would destroy the Ninevites. Jonah eventually obeyed, went to Nineveh and preached God's message of repentance. God was in control—the king and the entire city repented and were delivered from God's terrible punishment!

In the four chapters of this short book, we see the full picture of God's love and compassion, and realize that no one is beyond redemption. God's love and His non-discriminating mercy are for all who believe. Jonah had yet to learn that the Creator's love and forgiveness are available to everyone in the universe. Despite his behavior, God did not reject Jonah. He loves each one of us, even when we fail Him. We must also learn, as Jonah did, to accept all those whom God loves. We will find it much easier to love the unlovable when we love God.

Naturally, unbelieving minds do not accept the book of Jonah as factual. Some call it fiction, and allegory or a parable. Jesus regarded it as historical fact (Matt. 12:39 – 41). Jesus called it a "sign" of His own resurrection. He put the fish, the repentance of the Ninevites, His resurrection and judgment day in the same category. He surely was talking of reality. It was a miracle, a divine attestation of Jonah's mission to Ninevah. If such an astounding miracle had not occurred, the Ninevites would have given little heed to Jonah (Luke 11:30).

One good thing can be said for Jonah. When swallowed by the great fish, he prayed to God: "I cried out to the Lord because of my difficulties and He answered me" (Jonah 2:2). He was delivered in a most spectacular way, and was overwhelmed by God's grace.

To walk in our own selfish ways is to run away from God. God's commission is a lifetime mission. If any of us, like Jonah, has deliberately run away from the Lord, we are called home. We must trust God and not wait for one of life's storms to awaken us to our need. We have a forgiving God. His help is only a prayer away. The One who delivered Jonah can certainly deliver us as well.

Some people stop working conscientiously when they get a job. The following is a true story I'd like to share with you.

Mr. A, who worked at a hardware store, was lazy and impatient with customers. On a few occasions his boss was tempted to fire him. He did not go through with it, however, because of his concern for Mr. A's wife and children who would suffer as a result. A customer stopped by one day and noticed Mr. A's absence. When he asked the manager, he was told that Mr. A had found another job elsewhere. The customer then asked if they planned to replace him. The manager said that there was no need because Mr. A did not leave a vacancy. His work was of such poor quality that the business was better off without him. What a sad report! This should never be true of any employee, much less a Christian, and even less of an Armenian!

Countless verses in the book of Proverbs praise diligence and the profit it brings, and condemn laziness as a cause of hunger and poverty. "Lazy hands make a man (and woman) poor, but diligent hands bring wealth" (Prov. 10:4). Proverbs makes it clear that diligence is a vital part of wise living. We work hard, not necessarily to become rich, famous, or admired—although those may be by-products—but to support ourselves and our loved ones, serve God with our best, be productive and enjoy purposeful lives.

The Apostle Paul urges servants to be obedient to their masters. He says in Colossians 3:23, "Whatever you do, do it heartily as to the Lord, and not to man." If God expected Christian servants in St. Paul's day to work diligently for their masters, how much more should we give our employers an honest day's work for an honest day's pay. It is the right thing to do, and it strengthens our lives as Christians.

The Apostle's instructions encourage responsibility and integrity on the job. Christian employees should do their jobs as if Christ were their supervisor. And Christian employers should treat their employees fairly and with respect. Do we do our best even when the boss is not around? Do we work hard and with enthusiasm? This is especially important for our youth who take summer jobs. No matter whom we work for, and no matter who works for us, the ONE whom we ultimately should want to please is our Father in heaven.

Real success is achieved by maintaining personal integrity. If we are not a success by God's standards, we have not achieved true success. A good way to test the quality of our work is to ask ourselves this very simple question: If I were to quit my job, would that create a vacancy?

*M*ost of us have experienced the sharp sting of a bee at one time or another. It can be quite painful, and for a short time, we hate bees. Yet we all well know that the same little bee that sometimes stings also produces the sweet honey we enjoy.

No Christian can hope to reap only the good that comes from life that is God-directed without also feeling the aches that are part of God's loving plan for our lives. Along with the sweet part of life, we must also accept the "stings." The key is in calling on God's grace so that we are content with what He allows into our lives, and to respond appropriately.

The Apostle Paul writes to the Philippian faithful, "I have learned in whatever state I'm in to be content. I can do all things through Christ who strengthens me" (Phil. 4:11, 13). Are we content in the circumstances we face? St. Paul knew how to be content whether he was persecuted and in pain, whether he had plenty or was in need. His secret was drawing upon Christ's power for strength.

A few more examples from God's wonderful creations come to mind. It is the bruised rose that releases a sweet fragrance, and it is from the crushed grapes that delicious juice is extracted. A grain of sand is an irritant in the body of an oyster, and from that irritation a wonderful pearl is formed. As for new life, the pains of childbirth are compensated by the joys of motherhood!

Most of us of course would rather avoid all the stings of life. We may not get all that we want, but by trusting God, our attitudes can change by accepting His provision in our lives. Although St. Paul was writing this letter to the Philippians from prison, joy is a dominant theme in the epistle. The secret of his joy is grounded in his relationship with Christ.

We all want to be happy but we are often tossed and turned by daily successes, failures and inconveniences. We can have joy, however, even in hardship. Joy does not come from external circumstances, but from our inner strength. As Christians, let us not rely on what we experience at the moment to give us joy, but our joy should come from Christ's Spirit within us!

I have inherited my love for plants from my grandmother. Some of the rooms in our home are beginning to resemble a nursery. There is something warm and inviting about the presence of healthy, growing plants that I find very pleasant. While I care for their simple needs and watch their progress almost daily, I gained from my little green "friends" a new appreciation for the elements that make up the process of growth.

As Christians, we too resemble plants. In order to grow, we need to expand our roots daily, push through the earth, which is God's Word, spread our branches and burst into blossom.

Such growth and thriving conditions, however, aren't always evident in our lives. It is often easy to become bored with the routine of our daily activities. We lose our enthusiasm and motivation, and miss out on maturity and fruitfulness.

At time such as these, we find ourselves at a spiritual standstill. And when growth stops, decay begins. It is then that we must stretch our roots deeper into the Word of God. It is impossible to grow in the Lord without anchoring our roots around His Word. Only through God's Word can we receive our spiritual nourishment, and through His Light we grow radiant, beautiful and healthy. This is the most important step for every Christian. Then we will become fruitful plants, planted by rivers of Living Water, and our branches will extend, grow and blossom. (Psalm 1:3)

No matter where we are in our spiritual journey, no matter how mature we are in our faith, we still have much room for growth. As we grow closer to our Creator, we'll be better prepared by His grace to stand strong and healthy in any and all circumstances.

As we diligently grow in our faith, it will be evident in our behavior as Christians. Then our faith will culminate in love for our fellow man. Growth occurs only from being deeply grounded in the Word of God. We will then be able to practice what we have learned through His Word.

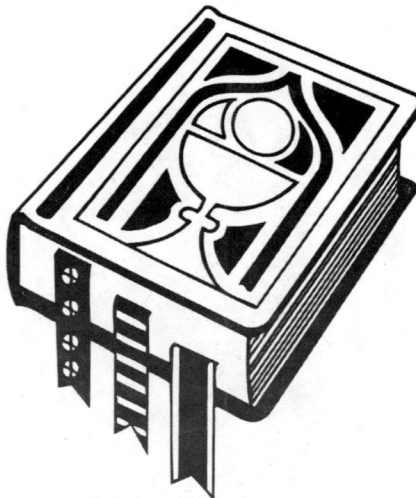

*I*s it possible to do what's right for the wrong reasons? The story is told of a young boy who did just that. His mother's birthday was only a few days away. Excited to have the opportunity to go shopping alone, he approached a sales person and asked to see some cookie jars. A large selection was on display at a counter, so the youngster carefully lifted and replaced each lid. His face revealed disappointment, however, as he came to the last one. "Aren't there any cookie jars with quiet lids?" he asked.

This delightful story could be a pretty accurate picture of human nature. It could also be a reminder that our right motives must follow our right actions. If not, it is possible to do what is right for the wrong reasons.

As children of God, we must examine our motives for doing what we do. A healthy habit such as this will bring into our lives the quality of sincerity. This was what the Apostle Paul prayed for on behalf of the Philippian faithful. He asked God that they might be able to discern what is best, and thereby be pure and blameless, so that their inner motives would correspond to their conduct (Phil 1:10). The Apostle knew the importance of sincerity in word and deed. God wants us to be honest and transparent in all our relationships.

As His followers, we must continue to pray for divine discernment so we can maintain our Christian values. Depending on God is a realization of our own powerlessness and our need for His constant presence in our lives. God is our source of strength, and we receive His help by being in touch, and by relying on Him daily.

Let's examine our actions. Why not ask God to show us our misdirected motives so that we'll be able to conduct ourselves with divine sincerity. And in doing so, we won't have to worry about "noisy lids."

Children, as we know, do not automatically become model men and women. Their development must be carefully nurtured. Raising children demands patience, diligence, determination, wise instruction, and loving correction.

The story is told that a friend visited Michaelangelo at his studio one day as he was putting, what seemed to be, the finishing touches on a sculpture. Later, when the friend stopped by again, he was surprised to find him busy on the same sculpture. Seeing no obvious changes, he asked the artist if he was still working on that same piece. The artist admitted he was retouching various parts; emphasizing a few muscle definitions, giving more expression to facial features, and more energy to the arms, etc. Surprised, the friend thought all that was so insignificant—just minute details. But Michaelangelo explained that minute details result in perfection, and perfection is not minute.

If a lifeless sculpture demands such care, attention, diligence and hard work, how much more do our own children require? It is natural for us to want to do our best. As parents we shape and mold the character of our children day after day. Children are like sponges. They soak up everything they come into contact with. We must be careful, therefore, to oversee what their minds absorb. What do our children and grandchildren see and hear in our homes? Have we created an atmosphere with a moral and spiritual foundation upon which they can build honorable lives? We must never forget the importance of our historical and spiritual heritage in raising our children. If we fail to do that, how will they ever know? We read in Prov. 22:6, "Train up a child in the way he should go, and when he is old he will not depart from it."

Wise parents don't expect absolute perfection from their children. Neither does our heavenly Father expect it from us. But He asks us to keep that as our goal. The values and attitudes our children absorb during their formative and impressionable years are sure to be projected into the world later. Let us make sure that those little "sponges" soak up what is pure and wholesome. This will bring glory to God and honor to our Armenian families and community. The proper upbringing of a child is the making of a masterpiece.

*W*e have created instant lifestyle. Twenty minute oil change. One hour photo processing. Instant cash. Same day dry cleaning. Drive through lunch on the go. No one likes to wait. If things don't happen within minutes, we become aggravated and impatient.

As Christians, we often direct our impatience toward God, especially when we experience trials. We wonder why our prayers haven't been answered. We know that God can make things happen in an instant—why doesn't He act?

In John 15:7, Jesus says: "If you abide in Me, and my words abide in you, you will ask what you desire, and it shall be done for you." The Bible is filled with answered prayers from Genesis to Revelation. We are commanded to pray, and God has promised to answer.

In the above scripture, there are two requirements for answers to prayer. First, we are to abide in Christ; that is, to stay close to Him, to remain in His perfect will at all costs (Rom. 12:2). Second, His words are to abide in us; they are to become an integral and vital part of our lives. We are to be filled with and guided by His words (Col. 3:16, 17). When we meet these two requirements, God promises to answer our prayers.

The answer to prayer is sometimes immediate. Peter walked on water to go to Jesus, and as he began to sink, he prayed, "Lord, save me!" The answer was immediate (Matt. 14:29 – 31). The answer is sometimes delayed. The resurrection of Lazarus is a good example of delayed answer to prayer (John 11:1 – 44). The answer may be "no." This is the hardest for us to comprehend. When we accept the answer "no" as His perfect will, God grants us patience to trust Him as our all-knowing God.

The answer may differ from our expectation. We may pray for patience, and God sends us tribulation; perhaps because tribulation produces patience. God answers all our prayers, not according to our wishes, but according to His perfect will. I have thanked God more than once years later for a "no" answer, or for a different answer than what I had prayed for. He knew what was best for me. If only I had realized it at the time!

Joy comes from a close relationship with our Creator. When our lives are intertwined with His, and we trust Him, we can go through anything and finish victorious. The joy of living a God-centered life will keep us level headed and patient, whatever the circumstances. God answers all our prayers according to His perfect will. God is never in a hurry, but His timing is always perfect.

*A*n aquaintance who is an airline pilot told me that as a boy, he enjoyed fishing on the river banks in his home town. Whenever a plane flew over, he would watch it until it disappeared, and wished some day that he would become a pilot. Many years later, now that he was a pilot, he wished he could be the boy fishing again.

How ironic! When we are young, we can't wait to grow up. When we are older, we look back longingly to our former years. Whatever our age, God intends that we enjoy each season of life as it comes, live it to its fullest, and be all that we can be. He desires that we follow Him, put our energy and resources at His disposal, and trust Him to guide us.

We can do plenty at any age. Our age has little to do with achievements and commitment. We are never too young or too old to use our talents. Age has little to do with dreams, determination, creativity and vision. When our desires conform to God's will, we are not likely to waste any time wishing for things that we once did in childhood. Real joy comes when we live purposeful, God-honoring lives.

Are we in life's springtime? We can work hard and trust God's timing to fulfill our dreams, just like the airline pilot. Are we in life's summer or autumn? We can face our daily challenges head on, making sure we are heading in the right direction. And if we feel winter's chill, we can concentrate on knowing God even better. His presence will make every season of life one of strength and beauty.

We read in Isaiah 40:31, "But those who wait on the Lord shall renew their strength; they shall mount up with wings like eagles, they shall run and not be weary, they shall walk and not faint." Waiting on the Lord means that we expect His promise of strength to help us rise above difficulties. We can call upon Him to renew us at any time of life.

Let us allow God to be our guide, and joyfully give of ourselves to His service. We can follow our dreams with determination and enthusiasm, and before we know it, we will be soaring like an eagle in any season of our lives.

A little encouragement can often spark great actions. We never know what effect a well-timed word of encouragement may have for someone we care about. It could mean the difference between giving up or going on.

Chilling winds of adversity and gray skies of a worldly environment can easily discourage us at one time or another. We can be more aware of this, and always try to encourage each other. Our hope is in God, and we know He is working in our lives. How fitting is this hope that is called an "anchor of the soul, firm and secure." (Heb. 6:19)

As children of God, we should make it a point, and even take pleasure in uplifting others, encouraging them on their gray days. By doing so, we actually show that pride hasn't entered our lives. A proud person is usually so preoccupied with self that he/she does not notice what others do, and has no desire to praise or encourage others. When we pay a sincere compliment, we show that our concern extends beyond ourselves, and that we care about encouraging others.

The Apostle Paul freely commended and encouraged the churches with uplifting messages of hope through his epistles. We too can serve Christ and bring joy to others by doing likewise. In Proverbs we read, "Pleasant words are like a honeycomb; sweetness to the soul and health to the bones." (16:24) Encouragement is truly a healing medicine – a physical, psychological and spiritual remedy!

Yes, every Christian's life can become discouraging at times. It is during these circumstances that one needs encouragement. They need those "pleasant words" that bring "sweetness to their souls." They need St. Paul's uplifting words through Christians like us.

Let us give people a pat on the back when they deserve it. Compliment the child who does something well. Encourage the man or woman who continually helps others by expressing our appreciation. It has been said: Praise loudly, blame softly. One of the best evidences of our faith in Christ is our kindness to others. Encouragement can mean the difference between giving up or going on. Let us take the time to do so. It is never too early to be kind, but it can be too late.

*T*he importance of communication is emphasized everywhere. Many are studying the field, others discussing its vital significance, and all of us practice it. Good communication, as we know, involves more than expressing our thoughts clearly. It also requires careful, attentive listening.

Christ, the master communicator, was often misunderstood. Although He spoke the truth clearly, His audience was often confused by His message, and then rejected it. Jesus says in the Gospel of John (8:43): "Why do you not understand my speech? Because you are not able to listen to My word." By answering His own question, He pointed out the reason for their confusion.

Why were they such poor listeners? Certainly not because Jesus failed to communicate. It was because His audience did not want to hear the truth. Listening and understanding would have meant a much needed change. Refusing to listen kept most of them from believing in Him. "They had ears but they hear not" (Ps. 135:17). They practiced "selective hearing."

For us today, careful listening is not only essential to communication, but often, just listening can indeed be an effective way to help others. What does active listening accomplish? Listening is a way of loving and respecting others. The art of listening conveys the message that we care. A caring heart, a listening ear, a thoughtful act, and even a loving tear comforts the broken-hearted and builds relationships. As Christians, our example also encourages others to have faith in God.

Attentive listening is also a means of learning the facts—a key element in clarifying misunderstandings between people. The wise King Solomon warned in Proverbs 18:13 that it is folly to answer a matter before hearing it.

Just as love for God begins with listening to His Word, so the beginning of love for our fellow men is to listen to them carefully and attentively. It is God's love for us, that He not only has given us His Word, but has also lent us His ear. Let us not be so driven to express our views or display our feelings that we don't really hear what others have to say.

Christ was always deeply interested in people and relationships. He showed warm concern for His followers and friends – men, women and children. His love for us is the "Good News" for everyone. We can learn so much through His teachings. As we take a quiet moment today and give God a listening ear, we'll be better prepared in the art of communication.

Our society places great value on physical beauty. It idolizes the so-called "beautiful people," such as models, popular film stars and entertainers, whose youthful faces adorn the covers of many magazines.

The influence of the West is very much evident around the world as well. While traveling in Europe some years ago, I recognized well-known, lovely faces of our American beauties in several countries, especially in Odessa (Ukraine, Istanbul and Rome, primarily advertising cosmetics. I must also say that the familiarity of these faces gave me a warm feeling of home.

It is easy to show partiality to physical beauty, but such attractiveness has nothing to do with the kind of beauty that delights our Creator. God wants us to place more value on what is in a person's heart than on superficial things; the physical skin-deep qualities of a person. By God's standards, a truly beautiful person is one who serves God's purpose.

Regardless of our outward appearance, and there is nothing wrong with good looks, all of us can be beautiful. By God's transforming grace, we can have the beauty and integrity that mirrors the character of His Son, Jesus Christ. As we devote ourselves whole-heartedly to the fulfillment of His purpose in our lives, we will develop the kind of God-honoring beauty that does not fade. (Prov. 31:30) That is the only way to become one of the truly "beautiful people."

Our Lord declares that man's real worth lies far beneath the surface. A child of God doesn't have to have a model's face to develop self-control, patience, wisdom, courage, unselfishness, mercy and compassion. Yet these are marks of a person's true value. They are the qualities of truly beautiful people. Neatness, good grooming and doing our best for our appearance are important. But even more important are a person's attitude and inner spirit. That is so precious in the sight of God.

When Christ is at home in a person's heart, even the most ordinary face shines with the beauty that comes from within. Nothing can dim that kind of beauty. Truly "beautiful people" are those who mirror Christ!

*S*omeone wise once said, "The person I have the most trouble with is the person I see in my mirror every day." This certainly is an honest admission! Is there a Christian who has never sincerely suffered over a few spiritual shortcomings? Or struggled with the tension of ambivalence and confusion?

The Apostle Paul, a dedicated follower of Christ, was intensely conscious of this tendency. Perhaps for that reason he wrote in his epistle to the Romans, "I do not understand what I do. For what I want to do, I do not do; but what I hate, I do. As it is, it is no longer I myself who do it, but it is sin living in me...For I have the desire to do what is good, but I cannot carry it out." (Rom. 7:14 – 25) Although we might take comfort from this thought, the Apostle is not saying that no goodness exists in him. Rather, he recognized the struggle of his imperfect human nature, and always turned to God for victory after victory.

"The devil made me do it!" was a popular expression of a comedian some years ago. This sounds like a good excuse, but we are ultimately responsible for our actions. From the Apostle, however, we learn how to be victorious. Instead of trying to overcome wrongdoing with human will power, we must take hold of God's tremendous power that is available to us. This is God's provision for victory. Our only way to freedom from wrongdoing is through the empowering of the Holy Spirit.

Being led by God's spirit involves the desire and readiness to obey God's Word, and the sensitivity to discern between our feelings and His prompting. The Apostle Paul struggled with this internal battle, and recognized that this would continue throughout his life. Yes, the struggle will continue, but we need not despair. If we acknowledge our need for God's Spirit, and consciously try to do His will, we will gain more and more victories, just as St. Paul did.

Jesus Christ, who conquered sin once and for all, promises to fight by our side. If we seek His help, we will never be alone. Why not let the reality of Christ's power lift us to a triumphant life. As we live each day, controlled and guided by the Holy Spirit, the words of Christ will be in our minds. His love will be behind our actions, leading us to victory. Then we will have no trouble with the person we see in the mirror every day.

*T*hree men were working at a construction site. Some one asked, "What are you doing?" "I'm mixing mortar," said one. "I'm building a stone wall," said the second. But the third one replied, "I'm building a cathedral for the glory of God!"

Most people work to earn a living, to reach some level of success or accumulate great wealth. There is absolutely nothing wrong with being immensely wealthy, if one earns it honestly and handles it correctly. But something is drastically wrong when one keeps it all to himself. God gives it to us so we could, in turn, give a portion of it back to Him, in His service. And yes, give it even in abundance!

In Luke 12:13, we see Jesus surrounded by a multitude of people. Someone asked Him about an inheritance problem he had with his brother. Jesus then talked about greed, and told the following parable: "The land of a certain rich man yielded plentifully. And he thought, 'What shall I do, since I have no room to store my crops?' So he thought, 'I will tear down my barns and build bigger ones, and there I will store all my goods. And I will say to my soul, "Soul, you have many goods laid up for many years; take your ease; eat, drink, and be merry." But God said to him, 'Fool! This night your soul will be required of you; then whose will those things be which you have provided?' So is he who lays up treasure for himself, and is not rich toward God."

There isn't a word in this parable or anywhere else in Scripture against well-earned or well-deserved financial prosperity. This farmer worked hard and was honest. Then, what is wrong? The man never thought that he might not live long; he talked to his soul as if he were immortal! Also, this farmer didn't really care about people. We only read about "Me, My, and I." Never once were others included in his thoughts. And finally, the man made no room for God. He lived a self-centered life as if God didn't exist. Imagine his shock when the Angel of Death said to him, "You fool! This very night your life will end!"

Jesus teaches us that the good life has nothing to do with being wealthy. The rich man in the parable died before he could enjoy life. Planning for retirement is wise. But if we accumulate wealth with no concern for helping others, we will enter eternity empty handed. Jesus challenges us to think beyond earth-bound goals, and to use what we have been given for God's Kingdom. Faith, service, and obedience to His Word are the way to become rich toward God.

Like the third man in our story, we need to see that what gives work eternal value is doing the job faithfully for God's glory. God commands us to work because it is good. Work also gives us Christians the opportunity to represent Christ to a skeptical world. By using our God-given abilities, we bring honor and glory to His Name. Is our work just a job? Or are we doing it for the glory of God?

I saw a portion of a movie on TV that involved auto racing. I was amazed and impressed to see a crew of some eight to ten men who worked on a race car as soon as it stopped at its designated station. In about the same time it takes most of us to get into our car, put on our seat belt and adjust the mirrors, this crew had changed four tires, filled the gas tank, washed the windshield, gave the driver a drink, and made vital adjustments under the hood. It happened so quickly and efficiently because each crew member knew his job, performed it skillfully, and had one goal; to send the car back into the race.

After seeing that, I thought, what if everyone in the crew wanted to drive? What if everyone wanted to wash the windshield? What if no one wanted to change the tires or fill the gas tank? The car certainly couldn't have gone very far in the race.

And so it is with the Body of Christ, the Church, of which Christ is the Head. As Christians we are all equipped by God with different skills and talents to do certain tasks efficiently and skillfully (Eph. 4:16). Using the analogy of the human body, the Apostle Paul emphasizes the fact that each part has a specific function that is necessary to the body as a whole. The parts are different for a purpose, and in their differences they must work together. If a seemingly insignificant part is taken away, the whole body becomes less effective. And so it is with the part each member plays in the Church—the Body of Christ.

As Christians we must avoid two common errors: One, being too proud of our abilities to offer them; and two, thinking we have nothing to offer. Instead of comparing ourselves to one another, we should use our God-given gifts and encourage others to use theirs. If we don't, the body of believers will be less effective.

God's Church is composed of many people from a variety of backgrounds with a multitude of gifts and abilities. It is easy for these differences to divide people. But despite the differences, all believers have one thing in common—faith in Christ. On this essential truth, we all find unity. Through the Holy Spirit, all faithful are one body of believers—the Church. As members of Christ's family we have one common goal; to serve, build and strengthen the Body of Christ.

The Apostle Paul stresses spiritual unity, asking the faithful to love one another, and to be one in spirit and purpose, serving with humility and love, as Christ taught us again and again. We can't all be pastors, teachers or youth directors. Some of us might have to "change tires" or "wash the windshield." Each job is just as important as the other. For the Body of Christ to fulfill its purpose, we each need to concentrate on our part and do our best as one efficient team.

*W*hile in heavy traffic, I noticed a bumper sticker in front of me that read, "The more I get to know the human race, the more I love my dog." Dogs are loyal, dependable, eager to please and quick to forgive and forget. Don't we wish more people were like that? Often, no matter how hard we try to have a good relationship with someone, it doesn't seem to work.

The Apostle Paul addresses that very issue in Romans 12:18 – 21. He says, "If it is possible, as much as depends on you, live peaceably with men." St. Paul knew that some "people problems" may never be resolved because, as we know, it takes two to quarrel and two to reconcile. If we do our part and the problem remains, there is a plan to follow. Paul suggests that we not harbor resentment or retaliate, but let God work out the problem. He continues, "If your enemy is hungry, feed him; if he is thirsty, give him a drink; for in so doing you will heap coals of fire on his head. Do not be overcome by evil, but overcome evil with good."

These verses summarize the core of Christian living. If we love someone the way Christ loves us, we will be willing to forgive. If we have experienced God's grace, we will want to pass it on to others. And let us remember that grace is undeserved favor. By giving an enemy a drink, we are not excusing the person's misdeeds. We are forgiving the individual and are being loving, in spite of everything—just as Christ did for us!

In this day of constant law suits and endless demands of legal rights, St. Paul's command sounds almost impossible. Why does he tell us to forgive our enemies? Because Christ taught us that in all four gospels. Christ Himself forgave even those who crucified Him! He is our prime example. Also, forgiveness may break a cycle of retaliation and lead to mutual reconciliation. It may also make the person feel ashamed, and may cause him or her to have a change of heart. By contrast, repaying evil for evil not only is unchristian behavior, but it hurts us just as much as it hurts the enemy.

Even if the individual never repents, forgiving that person will free us of a heavy load of bitterness. Our desire should not be to keep score, but to love and forgive. This is not natural; it is in fact supernatural. Only God's Holy Spirit can give us the strength to love as He does; to love our enemies and pray for those who persecute us. Only then can we overcome evil with good.

When we show love to those who don't deserve it, we reveal God's grace to them! Yes, the best way—the Christian way—to conquer an enemy is to make that person our friend!

*T*he story is told that a hotel in Texas on the shores of the Gulf of Mexico put the following notice in each room: "NO FISHING FROM THE BALCONY." Yet every day hotel guests threw their lines into the waters below. Finally the management decided to take down the signs, and the fishing stopped. Is there an attraction to the forbidden?

The above story reminds me of a cartoon I saw in the newspaper. The scene is at a restaurant. A lady seated at a booth while looking at a menu asks the waitress: "What is this 'stolen chicken'?" Waitress: "Just plain fried chicken." Lady: "Why do you call it 'stolen'?" Waitress: "It makes it taste better!"

Human nature is inherently rebellious. Give us a law and we will see it as a challenge to break it. In the Garden of Eden, Gen. 3, the serpent deceived Eve by taking her focus off all the freedom she had, and put in on that one restriction God had made. Ever since, we have all been rebels. Wrongful acts often look good to us precisely because God has said it is wrong. Instead of paying attention to His warnings, we often do the opposite.

When we are tempted to rebel, we need to look at the law from a wider perspective—in the light of God's grace and mercy. If we focus on His great love for us, we will understand that He only restricts us from actions and attitudes that ultimately will harm us. As in the Garden, we are free to choose between two masters, but we are not free to manipulate the consequences of our choices. Each master pays with his own kind of wages. The wages of sin is spiritual death. That is all we can expect or hope for in life without God. Christ's wages is eternal life—new life with God that begins on earth and continues forever in Heaven.

Eternal life is a gift from God, not something that must be paid back. A gift cannot be purchased by the recipient. A more appropriate response to a gift is gracious acceptance with gratitude. As children of God, we have eternal life because of His mercy, not because of any righteous act that we have done. Serving God is the fruit of our love and faith in Him.

The Apostle Paul says in Gal. 5:24, 25; "Those who belong to Christ Jesus have crucified their sinful nature with its passions and desires. Since we live by the Spirit, let us keep in step with the Spirit." For a child of God, control by a sinful nature is a condition that belongs to the past. Christ, through His death on the cross, resurrection and ascension, has forgiven all our wrongful acts and has sent us His Holy Spirit that produces in us the fruit of the spirit.

The Holy Spirit daily produces in us what the Bible calls the fruit of the spirit. These are: love, joy, peace, patience, kindness, goodness, faithfulness, gentleness and self-control (Gal. 5:22, 23). May God's Spirit guide us so that we develop these virtues to their fullest. Forbidden fruit may taste sweet but has bitter consequences.

A small spark from a match lights the tinder. This flame grows, fueled by wood and air, and soon spreads, consuming the wood. The little orange tongue of flame has become a fire.

Some 2,000 years ago, on the Day of Pentecost, 50 days after the resurrection of Christ, a spiritual "match" was struck in Jerusalem. At first, only a few in that part of the world were touched by God's spirit. But that fire soon spread beyond the Holy City and out to the world to all people. The birth and spread of the Church had begun.

When the risen Christ returned to the Father, He entrusted the proclamation of all He had accomplished to a few dozen men and women who had been His disciples during His earthly ministry. What was the message that turned the world upside down? It was the message foretold in the Old Testament that the Son of God, the Messiah, would come. He would live amongst men (Emmanuel; God with us), die and be resurrected. He was Jesus the Christ. It is only through Him that mankind can obtain forgiveness for all wrongdoing and find peace with God, by faith.

This small group of spirit-inspired evangelists began their apostolic mission, first in Jerusalem, and eventually spread the message of Jesus Christ over most of the Roman Empire. God broke down centuries-old barriers of race and culture. Empowered by the Holy Spirit, these courageous apostles boldly preached, taught, healed and demonstrated love to all people wherever God sent them, despite persecution. As a result, lives and history were changed. If persecution meant being driven out of town, the apostles went to another. If it meant jail, they preached in jail, rejoicing that God considered them worthy of suffering for His sake.

Apostle Paul's three missionary journeys are focused primarily on many countries north of the Mediterranean Sea. God's Word could not be confined to one corner of the world. This was a faith that offered hope to all humanity.

The Book of Acts, written by St. Luke, tells the history and spread of Christianity; the beginning of the Church. The Church did not start or grow by its own power or enthusiasm. The apostles were empowered by God's Spirit. The Holy Spirit was the promised Counselor and Guide sent by God when Jesus ascended to Heaven.

The message remains the same. Christ's glorious proclamation is ours as well. "You shall receive power when the Holy Spirit has come upon you; and you shall be My witnesses to the end of the earth" (Acts 1:8). Surely most of our generation needs Christ's proclamation just as Apostle Paul's did.

*W*e don't forget anything we memorize at an early age. I was in a supermarket line. A young lady in front of me had a slight disagreement with the female cashier about her bill. Suddenly the customer began calculating out loud in German. When she had it all figured out, she gave the results to the cashier in English, who was totally bewildered. The problem was eventually solved, and the customer departed with a smile. I understood completely what the German woman went through. In whatever language one learns the multiplication table as a child, that becomes the basis of all mathematical calculations. When I reached the register, I told the cashier that my bill was simple, but if I had to calculate anything, it had to be in Greek. She smiled and said, "I know none of that. I'm just a plain Yankee—give me a calculator." We both laughed.

Anything I learned to memorize as an adult, however, I must repeat often so I won't forget. The 66 books of the Bible, for example, from Genesis to Revelation, I repeat about once a week as I drive or wait at a red light. The 23rd Psalm is another one I don't want to forget. This Psalm is perhaps the best known passage in the Old Testament. Over the generations, it has comforted more readers than all the philosophies of the world. It is a testimony by David to the Lord's faithfulness in his life. It pictures the Lord as a shepherd. David is confident he will never be in want.

In describing the Lord as a shepherd, David wrote from his own experience. He had spent his early years caring for sheep. The New Testament often calls Jesus the Good Shepherd. As such, we are His sheep—wisely following the One Who will lead us in the right ways.

When we allow God, our Shepherd, to lead and guide us, we have safety from a threatening environment. God nourishes us spiritually and emotionally. Our Shepherd knows the "green pastures" and "still waters" that refresh and restore our spirit. In verse four, death casts a frightening shadow. We are helpless in its presence. We can struggle with our enemies—pain, suffering, disease—but strength and courage cannot overcome death. Only One Person can walk with us through death's dark valley and bring us safely through it—the God of life, our Shepherd. Only He can offer us eternal comfort, while His rod and staff are viewed as instruments of protection and direction.

The imagery of anointing is frequently associated with blessing. In the final scene we see that believers will dwell in the house of God, the perfect Shepherd and Host. With only six verses, this Psalm is a delight to the reader. By memorizing and repeating it often, it will remain with us forever.

We don't easily forget anything we memorize as children. Therefore, as parents and grandparents, we must do our best to teach our youngsters all we can—our language, tradition, our faith, our history. They will be enriched and grateful in later years for that.

*T*he image of fresh, cool water is a familiar sight in both Old and New Testaments. A cup of water offered to a guest or a stranger was a simple and expected sign of hospitality. In John 4: 1 – 26, Jesus uses earthly water to introduce "Living Water."

Jesus was passing through Samaria on his way to Galilee. Jews hated the Samaritans. But if we need an example of someone who overlooked racial barriers, we can turn to Jesus. Approaching a village, He came to rest at Jacob's Well. His disciples had gone to buy some food. Soon a Samaritan woman came to draw water. Jesus surprised her when He asked for a drink, and used the occasion to say: "If you knew the gift of God, and Who it is who says to you, 'give Me a drink,' you would have asked Him, and He would have given you Living Water." By this, Jesus was claiming to be the Messiah, Christ, the Anointed One. Only Christ could give this gift that satisfies the soul's desire. He used the term "Living Water" to indicate eternal life. Jesus also said, "Whoever drinks the water I give him will never thirst…"

Two thousand years ago, a thirsty woman questioned Jesus about His source of fulfillment. She was a Samaritan, of a mixed race, hated by Jews, known to be living in sin, and was in a public place. No respectable Jewish man would talk to a woman under such circumstances. Jesus ignored all that. God's Word is for everyone, no matter what one's race, social position or past sins.

The woman exclaimed, "Sir, give me this water so that I won't get thirsty and have to keep coming here to draw water." She did not immediately understand. She confused the two kinds of water, perhaps because no one had ever talked to her about her spiritual hunger and thirst before.

We do not deprive our bodies of food and water when we hunger and thirst. Why then should we deprive our souls? The Living Word, Jesus Christ, and the written Word, the Bible, can satisfy our hungry and thirsty souls.

Jacob's well is still there, a hundred feet deep, nine feet in diameter. It is one of the few places where an exact spot connected with Jesus can be identified. This is a beautiful story from Jesus' life and the Samaritan woman who found her "Living Water."

What water is to the body, the Word of God is to the soul. Are we spiritually thirsty? Why not take a drink from the spring that never runs dry. God is the Fountain of the Living Water. And Jesus offers us the life-giving water of eternal life.

*H*e was skeptical and full of doubt. Moses was told by God that Israel had suffered long enough under the Egyptians. It was time to send a deliverer, and he was the one chosen by God.

Moses had tried that deliverance task on his own 40 years earlier, while still a prince living in Pharaoh's palace. In order to defend a fellow Israelite who was being beaten by an Egyptian task-master, Moses struck and killed the Egyptian.

We all know what happened. Fearing for his life, Moses fled Egypt and went to the land of Midian. This prince and well-trained soldier, who had the best education available of his time, became a shepherd. Humbled and completely content tending sheep for 40 years, he was now, at age 80, called by God to be that deliverer! Moses said to God, "Who am I, that I should go to Pharaoh and bring the Israelites out of Egypt?" (Ex. 3:11) Despite his reluctance and five excuses, he accepted the mission, and God promised to be with him at all times.

Most of us have felt uncertain and full of doubt like Moses at one time or another. Are we presently facing a seemingly impossible task or assignment? It could be at work, at school, or perhaps a broken relationship that we wish to heal. Why not do what Moses did? He trusted God. He committed the task to the Lord and God was with him every step of the way.

Are we willing to trust God, pray for His guidance and wisdom and do our best? Why not think of that specific challenge which we might be facing right now. Have we committed it to the Lord? It takes humility to recognize and admit our need for God. Let's keep in mind that Moses was called to be a deliverer, not while he was a prince, but later when he was an humble, ordinary shepherd! God had prepared him in the desert for 40 years for that very special task. Now Moses was ready for another 40 years of desert life in the wilderness, but this time as an experienced leader and deliverer.

God often chooses ordinary people like you and me to accomplish extraordinary tasks in His service and for His glory. When we face seemingly impossible challenges, why not depend on God's strength, pray, and do our best. God is with us always and nothing is impossible for Him. With divine help, success is certain.

*S*omeone asked the president of the American Bible Society how one could keep a leather-bound Bible from stiffening and cracking. He gave this interesting reply: "There is one oil that is especially good. In fact, it will ensure the cover's good condition for a lifetime. This oil is not sold, but can be found only in the palms of human hands!"

Just as physical life is sustained by nutrients, so is our spiritual life nourished by reading and obeying the Word of God. It is an essential part of a healthy, spiritual diet. If we neglect God's Book, we become weak, spiritually anemic Christians. How fortunate we are to have God's Word available to us daily. The Bible is the most important book anyone could own. Do we appreciate the availability of God's Word to us? Are we thankful that we have at arm's reach the Book that offers the truest source of wisdom known to man? Do we treasure God's Word and recognize it as the ultimate resource to guide our lives? Do we recognize its superiority to all other books? "God's Word is a lamp to our feet and light to our path" (Ps. 119:105). It provides illumination to allow us to walk through life without stumbling—light enough for each step in making moral decisions.

The facts of the Bible never need updating, and neither do its teachings need revision. In fact, the Bible says in both the Old and New Testaments: "Whatever I command you, be careful to observe it; you shall not add to it nor take away from it" (Deut. 12:32 and Rev. 22:18, 19). The warning is given to those who might purposefully distort the message of God's Word. We must handle the Bible with care and great respect, and study its truths so that we do not distort its message, even unintentionally. When we know the truth of God's Word well, we'll be able to identify the false immediately. In fact, government officials who are trained to identify counterfeit money, know and have studied the genuine so well that they can identify the false at once.

As we read the Bible and meditate on its truths, we should also put its principles into practice. God's Word assures us of His great love and forgiveness through His Son Jesus Christ, Who is the Light and Savior of the world. "For God so loved the world that He gave His only begotten Son, that whoever believes in Him should not perish but have everlasting life" (Jn. 3:16).

Why not, then, put aside some time daily to read His Word in order to maintain our spiritual diet. And while we are doing that, we can be assured that our Bible's leather cover will be "well oiled."

$\mathcal{M}$ark Twain often took great pleasure in revealing the foolishness of human behavior. He once said, "Always do right. This will gratify some people and astonish the rest."

People are often surprised when someone does what is right. We had the following experience in our family. A few years ago, my husband Steve went on a trip to Boston. Before he even arrived in his hotel room, he discovered he had lost his wallet. He had dropped it after paying the cab driver. A young man found it. He looked through it, saw the business cards and realized the owner was from Los Angeles. He called Steve's office, informed his secretary, and left his name and phone number with her. The secretary called me with the information. When Steve called me later that day to say that he had arrived safely and that all was fine and well with him, I had all the information he needed. He didn't mention the subject of the wallet at first, so I wouldn't be concerned. But when I told him I knew and had all the information, he was surprised. He called the young man who met him at the hotel, returned the wallet completely intact, and received a generous reward.

Were we all astonished? You bet! The young man returned the wallet so he could keep something much more valuable—his integrity. Amazing! Yes, we are often surprised when someone does what's right. Doing what's right is not a new idea; unfortunately, neither is doing the opposite. Therefore, the Apostle Paul has written in his epistle to the Philippian faithful, "...become blameless and pure, children of God without fault in a crooked and depraved generation, in which you shine like stars in the universe..." (2:15).

We are faced with choices daily. Mark Twain reveals human behavior with humor. What will it cost us to do right? A long distance phone call? Some travel time on the freeway for obeying the speed limit? As Christians, we are chosen to be ambassadors of Christ on earth. We are challenged to live lives worthy of that calling. What an awesome privilege! Are we exemplary representatives? When we walk in His Light, and spiritually renew ourselves daily, we will naturally do what's true and right. Then we will "shine like stars in the universe."

*M*ost of us have looked into distorted mirrors, popular in country fairs. These fun mirrors are designed to distort the image they reflect. If, for example, one is tall and slender, a distorted mirror not only will show that individual short and stocky, but with a body totally out of proportion.

These mirrors could be a metaphor to illustrate the human heart, which without God, is totally unreliable to reflect a God-honoring spiritual condition. We read in Proverbs 28:26, "He who trusts in his own heart is a fool." There is only One Who is able, by His mercy and grace, to effect in us true spiritual changes. We also read in Proverbs 3:4, 5; "Trust in the Lord with all your heart, and lean not on your own understanding. In all your ways acknowledge Him, and He shall direct your paths."

Solomon, the third king of Israel, son of the great king David, reigned during Israel's golden age. God appeared to Solomon in a dream one night and said that He would grant him whatever he wanted. "Ask! What shall I give you?" Solomon asked for an "understanding heart," so that he may judge the people properly and may be able to discern between good and evil (1 Kings 3:5 – 14). God was pleased with this request, and He not only made Solomon wise, but He also gave him great wealth, power, long life and an era of peace and prosperity. Solomon built the glorious temple in Jerusalem and wrote most of the books of Proverbs, Ecclesiastes and Song of Solomon.

While God does not promise riches to those who follow Him, He gives us what we need if we put Him and His principles first. If we do that, He will satisfy our deepest needs. About a thousand years later, Jesus emphasized this same truth in Matthew 6:33, "But seek first the kingdom of God and His righteousness, and all these things shall be added to you."

In this age of information, knowledge is plentiful, but wisdom is scarce. Wisdom means more than simply knowing a lot. It is a basic attitude that affects every aspect of life. Wisdom means practical discernment. It begins with knowing God, which leads to righteous living and results in increased ability to discern between right and wrong.

Wisdom begins with God, and His revealed Word is the source of knowledge and understanding. In one sense, wisdom is God's gift to us. But He gives it only to those who earnestly seek it. Christians don't have to grope in the dark, hoping to stumble upon answers. We can ask for God's wisdom to guide our choices, and God will give it to us. Then we will not only be pleasing in His sight, but we will each be perfect mirrors projecting only spiritually undistorted reflections to all.

*M*ost of us are aware of the Summer Olympic Games that take place every four years in different countries around the world. It is exciting to watch athletes in peak physical condition compete in their chosen sports.

In the summer of 1997, I noticed an extreme example of this Olympic excitement in Rome. Italy was one of several countries that was bidding for the Summer Olympics for the year 2004. While the decision had not yet been made as to which country would host it, the Italians were already caught up in that excitement, selling T-shirts for the 2004 Olympics.

A Christian's life can be as exciting as an athlete's as well. One of the most descriptive pictures of a Christian's life in the Bible is that of an athlete competing in a "race." The Apostle Paul tells us that discipline is the key to winning (1 Cor. 9:24 – 27). We are encouraged to lay aside anything that might hinder our spiritual development and fitness while we stay focused on Christ. He also teaches us to press on, forgetting those things which are behind, including past failures, and reach forward to those things which are ahead (Philip. 3: 12, 13).

St. Paul did not take his commitment to the Gospel lightly. He gave himself to the task of serving God with the same dedication and determination that an athlete devotes to prepare for competition. While athletes train for temporal prizes, the Apostle endured tremendous hardship to win an eternal reward. With faith and determination, he always gave his best while his focus remained on Christ; a true "champion" for God.

Do some of us at times feel like quitting because of hardships in our lives? Let us keep in mind that we are Christian "athletes," and that the essential discipline is to stay focused on God's Word. As we study and train, alone or with other fellow faithful, the training will equip us with the faith to reach our full potential, and enter the "race" of a Christian's life with enthusiasm, stamina and joy.

Taking care of our physical fitness is important, but even more important is to care for our spiritual fitness by walking with the Lord. Now <u>that</u> is a fitness program with eternal value!

*T*he story is told that on Arturo Toscanini's 80th birthday (1867 – 1957) an acquaintance of the famous Italian musician and conductor asked his son what he considered to be his father's greatest achievement. The son said there wasn't such a thing for his father. He replied, "Whatever he is involved in at any moment is the biggest undertaking of his life—whether it is conducting a symphony or pealing an apple."

What a great attitude! If Toscanini devoted himself so deeply to every venture he undertook, how much truer should that be for us. As children of God, we too must demonstrate similar zest, discipline, dedication and deep devotion in all deeds of love we do for the Lord and others. The Apostle Paul writes to the Colossian faithful, "Whatever you do, do it heartedly as to the Lord and not to men" (Col. 3:23). God's love must so permeate our motives that we should always do our very best with gladness and for His glory.

Christ Himself says in Matthew 20:23, "The Son of man did not come to be served but to serve." Here Jesus described leadership from a new perspective. The world's system of leadership is very different from the leadership of God's kingdom. For Christians the leader is to be the one who serves the utmost with zest and enthusiasm. There are different styles of leadership. Some lead through public speaking, some through administering, some through organizations, etc. But every Christian, leader or not, needs a servant's heart. Christ demonstrated this throughout His earthly ministry. Can we ever forget Him washing the feet of His disciples?

We should begin and end each task with enthusiasm, doing it as to the Lord and not to men. By following Christ's example, Godly leaders serve wholeheartedly and with humility. They are driven, not by selfish ambition, but by a burning desire to care for their fellow man and accomplish God's purpose on earth.

By yielding to the Holy Spirit, we can all have such a strong assurance of doing the Father's will. Each of us has different gifts according to the grace that is given to us by our Creator. Let us seek God's purpose for our lives and use these gifts to the best of our ability to achieve His plan on earth for His glory.

Whether we are engaged in a project of great magnitude, or we are one of many in a teamwork effort, or simply helping a neighbor, we must see it as our responsibility to God and man. Anything we do for the Lord, large or small, should be, as Toscanini considered it, the biggest undertaking of that moment. It's a great thing to do even little things well. Even little is plenty when it is done for the Lord!

Our children are a gift to us from God. They are on loan to us for only a number of years, to train and nourish them in the Lord until they are grown and on their own. The following few lines were written by a father to his grown son:

"I took care of some errands in my new truck today...alone...with nothing more than lots of memories of Saturdays a long time ago. My new truck is everything I always wanted. However, I would give it up in an instant if I could turn back the clock 20 years, when I would load up the old blue truck with my two helpers." Those two helpers were his two young sons, who would happily bounce around in the front seat, out on a ride with dad. The old blue truck is now just a wonderful memory for those three men. It's been replaced with a brand new one, and the two sons are now grown and on their own.

These sentimental few lines emphasize once again, how quickly time passes, and that we must value every precious hour of each day. This father realized the early years were not wasted! Special moments by parents and children can never be repeated, but the effects live on forever. Many of us, I'm sure, treasure such precious days of long ago. Time spent with children, especially by Christian dads, can make all the difference in a child's decision to love and to serve the Lord as an adult.

We read in Psalm 118:24, "This is the day the Lord has made; we will rejoice and be glad in it." Do we appreciate God's gift of life? Do we live each day to its fullest for the Lord so that one day we can look back with no regrets? Today's wise decisions create tomorrow's awesome memories. For most of us, there are days when the last thing we want to do is rejoice. Our mood might be blue, our circumstances difficult. We can relate to a few sad psalm writers who often felt like us. But no matter how low the psalmists felt, they were always honest with God. And as they talked it over with Him, their prayers ended with praise.

If we do the same, we will find that the Lord will give us reasons to rejoice. Psalm 90:12 says, "Teach us to number our days, that we may gain a heart of wisdom." To number our days means that our time is short. We are to place each day in the balance, and make the scales tip in a way that will bring glory to God and blessings to the lives of others.

To have no regrets at life's end, we must make the most of every opportunity. We should treasure each hour as a precious gift from our Creator. We must keep our Christian standards high, act wisely and do good whenever and in whatever way we can. Instead of counting our days, we can make our days count. Our attitude will determine our altitude—how high we will rise or how low we might fall.

Could it be that we are too busy with future plans so that we ignore this day? Or perhaps we are too involved in the past so that the present is blurred. The past is history, our future is a mystery; the present is all we know and have—this moment! Let us see time as God's gift and seize every opportunity to live and serve Him diligently.

I walked into the parking lot towards my car. I noticed a car was pulling out while another car with its signal on was waiting to pull in. That's when the unexpected happened. Yes, the car pulled out and left, but before the female driver of the waiting car had an opportunity to pull in, another car quickly cut in front of her and took the space! A man quickly came out of that car holding the hand of a boy of about 8 or 9 years of age, and walked away between cars. The female driver was stunned, then furious at the injustice. When she saw me, she asked twice, "Did you see that?" I said to her that my car was nearby and was leaving. That calmed her down somewhat and said that I was a God-send.

As I drove away I thought of the man with the boy. If that child was his son, what a poor example he had just exhibited as a father! More importantly, this incident caused me to think of what our children and grandchildren learn from us at home and at the various places we go together. These tender minds learn much more from observing our behavior than what we teach them.

Our little ones do not automatically become model men and women. Raising children calls for patience, diligence, wise instruction, loving correction, and above all, good examples of an honorable character. The Bible says in Ephesians 4:6, "Fathers (mothers) do not provoke your children to wrath, but bring them up in the training and admonition of the Lord."

We all know that actions speak louder than words. As we teach our youngsters principles of God's Word, we must set that honorable example ourselves. All the words of instruction will not erase from that child's mind what he witnessed in the parking lot. I wonder if the father later said to his child, "Don't do what I did, but do what I say." Which will the child remember?

If we want our children to be exemplary citizens and bring honor to us as Christians, we must make God's Word and its principles part of our every day experience in all aspects of life. What we do speaks louder than what we say. Our little ones learn values, morals, and priorities by observing how we act and react every moment of the day. If there were any children watching us today, what would they learn? This leads us to the next question: When some day we are gone, by what words or actions would we mostly be remembered?

As Christian parents, let us not forget the example of our faith. We need to pass on words and deeds that honor and glorify our Lord. As ambassadors of Christ, let us make sure that we leave behind a rich spiritual legacy—one that they in turn will pass on to succeeding generations. The character of our children and grandchildren is shaped by what they learn from us today.

A Chinese artist was commissioned to portray a painting of the Prodigal Son. Giving it considerable thought, he chose to paint that part of the story where the rebellious son returns home in rags after having wasted his wealth in reckless living. He depicted the father standing by the gate waiting for his son, who could be seen approaching in the distance. When the artist showed the painting to a Christian friend, the man exclaimed, "Oh, no, you don't have it right at all! The father shouldn't be standing still. He should be eagerly running to meet his son!" Surprised, the artist responded, "But no Chinese father would ever consider doing that to a son who had been so self-willed."

"Ah," said the Christian, "But this parable depicts the heart of God. He is far more loving than even the very best of human parents."

How wonderful is God's love for all repentant sinners! When Jesus told the parable of the "Lost Son" in the Gospel of Luke (15:11 – 32) to His listeners, the father's actions, no doubt would have been unthinkable in first century Jewish culture. We all know the parable of the Prodigal Son. Jesus described the father eager to forgive his repentant child. Therefore, the most beautiful and meaningful point of this parable is in verse 20: "But while he was a long way off, his father saw him and was filled with compassion for him."

There is nothing truer and more blessed for us than to be told that our Heavenly Father also sees us while we are still a long way off from Him, and has compassion for us. What a heart-warming picture—what comfort, encouragement and hope!

We also see in this parable that regardless of the son's behavior, he departed as a son after receiving a son's inheritance. Upon his return, he was still accepted as a son, embraced, kissed and restored into his father's household. What maintained the father's love toward his son? He certainly didn't manifest any signs of "sonship," and yet, in his father's eyes and heart he continued to occupy a very special place. The father's love and acceptance of his son were not contingent on his son's behavior. The father's love was unconditional!

That was Jesus' point in the parable. The father didn't disown his rebellious son. God is not looking for people He can throw out of His family. He continually looks after them through all their ups and downs. He is the *Good Shepherd* and the *Compassionate Father*. If we have faith that Christ's death on the cross was payment for our sins, we are eternal members of God's family. Our good works didn't get us in, and neither being disobedient will get us thrown out. God's unconditional love is eternal.

Do we at times feel a long way off from our Heavenly Father? Let us remember the painting as it should have been rendered and the heart of God. Let us be assured that God eagerly waits to welcome us. He is eager to accept all His repentant children with open arms and to forgive their sins. God, we know, hates sin—but He loves the sinner! He loves each one of us. **What Grace!**

*F*athers are special. Growing up in Greece without a dad from age 8 made the memories I have of my father even more special. He died of cancer at age 42. My mother was faced with the responsibility of parenthood alone for my two brothers and me. We lived in Greece. I have great compassion for all mothers who raise their children alone. Therefore, although it is Father's Day week, this article is in part for all those courageous moms as well.

After becoming a mother myself in the U.S., I appreciated my mother's sacrifices even more. She lived in Fresno. As soon as she was eligible she became a U.S. citizen. She was elated! That was 1960. She said to me, "I am tired of learning foreign languages. This is my last move. My next move is up, to meet my Lord!" What kept this courageous woman going? Her faith in God. She did her housework singing sharagans and hymns. The Lord was her shepherd and strength.

One Sunday morning while visiting her in Fresno, we all got into our VW minivan to go to church. My older son Jim was our driver. Mom exclaimed, "What a blessing! I never thought I'd live to see this! My grandson is driving the family to church!" When she was ill in the hospital, I sat next to her bed holding her hand. Opening her eyes, she said, "You look so sad. If it is my time, and my Lord is calling me, I'm ready. I know where I'm going. Why do you look so worried?" Sadly, she went to meet her Lord in 1982. I will always miss her.

My father was a student at Roberts College in Turkey. His education was interrupted by the Armenian genocide by the Turks. I still have few pictures of him in his dorm. The family fled to Greece. In time, he met my mother, and they were married. Both my parents were born in Adapazar, Turkey. Years later, when my father was ill in Greece, I remember he had a large map of Europe taped on the wall next to his bed. Businessmen came to visit him often. They always discussed politics. With a ruler in his hand, my father would point to various countries and talk about world events.

My mother served coffee, and I would follow her with sweets. I was only 7 years old. A friend visiting commented how nicely I was growing. My father took great pride at that and said, "Oh, she is the ornament of our family!" I never forgot those words. After his death, I felt the awesome responsibility of my father's beautiful statement. I kept thinking, "Am I still that 'ornament' my father considered me?" As the years passed, I came to apply that thought to my Christian walk. Am I an "ornament" in my Heavenly Father's eyes? Do I shine and bring honor to His name? My dad's statement is with me always.

What if painful words were stored in my heart, and my father was no longer alive to heal or correct the damage? Apostle Paul says in Eph. 6:4, "Fathers, do not provoke your children to wrath, but bring them up in the training and admonition of the Lord." The importance of a father in a child's life is monumental. He is to nurture his children with Godly advice and wisdom. But a father can't do that if he is not available. In today's busy world the greatest gift a father can give to his children is of himself! A Blessed and Happy Father's Day to all fathers!

*W*hile at the supermarket, a gentleman not far from me was also doing his shopping. Suddenly we heard a child's voice nearby calling, "Hey, Dad!" The man instantly turned. Then he smiled and said to me, "My son isn't even with me. It must be an automatic response to the name 'Dad.'" I smiled back and said, "It still happens to me occasionally. When I hear the call 'Mom,' I instinctively respond, even though I'm a grandmother now."

This reminded me of the fact: Once a parent, always a parent. What an incredible responsibility and great privilege it is for young parents! All those men who answer to the call "Dad" have at least one child who looks to them for love, protection, guidance, friendship, discipline, and so much more. I truly can't think of a more rewarding job. One of the most quoted parenting principles in the Bible is found in Proverbs 22:6: "Train up a child in the ways he should go, and when he is old he will not depart from it." Experienced parents would also add, "But make sure, Mom and Dad, that you go in that direction yourself." Actions speak louder than words. This early training will remain with the child for the rest of that child's life.

The above verse, however, is a proverb and not a promise. Good parenting doesn't always guarantee good children. It only assures that our children will have the tremendous advantage of having had Christian parents who gave them a good Godly foundation. Let us look for a moment at the example of our heavenly Father and creation. He was a perfect parent. Adam and Eve were placed in the best of environments. Yet they chose to throw it all away and go in the way of the serpent! Yes, and one of their children became a murderer. Poor choices indeed! Life is a series of choices for each one of us. We have the privilege to choose, and unfortunately we sometimes choose incorrectly. Therefore, God's Word must be our moral and spiritual compass—our roadmap of life to guide us daily. The Bible instructs us to teach God's Word to our children, when at home, or when we walk along the road, when we lay down and when we get up (Deut. 6:7).

We will never know the love of a parent until we become parents ourselves. Our heavenly Father loves us so much He sent His only Son, Jesus Christ, to teach us true love. Jesus loves children very much as well. We see in Mt. 19:13 – 15, that when children came to Jesus, the disciples rebuked them, viewing the children as a distraction to Christ's ministry. But Jesus welcomed them. He laid His hands on them and blessed them, not only because of their innocent trusting and humble nature worthy of His kingdom, but also as His representatives and disciples to the next generation. They would one day become the ambassadors of His Good News. Since entrance into the kingdom is by God's grace, and not by human achievement, these dependent, teachable little ones always have a special place in God's kingdom.

What a privilege and necessity it is, today more than even, for fathers to share the heritage of our Christian faith with their children. God knows the responsibilities and joys of fatherhood because He is our heavenly Father. Only when fathers submit to God's training and instruction can they receive divine wisdom to bring up their children in His ways.

*L*ove and loyalty in human relations is most heartwarming. During our recent cruise, my husband and I shared a table with two women while having a snack. After a few moments of pleasant conversation, I asked if the two were related. The young lady looked affectionately toward her companion and said, "Oh, she's my mother-in-law." I was amazed, especially after I heard their story.

While the young lady was still a new bride, tragically her husband was killed in an airplane crash. Although presently independent from each other, they remained close. Their tender love and care for each other was clearly evident. At one point the mom said, "We are like Ruth and Naomi." I was intrigued by that comment and said, "Ah, where you go I'll go, where you stay I'll stay. Your people will be my people and your God my God." I saw a bright smile on her face, then she said, "You know your Bible!"

I am constantly amazed by God's delightful surprises. What a unique way to meet two devoted Christians! The mature lady's comment was wise. She didn't know me, yet she uttered that remark to see what would happen. As a result, we became friends and spent some time together.

The book of Ruth is a beautiful story of a lovely woman and a charming picture of domestic life. A Bethlehem family, Naomi, her husband and two sons, went to Moab, east of the Jordan River, on account of famine. Moabites were idolatrous people. The two young men married Moabite girls. After ten years, Naomi's husband and both sons died. Since the girls were childless, Naomi asked her daughters-in-law to return to their mother's house and perhaps remarry, while Naomi planned to return to Bethlehem. One daughter-in-law took her advice, but Ruth clung to Naomi and said, "Don't urge me to leave you or turn back from you. Where you go I will go, and where you stay I will stay. Your people will be my people and your God my God. Where you die I will die, and there I will be buried. May the Lord deal with me, be it ever so severely, if anything but death separates you and me" (Ruth 1:16 – 17).

Ruth, a gentile, a foreigner, vowed her commitment to Naomi in the name of God, acknowledging Him as her God. Returning to Bethlehem, Ruth's life exhibited admirable qualities. She was hard working, loving, kind, faithful and brave. God led this young Moabite widow to a man named Boaz, a wealthy land owner and relative of Naomi. Boaz extended protection to Ruth, whom he eventually married. The book of Ruth is also the story of God's grace in the midst of difficulties. God will use anyone who is open to Him to achieve His purpose. Ruth, a Moabite, through this union with Boaz, had a son Obed, who continued the family line through which Christ came into our world. Ruth became the great-grandmother of King David and an ancestor in the line of the Messiah (Matt. 1:5).

Anyone who reads this charming short book will be encouraged. The universal scope of the gospel comes to light as Ruth finds the blessings promised to all nations. Ruth becomes an ancestor of Christ, who later Himself will reconcile all nations to God. What a profound impact Naomi's life had made!

*W*e often take our lead from admirable or famous characters and personalities of the world. But we can often learn amazing truths by observing the order and harmony in creation. Proverbs 30:24 – 25, for example, points out that we should look at the virtues of the lowly things around us; the ants! We read, "Ants are creatures of little strength, yet they store up their food in the summer."

Ants know instinctively that winter is coming, so they take advantage of the warm weather as a time for preparation. They utilize their energy and resources economically. They attend our picnics, B.B.Q.'s and even invade our kitchens if they find the opportunity. These little creatures aren't very strong, but they sure are persistent, and almost nothing can stop them.

Ants are "exceedingly wise" in another area as well. Their wisdom is seen in their ability to work together as they gather their food in the summer. One ant alone cannot accomplish much. Perhaps it can move a few crumbs around and dig out a few grains of soil, but it can never construct a vast underground community by itself. That requires communication and cooperation. Ants are experts at teamwork, and that is another admirable point.

As Christians are we working together with our fellow faithful to accomplish God's work? Or are we trying to do it all alone, risking burnout and failure? God's work done in God's way requires teamwork. Scriptures teach that by God's design we have been made dependent on one another. We can't fulfill our high calling as members of the body of Christ until we realize that we all have a vital part to play. As members of HIS family, we need each other. Joining together is a beginning, staying together is progress, working together is success!

If we also were to display our wisdom, we'll prepare for "winter." We can equip ourselves for difficult times by storing up God's Word in our hearts. Then, when we face the storms and blizzards of life, we'll know right where to find nourishment for our soul. The time to prepare for tomorrow is today.

Next time we see an ant, let us remember that "winter" is not far away. Are we prepared?

*M*any people use the word "awesome" freely these days to describe athletes, one's own experience of an amazing event, or even to describe friends. There is nothing wrong with the word. If, however, one visits some of the well-known landmarks of this country, such as the Grand Canyon, Yellowstone and Zion National Parks, and experiences the natural beauty and panoramic views of these locations, it is impossible not to feel a sense of awe.

That was how I felt when we visited these locations. Although the natural scenery itself is breathtaking, my feeling of awe was more related to God than with the spectacular beauty of nature. I had the sense of being in the presence of the ONE who created these wonders—the Master Designer Himself. I was surrounded by the awesome beauty of the slopes, majestic mountain peaks and indescribable wonders of God's creations.

Often in our daily lives, we tend to become indifferent to the wonders of God's creative awesome work, such as a golden sunset at day's end, a spectacular cloud formation, the warm rays of sunshine, or something as common as a beautiful wild flower growing in the crack of a sidewalk. May we never become to busy or apathetic to appreciate the wondrous gifts of nature we have been given by our Creator. Rather, each day let us single out some awesome gift we have taken for granted and offer gratitude.

St. Matthew writes, "God causes His sun to rise on the evil and the good, and sends rain on the righteous and the unrighteous." (Mt. 5:45) God's awesome wonders of creation are for all to enjoy, but how much more meaningful they are to us who know the Creator intimately—the Master Creator and Designer Himself! That is when we utter, "What a great and awesome God we have!"

*P*rayer is as instinctive as breathing. It is a need that emerges from the heart; a need beyond our ability to understand. Prayer is our acknowledgement that there is a being higher than ourselves—our mighty Creater Himself.

The story is told that the installation of the first telegraph lines off the coast of some underdeveloped islands of northern Europe prompted unusual responses by some local citizens. While one man stood looking at the wires being installed, a second man endlessly praised the wonderful new invention. Excited, he exclaimed that once it is completed, they will be able to send messages many miles away, and get the answer within hours!

The first man seemed unimpressed, saying there was nothing great about that. Annoyed by this man's response, the second man asked if he knew of anything that was better or faster.

The first man asked if he had ever heard of getting an answer before the message is sent. He then quoted Isaiah 65:24; "Before they call I will answer; while they are still speaking I will hear." The second man looked puzzled, thinking it was just an odd meaningless comment. He had not realized the Biblical truth behind that reply.

It is true that God reads our hearts and always knows our every need. Often when it is His will regarding a need, even while we are speaking, the blessing prayed for is granted and on its way! It is a privilege to pray because it brings us into a close relationship and fellowship with our Creater. We admit our need for Him and our utter dependence upon Him.

We can talk to God any time, day or night. What if we could only pray to Him during restricted hours? What if we had odd/even praying days? We can rejoice and praise God again and again that we can call Him any time we wish. We have access to our Heavenly Father at all times, and when it is His will regarding our needs, the blessing is ours.

Yes, prayer is faster than any modern means of communication, including fax and E-mail. We can be assured that there is no time or place when He'll withhold His love and grace from us. Night or day, God hears as we pray!

$\mathcal{N}$ot long ago, I helped an elderly woman, a stranger to me, cross a busy intersection to the bus stop. After she sat on the bench, she thanked me, smiled, and with a twinkle in her eyes, she said jokingly, "Never grow old, my dear, never grow old." I smiled back and we parted.

As I walked to my car, I thought about her joking comment. Do we really have a choice? The only way to avoid getting old is to die while we are young. Yes, aging brings with it some aches and pains, but it can also be a wonderful time of life. Those who maintain fellowship with the Lord through life's ups and downs can possess a greater serenity than those who are younger, but have lived without knowing God intimately. We read in Psalms 92: 12 – 14: "The righteous shall flourish like a palm tree, and those who are planted in the house of the Lord shall flourish in the courts of our God. They shall still bear fruit in old age, they shall be fresh and flourishing."

To flourish like palm trees means to stand healthy and tall and live long. The faithful then, are seen as strong and unshakable by the winds of circumstances. All those who place their hopes and faith firmly rooted in God can have this strength and vitality.

Devoted Christians can produce spiritual fruit at any age. There are many faithful, precious, aging individuals who continue to have a fresh outlook, and can teach us from their life experiences of serving God. I personally know many such precious individuals who continually inspire me by their works and conduct. We can each seek counsel among our aging friends and relatives, and ask about their experiences with the Lord. That will challenge us to new heights of spiritual growth and maintain contact between generations. In return we will be blessed tremendously!

Whatever age group we might be in, we can praise God for the gift of life. We can also thankfully accept each passing year as a new gift for opportunities to bear fruit for His glory. Rather than counting our passing years, let us make our years count for the Lord.

*O*n a weekday morning a businessman called the office of a large company and asked to speak to an acquaintance who was an executive in that corporation. The secretary informed him that the person was not in the office, but "in school" that day. When the caller, rather surprised, asked if the executive wasn't a bit old to be going to school, she replied, "In this company, he is not!"

If that is true in the business world, it is even truer in the Christian realm. As Christians we should also have that same attitude. No matter how long we have walked with the Lord, or how much knowledge we have gained of His Word, we are still learners.

The Apostle Paul had acquired great spiritual knowledge, yet he was not content to rest on what he already knew. In Philippians 3:12 he says, "Not that I have already obtained all this, or have already been made perfect, but I press on to take hold of that for which Christ Jesus took hold of me." The challenge of spiritual growth lay ahead of him throughout his life.

Just as in the business world, we can look forward to a lifetime of continual learning. In the same manner the challenge of our spiritual growth is limitless through our entire life. Let us make it then, a goal to be "in school" by spending time studying God's Word. We never grow too old or have gained too much knowledge to be able to learn new spiritual lessons from God's classroom of life. As followers of Christ, there are unlimited truths to learn in the life of faith. It is the pathway to wisdom and the key to successful, happy and spiritually strong living.

*S*ummer BBQs and picnics reminded me of an article I read a few years ago suggesting a way of serving square hard-boiled eggs! I found the thought quite amusing. Why would anyone wish to serve square eggs? Perhaps for its uniqueness, they certainly would be the talk of the party, but the article pointed out that they are easier to store in the refrigerator.

The directions suggested the following. The eggs were to be hard boiled first, then the shells removed immediately, and while they were still hot, pressed into a box with six small square compartments. The lid would be closed tightly and the box stored in the refrigerator overnight. In the morning we would have cool, square eggs! Imagine, it took a chicken 24 hours to produce a perfectly oval egg, and we were to invest another 24 hours to reshape it into squares! Oh yes, the plastic boxes, of course, were available for sale.

This reminds me of the forces in our environment and the world that press its influence on us and attempt to shape us. Therefore, the Apostle Paul tells us in Rom. 12:2, "Do not be conformed to this world, but be transformed by the renewing of your mind." The Apostle urges all faithful to not conform their lives and conduct to those around them. But we are to allow the transforming Word of God to work within us and produce outward results, rather than to permit external pressures to shape us.

One can play the role of what their environment presses onto them for only so long. Why pretend to be someone we are not? As transformed people, when we meditate on God's Word daily, it will influence our thoughts and actions, and help us grow spiritually. Then our conduct and manner of living would be pleasing to God. Our Heavenly Father is committed to the task of conforming us to the image of His Son—in character, in patience, in goodness, in truth, in discipline.

As Christians, we must live and be guided by that small voice within us, which is the guidance and direction of the Holy Spirit, our moral and spiritual compass which keeps us as God's transformed people!

The English word *metamorphosis* comes from the Greek, which connotes a change of appearance. St. Matthew uses the same word to describe the Transfiguration in Mt. 17:2. Just as Christ briefly, and in a limited way, displayed outwardly His inner divine nature and glory at the Transfiguration, Christians should outwardly manifest their inner, redeemed nature, not once, but daily. The renewed mind is one saturated with and controlled by the Word of God.

It is interesting how the oval hard-boiled egg conformed to the shape of its environment when pressed while still hot. It then turned into a square overnight! Many temptations in today's environment will continue to try to shape our character as well, but they will not succeed in molding us into anything if God's Word continues to transform us from within daily! When we are transformed by the Word, we won't be conformed to the world.

*I*ndoor plants grow beautifully when planted in special flower pots that absorb nourishment from a transparent section at the bottom. Water and nutrients are added there, and the plant draws daily according to its need. The supply lasts for weeks. God-given intelligence has helped creative thinkers to invent this to keep our indoor plants well nourished and healthy.

Faith in God is like a tender plant that needs the Scriptures for its nourishment if it is to grow strong and healthy. If faith is not fed and watered with the Word of God, it withers quickly in the dry atmosphere created by a closed Bible. Using the analogy of a vine and its branches, Jesus told His disciples, "I am the vine, you are the branches. He who abides in Me, and I in him, bears much fruit; for without Me you can do nothing." (John 15:5)

Jesus tells his disciples and us that we should depend on Him as our life source. Without being in contact with Him, we are ineffective, unproductive Christians. Christ is the true Vine—our source of spiritual nourishment. The faithful believers are the branches and they are powerless to produce fruit if they do not abide in Him. Those who do, however, produce much fruit by their exemplary lives. To abide in Him is to continue to remain in His perfect will at all costs. His Words should abide in us also and become a vital part of our Christian way of life.

If we wish, then, to become well-nourished healthy Christians, we must be in continual fellowship with Christ. Our faith is renewed through prayer, praise, study and obedience to His Word. It is often said that a well-read Bible is a sign of a well-fed soul. As we feast on the Scriptures we will receive his inexhaustible power and take fresh delight in its truths.

If we are to serve God effectively, and have a fruitful, power-filled life, we need to stay connected to Christ—our true Vine; our power source. When Jesus told His disciples, "Without Me you can do nothing," He was really saying, with Me you can do everything, including bearing much fruit! What an uplifting promise!

*M*any of us might be amazed if we could see how little turns in the road of life and unexpected circumstances have shaped the course of our lives. All of these events, no doubt, have been directed by the unseen hand of our loving Heavenly Father. The following event is one such example.

The British hymn writer, William Cowper, often suffered great mental anguish. At times, he even considered taking his own life. One night when in such a mood he called a horse-driven carriage and asked to be taken to the Thames River. The city of London was covered with such a thick fog that the driver lost his way. Cowper, impatient, jumped from the carriage, determined to find his cold wet grave on his own. Searching through the fog, he was amazed when he discovered that he was back at his own doorstep! Falling to his knees, he thanked God for the fog He had sent over London that prevented him from committing suicide. Realizing that God, in His grace, had directed this turn of events, Cowper wrote the words of the well-known hymn, "God moves in a mysterious way His wonders to perform; He plants His footsteps in the sea, and rides upon the storm...."

When we encounter surprising turns of events, disappointments, delays, detours, fulfillment of dreams—are these coincidences? Of course not! God has a purpose for everything that comes into our lives. We may not be able to comprehend the "why" at the time. Of one thing we can be certain, and that is that He leads us in times of great distress.

A verse from Romans 8:28 comes to mind. Faith is knowing that "All things work together for good to those who love God, to those who are called according to His purpose." Faith is not believing that all things are good, or that all things work well, according to our perspective. It does believe that all things, good or bad, work together for good according to His plan to those who love God.

The full dimension of God's love and care are beyond human comprehension. As children of God, we don't have to know the "why"—we don't even need to see through the "foggy" way, as long as we stay close to the One who does.

*A*n interesting expression was used by someone in my presence, describing an individual's attitude of unforgiveness. This person said, "He never forgets slights done to him, which is his basic weakness. Oh, he might give the impression that he has buried the hatchet for a time, but you can be sure that he has marked the spot, ready to dig it out at the appropriate time." Not having heard the expression quite like that before, I could hardly keep a straight face. If it weren't sad, I would have laughed. It struck me so funny that I excused myself and walked away.

When people hurt us, and even apologize later, we may say that we forgive them, but we often let our minds dwell on those past hurts. We find it hard to let go. But the Word of God teaches us that love does not keep score or a record of wrongs. Love excludes evil. Instead, love forgives and forgets. That is Christ's law of forgiveness as taught in the gospels and in our Lord's Prayer: "Forgive us our debts as we forgive our debtors" (Mt. 6:12 – 15). God does not forgive us because we forgive others, but solely because of His great mercy. Those who are unwilling to forgive have not become one with Christ, Who forgave even those who crucified Him (Lk. 23:34).

The Bible doesn't tell us that we shouldn't feel angry, but it points out that it is important to handle our anger properly. If vented thoughtlessly, anger can hurt others and destroy relationships, often for life. If bottled up inside, it can cause us to become bitter and destroy us from within. The Apostle Paul tells us to deal with our anger immediately in a way that will restore the bridges of our relationships with others, rather than destroy them by building walls. The challenge of the New Testament is that we should change our way of thinking and be transformed by the renewing of our minds (Rom. 12:2). In time, renewed patterns of thinking result in changed feelings, giving us the power to control our anger and past hurts.

When we commit our circumstances into God's hands, not only have we taken the first step in overcoming our anger, but also God's divine influence grants us a new restrained kind of self-control. As we read in Gal. 5:22, 23, "The fruit of the spirit is love, joy, peace, patience, kindness, goodness, faithfulness, gentleness and self-control." If we want the fruit of the spirit to grow in us, we must read God's Word more often. As a result, we will be fulfilled and become healthier, happier, blessed individuals! We can choose to take that step today.

With God's help we can be bridge builders, not only in our personal lives, but also help others who are separated by walls. Let us bury the hatchet for good, and not mark the spot where we buried it. Christianity is about Christ and His loving, forgiving and compassionate gift of eternal life. Let us allow Him to shine through us so others can see His Light.

*D*riving in England can be a trying experience for Americans. The British drive on the left side of the road and sit on the right side of the car. Most challenging are some intersections called "roundabouts" that have no stoplights. Before one enters these fast moving traffic circles, one must know which lane leads where. The outer lane, for example, leads to the first exit. The middle lane half way around, and the inside lane, some three quarters of the way around. If a motorist happens to get in the wrong lane, he or she may end up going to an unintended road, or continuing in circles. It is easy to make a mistake.

Many people today can make a mistake when faced with a decision whether to choose God's way or the way they desire. It is easy to make a mistake in this roundabout of life as well. We can try to chart our course ahead of time, but to whom do we turn when the twists and turns, or unexpected detours of life come upon us?

In the Gospel of John, Christ says, "I am the Way and the Truth and the Life." (14:6) He is not one way among many, but "The Way"! This is one of the most basic and important passages in Scripture.

Often our environment could influence us to follow the wrong path. Especially when we are young, we want to be accepted. Therefore, we find it difficult to believe that friends and acquaintances could be luring us into taking the wrong path. While we should be accepting of others, we need a healthy skepticism about human behavior. When we feel that we are being heavily influenced by those around us, let us proceed with caution. God did not create us to live a life of failure, but of success. As long as we follow His Way, do His Will, allowing Him to work in our lives, we cannot fail.

When we trust our Creator, we can be confident that He knows the way because He is "The Way," and ready to travel along with each one of us. Why not then confidently choose to follow His Way through life's roundabouts to a life, not of failure, but to a life of success!

*W*hile in line at the supermarket, a total stranger strongly complained to me about the hot weather. I smiled, then I said, "Personally, I thank God for this beautiful weather. What if we had a terrible earthquake instead. Think about it. Let's not be complainers." He looked surprised by my response, smiled, then he said, "You're right about that, but I still like to complain." Some people are not happy unless they are unhappy. This incident reminds me of the following story.

A nearsighted man visited a museum with his wife and friends. Although he had forgotten his glasses at home and couldn't see clearly, that didn't stop him from expressing his strong critical opinions about the exhibit. Standing before what he thought was a full length portrait, he began to criticize it. Nothing seemed right; the frame was all wrong, the man in the portrait was too shabbily dressed. And why had the artist chosen such a subject for his portrait, etc. As he went on and on, his wife pulled him aside and whispered, "My dear, you are looking in a mirror."

Why is complaining so harmful for us Christians? Because if that's all people see in us, they would get a false impression of Christ and His Church. If as Christians we constantly complain about people and conditions within or out of church, it would only demonstrate that we lack the unifying power of Jesus Christ.

The Apostle Paul teaches us to do all things without complaining and disputing, that we may become blameless children of God without fault, in the midst of a crooked generation, among whom we shine as lights in the world (Phil. 2:14, 15). Believers are expected to demonstrate their character in the midst of a dark culture, and shine as the sun, moon, and stars in an otherwise dark sky; a metaphorical reference by St. Paul to our Christian character.

Are we shining brightly, reflecting Christ's light in our environment, or are we clouded by complaining and disputing? God expects us to have the right attitude in pursuing wisdom in His Word. Faultfinders are not reliable factfinders. The enemies of Christ even tried to find fault in the only One Who ever lived a perfect life. Because they looked for the worst, they were blind to the best.

Jesus said, "Why do you look at the speck in your brother's eye, but do not consider the plank in your own eye?" (Matt. 7:3) We must examine our own motives and conduct instead of judging others. Rather than complaining or criticizing the shortcomings of others, let's look in the mirror of God's Word and ask Him to help us see our own faults clearly. As we learn to see people through the eyes of Christ, which is love, we won't be so quick to point out any specks in others—even such simple things as complaining about the weather!

*M*ost of us would agree that God has created us with the need to be needed. Knowing that we have something to offer can keep us going, even under the most difficult circumstances.

The following story is told of Mr. X, who had given up on himself and on life. Even though he was barely fifty years old, he had been through seven heart surgeries that settled him into a pattern of depression. He felt he had nothing to live for, except being in and out of hospitals.

One day, however, while walking depressed near a dock along the shores of Florida, he noticed a dying pelican lying helplessly on the rocks. Mr. X nursed the pelican back to health, and he continues to do the same ever since, for more than 2,400 birds. He is known now to many as the "Pelican Man." He has devoted his life to nursing birds that have been injured by motorboat propellers and other accidents. This has indeed resulted in a two-fold healing process. Not only have thousands of birds been helped, but Mr. X has found a reason and purpose for living.

The Apostle Paul experienced the pain and loneliness of imprisonment, and often longed to be with Christ in heaven. But he knew that others desperately needed his teaching, encouragement and prayers. His whole purpose in life was to bring the Gospel to as many as possible. He considered this awesome commitment a privilege. This was his purpose for living, and he chose to do so with joy.

His words continue to encourage us today. He teaches us, as he did to the Philippian faithful, to be unified, as we stand fast in one spirit, with one mind, striving together to live a purposeful life (Phil. 1: 23 – 27).

Why not then, take his advice and consider this commitment a privilege. Nothing is hopeless when our hope and faith are in God. We can make a difference to so many; in our churches, schools or wherever we are called to serve our Armenian Community. We can begin while we are in good health, and praise God for it! We are all very much needed indeed!

*T*he ironies of history are often overwhelming and difficult for us to comprehend. But God has His amazing ways of turning evil into glorious victories. The following historical facts are good examples of such truths.

The French writer and philosopher, Voltaire, whose anti-Christian beliefs are well-known, had predicted that Christianity would disappear from existence within 100 years. Yet, only 50 years after he died in 1779, the German Bible Society occupied Voltaire's house and used his printing press to produce stacks of Bibles!

During World War II, Adolf Hitler had built an impressive structure in Monte Carlo. It was to be a radio station to broadcast Nazi propaganda into Europe and North Africa. Today, from that very same building, Trans World Radio beams the gospel of Christ's redeeming love all across Europe, the former Soviet Union and Africa.

Some time ago, on the "Hour of Power," the Christian television ministry of the Rev. Dr. Robert Schuller, a Russian Christian young man was introduced who happily announced that a Russian satellite, which once broadcast Communist propaganda daily, was now proclaiming the Word of God to the Russian people.

Could our human imagination have ever conceived of these ironies? God has His ways of turning the tables on evil, transforming such events into unexpected glorious victories. Apostle Paul wrote of a day when every knee shall bow, and every tongue shall confess that Christ is Lord, to the glory of God (Phil. 2:10 – 11).

Closer to home, our people in Armenia are free to worship God once again without repression. Our anointed and blessed spiritual leaders nourish our people with our Christian faith, teach them of God's love and satisfy their spiritual hunger. Who would have thought a few years ago that the Soviet Union would have fallen apart! We praise God for His amazing miracles! One cannot help but wonder why our forefathers, who were the very first to accept Christianity as a nation, suffered for so many years. Countless of our courageous Christian brothers and sisters lost their precious lives for their unshakable faith in God. Others experienced terrible hardships and persecution. Some still do in various non-Christian countries. Why so much grief and torment, we ask.

Again, the Word of God teaches us from Isaiah 55: "For My thoughts are not your thoughts, neither are your ways My ways. As the heavens are higher than the earth, so are My ways higher than your ways and My thoughts than your thoughts." God's mysterious and miraculous ways are indeed inconceivable to our human wisdom and understanding. We can only trust Him and His Word, and walk by faith and not by sight.

The ironies of history are overwhelming and comforting indeed. It is assuring that the righteous will be vindicated, and God will have the final word in His time and in His way, timed by His clock. Nothing is too small for Him to notice, and nothing is too big for Him to accomplish. He has the big picture and has a divine plan for each one of us. He still moves mountains!

*S*ports and competitive athletic games have been an important part of human life in most cultures. Someone always seems to break the world record for one thing or another. The joy of victory is indeed sweet for the recipients of medals, trophies, cups, etc.

Sports were seldom mentioned in the Old Testament. It had no significant place in ancient Israel. From ancient times, however, the Greeks had promoted athletic contests. Their sports included boxing, wrestling, discus throwing, racing, etc. The victor was awarded a crown; a wreath made of olive branches—a most desired prize in ancient Greece.

The Apostle Paul makes use of the Greek athletic games to illustrate the spiritual race of the believer. In 1 Cor. 9:25, he says, "They do it to obtain a perishable crown, but we do it for an imperishable crown." All through his teachings, we clearly see the determination of a disciplined spiritual champion! Expecting his imminent departure to be with Christ, the Apostle declared, "I have fought the good fight, I have finished the race, I have kept the faith." (2 Tim. 4:7, 8) He had completed the work that God had given him to do, and as a reward he anticipated the "crown of righteousness."

Christian life resembles the life of an athlete. Disciplined life is the training ground for Christian maturity. When we are empowered with the Holy Spirit, we must not just observe from the grandstands as spiritual spectators, but enter the "race" with joy. As Christian "athletes" we know that the essential disciplines of prayer, Bible study, worship and fellowship with other Christians equip us with the faith to run with enthusiasm, stamina and joy. By this we can also be a shining example to others who might wish to join the race.

In all competitive races, only one wins the prize, only one is crowned. In our spiritual race, all men, all women, people of all nations can be winners through faith in Christ. We can all be victorious and worthy of the "imperishable crown of life!" Are we ready to enter the race? Let us run with perseverance—let us run for the gold.

*D*riving through a busy intersection in Rapid City, South Dakota, we saw a huge billboard that read, "Have You Encouraged Someone Today?" By the time my husband and I had seen it, we had already passed it. It was large, red, with big white letters; definitely an eye-catcher. Who was promoting this we had not seen. Even though we were on our way to Mount Rushmore, we drove around the block to look again. In the lower right hand corner we saw a very small sign for a popular fast-food chain. We were amazed and impressed. What clever advertising! Five simple words, and yet it caught everyone's attention and made us think. Have you encouraged someone today? What a wonderful suggestion!

Sometimes it doesn't take much to get us down. Even on the sunniest day, an unkind remark from someone or bad news of some sort could discourage us and put a cloud of gloom over our day. Discouragement makes simple tasks a struggle. Some of us might also be discouraged because the work that God has called us to do is off to a slow start. We know as Christians that we should be joyful, and yet often times, something seems to be working against us. It is at times like these, we must remember that some of the most wonderful inventions we enjoy today got off to a slow start.

The first electric light, for example, was so dim that a candle was needed to see its socket. One of the first steamboats took 32 hours to make its way from New York to Albany, a distance of 150 miles. Wilbur and Orville Wright's first airplane flight is said to have lasted only 12 seconds. And the first automobiles traveled two to four miles per hour, and broke down often. Carriages would pass them with their passengers shouting, "Get a horse!" But look at what these inventions are capable of today! What would have happened if these people had given up.

All of us need a word of encouragement from time to time, especially when we are facing new challenges. We also need words of appreciation as we carry out our daily responsibilities, whether at home or at work. A word of approval, recognition, a friendly smile and an honest expression let them know we care.

Barnabus, a disciple of Christ, is a good example. The apostles called him "Son of Encouragement," because that's what his name meant, and he lived by that reputation. Apostle Paul probably never forgot how Barnabus had accepted him, encouraged him, while the other apostles remained skeptical of the newly converted Saul (Paul) of Tarsus. Barnabus had the gift of discernment. He saw beyond the surface, recognized Paul's God-given ability of evangelism and encouraged him. And God used Paul in a mighty way by guiding him to bring the Gospel to Asia and Europe.

Encouraging our fellow man can make the difference between giving up or going on. It may only take a few moments, but the results can last a lifetime. Is anyone among us off to a slow start? Let us not allow a rough beginning get us down. Let us look up and trust God. He can make a great finish out of a slow start! In the meantime, let us determine to encourage, not flatter, at least one person every day. It may not seem important to say a word or two, but to a discouraged person, what wonders it can do!

*B*lessed is the nation whose God is Lord!

The remarkable document known as the Declaration of Independence, approved by the members of the Second Continental Congress, declares belief in God. The writers of this notable proclamation knew that the unrestricted freedoms they were proposing could work well only in a society where the Creator is acknowledged and revered. They confirmed that God has granted people with the right to "life, liberty, and the pursuit of happiness" because He esteems values and loves each one of us.

President Thomas Jefferson (1801 – 1891), who mistakenly is often called an agnostic, was quite grieved by the injustice and wrongful acts he saw. He wrote, "I tremble for my country when I reflect that God is just." These are words of a truly troubled leader. If he trembled then, we can imagine what he would have written or said about this generation in his beloved country, the United States of America.

This country has been blessed because it was founded on biblical principles. But we are gradually losing our God-granted freedoms because unfortunately, society is denying that God is Lord. With the refusal to acknowledge Him, an attitude which grows worse with every succeeding generation, it is no wonder violent crimes in the USA have climbed to unbelievable levels. The Apostle Paul advises the Galatian faithful in 5:13, "Do not use liberty as an opportunity for the flesh, but through love, serving one another."

Freedom is dangerous in the hands of those who abuse it. The human spirit longs for freedom. But for some people, the pursuit of freedom leads to greater bondage. A body tortured by cravings of alcohol, drugs, or wastes away with some other addiction hardly sounds like freedom. Right living gives freedom from disastrous consequences. Unfortunately some people often use freedom's luxury to live selfishly or claim ownership of what God has merely entrusted to all.

For a follower of Christ, freedom comes only within the sphere of honoring God and His Word. Jesus said, "If you abide in My Word, you are my disciples indeed. Then you will know the truth, and the truth shall set you free" (John 8:31, 32). True freedom can never be enjoyed by people who refuse to acknowledge God. One of the most endearing verses from the Old Testament is in 2 Chronicles 7:14; "If my people who are called by my name will humble themselves, and pray and seek my face, and turn from their wicked ways, then I will hear from heaven and will forgive their sin and heal the land." True repentance means changed behavior. Let us pray for our nation, that its citizens will live as God's people should. Freedom is not getting our own way, but doing things God's way.

*A*ll seemed calm and business continued as usual, but there was a fire engine in front of a fast food restaurant. I stopped to get a soft drink. The problem was in the children's play area. A small child, during play, had wandered into the highest section of the colorful tubes and couldn't find his way down. Directions from his mom below didn't help. A slender fireman went into the tube and brought the four-year-old down. The child wasn't in any danger—just frightened.

Children with the spirit of adventure often get carried away. They cannot calculate the final outcome of their actions. It is natural. Children will always be children. But in the gospel of Luke 14:28 – 33 Jesus gives us adult Christians some valuable insights about the cost of being a disciple. He says, "Suppose one of you wants to build a tower. Will he not first estimate the cost to see if he has enough money to complete it? For if he lays the foundation and is not able to finish it, everyone who sees it will ridicule him…Or suppose a king is about to go to war against another king. Will he not first consider whether he is able with 10,000 men to oppose the one coming against him with 20,000? If he is not able, he will send a delegation and will ask for terms of peace. In the same way, any of you who does not give up everything he has, cannot be My disciple."

The multitudes who were with Jesus were positive but uncommitted. Therefore, Jesus was setting up an extreme condition to make a point. He set the cost of discipleship as high as possible, and encouraged them to take careful inventory before declaring their willingness to follow. Jesus was establishing priorities. Calculating the cost is certainly important before undertaking any serious project. Only those willing to carefully assess the cost and invest their will, time and treasure to His kingdom are worthy to enter.

What are those costs? Christians may face loss of social status or even wealth. This still happens in some countries. They may have to give up control of their time and part of their career. They may have to give up their comfortable lives, their time of leisure or retirement, to travel to foreign countries to help those in need. Serving Christ is not, by any means, a trouble-free life. We must carefully count the cost of becoming Christ's disciples so that we won't be tempted later to turn back. It is an unconditional commitment to Him without reservations; each of us according to our God-given gifts and talents.

Jesus did not want a blind, naïve commitment that expected only blessings. That would be childish. As a builder estimates costs, or a king evaluates military strength, so should a person consider what Jesus expects of us. As Christians we owe an unqualified loyalty and love to God. Then, because we put Him first, we are to love others. The two go hand in hand.

*G*reat spiritual endurance is essential to great achievements. Christian missionaries come to mind. Often these individuals sacrifice a comfortable lifestyle to share the message of Christ with those who have never heard it. Why? Because of their burning desire to obey God's calling.

The story is told that such a well-established missionary work had started in India by a man I'll call Mr. Z. His supporters in England sent a young man to assist him. Soon they were turning out portions of the Bible for distribution. Mr. Z had spent many years learning the language so that he could produce the Scriptures in the local dialect. He had also prepared dictionaries and other grammar books for future use.

One day, while the two were away, a fire broke out and completely destroyed the building, Bibles, and all manuscripts. When Mr. Z returned and saw the tragic loss, he showed no sign of despair. Instead, he knelt and thanked God that he still had the endurance to do the work over again. He started at once, wasting no time in self pity. Before his death, he had duplicated and even improved on his previous achievements! It is admirable when one has the ability to meet such tragic loss with such an attitude of strength. It is evidence of a faith that has not only been well tested, but a faith firmly rooted in God.

The Apostle Paul tells us in Romans 5:3 – 5 to "...rejoice in your sufferings because we know that suffering produces perseverance; perseverance character; and character, hope. And hope does not disappoint us, because God has poured out His love into our hearts..." St. Paul tells us to rejoice in suffering, not because we like pain or deny the reality of its tragedy, but because we know God is using life's difficulties to build our character.

Perhaps some of us find our patience tested in some way every day. We are advised to thank God for those opportunities to grow, and deal with them in His strength. That is why Mr. Z knelt and thanked God that he still had the strength to start over.

The written word can be lost, burned, destroyed, but not the Living Word! That is in our hearts. That is Christ Himself.

*I*s there a striking contrast between the behavior of Christians on Sundays in church and on weekdays out in the world? The story is told of a young man who was being interviewed for a position in a small business firm. The applicant had a neat business appearance and made a good impression on the owner. He had also prepared an excellent resume in which he listed as references his pastor, his Sunday school teacher and a church deacon. The owner of the business studied the young man's resume for a few minutes, then said, "I appreciate these recommendations from your church friends. What I would really like, however, is a word from someone who knows you on weekdays."

It is unfortunate that in some instances there is a remarkable contrast between the behavior of Christians in church on Sundays and out in the world on weekdays. God's principles that we hear on Sundays, and have known from childhood in our homes, should be practiced consistently all through the week.

Daniel's life from the Old Testament comes to mind. He was an ideal model in his relationship with both God and man. He did not practice double standards. His daily conduct was consistent with his spiritual values. His enemies tried to find some charge or fault against him, but nothing could be found! His walk before the world was in harmony with his walk with God. (Daniel 6:4)

Would our church friends be shocked if they observed our actions, attitudes, and heard our speech at our jobs or in some other environment? If we are faithful "Sunday Christians," we will be faithful "Weekday Christians" as well. We must be rooted in God's Word and principles continuously so we won't be shaken by circumstances. Our spiritual nourishment will provide divine wisdom to sustain us, and provide stability in our daily lives under all circumstances. Then there will be no contrast in our behavior in church and out in the world. A good "Sunday Christian" will also be a good "Weekday Christian."

*P*romotions and blessings are known to go to those who are faithful in little things. God places us in positions of service best suited according to the talents He has given us. As Christians we are to develop our talents and do our best by using our God-given opportunities, no matter how small they may seem. When God wants to promote us, He'll do it in His own way and in His own time.

American botanist, George Washington Carver's life story is an example. He was the son of slave parents. In spite of poverty and race prejudice, he obtained an education and devoted it to scientific research. He created countless new uses for old products which the Southern soil yields, including 300 manufactured products from the humble peanut! He called his chemistry laboratory "God's little workshop," and considered himself God's working partner, forgetting all the hardships he faced daily in the joy of his work.

The story is told that he once asked God to tell him about the universe. According to Carver, the Lord replied, "George, the universe is just too big for you to comprehend. Suppose you let Me take care of that." Humbled, Carver asked, "Lord, how about a peanut?" The Lord said, "Now, George, that's something your own size. Go to work on it, and I'll help you." When Carver had completed studying the peanut, he had discovered more than 300 products that could be made from that simple peanut!

That is not to say that we should not be thinking big and wanting to do something extraordinary or important. But as Christians, we should bring our goals and dreams to God in prayer, asking for His will to be done through us. We must also be willing to start at the bottom with little things, if that is His plan for us. We read in the Gospel of St. Luke 16:10, "Whoever can be trusted with very little can also be trusted with much." We have been given excellent resources and are expected to use these talents so that they multiply as we serve faithfully the Giver, our Creator. When we don't allow our integrity to slip in small matters, it will not fail us in crucial decisions as well. In God's service, promotions to greater trustworthiness go to those who are faithful in little things—to those who are willing to start, even with "peanuts."

*S*moke detectors are a must in every household. An inspector came to our neighborhood, explaining the law regarding smoke detectors, and informing us that he would be back a few weeks later to see if every room and hallway had one. And he did! Yet, how often do we read or see on TV news of lives lost due to fire that swept through an apartment as people slept. One fire incident was reported that while the house was equipped with several smoke detectors, the fire inspectors concluded that the devices had been deactivated for a party the night before. This was done to keep them from sounding off due to smoke from cooking and candles!

There is an interesting parallel to the smoke detector's alarms and the voice of our conscience. As Christians, our conscience is very much like an active smoke detector that warns us when we are about to take wrong actions or are headed in that direction. We must never ignore or deactivate the alarm system in us because the consequences can be very serious.

In Old Testament times, God often communicated in tangible, visible and audible ways—the burning bush, the Ten Commandments on tablets of stone, pillar of fire, a still small voice—to name a few. But when Jesus came, all that changed. He told His disciples that God's Spirit would live, not only among them, but also within them. Before His Ascension to the Father, Jesus promised His disciples that He would not leave them comfortless or as orphans, but would come to them through His Holy Spirit. The Holy Spirit did indeed come on the Day of Pentecost (Acts 2), not only upon the disciples, but also in the hearts of all those who believed and put their trust in Him. To have the Holy Spirit is to have Christ Himself in us!

As children of God, we must believe that the Holy Spirit was not sent to annoy or irritate us like a sensitive smoke detector. It only guides us as a moral compass pointing us towards the way which we already know we should take. The Holy Spirit does not send false alarms and neither do His batteries ever expire or run low. What a blessing it is to have that warning – the principles of God's Word!

Interestingly, the Apostle Paul, knowing human nature well, advises the Ephesians and us that if we want to avoid being tempted by any wrongful acts, to wear the armor of God at all times. He says, "Be strong in the Lord and in the power of His might. Put on the whole armor of God, that you may be able to stand against the wiles of the devil" (Eph. 6:10, 11). To withstand evil attacks of any temptation, we must depend on God's Holy Spirit's strength and use every piece of His armor.

To turn a deaf ear to the voice of our conscience is to invite trouble. Therefore, let us be even more aware of that "still small voice" in us, the Holy Spirit, and allow Him to guide us daily, and praise God for it!

*W*ise planning is something we all like to do. Students plan ahead for higher education by carefully choosing schools in their field of study. Those who wish to build a house consult architects and builders, visit model homes, or even wait for the best market conditions to act. Others may already be thinking ahead to their retirement years and plan accordingly.

The Bible encourages wise planning. The book of Proverbs contains many statements that counsel this. "The plans of the diligent lead to profit, as surely as haste leads to poverty." (12:15) Careful planning is wise. Including God in our plans and seeking His will is even wiser. This kind of planning brings forth blessings.

It is sensible to make plans for the future and seek God's will, but we must do this with an awareness of life's uncertainty. The Apostle James brings forth the actual and simple realities of life. We read in 4:13 to 15, "You who say, today or tomorrow we will go to such and such city, spend a year there, carry on business...whereas you do not know what will happen tomorrow. For what is your life? It is even a vapor that appears for a little time and then vanishes away. Instead you ought to say, if it is the Lord's will, we shall live and do this or that." The Apostle is pointing out that by including God in our plans, we acknowledge Him in our preparation for the future.

It is commendable and wise to have goals, but goals will disappoint us if God is not included in our plans. There is no point in going forward as though God does not exist. Our future is in His hands. When we make God's will the center of our plans, we will never be disappointed.

We are, after all, included in His plans—why not include Him in ours. That will be wise planning.

𝒫eople often use the expression that they are "searching" for God, or that they have "found" God; as though the Creator of the universe is playing a game of hide-and-seek with them. God's love and presence is with us always. While we are often told to seek God, this does not mean that God is lost, nor is He hiding. If anyone is lost, it's us, the people—separated from God by sin. Therefore, God sent His only begotten Son to show us the way to the Father. Jesus says, "I am the Way, the Truth, and the Life. No one comes to the Father except through Me" (Jn.14:6). He gave His life on the cross for us so that we could have the forgiveness of sin and a new relationship with God.

The Apostle Paul's enthusiastic preaching and devotion stirred up plenty of persecution. In Thessalonica and Berea, his life being in danger, he escaped to Athens, Greece (Acts 17:10 – 20). Athens, with its magnificent temples and the many gods that the Greeks worshiped, was the center of culture, philosophy and education.

In Athens, the Apostle Paul was greatly distressed to see that the city was full of idols. Here was a nation so advanced in culture and education, yet, they did not know the One True God! They were certainly "searching," but were not aware of their true Creator. These philosophers were always ready to hear and discuss something new, so they invited Paul to speak to them. The Apostle spoke respectfully to his pagan audience, even affirming the words of some of their poets.

Then Paul, having seen an idol the Athenians had built to an "unknown god," because of their fear of missing blessings or of receiving punishment, took advantage of this inscription and used it as a point of entry for his preaching about the One True God! He proclaimed to them the good news of Jesus Christ, His ministry, death and resurrection. Unfortunately, the spiritual eyesight and understanding of Paul's audience were shut tight. They were blinded by scales just as Paul (Saul) himself was blinded while on the road to Damascus several years earlier (Acts 9). The Athenians sneered at him and called Paul a "babbler" with strange ideas. Although few became followers of the Apostle and believed, there is no record that Paul ever established a church in Athens. This was around 50 – 57 A.D.

Accepting Christ as our Savior is a step of faith. Maturing in Christ is a journey of faith – an ongoing lifelong process that involves reading and studying His Word. As we mature in God's Word, veils will fall from our eyes, layer after layer, so we will be able to see more clearly the wonders of His Truths. So let's be patient with our new friends in Christ as we go along our journey of joyful discovery to the divine truths of His Word.

On a TV show, the host interviewed several lottery winners who had won millions. The important question he focused on was: "Are you happy now that you are millionaires?" Some confessed that after their first extravagant spending spree and a few exotic vacations, their happiness had faded somewhat. Others said that they had lost a number of friends when they stopped giving out gifts. And still others reported that money had created a whole new set of problems with some family members, including divorce. But one woman summarized the "Are you happy?" question with "Yes and no." Then she added, "I now can buy whatever I want, but a few weeks later, the emptiness in my soul comes back. Then what?"

Most of us know that true happiness doesn't come as a result of the things we have. Even a brand new car loses most of its power to thrill us after a while. Bigger and better does not make it best. And although we claim to trust in God, we act otherwise. A limitless budget seems more secure to us than God's promises to provide. But the Apostle Paul assures us that money is the uncertain part. Indeed, it is possible to run short of money, but we'll never run short of God's power to provide both essential and enjoyable extras.

To appreciate God's limitless power to provide, it is useful to consider the limitations of money with the following wise thought-provoking words: "Money will buy: a bed, but not sleep; food, but not appetite; a house, but not a home; amusement, but not happiness; a cross, but not a Savior; a church pew, but not heaven." What money can't buy, Christ gives freely!

We all know that happiness and wealth are not synonymous. Lasting joy comes when we put Christ first and serve Him. The Apostle Paul advises young Timothy, "Godliness with contentment is great gain. For we brought nothing into this world, and it is certain we can carry nothing out" (1 Tim. 6:6, 7). This statement is the key to spiritual growth and personal fulfillment. Apostle Paul had "learned" to be content in whatever state he was. He said he learned it because it does not come naturally to any of us. He had discovered that one great joy – the joy of knowing and serving Christ.

As I was growing up, my wise Christian mother often quoted to me Proverbs 17:22. "A joyful heart does good like medicine, but a broken spirit dries up the bones." She usually said this when I needed to change my attitude. That was it! No sermons, no lecture, just one verse about the phenomenal value of God-produced happiness that springs from the heart. Just one verse, and we didn't even have a Bible. In fact, no one in the entire Armenian community of 60 families in Larissa, Greece, owned one! Nevertheless, my mom knew that the state of my heart would reveal the look on my face.

The millionaires confessed their sets of problems. But St. Paul held the secret to lasting joy. It is in knowing and trusting Christ, and being rich in good works! Content people are never poor; the discontented are never rich!

*M*ost of us remember studying about the Minutemen. During the American Revolution, ordinary citizens banded together to form an effective army. These patriotic citizens were from all walks of life; farmers, businessmen, bankers, blacksmiths, carpenters, etc. When they heard the threat of war, they dropped their work, took their guns and headed into battle. They wasted no time searching through their attics or basements looking for their guns. They did not stop to clean or test them. They were prepared, ready for action in a minute!

These Minutemen bring to mind the dedicated workmen of Nehemiah's days who held their tools in one hand and their swords and spears in the other (Neh. 4:17). They were there to rebuild the walls of Jerusalem, which were in ruins. They encountered opposition from their enemies who wished to see the city unprotected. But Nehemiah, with faith in God, skillfully armed and arranged his men, and worked day and night. The wall was built in record time (52 days) despite opposition, and even their enemies fearfully admitted that God was with these builders (Neh. 6:16).

Preparation and readiness is everything. How do we rate as God's "Minutemen" and "Minutewomen"? Are we prepared and ready for action to be useful to our fellow man and community? Are we ready to display our Christian values and principles at any moment of the day? Perhaps a friend, a co-worker, a neighbor might ask for our opinion or input on a personal matter. Are we ready to give honest, practical answers based on biblical principles and values. Anyone can give answers based on what the other person wants to hear.

It takes preparation to be minutemen and minutewomen for Christ. If we wish to be one, readiness is imperative. Let's not store our Bibles on the shelf, but store God's Word in our hearts, wear it as our armor, and always be ready in His service. Our church and community need us as well. Are we ready and available? In God's service our greatest ability is our availability. God is working through His people to accomplish seemingly impossible tasks. He often shapes us with experiences that prepare us for His purpose. God prepared and positioned Nehemiah to accomplish one of the Old Testament's seemingly impossible tasks.

Some of us might feel we can do nothing great for God. But most great accomplishments are done by dedicated people working side by side; such as the American Minutemen and Nehemiah's workmen. People under God's direction can do what most would consider impossible tasks. Let us not be discouraged and always keep in mind Philippians 4:13; "I can do all things through Christ Who strengthens me." Let us be ready to be God's minutemen and minutewomen with joy!

*B*read was a principal commodity of life for all people in biblical times. No doubt, the term "bread" was often used to denote food in general. Bread was made primarily from wheat or barley, the latter being eaten mostly by the poor. In fact, bread was so basic a food that it became synonymous with life itself. "Eating bread" was the equivalent phrase for "having a meal." For example, we read in Gen. 43:31 – 32, "….the Egyptians could not eat bread with the Hebrews."

In the New Testament, bread was also the one basic food in everyone's diet; a symbol of life's necessities. It represented nourishment in its many forms. Therefore, we see it in the Lord's Prayer as well, "Give us this day our daily bread" (Luke 11:3). It is a prayer for daily provision of food itself. Bread was something so basic that Jesus referred it to Himself. "I am the Bread of Life. He who comes to Me shall never hunger" (John 6:34, 35). His audience responded, "From now on Lord, give us this bread always." This statement, once again, demonstrated the blindness of the crowd, for they were thinking of some physical bread, and failed to understand the spiritual implication that Jesus was that "Bread."

Christ is the sustenance of our lives. The life He gives is eternal; not something to be achieved, but to receive by faith in Him. Yes, we eat bread to satisfy physical hunger, and nowadays we have a vast variety to select from to sustain physical life. But we can only satisfy spiritual hunger and sustain spiritual life by a right relationship with Christ. Jesus further says, "I am the Living Bread which came down from heaven. If anyone eats of this bread, he will live forever" (John 6:51). Christ refers here prophetically to His impending sacrifice on the cross. To eat "Living Bread" means to accept Christ into our lives and allow His spirit to reside in our hearts. We must believe in His death and resurrection, live according to his teachings, and trust His Holy Spirit's power. By participating in communion, Christians also receive the Living Bread in memory of Christ.

There is a deep spiritual hunger within all of us. Sigmund Freud believed people are hungry for love. Karl Jung wrote that we crave security. But Christ declared, "I am the Bread of life." If we want the deepest hunger of our lives and souls satisfied, we need to go to Him to be filled. The bread that Christ offers symbolizes His promise to provide for every person who has chosen to obey Him, and to depend upon Him for all their needs. Christ is our only life-producing, Living Bread Who satisfies all our spiritual hunger! He is the Bread of Life.

*B*arney, the great big purple dinosaur, is very popular with most four-year-olds and younger. The creators of Barney's videos must be doing very well with sales. My grandson, when he was not quite two, is a great fan of this wholesome giant dinosaur, Barney.

The story is told that a four-year-old was taken to the doctor for a check up. The pediatric nurse allowed the child to use the stethoscope and listen to his own heart. At one point the nurse said, "Let's listen if Barney is in there knocking." The child replied, "But only Jesus is in my heart." The child was taught correctly.

Yes, Christ comes to live in every believer's heart when we invite Him in, and make Him the Lord of our lives. Out of unconditional love, Christ also eagerly knocks at the door of every human heart who has not yet turned to seek Him. That is why Christ is portrayed as standing outside the door knocking; a famous metaphor familiar to all of us.

Through His Holy Spirit and the teaching of His Word, Christ knocks at the door of our spiritual consciousness. "Behold, I stand at the door and knock. If anyone hears my voice and opens the door, I will come in to him and dine with him, and he with Me" (Rev. 3:20). Those who have seen the painting have also noticed that there is no doorknob. The door can only be opened from the inside. Are we willing to respond and open it? How incredible that Christ should be kept outside waiting! How gracious that He should still seek entrance! Christ is appealing to all those who have not yet turned to Him. He wishes to purify us, renew our minds through His Spirit, and build an intimate relationship with each of us.

Our heart is the very core of our being, the controlling center of our decisions and choices. When His Spirit enters into our lives, it becomes obvious to all. Can we each say our life is exemplary? Yes, it should be, so that when people get to know us, they will also want to know Christ as well. We read in Luke 6:45, "A good man (woman) out of the good treasure of his heart brings forth good....For out of the abundance of the heart the mouth speaks."

Jesus reminds us that our speech and actions reveal our true beliefs, attitudes and motivations. The good impressions we try to make cannot last if our hearts are deceptive. What is in our hearts will eventually come out in our speech and behavior.

Christ's invitation is three fold; if anyone hears, if anyone opens the door, if anyone is willing to dine with Him, He is ready to fellowship with each one of us. He is patient and persistent, but never forceful. He responds only when invited, allowing us to decide. Letting Him in is our only hope of lasting fulfillment. Christ's loving kindness is everlasting. Blessed are those who respond to His knock early in life.

*P*rayer is everyone's privilege. The gift of prayer is offered to all, and each of us may call upon the power of our almighty God. Often, however, when we make time to read the Bible and pray, we feel as though we are doing God a favor. We think that the primary reason we spend time with God is to please Him.

But when we examine the devotional life of Jesus, we see that although He is the Son of God, during His ministry on earth, He had felt dependent upon a power higher than Himself, and prayed a great deal. In all recorded prayers Jesus addressed God as "Father."

St. Mark in 1:35 describes this about Jesus: "Having risen a long while before daylight, He went out and departed to a solitary place; and there He prayed." As Jesus' public ministry gained fame and popularity, people flocked to hear Him preach and to have their infirmities healed. Therefore, Jesus often withdrew from the multitudes, seeking solitude in order to come into God's presence and pray.

If Jesus Himself needed solitude for prayer and renewal, how much more is this true for us? We must guard our time and not become so busy that life turns into a flurry of activity, leaving no room for quiet fellowship alone with God. Seeking solitude in prayer was an important priority for Jesus. He demonstrated what it means to live in complete harmony with the Father's will. His consistent prayer life provided a living example for His disciples and enabled Him to identify with our humanity.

Christ also prayed before significant events. The following are a few of the many recorded in the Bible: at His baptism (Luke 3:21); all night before choosing the 12 disciples (Luke 6:12); at the feeding of the 5000 (John 6:11); when He gave the Lord's Prayer to the disciples (Matthew 6:9 – 13); before raising Lazarus from the dead (John 11:41, 42); at the Last Supper (Matt. 26:26, 27); in the Garden of Gethsemane (Matt. 26:36 – 44); and on the cross (Luke 23:34).

We clearly see the pattern. Jesus drew aside often and prayed, and then went out to help others. Likewise, our time alone with God should urge us on to good works as well. Devotion to God leads not to lonely, fruitless living, but to a life dedicated to helping others with God's power. Prayer is the fuel for service!

Yes, prayer in church in fellowship with other faithful is very important. But private daily prayer is strictly a very personal matter between ourselves and God. If we do this often we will soon realize that there is no other single habit that will do so much to give us joy in life, and nourish and strengthen us for every emergency.

*W*e are driving on the freeway at about 55 – 60 miles per hour. If we were to take our eyes off the road for a second or two, what do we feel? Strong vibrations caused by the small bumps that are closely spaced on the pavement. These bumps along the shoulder of the road and separating the lanes warn us that we have drifted off to the side. Knowing the danger involved, we immediately come back to the center. The warning was well taken.

The Bible tells us about similar vibrations that God uses to correct us or warn us when we begin to drift away from Him. As followers of Christ, a similar principle is at work inside us. The Holy Spirit that dwells within us monitors our spiritual performance. He measures our thoughts, our speech and deeds by the standards of God's Word. When we drift away, the Spirit sends us signals to bring us back on course. These warning signals often may come to us from parents, through faithful Christian friends, prayer, the Scriptures, our conscience, from our pastor's messages, etc. But behind them all is the loving and faithful voice of God's Spirit and love.

In John 14:15 – 21, we see that Jesus would soon be leaving His disciples and this earth. But He promised to send His Holy Spirit to come and dwell in the hearts of all believers as a Counselor, Helper, Comforter. He gave His disciples the regenerating power of the Spirit just before His ascension (John 20:22), and the Holy Spirit was poured out on all believers on the day of Pentecost (Acts 2).

God always sends warnings to protect us. His Spirit guides us and urges us to make God–honoring choices. Are we sensitive enough to know and act on His divine warnings? We read in Prov. 10:17; "He who keeps instruction is in the way of life, but he who refuses correction goes astray."

Sometimes we drive ourselves beyond our physical and emotional limits. Our bodies weaken and illness may surface. That could also be a warning. By our own deeds, ambitions and excessive hours of work, our relationships with our loved ones often become strained or begin to break down. That also could be a warning.

Our prayer should be that God grants us discernment to be sensitive and act on His Spirit's warnings and not ignore them. We should open our hearts and minds to God with a teachable attitude, so when we feel the bumpy vibrations on life's freeway, we will know what to do. When we make God-honoring choices, we can travel smoothly and at top efficiency with God's blessings and the guidance of His Holy Spirit. It's the only way to go!

There are special nuggets of gold tucked away in the folds of every soul. They need only to be taken out, polished and used to serve humanity. Often the best thing that can happen to someone may appear to be a misfortune or an unexpected adversity. Through it they discover hidden resources, and give the world precious gems created by their hand, mind and heart. They find their special, tucked away treasures, turn their calamities into experiences of value and beauty, and come out victorious. It has been said, "People are like tea bags; they never know how strong they are until they get into hot water." The following individuals did just that.

After several financial failures, a Pennsylvania man developed a new kind of caramel candy. He believed there was a big market for a good five cent milk chocolate bar. Money-wise men scoffed at the idea. But that did not stop Milton S. Hershey from building a chocolate bar empire.

A fifteen year old boy was censored and asked to leave school because of lack of interest in his studies. His teachers thought he had a bent for mathematics, but he failed to pass the exam at the Swiss Federal Polytechnic School of Zurich. He finished training in another school, but was rejected as a teacher. This string of failures is the record of Albert Einstein.

Pierre and Marie Curie had conducted over 450 experiments to try to separate radium from pitchblende. All had failed. Finally, Pierre Curie said, "It can't be done. Maybe in a hundred years, but never in our life time." Madame Curie replied, "If it takes a hundred years, it will be a pity, but I dare not do less than work for it so long as I have life."

Rejection and scoffing hurt, and are very discouraging. Often, however, the best thing that can happen to us is a calamity; getting into "hot water." Through it we discover our hidden resources, and only then can we give to the world our precious hidden gems. "All things work together for good to those who love God" (Rom. 8:28).

Yes, there are times when various challenges of life set before us seem too overwhelming. We often forget that we are not alone, and that there is much more strength available to us than just our own. God is always with us. We must learn to draw upon that high divine power, and believe in ourselves as well. "According to your faith be it unto you" (Matt. 9:29) is a basic law of successful living.

Even when we feel that we have given our last ounce of strength, we must keep on going. Let us allow Christ to recharge our spiritual batteries. He is our divine power source. So, when we feel the deep hurt of rejection or discouragement, we can always look to Christ. He understands. He was scorned and rejected by many, especially His own countrymen. Those who trust in Him will never, never be rejected. He is the truest high power source we need.

*O*n our way home from a social function late one night, my husband and I stopped at a coffee shop for a quiet cup of coffee. The paper placemat caught my attention. Three colorful pictures of mouth-watering desserts were staring at me. These pictures were a challenging temptation, even to the most disciplined person on earth. I could not take my eyes off them. Their names were attractively written above each, and at the bottom, across the entire mat, I read what was written in big purple letters: "If there are seven deadly sins, then here are 8, 9 & 10."

Were they ever! What clever advertising, I thought. At the same time I realized that someone in this chain of coffee shops knew something about the seven deadly sins. I was even more impressed by that. When the waitress came, I asked her if I could have an extra place mat to take home.

At the first opportunity, I opened my Bible to the sixth chapter of Proverbs. One of the most serious lists in the Bible is God's itemization of the seven things He hates. Using the human body as a memory device, Solomon described seven things God hates. As the wisest of men, he wrote: "There are six things the Lord hates, seven that are detestable to Him: haughty eyes, a lying tongue, hands that shed innocent blood, a heart that devises wicked schemes, feet that are quick to rush into evil, a false witness who pours out lies, and a man who stirs up dissension among brothers." (Prov. 6:16 – 19)

At first glance, Proverbs seems to be a book of practical ethics. A closer look, however, shows how prominent and personal God is—a Creator Who loves us and longs for us to live honorably. This God-centeredness is stated in the key verse of Proverbs: "The fear of the Lord is the beginning of knowledge, but the fool despises wisdom and discipline" (Prov. 1:7). Fear, in this context, means a loving reverence and awe for God, and submission to His will.

In this age of information, knowledge is plentiful. But true knowledge and wisdom begin with God. When we choose to trust God, He grants us wisdom. A personal close relationship with God is everlasting. All else is perishable. Truly wise individuals seek to know and love God!

As for the mouth-watering, yummy desserts, I wouldn't exactly call them sinful. We could not resist—my husband and I shared one

$\mathcal{T}$he discussion was on sports as I approached a group of friends at a social gathering. One of them suddenly asked me what was the most adventurous activity I had ever participated in. Not being involved in any hazardous sports, I mentioned the one daring activity I had tried some thirteen years ago at a resort in Macedonia, Greece— parasailing. In a highly excited mood, I anticipated my turn to "fly." I wanted to experience the feeling of a bird. It was great! The discussion went on and all agreed that there was a time when skateboarding, surfing, and free style skiing were considered adventurous sports. Today's excitement has turned to a new category of adrenaline-pumping sports, like paragliding, rock climbing and bungee jumping. Life on the edge seems to have shifted to extreme adventures in sports for many.

Christianity is not a sport, but it certainly qualifies as life on the edge. Jesus calls each one of His followers to the ultimate life of adventure: "Whoever desires to come after Me, let him deny himself, and take up his cross, and follow Me. For whoever desires to save his life will lose it, but whoever loses his life for My sake and the gospel's shall save it." (Mark 8:34, 35)

Adventurous? Daring? You bet! Following Christ is the greatest risk to the selfish, to the "me-first" attitude held by so many. Hazardous? Extreme? No question about it! Self denial for the cause of Christ seems illogical, absurd in a world that urges us towards self indulgence. Exhilarating? Exciting? Absolutely yes! Serving God at any level brings the awesome rewards of His presence and power. Obeying God by faith puts us in partnership with the One Who changes lives.

Jesus uses the image of carrying the cross to illustrate the ultimate submission required of His followers. He is not against enjoyment or fun, nor is He saying that we should seek pain needlessly. He is talking about the heroic effort needed to follow Him, moment by moment, day by day, to do His will, even when the work is difficult. Jesus wants us to choose to follow Him, rather than to lead a life of self gratification.

Christ calls each one of us to a life of adventure! To say we are not our own, but His, is to have reached a great point in spiritual maturity. We are called to willingly give of ourselves to Christ's sovereignty. Our Lord makes disciples of His followers. He is accomplishing His work through us. That is a life of adventure! Do we want to be His followers? Are we ready to surrender our will to His? His call is, "Follow Me." Now that's an adventure with blessings!

*I*t was perhaps hard for the people of ancient times to imagine that the monuments which we call "The Seven Wonders of the World" would ever vanish. But except for one, they have all crumbled. The single remaining one is the pyramid of Cheops at Giza, Egypt, about eight miles from Cairo. It was built about 5,000 years ago as a tomb for a pharaoh.

The second wonder was the Hanging Gardens of Babylon, in what is now Iraq. Built about 600 B.C. by King Nebuchadnezzar for his Median queen. The walls were about 335 feet high, and its beauty described as beyond imagination. Today they are just a mass of ruins.

The third wonder was the statue of the god Zeus at Olympia, Greece. The figure was about 40 feet high, ornamented with gold, ivory and precious gems. No trace of it exists.

The fourth wonder was the temple of the goddess Diana at Ephesus, in what is now Turkey. Stone columns 60 feet high supported the roof. The temple contained some of the finest Grecian art. It was burned by the invading Goths in 262 A.D.

The fifth wonder was the tomb in the city of Halicarnassus in what is now Turkey. It was built for King Mausolus, who died in 353 B.C. It was such a splendid structure that we now call any elaborately decorated tomb a "mausoleum."

The sixth wonder was the Colossus of Rhodes, a bronze statue of Helios, the sun god. It was 105 feet high and straddled the island's port. It was destroyed in an earthquake in 224 B.C.

The seventh and last wonder was the Lighthouse of Pharos, begun in 283 B.C. on the island of Pharos off the coast of Egypt. It was about 600 feet high above its base, and its light guided ships to port. The beacon served for more than 1,500 years before it was destroyed by an earthquake.

Why has only one of the Seven Wonders of the World survived? Because of its foundation. The pyramid's foundation is wide, deep, unshakable. As recorded in Matthew 7:24 – 27, Jesus spoke of the wise and foolish builders. He stated that anyone who hears His words and puts them into practice is like a wise man who built his house on the rock. Rain, storms and winds beat against his house, but it did not fall, because its foundation was on the rock. On the contrary, the house built on sand by the foolish man, did not withstand the storms, and it fell with a great crash.

To build "on the rock" means to be a responding disciple of Christ. Practicing obedience to the Word of God is our solid foundation. For Christians, the precious cornerstone is Christ Himself. Although the houses of the foolish and the wise may, for some time, appear equally secure, when the storms come, the destruction of the foolish is total, just like six of the Wonders of the World. Like a house of cards, the fool's life crumbles.

When life is calm, our foundations don't seem to matter. But when crises arise, our foundations are tested. Only those who built on the firm foundation of obedience and trust in God's Word will stand. Genuine faith produces trust and obedience. Blessed are those who build on solid foundations. They build for eternity!

A seven-year-old girl won the competition! "How did you learn to skate so well?" someone asked. As naïve as this question is, the child's simple reply touched a profound reality. She said, "By getting up every time I fell down."

Our Christian life can also be a series of falling down and getting up again. When we experience failure, we are discouraged, and often we don't even feel like getting up. But as Christians we must never give up because our Lord is the God of new beginnings. Failure should never be final for those who begin again with God.

As believers of the Word, the strength of our faith can be measured by the ability to bounce back. Although failure is painful—and who hasn't experienced that pain—it offers us an opportunity to reaffirm our heart's devotion to Christ. Perhaps the Lord may allow us to fall down so that we'll learn to look up. We can learn by the simple answer the little skater gave, and get up every time we fall down.

People often ask why God allows difficulties to come into the lives of those who love Him. Experience has taught us that affliction comes not to make us sad, but sober, not to make us sorry and discouraged, but wiser. Even the plow that breaks the earth enriches the field so that the seed multiplies a thousand-fold. So, affliction should magnify our joy and increase our spiritual harvest.

God never calls our failures as final. In whatever area we might have failed, God by His grace, can bring good out of our greatest defeats. In Romans 8:28 we read, "...All things work together for good to those who love God." What a helpful mystery! There is a purpose for everything—His purpose! God often allows difficulties and heartaches to come into our lives to develop our character. When God permits trials, He also provides comfort.

How are we handling our difficulties? We may shrink under our present adversity, or we may let God's comforting love soften our hearts so that the Holy Spirit will be able to stretch us to new dimensions. Self-pity, complaining and rebelling will hinder our growth, but praise, submission and vibrant faith in God's loving purpose will produce in us a growing likeness to Christ.

If some of us are being tested by disappointment, let us not become bitter nor too proud to try again. Pride destroys individuals as well as nations. Pride makes us self-centered. We can be released from our pride by humbling ourselves before our Creator. "God opposes the proud but gives grace to the humble" (Js. 4:6). The Bible says, "Cast your burdens on the Lord, and He shall sustain you" (Ps. 55:22).

Failure is never final for those who believe and begin again with God. Even when our trials seem beyond our understanding, we can trust the Lord. He will show us that He is the God of new beginnings!

*W*e often hear the expression "New and Improved." But is it really improved? There are a few things better left alone because they can't be improved upon. That is not to say that people have not tried. There is one tiny item that inventors attempted to dress up, make it colorful, more expensive, but they can't make it better because there is no room for improvement. Why would anyone try to change its simplicity? Years have passed, and that tiny device continues to work well, providing countless people with the simple, practical service for which it was originally created. Well, I'm talking about the simple paper clip! That little metal curlicue that holds sheets of paper together. It is simple, straightforward, and it works!

There is something else that is simple and straightforward—the Word of God! The Bible! In it we read the most beautiful story ever told. The birth, life and ministry of Jesus Christ—the Son of God. And why should spiritual enlightenment be complicated? Christ lived a perfect life on earth. He was crucified—taking upon Himself the sins of all the people who would accept Him as Savior. He was buried; He rose from the grave to give us a new life eternal.

The Apostle Paul tells us in 2 Tim. 3:16, "All scripture is God-breathed..." When God revealed His truth for human writers to record, He breathed out His Word. Scripture is not inspired like a sculpture by Michelangelo, not inspired like a great composition by Handel, not inspired by a great sonnet by Shakespeare, but inspired as in God-breathed; as we Armenians appropriately call the Bible the "Breath of God."

The Bible and the work of God's Holy Spirit are to us like a map, and our moral and spiritual compass to direct our lives. In a world where we are encouraged to behave as we wish (If it feels good, do it!), the Bible addresses that which is right and that which is wrong. It tells it just as simply as that. It provides the kind of solid foundation that we all need. Many books can inform, but only the Bible can transform lives. To live the Christian life successfully, we need more than a spiritual "snack" on Sundays. No matter how inspiring a sermon, or how uplifting the worship service may be, we need spiritual nourishment from God's Word throughout the week to help us remain faithful, and to know God in a more intimate way.

Yes, the Bible is God's Book, but He doesn't want it back. He wants us to keep it, to meditate on it, to understand it, to believe it, and to obey its message. When we do that, we become one of His chosen sons and daughters, and we begin a fresh, vibrant relationship with Him.

Some people can't take the simple gospel as it is and trust it. They want to complicate it—improve it—like those who try to make a better paper clip. They try everything but what works. God's Word comes highly recommended, but don't take my word for it. Begin to read it. Take a "taste," test it for yourself. And come back again and again. Satisfaction guaranteed. Nothing in the world is better! A well-read Bible is a sign of a well-fed soul.

Our culture seems to value young people more than the elderly. In the workplace, for example, mandatory retirement policies restrict the age at which an employee may continue to work. As Christians, however, we need not feel unproductive after reaching a certain age. The best years are still to come. As the years pass, we should become even more effective and stronger in our faith. Just as autumn is the time of abundant fruitfulness, so it can be with us. The Apostle Paul writes in 2 Cor. 4:16, "Even though outward man is perishing, yet the inward man is being renewed day by day."

This was true with St. Paul. As he served the Lord, he faced many hardships. He recognized his human frailty, and as his body became weaker, his spirit became even stronger. As he grew older physically, he grew more vibrant spiritually. As Christians we know that our bodies are perishable, but we also know that God's limitless power and spirit dwell in us.

Are we growing in the grace and knowledge of our Lord? The wise psalmist wrote: "The righteous shall flourish like a palm tree...Those who are planted in the house of the Lord...shall still bear fruit in old age; they shall be fresh and flourishing" (Psalm 92:12 – 14). Palm trees are known for long life. To flourish like a palm tree is to stand tall and to live long. The psalmist saw the faithful strong and unmoved by the winds of circumstances. Those who put their faith firmly in God can have this strength and vitality. Serving God is not limited to young people alone, who seem to have unlimited strength and energy. There are many dedicated, mature people who continue to have a fresh outlook, and can even teach us from a lifetime's experience of serving God.

The story is told of a woman facing the trials of growing old who asked her pastor, "Why does God let us grow old and weak?" Her pastor replied, "I think God has planned the strength and beauty of youth to be physical. But the strength and beauty of old age is spiritual." We gradually lose the strength and beauty that is temporary, so we'll be sure to concentrate on the strength and beauty that is forever. Although some of us at times may think we are at the end of our rope, we are never out of hope. Our perishable bodies are subject to suffering, but God never abandons us. Christ has won the victory over death. As Christians we have eternal life.

Are we in life's springtime? We must trust God's timing to fulfill our dreams. Are we in life's summer or autumn? We can face our daily challenges head on. And if we feel the chill of winter, we can strive to know God even better. His presence can make every season of life one of strength and beauty. Whatever our age, our challenges are opportunities for Christ to demonstrate His power and presence in and through us! To all mature men and women: WE ARE NOT ANTIQUES, BUT TROPHIES IN GOD'S EYES!

*T*o receive daily nourishment, the food we eat must be properly digested. This process begins with chewing. The same is true of our intake of spiritual food—the Word of God. As we study the Bible, we must digest its truths and meditate on it daily in order to derive all spiritual benefits possible.

It has been suggested that we read the Bible, not as any other book, but as a letter from home, or a letter from a loved one. Is it not with great joy that we open such a letter? And how delighted we are reading its content!

Although this was many years ago, I will never forget my mother's joy and happiness every time she would receive a letter from my brothers, who were both serving in the U.S. Army. I was single then, living at home. It was first my older brother who was a paratrooper with the 82nd Airborne Division stationed at Fort Bragg, North Carolina. How precious were his letters to us, and especially to Mom. After reading each new letter several times, she would keep it in her dress pocket. During the course of the day, she would read it again and again. Just before bedtime, she would read it one more time and finally put it in her Bible next to her bed. This was repeated almost daily till a new letter arrived.

Not only can the Word of God be just as exciting and delightful as that, but much, much more! The four Gospels and the Epistles are God's letters written with love, and addressed to each one of us personally. The Bible tells us that, "All Scripture is given by inspiration of God....." (2 Timothy 3:16) His love and forgiveness, as well as instruction, are evident in every Gospel and Epistle for our benefit. As we read His Word and meditate on its truths, the Holy Spirit will guide us, will renew our hopes, and give us courage to face any battles that may lie ahead. It has been said that a well-fed soul results from a well-read Bible.

When we make Christ the center of our lives, the Word of God becomes a spiritual banquet to feed our souls. Let us read His letters with prayer and meditation, and take delight in its content. We will be blessed.

*A*irplane trips can present opportunities for interesting conversations with total strangers. I was reading my Bible on the plane recently when an amusing thought struck me. If anyone would recognize it was the Bible I was reading, they might think I was so afraid of flying that I was praying continuously. Interestingly, a woman next to me might have thought just that, and suddenly she confessed her fears of flying. Then she added, "I try to stay calm, but then I remind myself, 'Oh well, I have had a full life, and if I die, I die'." We both laughed. I closed my Bible and we just talked. I think she felt better.

The simple truth is that faith fades fear. We must trust our Heavenly Father. Jesus Himself says in John 14:27, "Peace I leave with you. My peace I give to you; not as the world gives do I give to you. Let not your heart be troubled, neither let it be afraid." Unlike worldly peace, which is usually defined as the absence of conflict, this peace is confident assurance in all circumstances. With Christ's peace in us, we have no need to fear the present or the future. If our lives are full of stress, we can allow the Holy Spirit to fill us with Christ's peace.

Modern society longs for peace of mind. They search for that peace in all directions, except in God's Word. Yet the Bible has clear cut instructions on how to attain that peace. If we love God, obey and meditate in His Word, we will have His peace. It is the greatest antidote to anxiety at any time or place. We must trust God Who alone is above all circumstances of life.

The Apostle Paul also reminds us, "Be anxious for nothing, but in everything by prayer and supplication, with thanksgiving, let your request be known to God; and the peace of God, which surpasses all understanding, will guard your hearts and minds through Christ Jesus" (Philip. 4:6, 7). Imagine never being anxious about anything! We all have worries or anxieties on the job, at home, at school, and for some, even on an airplane. But St. Paul's advice is to turn our worries into prayers. Fret and worry indicate lack of trust in God.

Do we want to worry less? Then we can pray more wherever we are. God's peace is not found in positive thinking or in absence of conflicts. It comes from knowing that God is in control. We can experience victory when we let God's peace guard our hearts against all anxiety. It has been said that sorrow looks back, worry looks around, but faith looks up.

"Peace" is a common Hebrew greeting which Jesus uses in a unique way. The term speaks in effect of Christ's redemptive work; a total well-being and inner rest of spirit with those in fellowship with God. True peace is His gift. It is the supreme remedy that dissolves all fears and rules in the hearts of God's people. God, Who holds the universe, is our God Who is holding us in His care.

$\mathcal{M}$ost of us have been on a camping trip, at least once in our lives. I have been just once. I remember that in order to walk safely in the woods at night, we need a light so that we don't trip over tree roots, etc. We carry a flashlight or lantern which lights only one step ahead. With each step we take, the lamp moves forward and another step is made visible and safe. This way we reach our destination safely without once walking in darkness. Amazingly, we have been walking in the light all along, but only one single step at a time! This is exactly the method of God's guidance.

In our daily life, we also walk through "dark woods," often surrounded by a threatening environment. As Christians we know our ultimate destination and we are assured of our safe arrival, and yet, the darkness of the unknown can conceal our pathway. Possible difficulties and unseen dangers often upset our walk, making us wary and deprive us of the peace and confidence God intended for us to enjoy.

But the Word of God can be our light to show us the way ahead, provide illumination so we won't stumble. God's guidance through His Word can clearly reveal to us the false values and philosophies which might surround us.

The Apostle Paul says to the Corinthian Christian faithful, "For we walk by faith, not by sight" (2 Cor. 5:7). God's children should not worry about tomorrow and trust Him for today. Their confidence in God and His Word should be a lamp to their feet and light to their path. Even as a lantern illuminates each new step on a dark path at night, so does the illumination of Scripture provide light on our path of life. Then let faith, hope and love for God give us confidence and inspire us to faithful service through His guidance and for His glory. As we meditate on His Word we will be able to see our way clearly enough to stay on the right path.

It isn't necessary to see beyond what the Lord reveals. When we follow His leading there is always enough light for each step of the way. Why fear the darkness of tomorrow if we are walking in His light today? True faith is not based on evidence, but on divine assurance, and it is a gift of God!

*W*hile visiting the Rocky Mountains in Colorado, I learned of an amazing plant known as saxifrage. This bright green bush grows on the bare surface of steep rocky slopes. Although the saxifrage can withstand winds and violent storms, it has no soil to anchor its roots. How does it stay firmly rooted on the rock? This amazing plant makes its own soil. Its seeds contain a strong acid which decomposes the rock, preparing the needed soil for its roots! As for moisture, it draws water from the rock layers that absorb from nearby streams and waterfalls. This beautiful bush is another miracle of God's wondrous creation!

What a refreshing secret for us to take note of! What a valuable lesson! As children of God, we too, through faith in Christ, can create our own fertile soil that can produce hope, courage and perseverance to overcome life's challenges. We too can become fruitful and productive when we build our faith on the firm foundation laid upon a rock, our mighty Creator Himself.

In Romans 12:2 we read, "Do not be conformed to this world, but be transformed by the renewing of your mind." We can only redirect and renew our minds through our faith in Christ. To strengthen our faith, however, we need to know God's Word. We must read His textbook, the Bible, learn its principles and God's promises to us. This is the only way to develop faith—faith that moves mountains of fear and doubt, faith that can produce the "soil" we need with endless possibilities to flourish.

Yes, each new day will bring challenges, excitement and opportunities for success or setbacks. We truly don't know what winds or violent storms might be around the corner. But we do know that we can be joyful at each turn, even if the conditions are rough. Our journey begins by knowing Christ. He is our life's only solid foundation of yesterday, today and forever. Let us anchor our lives firmly on Him, our Rock, as we walk in faith and obedience.

Faith does not make all things easy, but it does make all things possible— even producing our own "soil" of faith in which we can flourish!

*W*e were on our way for a cruise to Alaska. Our flight from LAX to Vancouver, Canada, was delayed 2? hours. Our concern now was that we might miss our cruise ship. We had made arrangements to be picked up at the airport by cruise line representatives. My husband Steve called from the plane to inform them of the delay. They were aware of the situation. The co-pilot was also aware of our concern. When the plane landed he asked that all passengers remain seated until we exited first. The cruise representatives were waiting for us. We ran through the airport and into a waiting taxi. We boarded the ship just before the gangway was removed!

We were aboard, but our luggage was not. It was delivered to us two days later in Juneau. In the meantime, we were treated royally. We were each given a bag of toiletries, a T-shirt, and were provided with formal wear for that evening's events—all complimentary!

The top officers of this cruise line, from the captain on down, are Greek. The following day, seeing a young officer, I expressed to him in Greek our gratitude for their gracious hospitality. It turned out he was the Hotel Manager, second in command to the Captain. He was delighted! He gave us his card and asked us to meet him the following day. Later that evening a bottle of champagne, a basket of fruit and a box of chocolates were sent to our cabin. We were surprised! I wrote him a thank you note and included a copy of one of my Armenian Observer articles. The following day we were invited to his luxurious office! After a few minutes of conversation, he exclaimed, "Let's celebrate—today is my 37th birthday!"

While seated in the cocktail lounge he said, "I read your article and I liked it. Are these weekly spiritual articles an assignment for you?" I answered that it was not, and am delighted and praise God for the opportunity to share His Word with so many! To my surprise, he said, "That's good, that is very good!" Then I was amazed at how this young man opened his heart and spoke to us about his faith.

We learned that he had just been promoted to Hotel Manager. Before he took this responsibility, he spent some time with his parents in Greece. Then he arranged by permission to enter a monastery for two days, devoting himself to prayer, fasting and meditation. He spoke of consecrating his heart to God, seeking wisdom and guidance as he was about to accept his new position. Steve and I were captivated as he spoke for some time of his faith and his desire to do his best.

This brought to mind King Solomon who, as a young ruler, prayed to God for a discerning heart, to be able to govern his people with wisdom. God was so pleased with his humble prayer that, not only did He grant King Solomon wisdom, but blessed him with wealth and much more (1 Kings 3: 7 – 15).

I was thrilled to have met this wise and godly young man. And to think that my spiritual article had unlocked his sensitive heart. It was an unforgetable cruise. At the last formal night, we were invited to the Captain's Table. My place card was next to the Hotel Manager. He was a gracious host. The grace of God was indeed upon this young Greek man.

*S*ome of us are familiar with the film "Indiana Jones and the Last Crusade." The ancient city of Petra and its monumental reddish sandstone architecture, a mixture of Greek and Roman classical styles, was the setting in parts of the movie. Petra, once a capital of the Nabatean kingdom, is located 47 miles southeast of the Dead Sea, in what is now the country of Jordan. The architecture is more remarkable for its scale and the fact that all the buildings are carved out of solid rock, than for its creativity. It is nevertheless profoundly impressive in the middle of the Edomite (Idumean) desert.

According to the Bible, Edomites are descendants of Esau (Gen. 36:1 – 9), Jacob's brother and older of the twin sons of Isaac and Rebekah (Gen. 25:19 – 26). To support the population of these desert cities, highly sophisticated water gathering systems were invented by its people. Petra, their capital city, was also the center of trade routes. They controlled the major caravan routes carrying spices, incense and their exquisitely painted "eggshell" pottery to Palestine, the Mediterranean countries, Egypt and Syria.

The people boasted that their country was so well protected that they could never be taken. Towering cliffs and a winding narrow entrance was and still is the only way into Petra. The entrance, about a mile long, is so narrow that one can only pass through on foot or by horseback. Petra is surrounded by massive rocks, some as high as 700 feet! Edom thought that it was invincible.

Nations and individuals can often be blinded by pride. They become self-sufficient and forget that God is the source of their strength. The Edomites failed to consider one basic thing: "God resists the proud, but gives grace to the humble" (James 4:6). Pride makes us self-centered. When people grow strong with a sense of their own sufficiency, eventually they are brought to their knees, humbled before the Creator of the universe. Proud people often take little account of their weaknesses and don't anticipate stumbling blocks.

What happened to Petra? Edom was taken because of traitors within. By the discovery of a hidden passage, an Islamic invasion in the 7th century A.D. brought an end to this desert stronghold. Petra also suffered a series of disastrous earthquakes from 110 to 750 A.D., and was gradually forgotten by the civilized world until its rediscovery in the 19th century. Excavations in Petra have been carried out since 1965 by British and American archeologists. Because of their seemingly invincible rock fortress, the Edomites were proud and very self-confident. But God humbled them, and their nation disappeared from the face of the earth.

Any nation that trusts more in its power, wealth, technology and wisdom than in God, will be brought low. All who are proud will one day be shocked to discover that no one is exempt from God's justice. Knowing God makes us humble— knowing ourselves keeps us humble.

*T*he old town clock in Halifax, Nova Scotia, Canada, is one of the city's symbols that captures the visitor's attention. It stands tall like a tower keeping watch over the harbor. It was built on the orders of Prince Edward, Duke of Kent. The clock arrived from England in 1803. When I commented to our guide that the beautiful clock had four sides, and that one could see time from every angle, she said that the people in Halifax are not much concerned about time. Perhaps the town clock was given to them to make them more aware of it, but she admitted that it hadn't changed their lax ways.

I was amused by her response. "Use time wisely" was all I heard from my grandmother as I was growing up, even before I knew what it meant. Time is the most important, valuable capital we own. We can lose great fortunes, and if we are lucky, we may gain them back. But time, once spent, is gone forever. Napoleon, at the height of his power, is believed to have said, "Ask me for anything, and I will be able to give it to you. Anything, that is, except time."

If we realized the value of our days, we would live in more meaningful ways. We should treasure each hour as a gift of great value from God, and use it in a purposeful and productive way. We read in Psalms 90:12, "Teach us to number our days, that we may gain a heart of wisdom." Realizing that life is short helps us to use time wisely and for eternal good. We are to place each day in the balance and make the scales tip in a way that will bring honor and glory to God, and blessings to the lives of others.

The way we choose to live, our ability to love others and be loved, determines the true value of the time we have. As the clock keeps ticking away, our responsibility is to put as much meaning as possible into the intervals between each tick. We must live and act wisely, keep our standards high, serve God and do good whenever we can. There are, of course, times when we must rest and relax. Even Jesus did that with His disciples (Mk. 6:31). But that was using time for restoration. After they had rested, they could be more fruitful and productive.

To have no regrets at life's end, rather than count our days, we can make our days count. The clock of life is wound but just once, and no man has the power to tell exactly when the hands will stop. Therefore, if there is something important we want to do, we must not put it off for a better day. If there is someone we love, we must tell that person. If we need to forgive, we must do so, or praise someone who deserves it. Perhaps we have recently distanced ourselves from the Lord. It is never too late to come back. Christ is knocking at the door of our hearts. Let's not neglect what is truly important. It is ironic that people spend so much time securing their lives on earth, and give so little time and no thought as to where they will spend eternity. To spend time wisely, we must invest in eternity!

A university student, having difficulty with his studies, asked his professor's opinion. "I'm studying hard. I try my best, but I just can't retain what I read. Do you think it will help if I hire a tutor?" The professor replied, "No, I wouldn't recommend that at all. You don't need a teacher—you need a pupil." He knew that learning is enhanced when we share our knowledge with others.

The professor's advice reminds me of some children of God who know many Bible facts, but have a poor understanding of the applicable scriptural truths. They may attend church on Sundays, listen to religious broadcasts, even enroll in Bible correspondence courses, yet they still seem to lack applicable knowledge of the Bible. Why? Because they never use the knowledge they possess. These individuals don't need to be taught more; they need to tell others what they have learned. As they teach what they know to others, they will grasp it better themselves, and be blessed in the process.

The Apostle Paul advises young Timothy, whom he considered his spiritual son, "The things that you have heard from me among many witnesses, commit these to faithful men who will be able to teach others also" (Tim. 2:2). St. Paul, aware that the end of his life was near, passed the responsibility of the ministry to Timothy, and urged him to continue his duties faithfully. Timothy was to take the divine revelation he had learned from the apostle and teach it to other faithful men – men with proven spiritual character and spiritual gifts, who would in turn pass those truths to another generation.

That process of spiritual reproduction, which began in the early church, is to continue until the second coming of Christ. Isn't that exactly what Christ Himself commanded His disciples to do, which is called the "Great Commission"? (Mt. 28:19 and Mk. 16:15) "Go and make disciples of all nations…in the name of the Father, and of the Son and the Holy Spirit, teaching them to observe all things that I have commanded you; and lo, I am with you always, even to the end of the age."

When someone is dying or leaving us, his or her last words are very important. Jesus left the disciples with these last words of instruction: They were to teach new disciples to obey Christ, and He would be with them always. In previous missions, Jesus had sent His disciples to the Jews only (Mt. 10:5, 6), but hereafter their mission would be world wide; to all nations. St. Paul, at the end of his life, was now asking Timothy to do the same.

We are not all evangelists or teachers in the formal sense, but we all have received gifts from God that we can use to help fulfill the "Great Commission." We can be a light for Christ in every dark corner of our community. And as we do that, we will have the comfort of knowing that Christ's Spirit will be with us always.

Do we share the truth of God's Word with others? Do we share or teach others, using some of the gifts and talents we have been given by God? If not, it is time we stopped being just students, and start being teachers. When we share with others what we know, not only will we grasp the knowledge better ourselves, but we will also be blessed abundantly!

Some of the most delightful experiences often catch us by surprise! I was delighted to see a copy of the famous check for $7,200,000 (seven point two million dollars) which the United States paid Russia for the purchase of Alaska! The check copy was on display in the museum in Juneau, capital of Alaska! William Henry Seward, U.S. Secretary of Sate at the time, brought the purchase to a successful conclusion on March 30, 1867. As I stood there, amazed and amused, I noticed a full-page cartoon on display near the check depicting President Clinton on the phone saying, "I need the receipt, the Russians want Alaska back!"

Many American politicians and journalists criticized the purchase of Alaska at the time, dubbing it "Seward's Folly" and "Icebergia." But it was after the purchase that Alaska proved to be rich in minerals; petroleum, coal, iron, and gold! We took a few guided excursions inland from the various ports that we visited. The stories our guides seemed to enjoy sharing the most were of the gold rush in Alaska and the Yukon. They said that some did very well. For others, the excitement in the pursuit of gold seemed most exhilarating, and many died, never finding the gold they dreamed of.

One of the stories we were told was about a handful of gold miners who discovered gold. But not having the proper tools they needed, they decided to go to town and buy some. They also took an oath not to say a word to anyone about the gold so they wouldn't have to share it with others. Although they kept their promise, their happy disposition and joyful faces gave their secret away. Those who saw them knew they were up to something! When they returned to their claim with the tools, the townsmen followed them, and it was all revealed.

The above story demonstrates that there is a powerful link between facial expression and emotion. As children of God, do our faces express the joy we have in the Lord? Do we reflect that "Light" we have received through Christ? Does the fact that we have Christ in our hearts give away the joy we have within? Our Lord teaches us to let our light shine for all to see (Mt. 5:16). As Christians we are to be the light in the world around us.

Each one of us is precious in our Creator's eyes. Even if we think of ourselves as ordinary believers, all of us can, by God's grace, be a shining light that glorifies our Father in heaven, and point others to Christ. Perhaps unknown to us, we already may have influenced others by our Godly attitude and actions. If we have the joy of Christ in our hearts it will show on our faces, just as the excitement the gold miners displayed. But we have much more than gold in our hearts. We have the precious Holy Spirit of Christ!

Even when we don't feel particularly happy, we can be joyful in the Lord. It's not a matter of pretending, but practicing an outlook on life that reflects our faith in Christ. "Rejoice in the Lord always," Apostle Paul wrote from prison! "Again I will say, rejoice!" (Phil. 4:4) A cheerful attitude begins with a merry heart and spreads quickly to a joyous face.

The freeways of Los Angeles often seem to be in a process of being widened. Frequently the state is adding another lane or create a "Diamond Lane" to alleviate congestion and make life easier for motorists. The freeways of life can sometimes be just as difficult as overcrowded freeways. We tend to get frustrated because trials and difficulties hold us back. Our progress seems to slow down to a turtle's pace. We don't feel we are accomplishing what we think we should, or as fast as we should. Possibly we too need to open another lane; an express lane that will allow our praise to make its way to God.

Apostle Paul tells us to give thanks in all circumstances, for this is God's will. (1 Thes. 5:18) The truth is that we all do pretty well in praising God on "sunny" days, when things go right, but it is not so easy to sing praises when things become difficult. Nevertheless, we are taught that praise should continually be in our mouths.

St. Paul is not telling us to deny the reality of a painful situation, but it is possible to have a prayerful attitude at all times, and trust God. He is instructing us to learn to see that God is good, no matter how bad the situation. Our prayers of thankfulness should not fluctuate because of our circumstances.

With that kind of an attitude then, our thanksgiving and praise will open new avenues of heavenly blessings. When the lane of praise is used, life caught in the traffic jam of grumbling, bitterness and frustration begins to move with new purpose.

Today then, why not make praise to God the fruit of our lips. It will free our life's gridlock and bring wonderful changes and new dimensions of joy into our lives. Let us use the express lane—the lane of praise.

*L*ily and I were classmates at the university I attended years ago. While working on a class project, suddenly, out of nowhere, she asked me if I had any serious fears in life. Puzzled, I asked what kind of fears she meant; fear from another person, high places, etc. "Any fears. Do you have any fears?" she asked again.

Still somewhat perplexed, I explained that there was a difference in our ages and family life. I pointed out to Lily that she was a girl just out of high school. I was already married with three small children, and because of my responsibilities, my thinking process was different from hers. Then, to answer her question directly, I confessed that I had only one concern. It was "My daily prayer to God that He continues to give me good health so that I'll be there for my children. I don't want my children to be raised by anyone else." She didn't seem surprised. "That's very good!" was her response.

Over the years I never forgot Lily's question. After my youngest child's eighteenth birthday, I thought of Lily's question again! I praised God once again for my health and the wisdom He granted me all those years to trust Him in every area of my life. And it suddenly occurred to me that now I didn't even have that one concern any more! However, I often still think of Lily and the impact her question had on my life.

Millions of people live with anxiety. Researchers say that the root of any anxiety is the fear of losing control of one's life. Any way we think about any thing, we must never forget that God is in control of everything. Trusting an invisible God can be frightening, especially for a new Christian. However, as we study God's Word, we clearly see His many promises to His beloved, faithful children. We read in Joshua 1:5, "I will never leave you nor forsake you." In Isaiah 41:10, "Do not fear, for I am with you; do not be dismayed, for I am your God. I will strengthen you and help you; I will uphold you with my righteous right hand." And Jesus said, "Take courage! Don't be afraid" (Mt. 14:27).

God knows all our concerns and fears, and He wants us to trust Him in all areas of our lives. In fact, I understand that all "fear not" related phrases are repeated in the Bible 366 times! We have one "fear not" command from our Lord to remember for each day of the year. Plus one extra to spare! Is this encouraging, or what? Do we have an awesome God, or what!

Perhaps there is someone facing some kind of fear today; sickness, financial crisis, broken relationship or loss of a loved one. Jesus tells all of us to take courage and not be afraid. He is in control of our fears and all of life's storms. Let us not give in as defeated victims, but as overcoming victors. We can go through anything knowing that God's presence is in us and He'll keep His many promises. God will carry us safely through any fear or storm of life. Unshakable faith and trust in God can dispel all fears!

*E*phesus was the largest and most important city in the Roman province of Asia, on the west coast of what is now Asiatic Turkey. It was an important port city, situated at the mouth of the Cayster River between Smyrna and Miletus. In the New Testament Ephesus and the Ephesians are mentioned more than 20 times. We also have the epistle to the Ephesian faithful, written by the Apostle Paul. Ephesus was noted for its active, crowded harbors, its broad avenues, its gymnasiums, baths, its huge amphitheater, and especially its magnificent temple of Diana (Artemis, in Greek), one of the seven wonders of the world.

But what happened to that metropolitan city, which was once one of the cultural and commercial centers of its day, to bring about its gradual decline? Was it destroyed by enemies, demolished by earthquakes? No, silt was its downfall – quiet and nonviolent, continuous silt which was at work for centuries. Over the years, fine sedimentary particles slowly filled the harbor. The alluvions carried by the river filled the bay, completely separating the city from the economic life of the sea traders. As the harbor silted up, the city declined. Ephesus, the largest and most important city of the Roman Empire in Anatolia was no more a port city or trade center!

Today, from the port of Kusadasi, Ephesus is 15 to 20 minutes away by bus. The city is uninhabited. Archeologists have excavated the magnificent 24,000 seat amphitheater, the Celsus Library, and many other public buildings, examples of the finest Grecian art of the first and second centuries A.D.; the time of the city's height and prosperity. Although it is believed that only 15 percent of what once existed has been excavated, Ephesus is still perhaps the most impressive ruins in Asia Minor. The modern visitor can still gain quite an impression of the city as it was known by St. Paul.

Meanwhile, Christianity was rapidly spreading through Apostle Paul's ministry beginning around 52 A.D., despite an ungodly environment. Years later, while a prisoner in Rome, the Apostle Paul writes to the Ephesian faithful to be children of the Light and live a life worthy of the calling they have received, because the days are evil (Chap. 4 – 5). We need the same sense of urgency because our times are also difficult. We must keep our standards high, act wisely, and as Christians and ambassadors of Christ, be that light by our exemplary lives.

Often, small wrongful practices, little acts of disobedience may seem harmless. But if we let the silt of sin gradually accumulate in our lives, we will find ourselves far from God, and our lives can become a spiritual ruin. Today if we were to look for Ephesus on the map in the back pages of our Bibles, we will easily find that dot, but the city is not a port any more. The history of Ephesus is long. After the Goths burned and destroyed Ephesus in 262 A.D., the city never relived her glorious days again!

*T*he following Biblical example focuses on God's provision of blessings we receive according to our faith and willingness to obey.

One of prophet Elisha's disciples died leaving his wife penniless and in debt. The creditor demanded his money, and was determined to take the widow's two sons as slaves. She came to Elisha crying and begged for help. Elisha asked what she had in the house. She only had a jar of oil. He advised her to go with her sons and borrow as many empty vessels and jars as possible from friends and neighbors. Elisha stressed, "Don't borrow only a few." (2 Kings 4:1 – 7) She was then to enter her house with her sons and pour out the oil she had from their one jar into all the empty vessels. She did as Elisha instructed.

When the vessels were all full, she asked her sons for more empty jars, but none were left. The oil stopped pouring only when they ran out of empty vessels. Countless more jars could have been filled had she borrowed more! When she told the prophet what had happened, he advised her to sell the oil, pay her debt, and there would be enough money left for them to live on. What a faith-inspired miracle! They had seen God's tenderness and care through Elisha, and the two sons were saved from slavery! The number of vessels they had gathered, however, was indicative of the depth of their faith. God's provision was as great as their faith and willingness to obey.

Are we limiting ourselves to receiving God's blessings? We should never think small because we have a great Creator! God's immeasurable love is available to all of us today. His supply of blessings is as large as the power of faith within us. Let us not put limits on all that can be abundantly ours. As we strengthen our faith through His Word, it will release an astonishing power in our lives to produce miracles. When we dismiss all negative, self-defeating thoughts, and have faith, wonderful things begin to happen. We can expect miracles by believing in all-powerful God, by believing in ourselves and do our very best. We have an enormous potential for miracles in us that is placed there by our gracious and loving God, our Creator Himself! Let's act on it and expect unlimited blessings.

*E*ncouragement is the oil that takes the friction out of our daily lives. Mark Twain is believed to have said that he could live for a whole month on one good compliment! Words of encouragement among Christians, however, are more than a compliment or a pat on the back, valuable as these can be. Encouragement and prayer support can be a powerful friend. It strengthens the weak, delivers courage to the faint-hearted, and gives hope to the hesitant.

One of the greatest ministries we can each have as children of God is to uplift the spirits of those we come in contact with, especially fellow faithful. Many Christians can become weary in their daily conflicts, faced with a variety of challenges, often tempted to give up in their spiritual struggle. Our motivating words, an expression of appreciation, the assurance of prayer support can bring an attitude of optimism and spark great enthusiasm.

Perhaps those who need our encouragement and prayer support are our sons, daughters and grandchildren. Everyone needs uplifting words and approval at one time or another. We can encourage by telling them what God has done in our lives. There is nothing more effective and refreshing than one's own personal testimony of faith. It will motivate them to double their efforts and come out victoriously.

The Apostle Paul gives this advice to the Thessalonian faithful: "...Brethren, appreciate those who diligently labor among you...esteem them very highly in love because of their work. Encourage the faint-hearted, help the weak, be patient with all." (1 Thes 5:12 – 14) Just as the Apostle Paul gave the churches uplifting messages of hope, we too can serve Christ and bring joy to others through thoughtful letters, notes, encouraging words. We are only human, and regardless of the level of work we do, we need the assurance that we are appreciated. Flattery is wrong; sincere words of praise are always right.

Do we know someone who needs uplifting words of hope, approval and prayer support? Let us act on it. It may not seem like much or important that we say a word or two, but when it is encouragement, what wonders it can do!

*W*e stopped to get some gas. While my husband was dealing with the ATM, I came out of the car to examine the various ways one can pay for gas. I am happy that I can still "prepay the cashier." I like to deal with people. As we drove away, I thought that modern society emphasizes efficiency and convenience, but minimizes personal interaction. But God calls us to operate from a different perspective. As Christians we should look for opportunities to interact.

The following incident is an example of the opposite extreme. A few years ago while my husband and I were in Greece, our friend Nick suggested we drive to see a friend who owned a restaurant. Although it was 10:30 p.m., we went. Nick explained on the way that he wanted to ask his friend for a favor—some of his special Greek feta cheese. Nick was going to entertain a few special friends, visiting several Greek islands on a yacht.

The restaurant owner greeted us personally. Steve and I were introduced, and the man sat with us. Coffee was served and pleasant conversation continued. No word from Nick about the cheese. They talked about their families, children, business, the economy, the weather. A few questions were directed to us about the U.S., and more on the weather. Still no word about the cheese! I was beginning to wonder if Nick forgot why we came. It was close to 1:00 a.m. when Nick thought it was getting late, and stood up. While the restaurant owner was escorting us out, at the doorsteps, Nick said, "Oh, by the way, could you spare me 5 kilograms of your feta cheese? I'll be entertaining." "Yes, certainly," was the response, and we parted. The following day Nick was to send a boy to pick up the cheese.

I was amazed! I had forgotten the cultural customs of the land. This visit was fascinating! While in America, we know that the shortest distance between points A and B is a straight line. In Greece, it's a long, long arc! The most fascinating thing of all was that Nick's friend knew there was a reason why we were there, and he patiently waited. Nick also knew that his friend was aware of this. Both were going through the motions. Most of us in this country would have called first, asked the favor, and later picked up the cheese, and still have fellowship.

Life is to be enjoyed, and people are very much part of it. As Christians we can find a way between the two extremes. Yes, we all live rushed lives, but we must never forget to keep that human touch in all our relationships. Jesus teaches us in John 13:34, 35 that when we take time to demonstrate our love to others, all will know that we are His disciples.

As Christians we must be willing to go against the flow of society. This takes love, courage, patience, and an attitude of availability. When we do things in God's way, people are never a means to an end—they are the end. Inefficient and inconvenient? Frequently! Unimportant and unnecessary? Never! This is not easy. That is why people will notice and know we are empowered by a supernatural source. What a privilege and blessing that is!

*F*or most of us, admitting wrong-doing is not easy. Some might even say that admitting guilt is not a smart thing to do these days. We want the blessings of forgiveness without a sincere commitment to turn away from wrong-doing. Faith in our God, however, involves a sincere permanent change of heart and mind. We often seem repentant, promising God we will change if He will only get us out of a tight spot. That often, however, becomes a desperate act until the pressing problem is gone. The following amusing story illustrates the attitude of seemingly regretful individuals, and how the shallowness of their repentance comes to light when the pressure is off.

Two shipwrecked sailors had been drifting on a raft for days. In desperation, one began to pray, "God, I know I haven't lived a good life. I have lied and cheated and done many things I am ashamed of. If you save my life, I promise I'll....." "Hold it, hold it!" interrupted his shipmate. "Don't say another word! I just spotted land!"

When John the Baptist preached repentance, he called for right action. Soldiers and tax collectors, for example, were not to intimidate anyone, nor accuse people falsely, and be content with their wages. (Luke 3:13, 14) These honest actions would prove the sincerity of their response to John's message. When we truly seek God's forgiveness, we also turn our backs on all wrong-doing. And if our faith is genuine, our actions would prove our sincerity as well. God stands ready with His gift of forgiveness to cleanse and restore us.

Prayer is the Christian's open line to Heaven. We can approach God any time, any day, no matter what the situation and be sure that our sincere repentant prayers will be received. No one should bear all burdens alone. Why hang on to unnecessary baggage? God loves us too much to let us remain under stress. As He forgives, He also forgets. What a great privilege! What grace!

*A*rmenian women are great hostesses. That is because their training begins at childhood. Mothers make sure to teach their daughters all they know, and by being an example themselves as they prepare their daughters in the graces of Armenian hospitality. Other cultures undoubtedly may say the same of their women. Hospitality is an art. Making sure a guest is welcome, comfortable and well cared for requires creativity, organization and teamwork.

We see this in Luke 10:38 – 42. The ability to accomplish these goals makes Mary and her sister Martha one of the best hospitality teams in the Bible. Here we see Middle Eastern hospitality in action. On His way to Jerusalem, Jesus stopped at Bethany, home of Mary, Martha and Lazarus. Like most attentive hostesses, Martha strove for perfection around the house, especially when the family's guest that they loved so much was Jesus. She was busy with meal preparation while Mary sat at Jesus' feet, absorbing His every word.

For Mary, hospitality meant giving more attention to her guest Himself than to the needs He might have. She would rather listen and ask questions than cook. She was more interested in her guest's teaching than the promptness of the meal. Besides, there was Martha. She let her older sister take care of those details.

Martha was discouraged. There was so much to be done, and Mary just sat there with Jesus. Martha didn't realize that in her desire to serve the best meal, she was neglecting her guest. At this point she came to Jesus and asked, "Lord, don't you care that my sister has left me to do the work by myself? Tell her to help me." But Jesus replied, "Martha, Martha, you are worried and upset about many things, but only one thing is needed. Mary has chosen what is better, and it will not be taken away from her."

The one thing necessary was exemplified by Mary; an attitude of worship and meditation, listening to Him with open mind and heart. Mary knew that being in Jesus' presence was an extraordinary opportunity which must be given preference. Martha is gently rebuked by Jesus for her excessive concern for practical details. She was no less devoted to Jesus than Mary. Her faithfulness to Him is recorded in the gospel of John 11:27. Concerned with the task of serving, she missed the greater importance of taking time to sit at His feet. Jesus was more interested in spiritual food for the soul rather than for the body. He didn't rebuke Martha about her household chores – He was only asking her to set priorities. Seeking God and working whole-heartedly both have their place. Nothing was wrong with Martha's hospitality. Her priorities were simply out of order.

What kind of hospitality does Jesus receive in our lives? For Martha, the heat of the kitchen and her busyness caused her to take her eyes off Jesus. Do we allow anything in our lives to take our eyes off Jesus? Christ is knocking on the door of our hearts. He wishes to enter and have fellowship with us. It is Mary's kind of hospitality that He seeks from each of us.

*W*hile on a trip, we stopped at a coffee shop off the highway. The view from the booth where we sat was spectacular. The hills were vivid, velvety green with patches of yellow and purple wild flowers blooming on the slopes. My husband opened the shutters completely so we could fully enjoy the view. It was a spring day at its best! In the next booth another couple was seated with the shutters closed. Since the cords were on my side, I asked that if they wished, I would be glad to open their shutters. "No, thank you," said the lady, "In a few months the hills will all be dry and yellow anyway." She was right about that, but why not enjoy the view today, this moment?

I didn't blame the woman for her attitude. Perhaps she had a difficult day. And yes, if we were to return even a few weeks later, perhaps it wouldn't be the same. As I thought about it, the words of prophet Isaiah came to mind. "All flesh is grass, and all its loveliness is like the flowers of the field...The grass withers, the flower fades, but the Word of God stands forever" (Is. 40:6 – 8). Isaiah compares people to grass and flowers that wither away. We are mortal, but God's Word is eternal and unfailing. Public opinions change, but God's Word is constant. His Word never fades nor dries up. Its treasures are there for us to appreciate each day.

Isaiah continues: "Have you not heard? The everlasting God, the Lord, the Creator of the earth, neither faints nor is weary. His understanding is unsearchable. He gives power to the weak, and to those who have no might, He increases strength...But those who wait on the Lord shall renew their strength; they shall mount up with wings like eagles, they shall run and not be weary, they shall walk and not faint" (40:28 – 31).

God's power and strength never diminish. Some of us may often think we are at the end of our rope, but we are never at the end of hope. Our perishable bodies are weak as the grass and the flowers that are here today and gone tomorrow. But because Christ has won victory over death, we have eternal life. Our trials could in fact become opportunities for Christ to demonstrate His power and presence in and through us.

When we think of ourselves as weak, we must remember that each generation had its own problems, but God's plan embraces all generations. He is the only One Who sees a hundred years from now as clearly as a hundred years in the past. When we have concerns about our lives, let's talk it over with our Creator in prayer. No where does the Bible teach that Christians are to be exempt from tribulation. It does teach that Christians can face tribulation, crises and personal suffering with a supernatural power that is not available to those outside Christ. With this power we can rise above our circumstances. We must trust God and His timing, and try to enjoy each day to its fullest in His service.

*T*he town's clock on the courthouse tower was being cleaned. the workmen were lifted and suspended by a crane over the face of the large clock. In the process of cleaning its face, the repairmen had stopped the movement of the clock's hands—but had not stopped time.

Even though most wristwatches don't have a ticking sound any longer, every tick of a wall's clock reminds us of the passing of precious time. The swinging of the pendulum of a stately old grandfather's clock quite loudly does the same. And if we were to step into a special clock shop, we would see the ticking of time in most unique and creative ways. What does all this mean to us? Time does not stand still. We cannot prevent the passing of time. We can however, use time wisely. Realizing that life is short helps us use the precious time we have wisely, and for good. This priceless gift that our gracious Heavenly Father has entrusted to our use must not be squandered.

The Apostle Paul in his epistle to the Ephesians, Ch. 5, tells them to exercise wisdom because the days are evil. He urges them to use time wisely, making the most of every opportunity in serving Christ and doing His will. We need that same sense of urgency, because our days are also difficult. We must keep our standards high, act wisely and do good whenever we can. Paul's instruction to the believers in Ephesus applies to us as well. We are to submit ourselves daily to God's leading and draw constantly on His power. An unknown poet wrote:

> Time that is past we can never recall,
> Of time to come we are not sure at all,
> Only the present is now in our power,
> Therefore, redeem and improve every hour.

God is our Creator and the Master of our time. Even though we are His children, we can not secure our next moment or hour, much less our tomorrow or next year. Only when we recognize that we live by God's grace, will we then realize the utter dependency of our existence. For only by the will of God can we live or do anything. The important question we should ask then is; what worthy act can we begin today that will also glorify God? And what steps could we take toward that goal? Setting goals is admirable, but goals will disappoint us if we don't include God in them. God-centered life will be enriching—never disappointing. In fact, delightful, surprising events might even come our way—events we had neither imagined nor even prayed for. With Paul's teaching in mind, let us exercise wisdom, use time wisely and walk in the will of God. Our Christian exemplary lives must demonstrate who we are and WHOSE we are!

Therefore, if we are led by God to do a kind act, to render a meaningful service, or restore a relationship, let us not delay one more moment, and do it. It will enrich our lives and will glorify our Creator. We will experience a renewed and refreshing vitality of our Christian faith. Let us use time wisely, walk according to God's will, and do good. Time is precious.

*T*he impact of our lives is the sum of impressions we make on others. We all leave a legacy in some way or another. We must never downplay the importance of good deeds. Jesus tells us in Mt. 5:16, "Let your light so shine before men that they may see your good works and glorify your Father in heaven." The beautiful story of Dorcas in Acts 9:36 – 42 comes to mind.

Dorcas was a devout Christian woman in Joppa. She was also known by her Aramaic name, Tabitha. Dorcas had made an enormous impact in her community for her generosity and compassion for the fatherless. She was also known for her talents, such as making tunics and other garments for the poor. In fact, the Bible refers to her as a disciple! But this Godly woman got sick and died. When the disciples in Joppa heard that the Apostle Peter was in Lydda, a town not far from Joppa, they sent two men to ask him to come at once. The faithful in Joppa believed that the Apostle Peter, through God's power, could raise Dorcas from the dead.

The Apostle went to them at once. When he arrived, the crying mourners showed him the garments that Dorcas made while still alive. Peter sent them all out of the room, knelt down and prayed. Then he said to her, "Tabitha, get up!" She opened her eyes, and seeing the Apostle Peter, she sat up. He helped her to rise, then called the faithful and presented her alive to them. The news spread all around Joppa, and many more came to believe in the Lord.

God used great apostles, like St. Peter and St. Paul, and others for His glory, but He also uses those who have gifts of kindness like Dorcas. God can also use people like us. Rather than wishing we had more gifts, we should make good use of the gifts God has already given us. Dorcas gave generously of herself to others, and her name today, 2000 years later, is synonymous with acts of charity. In fact, there now are Dorcas Sewing Societies worldwide.

Yes, we all leave a legacy. Some, like Dorcas, touch hearts and lives for good and for God. While some leave behind a rather vague, misty legacy of shattered dreams and disappointed loved ones. Let us think for a moment about our own legacy. After graduating a university, for example, or changing a job, or moving to another neighborhood, etc., how would people remember us? Will they have respect for our standards? Will they look fondly at the contributions we have made to those around us? Will our friends look across the years and recall our dedication to God, our kindness? Or will they remember us for things we know we shouldn't have done, said, or allowed to happen?

We must never forget who we are as Christians. Someone is watching us as we build a legacy. Someone will remember us for what we are doing today. Our Heavenly Father calls on us to make a difference in what we say, how we live, how we show love, how we demonstrate our faith, and how we maintain our purity. Let us continue to work hard and leave a legacy of ongoing, Godly values. In Proverbs 22:1 we read, "A good name is more desirable than great riches; to be esteemed is better than silver and gold!"

*T*he story is told of a water carrier who carried water to his master every day. He would come down the hill, fill his two ceramic pots with water, hang the vessels, one on each side of a pole, set the pole on his shoulders, and carry it back up the hill. But one of the vessels had a crack, and water leaked from it. By the time the man went to his master, the cracked pot was only half full.

One day the cracked vessel said to the water carrier: "I'm sorry to have wasted your efforts and energy all this time. I'm only half useful to you because of my crack. Why don't you ask your master to throw me away." The water carrier replied, "You are so concerned about your crack that you haven't even looked down the path I walk. You see, I asked my master if I should throw you away, and he said no! He advised me instead to get some seeds and spread them along the path I walk. Do you see the colorful flowers? They are the result of the crack!"

None of us is perfect. We are all "vessels" with cracks of one kind or another. Yet, God, with His love and grace, can use us just the way we are for His glory. Apostle Paul writes in 2 Cor. 4:7, "But we have this treasure in earthen vessels, that the excellence of the power may be of God and not of us." We are like "earthen vessels," that can be broken. But Apostle Paul reminds us "we have this treasure" stored in us—the glorious wisdom of the Word of God. In our human frailty, we are weak, but the divine power of God, the Holy Spirit, which lives in us, transforms us into strong and powerful servants of God. It is not our power, but His. These "earthen vessels," although frail, contain the divine treasures of our Potter's wisdom through His Word which dwells in us, helping us to live victorious lives.

Perishable bodies are subject to "cracks" and suffering, but God never abandons us. Our Lord can create a colorful flower garden, even from our weaknesses, when we faithfully devote ourselves to Him, as we see in the above story. St. Paul speaks of his own experiences. He was "hard pressed on every side, but yet not crushed; perplexed, but not in despair; persecuted, but not forsaken; struck down, but not destroyed" (2 Cor. 4:8, 9). Through the Holy Spirit he received power and always gave all the glory to God!

Yes, we might be like "earthen vessels," but we must never be concerned with our weaknesses. Our Potter can create amazing results in spite of our "cracks." We must trust and yield to the divine power of the Holy Spirit. Christ has placed the Light of His life within us. As Christians our responsibility is to work in His service and let His divine strength, power and light shine in us and through us.

*T*he "Egnatian Way" was a well-known highway in Biblical times, built by the Romans, that crossed northern Greece from east to west. It is certain that the Apostle Paul walked through it during his second missionary journey. Today Egnatia Boulevard is still a major downtown street in Thessalonica.

Similarly, on our trip to Damascus, Syria, we walked on the street called "Straight," which is associated with Saul's (Apostle Paul's) conversion. The street still carries the same name. At the end of it we saw three Romanesque arches, and nearby we found the chapel we were looking for.

Saul was a Pharisee who knew Jewish scriptures well and he persecuted Christians everywhere. He was on his way to Damascus to arrest Christians and bring them to Jerusalem in chains. But as he approached the ancient city, he discovered that God had other plans for him. We read in Acts 9:1 – 22: "Suddenly a light shone around him from heaven. He fell to the ground, and heard a voice saying to him, 'Saul, Saul, why are you persecuting Me?'" Saul asked this crucial question: "Who are You Lord?" From the answer, "I am Jesus," Saul instantly realized that the One he persecuted was truly Christ. Trembling in divine presence, Saul asked a second crucial question: "Lord, what do You want me to do?" Instantly he put himself in God's hands. The Lord said to him, "Arise and go into the city, and you will be told what you must do." Saul was led to Damascus. He was without sight for three days, and neither ate nor drank.

There was a disciple in Damascus named Ananias. The Lord said to him in a vision to go to the street called Straight, and inquire for a man called Saul of Tarsus. Ananias did as he was instructed. He placed his hands on Saul and said, "Brother Saul, the Lord Jesus, who appeared to you…has sent me that you may receive your sight and be filled with the Holy Spirit." At once the scales fell from Saul's eyes. He received his sight and was baptized. Now Saul had a far different view of his life's purpose. Now he saw Jesus as his only hope, and his highest goal was to become like Christ (Phil. 3:7 – 14). Saul was his Jewish name and Paul his Roman or Gentile name. Now using the name Paul, he later served Christ with devotion, the One he once sought to destroy!

The chapel of Ananias is an underground stone structure with precious reminders of Acts chapter 9. The verses are translated into six languages. On the walls icons depict the events of Saul's conversion. I was disappointed that none of the six languages was Armenian. But then I saw the cloth on the altar. In Armenian capital letters I read, "IN THE NAME OF THE FATHER, THE SON AND THE HOLY SPIRIT, AMEN." Also, "OUR FATHER IN HEAVEN, HALLOWED BE THY NAME." This is repeated around the border. I was pleased to see that.

God has a purpose for every life which leads to a real adventure for those willing to serve Him. God can use extraordinary means to carry out His plan – often when we least expect it. God can use you and me. As children of God, we also must ask our Creator the same question: "Lord, what do You want me to do?" Our eyes are already open to His Truth.

*O*ne of the best papers for watercolor painting is produced by the Fabriano paper mill of Italy. To appreciate its value, students of art are shown a film of its manufacture. It is fascinating to see the various stages rags go through; bleached and washed till all stains are removed, shredded into pulp and pressed until the pulp is transformed into a fine quality white paper. Rags experience amazing trials of change in the mill before they emerge into this new beautiful form!

Divine transformation, in a similar way, has its various stages as well. The unseen hand of God transforms us spiritually day by day, helping us to grow in His grace throughout our lifetime. The Bible provides many instances of God's children who have gone through such transformation to become victorious men and women of God, and served for His glory. Some examples are Job on a heap of dust and ashes, Joseph sold into slavery, the Samaritan woman at the well, Apostle John on the lonely isle of Patmos, Apostle Paul on his way to Damascus, and later with a "thorn in the flesh," just to name a few. Such testing can have a cleansing, transforming effect on men and women of faith.

In Philippians 1:6, Paul tells us to be confident that God, who began a good work in us, will carry it on to completion through our lifetime. This is the process of Christian growth and maturity.

If any of us at times feels as though we aren't making spiritual progress, or we are discouraged by our shortcomings, let us remember God's promises. He will help us grow in grace daily until he has completed His work in us. We must not let present conditions rob us of the joy of knowing Him and growing closer to Him. God is good. Are we called to do a hard task? Are we carrying a heavy burden? Why not trust God and move forward. Let's supply the willingness, and God will supply the power. We are being transformed into an image pleasing to our Creator.

*G*enius often depends upon our determination to persevere in spite of obstacles, and to overcome discouragement from critics who can shatter our dreams, undermine our talents and weaken our hopes.

A Kansas City cartoonist studied the sketches of a young man and told the hopeful artist that he had no talent. After securing a job drawing publicity material for churches, the young artist rented a mice-infested garage for a studio. It was then that Walt Disney got the idea of a Mickey Mouse series, became famous, and the rest is history.

A drama director in New York City told a young beauty who had just graduated from Cushing Academy, that she lacked seriousness. The director advised her to give up a stage career and study some other field. It was a crushing blow to Bette Davis, yet she became one of the most gifted dramatic actresses of our time.

Some might feel that the above individuals were unusually gifted, and succeeded in spite of obstacles. As children of God, we can be assured that the actions of our thoughts can be mighty powerful. The power of right-thinking is the power of faith. For it is only through absolute steadfast faith that we can use our God-given talents to be victorious.

In John 10:10, Jesus says, "I have come that they may have life, and that they may have it more abundantly." This is addressed to each of us. As we reread the above verse, let us replace each "they" with our name. That is how personal this verse is. Life in Christ is lived on a higher plane because of His overwhelming forgiveness, love and guidance.

I don't know what inner strength and drive Mr. Disney or Miss Davis possessed, each of whom was rightfully admired. I know, however, that we can create miracles in our lives by achieving goals which others with less creative minds, less faith and determination might say it can't be done. Let us not forget the well-known verse, "I can do all things through Christ who strengthens me." (Phil. 4:13)

The power of faith and perseverance is within us. We alone, by faith, have the key to successful living. We can reach for that abundant life and become victorious.

*T*wo of my grandchildren were over one evening. At the proper time they prepared for bed. As I tucked them in, I listened to their prayers individually. They put their little palms together in prayer and Lukas, who is age five, began first. In conclusion he added: "God bless all those we love, and God bless the United States of America. Amen." I was pleased and moved. Samantha, age three, repeated the same prayer as her brother, but added one more sentence by concluding: "And God, help me to be good to my Nana. Amen."

Laughing and moved at the same time, I thought what a diplomat Sammie is! She is sweet and loving, (Yes, I do sound like a grandma) as a typical, bright active three-year-old child. But the desire to please me and be the best she could be was touching. As I meditated on Sammie's last sentence, the words of the Apostle Paul came to mind. He says in Romans 7:15, 19, "For what I am doing, I do not understand; for I am not practicing what I would like to do, but I am doing the very thing I hate. For the good that I want, I do not do, but I practice the very evil that I do not want."

Being a Christian does not instantly stamp out all wrongful acts and temptations from a person's life. Living the obedient Christian life is a lifelong, continuous process. In fact, the apostle compares Christian growth to a strenuous race.

Apostle Paul is distressed by his self-analysis, and this struggle creates tension in him. This refers to man's fallen nature. He is not saying that no goodness at all exists in him, but the danger of disobedience is always possible. This indeed describes the experience of any Christian struggling to keep God's Word without the help of the Holy Spirit. We must never attempt to fight it with our own strength, but take hold of the tremendous power of Christ through His Holy Spirit that is available to us. This is God's provision for victory!

"The devil made me do it!" is a humorous expression popular since the 60's. It sounds like a good excuse, but we are responsible for our actions. That is why we should never stand alone. Jesus Christ, who conquered sin once and for all, promises to fight by our side. The Apostle Paul finally has comforting words for us. He says in 2 Tim. 4:7, 8: "I have fought the good fight, I have finished the course, I have kept the faith; in the future there is laid up for me the crown of righteousness, which the Lord, the righteous Judge, will award to me on that Day; and not only to me, but also to all who have loved His appearing." Paul not only fought the fight and kept the faith, but also passed it on to many millions, and we continue to learn through his epistles. He died for his faith!

As amusing as Sammie's prayer's concluding words were, she knew to Whom to turn for help. We can't depend on our human willpower. We need the divine help of the Holy Spirit daily to be victorious in our Christian race.

*E*xploring the western part of the United States has been an informative and educational experience. Last year my husband and I had the opportunity to take two driving vacations, and visited nine western states that I had never seen before. As we mingled with the local people, which is always fun, the moment they found out that we were from Los Angeles, they became excited and amazed. They told us that we must be so brave to be living in L.A.—that we people do nothing in a small way! Everything about us is sensational, catching world-wide attention! Then they named the various events; riots, fires, earthquakes, floods, mud slides evacuations, etc. This kind of response was repeated everywhere we went; whether we were in a small town in Montana, or a large city in Texas. Even though these events were all true, we thought their response was rather amusing.

Life is unpredictable no matter where one lives. We don't know what tomorrow will bring. We choose to remain confident of God's wisdom, love, power, and move on with hope into tomorrow. I read some time ago that Thomas Edison had lost his great New Jersey laboratories in a fire in 1914. Yet the very next morning, walking through the rubble of those buildings that had housed so many of his projects, Edison, then 67, said, "There is great value in disaster. All our mistakes are destroyed. Thank God, we can start anew."

No matter what hopes, dreams and relationships have been destroyed or snatched away from us, with God's help we can start anew. Prayerfully, we can follow not only the inspiring attitude of Edison, but we can also follow with determination the advice that the Apostle Peter gives to all Christians; "Cast all your cares upon God, for He cares for you." (1 Peter 5:7)

Why submit to circumstance, while we can trust God who controls all circumstances. Besides, if we let Him fight our battles, we can't lose! Great trials often precede great triumphs. Sometimes our Lord might have to liberate us from the past, even through a painful loss, in order to lead us into a more fruitful future. When we feel alone and discouraged, let us trust God and remind ourselves of His unconditional love. Fear might not suddenly disappear, but trusting Him will prevent panic, and strengthen us to go on. The best antidote to fear is faith – faith in our Creator. When we acknowledge our helplessness and cast our cares on Him, the battle is not ours any longer, but God's. And we know that nothing is too big for God to accomplish, nothing is too small for Him to notice.

We can start anew. We can cast all our cares upon Him, trust Him, pray and work hard to make our hopes and dreams thrive and come alive daily!

VERBAL POLLUTION

A personal experience was related to my husband by a friend. This gentleman was returning home to Los Angeles from a trip to New York. In the plane he saw a charming movie he liked very much. Upon his return, he noticed the same movie was playing at a local theater. Happily, he promised his wife and children a truly fun afternoon, and took them to see this entertaining film; or so he thought. It wasn't long before the entire language in that same film changed completely. Vulgarity and profanity dominated the screen. It reached the point where he and his wife could not stand it any longer, and left the theater with their children. As you might have guessed, the film seen on the plane was edited. The one in the theater was screened in its entirety.

Vulgarity seems to be everywhere in our environment, and it's getting worse as time goes on. Bad or rough language is used on campuses and during casual conversations among some youth and adults as well, all in the name of portraying "real life." It is considered "cool," and countless movies playing in our cities encourage it.

Pollution takes many forms. Profanity is verbal contamination of the world we live in, painful to our ears and completely unnecessary under all circumstances. It has reached a point that some peoples' ears have been so desensitized to this kind of pollution that they don't seem to mind. Others, I notice, have crossed lines of verbal compromise. How sad! I have the feeling that if those who freely use this "cool" language were to enter an experiment where they were not allowed to use any coarse talk for just a week, they would be surprised to learn how little they'll speak. They would have to relearn new conversational skills.

What do we do as Christians? This language gap provides us with yet another opportunity to demonstrate the difference Christ makes in our lives. If someone uses such a vocabulary in our presence, we shouldn't snap at them, but neither should we compromise our speech. God's Word calls for higher standards.

In Ephesians 4:29, St. Paul says, "Let no corrupt word proceed out of your mouth, but what is good for necessary edification, that it may impart grace to the hearers." St. Paul warns us against unwholesome language, and a lot more. It is amazing how many ways we can go wrong when we open our mouths. Ephesians chapter 4 includes many different ways for us to live as lights within a world of darkness. The only way others will be aware of Christ is by seeing Him in the lives of Christians. We are called and equipped by the Holy Spirit to reflect Christ's character. Our lifestyle and verbal communication should demonstrate our commitment to God, and perhaps even begin to clean up the verbal pollution in our environment.

*W*hen we went to the Holy Land a few years ago, I was amazed by the massive stone work of some of the old structures such as the Damascus Gate in Jerusalem, the Western "Wailing Wall," etc. Gigantic stones were used in the lower parts of the walls to form a massive foundation for buildings dating back to Herod's time, such as the Citadel Tower in Jerusalem.

In their early building experiences, the Israelite builders thought that they had no use for such massive stones, and rejected them. Only later did they discover that these huge stones were necessary as cornerstones to give strength to the entire building.

In the gospel of Matthew, Jesus Christ applies the following verses from Psalm 118:22, 23 to Himself: "The stone that the builders rejected has become the chief cornerstone. The Lord has done this, and it is marvelous in our eyes." (21:42) He refers to Himself as the "chief cornerstone," rejected by men but chosen by God. Although He was not accepted by many of His people, He is the "chief cornerstone" of our new structure, the CHURCH.

The Apostle Paul writes to the faithful believers of the Ephesian church that they are now fellow citizens with God's people, and members of His household, with Christ as the "chief cornerstone." (2:19, 20) Yes, the Bible declares Christ as the Head of the Church, and each faithful believer as a block that is part of the Church. The Christian Church is built up of individuals who, by faith receive Christ as God's unique Son, the Light of the world. In a metaphorical sense, we are "living stones," being joined together with Christ as our "chief cornerstone" who gives the structure completeness, strength and unity.

As Christians and members of His Church, we are reminded that while we are all different, we are one in the Body of Christ, with a variety of God-given abilities and gifts. Every child of God is obligated therefore, to recognize that particular talent or talents and to use them in His service, for His glory, for His Church. Let us give our very best and not settle for less. All structures, we realize, may eventually crumble, but Christ's Church is built to last!

*E*arrings have been worn by women since ancient times. Among other ornamental jewelry, earrings are the most commonly found items in ancient tombs. In recent years, numerous small earrings worn on the same ear has been the trend adopted by some women. It is amazing, however, that some men have also picked up the trend in the last several years. Having pierced one ear, and wearing one earring seems to be the "cool" look for men in some circles.

In the Old Testament, however, in Moses' time, a pierced ear and one earring worn by a man was not a fashion statement. Instead it showed a slave's devoted love for his master. The main reason for slavery was default on taxes and loans. The government taxed their subjects heavily, which was difficult on the poor and widows. In those cases, according to Mosaic law, creditors could enslave debtors and their children to work off a debt when they could not pay (Ex. 21:2 – 4). Those persons enslaved in this manner worked more often as domestic servants, rather than as agricultural labor.

Exodus 21 tells us that according to God's Law given to Moses, all slave owners were to free their slaves every seventh year. This was called the Sabbatical Year. In certain circumstances, however, if a slave loved his master and preferred to remain with that family, even after the required six years of servitude, he would then be given the opportunity to declare his intentions in the presence of judges. Upon this declaration, he would have his ear pierced at his master's doorpost, demonstrating his lifetime commitment to serve him (Ex. 21:6).

The Apostle Paul urges us to make the same kind of commitment to the Lord. In fact, St. Paul often refers to himself as Christ's servant, signifying the same slavery by choice. No, we don't have to pierce our ears to show our loyalty to Christ. Piercing or not piercing, our ears have nothing to do with it. Instead, we must demonstrate by our lives to everyone around us that we are God's servants for life—because He redeemed us through Jesus Christ, and because we want to serve Him.

Man was created in God's image, but ever since Adam and Eve, all mankind has been enslaved by sin and is under judgment. The purchase price of redemption was the sacrificial death of our Lord Jesus Christ. Believers are set free from sin through repentance. And as they put their trust in Christ, they are given the precious gift of eternal life from God. Everyone who accepts God's free gift of forgiveness is set free and becomes a servant of Christ, the Redeemer (Rom. 6:22).

In one sense, God offers us our freedom every day. We are free to either serve Him or to serve our own selfish desires. The challenge is for us to present ourselves to Him, and willingly serve Him. We are accountable for all that we are, all that we have, and all that we are yet to become. Christ paid an enormous price for our freedom. Do we serve Him out of gratitude? Christ gave His all for us. Are we giving our all for Him?

The Acadia National Park, near Bar Harbor, Maine, is a region of natural beauty on the shores of the Atlantic Ocean. The park, which is centered on Mount Desert Island, covers 41,642 acres. While touring the park by bus, our guide told us about the devastating fire they had a few years ago that burned out of control for several days. Today, however, Acadia Park looks better than ever.

This reminded me of the 1988 devastating fires of Yellowstone National Park in Wyoming that also burned out of control for months. Thousands of acres were blackened, ruining the beautiful national landmark. Scientists are now discovering, however, that the fire, which was believed to have been started by lightning, was the best thing that ever happened to Yellowstone. A film in the auditorium within the park explains why. Experts discovered that one species of pine trees reproduces itself only when a fire's heat opens the pinecones, sending spores and seeds onto the ground. Although the adult trees were burned, the seemingly disastrous fire brought forth a flourishing new crop. This became a food source for larger herds of elk, bison and moose as early as a year later. What seemed like a terrible loss brought new life to both national parks! Officials had decided to monitor naturally caused fires, but not put them out unless buildings and human lives were threatened.

Perhaps there are some of us who might feel that they too have fires of adversity burning in their lives. It might even seem as though God has forsaken us. We are discouraged, frightened, alone. Fires of adversity, however, can make us stronger, and bring us into closer dependence on God. As a result, we can bear more fruit in His name.

The Apostle Paul says in Romans 8:28: "We know that all things work together for good to those who love God, to those who are called according to His purpose." This does not mean that all that happens to us is good. Evil is present in our fallen world, but God is able to turn every circumstance around for our long-range good. Let us note that God is working to fulfill His purpose, which is not for everyone. The verse says that it can be claimed only by those who love God and are called according to His purpose.

Apostle Paul teaches us to be brave, faithful "firefighters" in God's service. Those who dwell only on their suffering never see the higher perspective. Suffering, however, can result in perseverance, character and hope when we allow God to work in our lives. We must surrender our will to our Creator, allowing us to be used for righteous purposes, and for the good of mankind.

If we are facing those kinds of fires, we must trust God and be confident that He has a plan for us. Unfortunately, we can't see the entire picture—but God does! And His plans are always good. Great blessings can grow out of ashes of adversity! We must believe this.

*I*f we wish to go through life with as little sorrow and pain as possible, then we must love no one. Because each time we allow ourselves to love, we become vulnerable and open the door to pain. When a person falls in love and marries, he or she may someday suffer and shed many tears over illness or death of a spouse. Becoming parents is also painful. Loving our children will also cause us worry and endless concern as we watch them grow up in the world. Friends and co-workers may also disappoint us. We will certainly save ourselves a great deal of pain if we don't allow ourselves to become emotionally attached to anyone. On the other hand, we will also miss out on some of the greatest joys of life. The more we love, the more we may suffer, and yet the path to selfless love is also the path to greatest joys! In spite of sorrows, we chose to love.

God also has chosen to love us in spite of our shortcomings. If we then, as imperfect individuals, know how to demonstrate our love to those we care for, how much more does our Heavenly Father love us in spite of our failures. Jesus says in John 13:34, 35: "A new commandment I give you: Love one another. As I have loved you....By this all men will know that you are my disciples, if you love one another". This instructs to love others based on God's standards of love! Have we given any serious thought to the depths of His love? The following story illustrates just that.

A Norwegian explorer tried to measure an extremely deep part of the Arctic Ocean. The first day he used his longest measuring line, but could not reach bottom. In his log book he wrote, "The ocean is deeper than that!" The next day, he added more line, but still could not measure the depth. So, in his record book he wrote again, "Deeper than that!" After several days of adding more and more rope to his line, he had to leave that part of the ocean without learning its actual depth. All he knew was that it was beyond his ability to measure.

God's love for us is also beyond our ability to measure. Our human measuring line is too short, and the depth of His love is incomprehensible to us. LOVE is an emotion that reveals itself in ACTION. Action is the fruit of love. God's word teaches us to unselfishly love our fellow man when it's not convenient, give when it hurts, devote energy to others' welfare rather than our own, and absorb ill-treatment from others without trying to get even. This kind of love is hard -- very hard. If we follow these instructions, people will notice and will know that we are empowered by a divine source!

Yes, loving others makes us vulnerable to pain and disappointment, but the rewards are great. God's love is our example, our measuring line. Let us then put our love into action. As we know, there are always personal rewards, growth and enrichment in the experience of demonstrating our love; and when we give freely, we are always the recipient.

*W*hile attending grade school in Greece, some of my notebook covers displayed the picture of Atlas—a gigantic, beautifully proportioned male with all his muscles strained, carrying the world on his shoulders. Its story is from Greek mythology. And since the figure of Atlas supporting the earth was often used in the title pages of early collections of maps, the name has come to be applied to a volume of maps.

There he was, a strong muscle-man, barely standing up under that great weight—the world. Now, that is one way to live, trying to carry the world's burdens on our shoulders. On the other hand, we can turn all our concerns and burdens onto the One Who is the great burden bearer. Are we straining under a mounting load of anxieties? St. Peter instructs us, "Cast all your cares upon Him, for He cares for you" (1 Pet. 5:7). In other words, conserve energy and trust the Lord.

Trust in God does not mean ignoring our own common sense. But common sense alone isn't enough to give needed direction for a particular decision. By grounding our common sense in His Word and prayer, we can then rely on Him to guide us through His Holy Spirit. God gives wisdom, and with it, the ability to make wise decisions.

We all encounter disappointments that perplex us, and we often cry out, "Oh Lord, why do You allow these things to happen?" But it's especially at times like these when we should cast ourselves into God's loving hands. Even though our present trials may be heartbreaking, the all-wise heavenly Father works through them to bring about ultimate good. God may have allowed the burdens and problems we experience, so that we may learn to cast them all on Him. Life's challenges are designed not to break us, but to bend us toward Him. Perhaps we should thank God for our burdens because they are often blessings in disguise. Clouds of testing can often bring showers of blessings. And what appears to be human tragedy often bears the seeds of divine triumph. All things can work together for good to those who love God, who are called according to His purpose (Rom. 8:28). Our afflictions should never diminish our faith or disillusion us. Yes, it's easy to loose heart and quit. But rather than giving up, we can concentrate on experiencing inner strength through the Holy Spirit.

Are we straining under a weight of burdens? It's always darkest just before dawn. Let us determine not to imitate the picture of Atlas, and give God the opportunity to demonstrate His power. Obediently, we can trust God in all our circumstances, even when we don't understand them. Instead, we must see tomorrow's triumphs beyond today's problems!

*D*riving through Northern California's Redwood Forest, I was amazed at the height and density of the redwood trees. It is an overwhelming feeling to enter the Drive-Thru Tree Park, seeing countless gigantic trees that measure more than 315 feet in height, and at least 21 feet in diameter. The tree in particular which is familiar to most is the one that has the hand-hewn opening at the base, through which full sized autos easily drive. The most amazing piece of information I received however, was that redwood trees have relatively shallow roots. How could they be so strong and healthy, stand so tall, and yet have shallow roots? Redwood trees, I learned, are connected to each other by their roots. Their roots are all woven tightly together, forming a network of underground strength! This is amazing and very meaningful.

Christians also need to stand strong and be connected to each other as those redwood trees, especially in times of stress. Sometimes the winds of adversity blow hard enough to topple us. To stand alone is difficult during challenging times. If however, we draw on the support of loving brothers and sisters in Christ, we will have the needed strength to withstand adversity.

The Apostle Paul, in his epistle to the Philippians, Ch. 6, expressed his gratitude for the way believers in Philippi stood by him in his time of need. Although Paul was writing from prison, joy is a dominant theme in his letter. The secret of his joy is grounded, of course, in his relationship with Christ. He is, however, overjoyed by the generosity and love of the Philippian believers. They had supported him financially while he was in prison. It was not the Philippians' gift, but their spirit of love and devotion that Paul most appreciated. He called it "A fragrant offering!" How comforting it must have been to Paul to have the assurance that fellow Christians cared! That is "redwood support—redwood connection."

When we give to those in need, the benefit is not only to the receiver, but to ourselves as well. As Christians we need to uphold one another with redwood support in times of difficulty. When we are unified and strongly connected, Christ's strength is most abundant. We can have joy, even in times of hardship. Joy does not come from outward circumstances, but from inward strength. Joy comes from knowing Christ personally, and depending on His strength rather than ours. Just like Paul, we also need to have the support of our fellow Christians. God used the Philippians' support to encourage and strengthen the apostle. He can do the same for us also. Christians rooted together are not easily uprooted. Yes, we are connected by the love that comes from God our Father, but we also depend upon the strength we draw from each other. Roots of stability and strength come from being grounded in God's Word and from being connected as Christians.

Do we wish to stand strong and tall as the immovable redwood trees? Let us get connected—give one another redwood support!

Someone has said, "There's nothing like the beauty of a loving heart, shining through a seasoned face!" I witnessed that a few days ago when my friend said to an elderly woman, "I think you are absolutely beautiful!" The woman replied, "I should be, my dear. After all I'm 85 years old!" Then she added with a smile, "And the Lord is my Shepherd, you know!" She was beautiful, and her walk with the Lord made all the difference. Her face shone and she didn't miss the opportunity to tell us of her Shepherd.

We often think of the springtime of youth as the most beautiful time of life. The body is strong, the mind is sharp, and there is a great curiosity and desire to learn. Yet the 70's and 80's are even more beautiful, according to Prov. 16:31, that says, "The silver-haired head is a crown of glory if it is found in the way of righteousness." So it is with all those who know the Lord and have invited Him to come into their hearts. When we walk with God, the years have a way of refining us. The sufferings of a lifetime mellow us and reveal the grace we received in Christ. The late autumn years can be beautiful years!

No matter how hard we try, none of us can hold back the natural process of aging. We can exercise, eat right, put on moisturizers, but years have a way of catching up with us. That undeniable truth is found in 2 Cor. 4:16, which states, "Our outward man is perishing, yet the inward man is being renewed day by day."

In 2 Cor. 5:1, the Apostle Paul refers to the human body as our "earthly house" and "tent" as a metaphor for the physical body. This imagery was quite natural for first century Christians because many people were nomadic tent dwellers. The Apostle himself was a tent maker (Acts 18:3) and knew much about a tent's characteristics. His point is that, like a temporary tent, man's earthly existence is fragile. But compared to eternal life, Paul is referring to a believer's security and permanence as opposed to the frail, temporary nature of a tent.

But there is good news! Although our bodies rush toward aging, we can still enjoy a beautiful vitality in our walk with God. Spiritual age does not have the same effect as physical age. In fact, it's the opposite. The longer we walk with God, the more spiritually renewed we feel day by day. "If anyone is in Christ, he is a new creation; old things have passed away; behold, all things have become new" (2 Cor. 5:17). As Christians we are brand new people on the inside. The Holy Spirit gives us new life. We are recreated, living in union with Christ.

For centuries people sought a fountain of youth, a spring that promised to give eternal life and vitality. It was never found. But the joy and wisdom in God's Word is a wellspring of life that can make a person happy, healthy and spiritually eternal. When we accept Christ into our hearts and lives, He washes away all effects and guilt of our past trespasses. The promise of eternal life gives us a joyful perspective in our present life. The fountain of youth was only a dream, but the wellspring of eternal life is reality. Our bodies may be perishing, but our spirit can be flourishing!

*T*he story is told of a young Chinese Christian named Lo who was given a New Testament. Delighted, he began to read it enthusiastically. When he read in the gospel of Matthew 28:20 the words of Christ, "Lo, I am with you always, even to the end of the age," he became very excited. He took this verse as a personal promise to him. Although he misinterpreted the first word of that text for his own name, Lo did not miss the impact of the verse. In fact, it became more meaningful and real to him.

As Christians, each one of us could, in fact, insert our own name into this promise of Christ as well. At this time Jesus was with the disciples physically, but soon after saying these words He ascended into heaven. After this, He was with them spiritually through His promised Holy Spirit—and His presence would never leave them. Christ gave these reassuring words to His disciples because He knew how lonely they would feel. Knowing the weakness of human nature, He consoled them with the truth that He would still be with them in the person of the Holy Spirit. He would assist them in preaching, teaching, and guide them as they began His Church.

There are times when the various challenges of daily life set before us seem too overwhelming. We often forget that we are not alone, and that there is more strength available to us than just our own. This personal and empowering presence of Christ is visibly portrayed in this verse, and is promised to all His followers. Those who trust in Christ and seek Him will find Him, no matter where they go or what problems they may face.

Christ is Christianity and Christianity is Christ. We certainly carry his name. We cannot belong to Christ nor be adopted into God's family without His Spirit. At the same time, we must keep this in mind: If we are to feel Christ's presence with us, we must be present with Him.

No matter how weak, humble or unimportant we might feel, He is our friend, our companion, our comforter—invisible but there. He is walking by our side, watching with loving interest every detail of life's struggle, trying so patiently to lead us to a place of joy and happiness. All this may seem like a beautiful fantasy to some. But it is a FACT—the one fundamental fact of Christ's promise. There is a touching echo at the beginning of Matthew's Gospel (1:23). When Jesus was born He was called "Immanuel"—which means "God with us." He remains with us, even to the end of the age!

One of the important lessons we learn from God's Word is that everything in nature, everything in life produces after its own kind. Vegetation, the animal kingdom, all produce according to their own classification. A farmer knows well that whatever he sows in his fields, that is what he will reap.

In 2 Kings 4:1 – 7, we read the story of Elisha and the poor widow who had nothing but a little oil. Yet when Elisha blessed it, wealth was produced for her, not in money but in oil after its own kind. In all four gospels; Matthew 14, Mark 6, Luke 9 and John 6, we read that when the crowds had no food to eat, Jesus took a few loaves of bread and two fish. After blessing them He was able to feed 5,000—there were basketfuls left over! Christ's blessings produced after its own kind.

It is the same with us. Our abilities given to us by our Creator are gifts. If we want to increase them we must put them to work by faith in God's service, and we will be blessed. In Matthew 25:14 – 30, we read the parable of the talents. Jesus tells us that the Kingdom of Heaven is like a man going on a journey who called his three servants and entrusted one with five talents of silver, another with two talents, and the third with one talent. Then he left. While the first two put their talents to work and doubled the amount, the third man was so afraid of losing his portion that he buried it in the ground. For his lack of initiative and faith, he was not only discharged from his job when his master returned, but was thrown outside into the darkness as a worthless servant.

Every one of us has talents and abilities, but so many have long buried their talents. We must use our time, talents and treasures diligently. God expects us to do so, and in using them we will multiply their effectiveness and touch lives for good. Yes, and in due time we will also be blessed. But the basic law of life is that we must first give before we can receive.

The farmer in the spring casts his seeds into the ground. Then he covers them with soil and waits for the harvest. He waits in perfect faith believing that nature's law will work for him once again. He does not go daily digging the soil to see what happened to his seeds. He knows that in due time he will receive. This law is just as dependable when we sow our good deeds for the Lord and for His glory. In due time they will come back to us many fold.

God's love and blessings are our inheritance because we are His faithful, obedient children. Christ says, "I have come that they may have life, and that they may have it more abundantly" (John 10:10). The law of cause and effect simply means that whatever we think and do in life will come back to us with interest. We reap whatever we sow.

One of my favorite paperweights on my desk is an oval flat stone. It has an almost silky smooth surface that is very pleasant to the touch. I picked it up as a momento two years ago while driving along Ocean Drive in Newport, a beautiful area on the rugged coast of Rhode Island. Although the ocean was relatively calm on that summer day, the waves broke onto the rocky coast with amazing force. As I walked along the shoreline, I saw stones the size of golf balls and others as big as a football. All of them however, were rounded and surprisingly smooth. The waves of the stormy sea had transformed over many years, once rough-edged rocks into rounded objects of beauty and wonder!

God does something similar to that with each one of us as well. He works on us through the various storms of life, shaping us into men and women who reflect His glory if we hold firm to His love. Although circumstances may be very difficult, God uses them to refine our character, making us patient, humble, and sensitive to His will. That is why it is not unusual, even as Christians, for us to endure severe trials.

In his epistle to the Romans, Chapter 5, the Apostle Paul writes, "We rejoice in suffering because we know that suffering produces perseverance; perseverance, character; and character, hope. And hope does not disappoint us, because God has poured out His love into our hearts."

Naturally we wish for life's seas to remain calm at all times so that we can live undisturbed. God, however, sees our rough edges and acts in grace to remove them. When we think of all those stormy, difficult times when we were tossed about like those rocks on Newport's seacoast, our all-wise, loving Heavenly Father had not deserted us. He was working all the while to smooth our rough edges and produce in us the beauty and loveliness of Christ.

It is not easy to rejoice in suffering, and yet, we are reminded that we are only being shaped and sculpted, and this is the Maker's process! Those who know the Lord have in Him a calm retreat in the storms of life, even while the winds of trial are sweeping over us from time to time. We can experience through His love, peace and calmness of spirit. Reasoning will not help us. We can only put our faith and trust in Him in all circumstances. Our confidence is in His faithfulness and everlasting love.

Let us not then be overwhelmed by the storms and waves we face from time to time. The secret to peace is to give every anxious care we have to God. He will give us peace through the storms we may face. And we know that He Who began a good work in us some time ago, will carry it on to completion. Why not rejoice. We are being sculpted and shaped into smooth beautiful beings of wisdom and wonder!

$\mathcal{T}$he story is told of a young woman who put aside a certain book she was reading because she found it dull. Not long after that, she met a young man whom she liked very much. They got to know each other, and some time later they became engaged. One day she said to her fiancé that she had a book written by a man with the same name as his. What an amazing coincidence! The man responded that it was not a coincidence—he wrote that book. That night she stayed up till morning hours reading the book she once found dull. It was now the most thrilling book she ever read. She had fallen in love with the author!

Is the Bible a dull book to some of us? Then perhaps we should meet the Author. The Bible is a book that will work wonders in everyone's life if its precepts are acted upon and obeyed in faith and sincerity. We read in 2 Tim. 3:16, "All scripture is given by inspiration of God, and is profitable for doctrine, for reproof, for correction, for instruction in righteousness, that the man of God may be complete, thoroughly equipped for every good work."

The Bible is the most remarkable book ever written. It is a divine library of 66 books, some quite long and others no more than 21 or 25 verses. These books include various forms of literature, history, biography, poetry, proverbial sayings, hymns, letters, directions for elaborate worship, laws, parables, allegories, prophesy, drama, etc. They embrace all manner of literary styles of human expression.

The Bible is not the product of human effort. The prophets, in fact, sometimes wrote what they could not fully understand, but were faithful to write what God revealed to them. The Holy Spirit is the divine author, originator and producer of the scriptures. Although the human writers were active rather than passive in the process of writing scripture, God's Holy Spirit directed them. Using their own individual personalities, thought processes and vocabulary, they composed and recorded without error the exact words God wanted written. Scripture therefore, is God-inspired, God-breathed, and without error.

The Bible contains light to direct us, spiritual nourishment to sustain us, and comfort to encourage us. It is the traveler's map, the pilgrim's staff, the pilot's compass, the soldier's sword, and the Christian's character. The Bible is a mine of wealth, the source of health, and immeasurable pleasure to the faithful. Illumination is given to all believers who seek to know and understand its divine written truths. Christ is the grand subject. It is designed for our good, and the glory of God is revealed from beginning to end, from Genesis to Revelation.

Someone has said of the Bible: Read it to be wise, believe it to be safe and practice it to be holy. Is the Bible a dull book to some of us? Then perhaps we need to know the Author better!

SMALL FOREIGN CAR

*W*hat are some of the most desirable features we look for in a car? For most of us, what we hope to get are reliability, good gas mileage and reasonably good looks; preferably in that order. The following amusing story was related to me not long ago.

The owner of a small foreign car began to irritate his friends by bragging constantly about his car's impressive gas mileage. Having enough of that, his friends devised a plan to bring the young man's boast to an end with a prank. Every day one of them would secretly pour a few gallons of gas into the car's tank. Soon the car owner was boasting of getting as much as 90 miles per gallon!

The mischievous friends enjoyed watching his excitement as he tried to convince people of the truthfulness of his claims. Needless to say, they had even more fun to see his reaction when his friends stopped refilling the car's tank. The poor fellow couldn't understand what happened to his car.

The story points out that bragging can have unpleasant results and leave one looking foolish. It is also very unattractive when a person advertises one's own good judgment or abilities. We read in Proverbs 27:2, "Let another man praise you, and not your own mouth; a stranger, and not your own lips." If we deserve praise, someone else will notice and will praise us. If we brag about ourselves, we are demonstrating pride and will soon turn others off, as the young man in the story. Besides, the praise of others carries more weight, since they are more objective about our accomplishments and character qualities. It has been said that people who sing their own praise usually do so without accompaniment.

How much better it is to find our security and sense of worth in a quiet, personal relationship with the Lord. God wants His people to be wise. When we choose God's way, He grants us wisdom. His Word leads us to live righteously, have proper relationships, and make wise decisions. Our speech is a test of our wisdom. King David says in Psalm 141:3, "Set a guard, O Lord, over my mouth; keep watch over the door of my lips." Knowing the power of the tongue, we would do well to ask God to guard what we say so that our words will bring honor to His name.

How much better it is to seek the praise of God rather than the praise or approval of man. Then we will be free to give God the credit. Self-praise is both meaningless and foolish. The only true, meaningful commendation comes from God. We may speak of our accomplishments only as a means of encouraging others by personal example who might need uplifting words. Such an approach will win notice and approval, and glorify God. "Let the words of my mouth and the meditation of my heart be acceptable in Your sight O Lord" (Psalm 19:14). As we begin each day, let us resolve that God's love and teachings will guide what we say and how we think.

*T*he story is told that an educator and comedian, Sam Levinson, was standing with a group of men who seemed to tower over him. Someone asked, "Sam, don't you feel strange surrounded by so many tall people?" He replied, "Yes, I do. I feel like a dime among a lot of pennies!"

Perhaps for some of us Christians there might be situations or places where we may not feel "tall" in the eyes of some. In fact, at times the world might look down on us. But regardless of how some people might make us feel, we are precious in the sight of God. The Apostle Paul says in Romans 8:16, "We are children of God, and if children, then heirs—heirs of God and joint heirs with Christ." For the first century believers, there was economic and social persecution, and some even faced death. In many parts of today's world, Christians still face persecution. But even in countries where Christianity is tolerated, or even encouraged, Christians must not become complacent.

God's ultimate goal for us as Christians is to make us more like Christ each day. It's a process that will progress throughout our entire lives. We already carry His name. How can we conform to Christ's likeness? By studying His Word, putting it into practice, attending church, learning more about His life on earth through the gospels, and by doing His work in the world. One of Christ's last instructions to His disciples was, "Go and make disciples of all nations ... teaching them to obey everything I have commanded you. And surely I am with you always, to the very end of the age" (Matt. 28:19, 20).

Christ promises to be with us. He says in John 14:18: "I will not leave you orphans; I will come to you." How is Christ with us? Jesus was with His disciples physically until He ascended into heaven, and then spiritually. The Holy Spirit would be Jesus' presence that would never leave the disciples. Christ is with us also through His Spirit, even today, even at this very moment. The Holy Spirit is a source of divine inspiration, direction, wisdom and courage for all faithful. He empowers us, not only for the mission of the Church, but also for the moral and ethical life appropriate for those who are people of God.

Are there persons who perhaps feel down on themselves? Some may admit that at times they felt unimportant or rejected; like being on the outside looking in. Let's remember that even when we are feeling low, God thinks highly of us. Regardless of how the world may think of us, or how small we may seem to others, we are precious in His sight. Through Christ we have immeasurable worth. The world may try to discount us, but in the sight of God, we are priceless! We are not "dimes," but precious "diamonds" among pennies!

*I*t made front-page news in the city's local newspaper. Two wealthy businessmen—philanthropists—had donated $150M to charitable causes over a period of ten years! It was certainly a sum worthy of headlines. It is wonderful that God blesses some individuals with great wealth to benefit others. But let us also keep this in proper perspective. If someone is a billionaire, the giving of millions represents only a small fraction of what he is worth.

The Bible gives us an example of another account of big giving that would also be worthy of today's front-page news. It is Jesus' evaluation of a poor widow as she dropped two mites into the temple treasury. In Mk. 12:41 – 44, we see that Jesus sat opposite the place where the offerings were put, and watched the crowd putting their money into the temple treasury. Many rich people put in large sums. But a poor widow came and put in two very small copper coins, worth only a fraction of a penny. For her it was a gift of astronomical proportions.

Calling His disciples to Him, Jesus said, "I tell you the truth, this poor widow has put more into the treasury than all the others. They all gave out of their wealth; but she, out of her poverty, put in everything—all she had to live on." In Jesus' eyes, this poor widow gave more than all the others combined, though her gift was by far the smallest. The value of a gift is not determined by its amount, but by the spirit with which it is given. A gift given grudgingly or for recognition loses its value. When we give, we must remember that a gift of any size is pleasing to God when it's given out of gratitude to Him, and with a spirit of generosity.

God measures not how much we give, but how much we retain. Jesus also points out that those with greater income have an obligation to return a larger amount to the Lord's work. God can use any amount and multiply it in His service to be a blessing to many, as we see in the account of the two fish and five loaves of bread. A boy willingly gave his poor man's lunch, which through Christ's blessing, fed 5,000 men, plus the women and children who were present; with twelve basketfuls left over! (Mt. 14:15 – 21). Our willful giving must be linked to God's divine power. Then, through Him, it will grow to bless more people than we could ever imagine. This includes our time, talents, treasure and love.

What we have is meaningless unless it is used for something meaningful. Such generosity has eternal value. Since God measures our giving by the degree of our sacrifice, many who have little to give in this life will be immensely rewarded in the life to come. Whether we are rich, poor or in between, let's be sure to invest in eternity. Our value is determined, not by what we have, but by what we do with what we have. Let's remember that God gave! He gave His only Son, that whoever believes in Him should not perish, but have eternal life (Jn. 3:16).

If Jesus evaluated our giving by the principle of sacrifice, would we make the headlines?

*T*he January 2001 issue of "Vanity Fair" magazine displayed 18 of photography's most enduring masters, now "clicking into their 80's and 90's. Jousuf Karsh, the internationally known Armenian photographer, now age 91, was featured among them. A full-page portrait depicts the artist's maturity with flair! A familiar portrait of Winston Churchill, taken by Karsh back in 1941, also skillfully displays the use of light and shadows, essential to a dramatic portrait. "With celebrity photography," Karsh notes, "the photographer too became an object of glamour." But the man who has had sittings with every president since Hoover says he no longer takes photos.

Karsh was interviewed by Mike Wallace on TV a few years ago. I vividly remember the following amusing point: Wallace said to Karsh, "You travel around the globe photographing world leaders and celebrities. What was your most recent assignment?" Karsh said that he had gone to Rome to photograph the Pope, and then he went to Paris for a photo session with Brigitte Bardot. "Ah," said Wallace, "you went from the saint to the sinner!"

The word "photograph" is taken from the Greek, which literally means, "written with light." When our photo is taken, we usually pose and smile. We want our best side to be seen. But let us visualize an imaginary candid camera taking photos of our lives. Click, click. What would the camera reveal? Jesus taught plenty about light and darkness. In John 8:12 He says, "I am the light of the world. Whoever follows Me will never walk in darkness, but will have the light of life."

"Light" and "life" are qualities possessed by those who respond to the gospel message of Jesus Christ—enlightened by God's Word and receiving everlasting life. "Light" refers to biblical truths, while "darkness" to error and falsehood. Morally, "light" refers to holiness and purity, while "darkness" to sin, wrongdoing and evil. The statement that "God is Light" means that God is perfectly holy and true, and that He alone can guide us out of the darkness of sin. Light is also related to truth, that is, light exposes whatever exists, whether it is good or bad. Jesus calls people out of darkness into His marvelous light.

All God's faithful can be described as "lights in the world," because they are enlightened by God's truth. As Christians, we must never forget the value of being an example—a model—a light in every dark corner of our environment. Whether we are at home, in the workplace or at school, we must never forget that we are constantly being watched. As Christians, we have the opportunity and responsibility to be an example. And that example is what will last and be remembered, even after we are gone.

If we live God-pleasing lives, we will glow like lights, showing an unbelieving world the way to Christ. If we go along with the crowd, we'll be hiding our precious light. Let us be beacons of God's truth wherever we are! Then we won't care who takes candid photos, and when. Click, click!

*T*en-year-old Johnnie and his eight year old sister Jill were excited to visit grandma who lived on a farm. While Johnnie was practicing with his slingshot, he accidentally hit grandma's favorite duck, which later died. Jill saw what happened, but said nothing to grandma. After dinner she said to her brother, "I will not help you with the dishes anymore." "But why?" asked Johnnie, "We always did it together." "Remember the duck?" whispered Jill.

Johnnie said nothing, and washed the dishes alone. This went on for a few days. Feeling guilty about the duck, and tired of his sister bossing him around, Johnnie went to grandma with the truth. After hearing Johnnie's confession and his remorseful words, grandma said, "I know. I saw what happened from the window, and I have forgiven you."

We are often like Johnnie ourselves. Rather than turn our burdens over to God, we carry the weight heavily in our hearts. But when we turn to God in repentance, He not only forgives, God also forgets! In both the Old and New Testaments, we read, "For I will be merciful to their iniquities, and I will remember their sins no more" (Jer. 31:34 and Heb. 8:12). God sees and knows our weaknesses, and He offers us His grace and forgiveness, not on the basis of any act we have done to earn it, but solely because of His grace.

We should never get the idea, however, that our wrongful acts are taken lightly by God. But when we acknowledge our guilt with true repentance, God stands ready to forgive because of what Jesus did on the cross for us. Following Christ's teachings, which are the foundation of our faith, gives us an opportunity to make a fresh new start, and establish a permanent personal relationship with God.

Holding onto a hurt creates more hurt. We must set ourselves free. To forgive is to set a prisoner free, and discover that the true prisoner was us! We must never allow the pain of a burden to grow. The Bible urges us to maintain honest, peaceful relationships with our fellow man. To ignore such instruction can surely affect our health.

Is there someone we need to talk to openly, honestly and humbly about our relationship? We can ask the Lord in prayer to help us speak the right words and listen to what the other person has to say. In light of God's great mercy and love, the issue that appeared so large in the past may not be that big after all. Christian community relations depend on members forgiving one another. We ask God in the Lord's Prayer to forgive us our moral debts, as we are also to forgive our debtors. Do we? Jesus is speaking here of daily forgiveness, which is necessary to restore broken communications.

Stifled anger, resentment and guilt burn flamelessly inside us. Forgiveness puts them out. Through Christ, we can experience the forgiveness that also forgets. We'll be free and restored. This is what St. Paul says in Eph. 4: 32: "Be kind and compassionate to one another, forgiving each other, just as in Christ God forgave you."

*A*ccording to a news report out of San Jose, California, about 100 former gang members took part in a program in which a plastic surgeon donated his skills to remove gang tattoos. J.K. was one of the hundred. He was tattooed a few years earlier to tell the world who he was. Now, he wanted to get rid of them because of who he wants to be. The distinctive marks turned off prospective employers, thereby threatening a new life he desired—one away from the streets.

For some, tattoos are identification badges, indicating to which gang they belong. They are looking for acceptance, which sooner or later, can get them into big time trouble. J.K. no longer wanted to be identified with the gang whose symbols he once so proudly wore. He is back in school, trying to build a solid future. Many laser surgeries and a lot of pain later, all 100 were free from their tattoos. Getting rid of them was a sign that their old life with the gangs with which they identified was behind them.

As Christians, when we accepted Christ into our hearts and lives, we too left behind an old life. It may not have been marked by physical signs, but it was marked by alienation from God, and an inability to grasp the truths of His Word. It may also have been characterized by undesirable habits that God's grace has freed us from.

The Apostle Paul writes to the Corinthian faithful, "If anyone is in Christ, he is a new creation; old things have passed away, behold, all things have become new" (2 Cor. 5:17). As Christians, we are brand new people on the inside. The Holy Spirit gives us new life, and we are not the same any longer. We are recreated, having a new life under a new Master, Christ Himself. Living the Christian life is a process. Although we have a new nature, we don't automatically think only good thoughts and express correct attitudes all the time. But if we continue to listen to God's Word, attend church on Sundays, we will be changing daily.

As we look back over the past year, do we see a process of change for the better in our attitudes and actions? Although change may be slow, it comes as we trust God to change us. We should put our old way of life completely behind us, like old clothes to be thrown away. People should be able to see the difference in our new transformed life, renewed through Christ.

Receiving Christ as Lord of our lives is the beginning of a Christian's life. As we continue to follow His leading by being rooted and established in the faith, Christ will guide us through His Holy Spirit to do right. Just as plants draw nourishment from the soil through their roots, so do we draw our life-giving strength and discernment from Christ.

God has chosen us to be Christ's representatives on earth. In light of this truth, we are challenged to live lives worthy of the calling we have received. As people watch our lives, what symbols do they see? Are we marked by faithfulness to Him? Can others see Christ in us? How well are we doing as His representatives?

*H*ow often do we respond with excuses when we are asked to do something in the service of God? We usually say, "I'm busy enough as it is," or "I'll have an opportunity to do that some time later," etc. Not wishing to cross our comfort zone, we develop excuses. Strange as it may seem, Jesus heard His share of excuses as well.

In Lk. 9:57 – 62, we read two opposite attitudes among His audience. It happened as Jesus and His followers journeyed on the road, when someone said to Him, "Lord, I will follow You wherever You go." This man volunteered to follow Jesus without any reservations. His problem was that he hadn't realistically counted the cost of discipleship. His enthusiasm based on his feelings of the moment would not sustain him during trials that lay ahead. Knowing this, Jesus warned the would-be disciple that Christ Himself didn't have even the ordinary comforts of home. And as the Jewish religious leaders became increasingly hostile toward Him, Jesus wanted His disciples to be prepared for the worst. Therefore, the decision to follow Jesus was not to be taken casually.

Then Jesus said to another man, "Follow Me." But this one responded quite differently. He said, "Lord, let me first go and bury my father." This didn't mean that his father was already dead. The phrase was a common figure of speech meaning, let me fulfill my obligation to care for my father until he dies, and then I'll follow You. If the man's father was indeed dead, the son would not have been with Jesus, but busy with burial duties. Jewish law requires that the deceased must be buried with 24 hours of death. Jesus knowing this, said to him to let those who are spiritually dead bury those who are physically dead.

Jesus understood the command to honor one's parents. He didn't teach forsaking family responsibilities, but He often gave commands to people in light of their real motives. Perhaps this man wanted to delay following Christ, and used his father as an excuse. Therefore Jesus added, "No one, having put his hand on the plow, and looking back, is fit for the kingdom of God. This makes it difficult to plow straight furrows." To bring this expression up to date: We are not fit to be drivers, if we continually look back while we drive the car forward.

What does Christ want from us? He is not looking for excuses. He wants our obedience—total dedication, not half-hearted commitment. We can't pick and choose and follow Him selectively. If we say we are fatigued, perhaps we should look at what is sapping our energy from our Christian responsibilities. Perhaps we spend too much time on the wrong things. Christ is not looking for excuses, but obedience to His call. We have to accept the cross along with the crown, judgment as well as mercy. We must count the cost of discipleship and be willing to abandon those things that gave us comfort in the past. Therefore, when we hear the call, "Follow Me," no excuse is acceptable.

A philanthropist and community leader was the speaker at a banquet, and this is the story he told his audience:

A few years earlier, he had been approached by an individual who informed him of a teen-age boy who desperately needed urgent medical care. The philanthropist was then asked if he would consider providing that help for the boy. The youth had been struck by a car and had not received proper medical attention. He would be unable to walk unless he underwent a series of surgeries and months of physical therapy, which his family could not afford. The philanthropist provided all the medical care the youth needed. Three years later, the young man, now an adult, walked into the philanthropist's office, completely recovered. He had come to meet and personally thank his benefactor. It was a moving moment for both men.

"Most of you might be wondering," the philanthropist continued, "whatever happened to the young man and where he is today. Is he at school getting an education? Learning a trade? Working for someone?" With deep emotion the speaker reported, "No, none of the above. Today the young man is in prison for a terrible crime." Then he added, "I was instrumental in helping him walk again, but there was no one to teach him in which direction he should walk."

Jesus says in John 14:6, "I am the way, the truth, and the life. No one comes to the Father except through Me." This is one of the most basic and important passages in scripture, and familiar to all of us. In this verse the exclusiveness of Jesus as the only approach to the Father is emphatic. Christ is the door and basis of all that is right.

Many people react negatively to the fact that there is no other name than that of Jesus to call upon for eternal life. Yet, this is not something that the Church determined. It is the specific teaching of Jesus Christ Himself. If God designated Jesus to be the Savior of the world, no one else can be His equal. No other religious teacher came to earth as God's only Son, Who died on the cross for our sins, rose from the dead and ascended into heaven. Our focus should be on Christ, Whom God offered as "the Way," so that we can have an eternal relationship with Him.

It seems that the young man in the above story never knew that, or knowingly ignored it. Perhaps there is still some hope for him, even in prison, but he still must pay his debt to society, and accept the consequences of his unlawful actions. Wrongful acts often have a way of enslaving us, dominating and directing our lives. And one poor choice can easily lead to another. Only Christ through His Holy Spirit can free us from this bondage that keeps us from becoming the person God created us to be. Life through Christ is lived on a higher plane because of His overflowing forgiveness, love, guidance, mercy and grace.

As Christians, our mission is to point people, especially our youth, to God. Only through Christ can those with broken bodies, broken dreams, broken homes and broken hearts experience wholeness in life. Jesus says, "I am the way, the truth, and the life." That is the direction we must walk.

*E*very household in Greece had at least one cat. We had two. Cats were not considered pets, but were there to catch mice. In fact, I was instructed by my mother and grandmother not to overfeed them so they wouldn't get lazy and stop hunting mice. One year, one of our cats had four kittens. We found homes for each one of them, except for one, which we kept.

Some time after the kitten was over six months old, a friend of the family visited us. When she saw the cute grown kitten, she asked if she could take it home. My mom was pleased. When the woman was ready to leave, my grandma put the kitten in a basket and covered it with a large piece of cloth. The woman left, holding the basket on her chest with both arms. By this time it was dark outside.

The next morning we heard a familiar meowing at the door. When we opened it, there was our kitten! We could not believe our eyes. The cat had found its way back home from quite a distance! Well, now we had three cats again.

What remarkable homecoming instincts God has given to some animals! On the spiritual level, why is it that a child of God who has chosen to walk away from Him has less instinct to return "home"? Even the storks and other migratory birds know their appointed seasons of migration and obey their God-given instincts. Yet, why do some rebellious children of God often demonstrate less sense? We have come into existence by a loving Creator Who has given us every reason to want to come home to Him.

Jesus says in Mt. 11:28, "Come to Me, all you who are weary and burdened, and I will give you rest." Christ frees people from all burdens. The rest that He promises is love, healing and peace with God. A relationship with God changes a meaningless life into a spiritually productive and purposeful one. In His presence there is hope, comfort and joy. Away from Him there is perhaps temporary pleasure, but eternal loss and despair.

It is never too late for anyone to come back home. God makes provision for all those who may have distanced themselves or turned their backs to Him. Christ's outstretched arms on the cross are still calling all His prodigal sons and daughters back to Him; to an embrace of comfort for every hurting heart. God's Word says in 2 Chron. 7:14, "If My people who are called by My name will humble themselves, and pray and seek My face, and turn from their wicked ways, then I will hear from heaven, and will forgive their sin and heal their land."

Whether we sin individually, as a group, or as a nation, following these steps will lead to forgiveness. And God will accept our earnest prayers. Our Creator longs to see willing hearts ready to accept His love in faith. He does not force His love upon anyone. "Come to Me." These must be the dearest words ever heard by mankind. It is never too soon for anyone to come back home to God. Therefore, we can now stop running, unless it is to come back to Him!

Close to the center of the Bible are two books that have been favored by people for over 3,000 years. They are the books of Psalms and Proverbs. The Psalms uniquely represent the vertical aspects of our relationship with God. The authors are expressing to their Creator their deepest feelings and aspirations of their hearts. The book of Proverbs, on the other hand, represents the horizontal aspects of relationships we should have with people.

Proverbs is a book of practical ethics—a book of wise sayings—and instructs us how to live godly lives. It teaches us how to attain wisdom, discipline, and to do what is right and just. In short, it teaches how to apply divine wisdom to daily life, and provides moral instruction. Most of it was written by King Solomon, son of King David, especially emphasizing righteousness and fear (respect) of God.

In Psalms we turn to our Creator with songs of trust, hymns of devotion and prayers which express the heart of humanity. David and other writers honestly poured out their true feelings, reflecting a powerful and life changing relationship with God. The psalmists confess their sins, express doubts and fears, ask for God's help in times of trouble, and worship Him.

The Psalms are 150 poems to be set to music for use in private life and public worship. There are several authors, but we speak of the Psalms as the "Psalms of David," because he was the principle writer and compiler. Some 73 are ascribed to him. David was a warrior of unprecedented bravery, a military genius, and a brilliant statesman who led his nation to its pinnacle of power. He was also a poet and musician, and he loved God with all his heart.

Jesus Himself was very fond of the Psalms, so much so that they became part of His mental nature, and He uttered words from them in His dying agonies on the cross. In Ps. 22:1 we read, "My God, My God, why have You forsaken Me?" Also Ps. 31:5, "Into Your hand I commit My spirit." They are very familiar to most of us because they are Jesus Christ's words in Mt. 27:46 and Lk. 23:46, uttered in His last moments of life.

Many years ago I was introduced to Ps. 121 at a family gathering. It is known as the "Traveler's Psalm." The head of the household was going to cross the United States by car, and this Psalm was read in prayer. "I will lift up my eyes to the mountains; from where shall my help come? My help comes from the Lord, Who made heaven and earth." The entire Psalm is only eight verses, and it ends saying, "The Lord will protect you from all evil; He will keep your soul. The Lord will guard your going out and your coming in from this time forth and forever."

The grandfather of the family explained to me that when he left the "old country" as a teenager to sail alone to the U.S., he was bidden farewell with this Psalm. Then he added that in his 82 years of life he experienced many "goings out" and "comings in." He enjoyed many happy days, but endured others that were dark and grim. How reassuring it is that God of all creation goes with every believer in Christ! When this grandfather went "out" for the last time, I believe he was singing Psalm 121. He traveled home to be with the Lord.

I like comedienne and author Erma Bombeck's humor. On traveling, she says, "When you begin to look like your passport photo, it is time to go home." A recent trip to New Jersey that my husband Steve and I took demonstrated just that. The occasion was Steve's 50th high school reunion.

We rented a car and visited the Statue of Liberty and Ellis Island Immigration Museum. More than a hundred million Americans can claim ancestors who came through Ellis Island. It is a moving historical sight worth visiting at least once. We also drove to Gettysburg, PA., and visited the famous Civil War battlefield and National Civil War Wax Museum.

The following day, September 11, we had an early start. By 8:00 a.m. Eastern time, we were on the road, leaving Gettysburg behind. Our destination was Newark Airport for an early afternoon flight to Los Angeles. We had the radio on to local news when suddenly, just before 9:00 a.m., we heard the breaking news that a plane had hit one of the Twin Towers in New York. Somehow I knew at once that it wasn't just a terrible accident, and related my thoughts to Steve. His response was, "We might have to spend the night here." As the tragic news continued to unfold, we were horrified, as was the rest of the nation. Within minutes, the second tower was hit, later the Pentagon, and the plane that crashed in Pennsylvania. We listened in disbelief. The airports were closed and all flights canceled.

We kept the car for another day and checked into a hotel, and contacted our children. All main streets and highways around Newark were jammed. Traffic stood still. With their engines turned off, people were out of their vehicles looking with horror at the dark cloud of smoke in the sky. We watched the TV news showing the unbelievable events of the day.

We listened to President Bush addressing the nation. At one point he quoted from Psalm 23: "Even though I walk through the valley of the shadow of death, I fear no evil, for You are with me." His words to the nation were comforting, encouraging and reassuring. A verse from Joshua 1:9 suddenly came to mind. "Have I not commanded you? Be strong and courageous! Do not tremble or be dismayed, for the Lord your God is with you wherever you go." The Word of God is always comforting in all circumstances.

I thought continuously of the tragic events of the day. I kept thinking of all the innocent people who perished. We were to take our flight from Newark on American Airlines just a few hours later than the one that crashed in Pennsylvania. Why were we spared? Only God knows the answer and the timing of every life. Even when we can't see God's purpose, we can choose to trust Him. Two days later, the airports opened with limited flights. American Airlines scheduled us for an afternoon flight. We turned the car in and were ready to fly to LA.

At one point, while in the ladies room at the airport, I glanced in the mirror and Erma Bombeck's words came to mind. I knew I had long passed looking like my passport photo! It was time to go home.

*M*ost of us Christians, when we speak of the near future usually say, "God willing, I'll see you…" and we name the day and place. That's exactly what my husband and I said to our children when we went to New Jersey for Steve's 50th high school reunion. "God willing, we'll see you Tuesday, September 11." Well, God was not willing, and we did not return to Los Angeles on the above date as we had planned.

Here we were at Newark airport, two days after the tragic events because American Airlines had rescheduled us on a 6:00 p.m. flight to LA. Our luggage was checked in and carefully x-rayed. We were meticulously screened, and just when we were about to board our plane, the flight was canceled. We were told that there is some hope that the check-in desk would reopen at 4:00 a.m. if we wished to wait and get a flight on stand-by basis. Our luggage was returned.

I convinced Steve to spend the night at the airport. The security was very tight. Uniformed guards with shotguns were guarding the airport. We had dinner at the coffee shop there. I was loaned a brand new blanket by an airport worker who was passing them around to those who stayed overnight. I was amazed. Is this a great country or what, I thought!

Wrapped in the blanket, I thought again and again of the tragic events of September 11. So many verses from God's Word came to mind. St. Peter, quoting from Isaiah 40:6 – 8 says, "All flesh is grass, and all its loveliness is like the flower of the field. The grass withers, the flower fades, but the Word of God stands forever." The Apostle reminds all faithful that everything in this life—possessions, accomplishments, people—eventually fade away and disappear. Only God's Word is permanent. He teaches us to stop grasping on the temporary, and focus our time, money and energy on the permanent; our eternal life with God.

Life is short, no matter how many years we live. Let's not be deceived thinking that we have lots of time remaining to serve God some day, to enjoy our loved ones, etc. Let's live for God today and get to know Him personally. Then, no matter when our lives end, we will have fulfilled God's plan for us. We know yesterday is gone—it's history. Tomorrow is a mystery. Today is all we have, this very precious moment, which is a gift from God. Therefore, we call it "present."

God is in control. And all our future plans are in accordance with His sovereign will which doesn't condemn wise planning, but rather planning that omits God. Also when we say, "If the Lord wills," we must not use it as a cliché, but as a sober reflection of an attitude of heart, recognizing that everything truly depends on God's will. Knowing this should instill in us humility, wisdom and perspective for each precious moment of our lives.

The possibility of a morning flight vanished. The airport remained closed indefinitely. At this point we made our decision. We rented an attractive new car right there at the airport, and after a good breakfast on the way, we drove home to LA across the beautiful USA! God Bless America!

*L*ife is filled with unpredictable experiences and events. When my husband Steve and I left Los Angeles on September 5 and flew to New Jersey, the thought of driving across the country to return home had never entered our minds. But in light of the tragic events of September 11, 2001, the chances of taking a flight home became very slim. After our rescheduled flights were canceled for the third time, we decided to rent a car and drive home across the beautiful U.S.A.!

Patriotism in America was reborn overnight. Almost every overpass crossing the interstate was decorated with huge American flags and banners that said, "God Bless America," or "United We Stand," or "We Are Praying For You." Even electronic flashing lights repeating all of the above were set along the highways. This display of patriotism was not only evident in cities and towns, but even in the middle of nowhere. We were so moved, and we enjoyed every moment of it.

We kept in touch with our children daily. They were delighted that we were driving home. It turned out that it was quite an educational geography lesson for our grandchildren. Although the oldest is only five years old and the youngest three, they were very interested in what states we were crossing. Every night we talked on the phone and gave a report of our whereabouts. They were so excited as their parents marked our progress on the map. Our daughter Julie was very helpful in taking care of my appointments. For example, I was scheduled to serve jury duty. That had to be rescheduled. Talk about making plans in advance!

Life is uncertain. We must constantly remind ourselves of this truth. We don't know what the future holds, but we know Who holds the future. The Bible, Old and New Testaments, has plenty to say about our short lives. It describes life as a puff of smoke, or one's breath that appears for a moment in cold air, and then is gone! It stresses the temporary nature of life. Psalm 90:4 – 6 says, "For a thousand years, in Your sight are like yesterday when it is past...In the morning it flourishes and grows up; in the evening it is cut down and withers." In the New Testament, James 1:14 says almost the same. Our time on earth is limited. God is in control and He knows the end from the beginning. In every conversation I had with my children while we were away, I found myself repeating the three magic words, "I love you!" We don't say it often enough to our loved ones under normal circumstances.

In the 42 years I have been in the United States I have never seen such unity, patriotism and prayer amongst its citizens. May God continue to bless and reward America. What nation gives food to the enemy that tries to destroy it? As soon as we arrived home, Steve displayed our American flag. The following day I went to a fabric store to buy some red, white and blue ribbons. There were sold out! I was moved, tears filled my eyes. I bought some yarn, however, and made a few tri-color, big pompoms for our cars until flags became available.

We enjoyed the five-day cross-country trip. In the total 15 days that we were away, we slept in seven different hotels plus one night at the airport; an adventure we'll not soon forget. It's good to be home!

*F*ollowing directions carefully is good practice. The story is told that a professor at a Bible college gave his students an hour-long exam. They were instructed to spend half of their time on the Holy Spirit, and the remaining half about the devil. One student wrote continuously through the entire hour on the Holy Spirit. When he realized time was up, he wrote at the bottom of his paper, "I had no time for the devil," and he handed in his exam.

That is not, of course, the way to get a good grade on an exam. But the student's last comment points out to us about how we should treat the devil. When we are in the study of God's Word, intimately communicating in prayer, and yielding to the guidance, wisdom and will of the Holy Spirit, we will have no time "...nor give place to the devil" (Eph. 4:27). If we are not on guard, however, the life of a Christian can be like a battle at times. To withstand the attacks of the devil Apostle Paul says in Ephesians 6:11, "Put on the full armor of God, so that you will be able to stand firm against the schemes of the devil."

The Apostle Paul gives this counsel not only to the Ephesian church, but to every child of God. To put on the full armor of God is every Christian's responsibility. He was in prison when he wrote this epistle, and being guarded by Roman soldiers, made him even more aware of the need for armor. He certainly had his armor on; God's Word, his firm faith, intimate fellowship with the Lord in prayer, and the guidance and will of the Holy Spirit. In Eph. 6, St. Paul names each part of the armor piece by piece.

The Apostle never underestimated the enemy and the worldly battle which Christians often face. Attacks can come in the form of insults, temptations of various kinds, lack of self-worth, discouragement, etc. In short, the world wants us to doubt God and ourselves. But the shield of faith protects us from the fiery darts, and the truth of God's Word guards every true Christian's integrity.

The full armor of God symbolizes the protection Christ gives us against all attacks. Scriptural truth is always our primary line of defense. The more our minds are filled with the truth of God's Word, the less susceptible we are to deception and temptations surrounding us.

Therefore, before we launch out into the world each day, and for whatever occasion we appropriately dress, why not symbolically put on the full armor of God, piece by piece. And above all, we must hold onto that shield of faith; a vital part of every Christian's armor. When we do that, then, as in the above story, we will not have time nor give place to the devil.

*W*e all know about the long lines at major city airports due to the extra security measures taken since September 11, 2001. Frankly, on previous flights, security at LAX was so lax that it left me very concerned.

I was concerned because I compared our security measures with other countries. For example, we have been to Israel twice in the past ten years. Although we have never flown directly into Israel, entering the country from both Jordan and Egypt by bus, security was very tight. We crossed the border from Egypt; a busfull of 52 Armenians from Los Angeles, Fresno and San Francisco. Talk about security! Knowing this, I removed every piece of metal I had before I went through the gate. It still beeped. I removed my watch and wedding band—it still beeped. "I don't know what else to do," I said to the young man in uniform. When he saw my concern, he said in perfect English, "Our machines are very sensitive, it's OK. Go." He then asked me to point my camera at the ceiling and take a photo. He wanted to make sure that it was truly a camera. As I waited for the rest of our group, I noticed the two small buckles on my boots. That's what had caused the beeping. I went and showed it to the young man. He smiled.

Our luggage was thoroughly searched in our presence. Next was the passport station. As we know, women in Israel serve in the military. A beautiful young woman in army uniform was at the gate, with naturally red curly hair and freckles all over her face and arms. We noticed her name on her badge. It was Armenian! All 52 of us went through her station. She never smiled, didn't say a word, never even made eye contact with us. The only time she looked up was to see that the passport photo matched the person. It was obvious she didn't want any conversation. She was all business!

All this might be somewhat extreme for us, but our airports will never be as lax as they once were. An entire generation will now be asking each other, "Where were you on September 11?" For thousands of people at the World Trade Center and Pentagon, the answer would have been simple: "At work." It had begun like any ordinary day. They had no idea that for many, their very next breath would be their last. Few—if any of us—wake up thinking, "Today may be my last day on earth." But sooner or later, one way or another, every one of us will die. Hardly any of us knows for sure just how and when our time will come.

On September 11, thousands of people suddenly entered eternity. Some of them were ready, some were not. Jesus says in John 11:25, 26, "I am the resurrection and the life. He who believes in Me will live, even though he dies; and whoever lives and believes in Me will never die." Those who believe in Christ have a spiritual life that death cannot conquer. What wonderful assurance this is for those who believe! Jesus also says in John 14:19, "Because I live, you will live also." Those are God's promises to His faithful. We can trust our all-knowing God about our unknown future.

$\mathcal{M}$y granddaughter Samantha, who just turned three, was visiting me a few days ago. I noticed she was having so much fun jumping up and down on the couch cushions, and then off onto the floor on a pile of pillows. After a while I told her to stop. But she was having too good a time to stop. At one point I said, "Sammie, I'm warning you, don't come crying to me if you hurt yourself." She smiled back and said, "Can I go to grandpa and cry if I hurt myself?" Amazing! She wanted to make sure that she had a secure, comforting place to go, just in case she hurt herself. And since she got my warning, she wanted to ensure the loving arms of her grandpa!

As I meditated on Sammie's words, I thought how much alike we all are. Don't we all like to have a place of comfort to retreat to, especially in time of trouble? Once again the tragic events of September 11, 2001, came to mind. In this country, when had we ever seen people of all walks of life stand shoulder to shoulder and cry together, pray together, extend love and comfort to each other, and openly express their spirituality? Even members of Congress stood shoulder to shoulder and sang "God Bless America"!

The outburst of spiritual renewal was also moving. Just a few blocks from "Ground Zero," a Prayer Center was organized a few days after the tragic event. They ministered to the spiritual needs of the men and women who had been devastated by this tragedy. They were there, available to pray with the people, share scripture and provide that secure, comforting place of hope that can be found only through faith in God and His Son Jesus Christ.

The September 11 tragedy has united us as one big family, with the government acting as our protective, concerned parent, doing its best to protect its family members (citizens). God perhaps is using this crisis to draw people to Himself in a new amazing way. This tragic event reminds us, once again, of the brevity and uncertainty of life. Why wait for tragedy, however, to turn to God? We all need that secure, comforting place every day of our lives. Even my three-year-old Sammie wanted to secure her grandpa's loving arms just in case, even before she hurt herself!

As difficult as it may seem for us now, this tragic event may be a message of hope – hope for the present because we desperately needed a spiritual renewal in this country. And hope for the future because of God's promises in His Word.

We may not see God's purpose in any of this, but we can choose to trust Him even when life seems at its darkest. Jesus says in Mt. 11:28, "Come to Me all you who labor and are heavy leaden, and I will give you rest." In both the Old and New Testaments, God's promises remain unchanged. He calls us into that secure place we all want to be. God is with us and gives us assurance of His strength, help, hope and victory with eternal life to all who put their trust in Him. God is our refuge and strength, that secure place every day of our lives.

*T*he road was empty and the crowds were gone. A ragged cloak lay trampled on a street in Jericho. It was left behind by a beggar named Bartimaeus in the excitement of receiving his sight, and in his eagerness to follow Jesus (Mk. 10:46 – 52). The cloak was the most important article of clothing a person could own in Biblical times. It was used as protection against the weather, as bedding, as something to sit on and as luggage. It could also be given as a pledge for a debt, or torn into pieces to show grief.

Beggars were a common sight in most towns. Because most occupations of that day required physical labor, anyone with a disability or disease was at a disadvantage, and was usually forced to beg for their livelihoods, even though God's laws commanded care for such people (Lev. 25:35 – 38). This cloak had been very important to Bartimaeus before he met Jesus. It was probably part of the trappings of his life of begging as well. He wrapped it around him as he begged, or he spread it on the ground to receive the coins tossed his way. But he threw his cloak aside when he followed Jesus. He begged and cried out for the last time to Jesus Himself saying, "Son of David, have mercy on me!" He asked that his eyes might be opened. Jesus said to him, "Go your way; your faith has made you well." And immediately he received his sight and followed Jesus!

In all the excitement of receiving his sight and his eagerness to follow Jesus, Bartimaeus didn't think he needed his cloak—no more than the two brothers, Peter and Andrew, need their fishing nets when they followed Jesus. Neither did James and John, another set of brothers, need their fishing boat after Jesus called them. Likewise, neither did Matthew the tax collector, who left a comfortable life behind when he was called by Jesus. Matthew left his desk and writing tools, but kept in memory all that he witnessed, and later wrote the gospel that carries his name.

When we become followers of Christ and begin to work in His service, we too must leave things behind; perhaps a few undesirable habits, cleaning up our speech, our behavior, our attitudes, etc. We must willingly choose to leave them all behind as we walk with the Lord. After all, our walk must match our talk. Bartimaeus' physical and spiritual eyes likely were opened at the same time. His outward healing reflected his inner renewal by recognizing and accepting Jesus as his Savior!

It is ironic that the blind beggar had more spiritual insight than the many who could see had missed—including the Jewish religious leaders who witnessed Jesus' miracles. They were spiritually blind to see Jesus as the Savior, the Messiah. Seeing with our eyes does not guarantee seeing with our hearts. Bartimaeus threw his cloak aside and came to Christ. As Christians, are there a few things from our past that we still need to cast aside?

On a recent trip to Halifax, Nova Scotia, Canada, my husband I visited Citadel Hill, a most visited national site. It was built by the British to defend the city from enemy attacks. The guards are dressed in 19th century regiment uniforms (kilts), depicting the life of the fortress of that time. We were just a few feet away when the changing of the guards occurred. As the incoming soldier took over, he received the following orders: "Keep guard over government property, ...etc." Then they continued with their formal traditional march.

This experience reminded me of our visit to the Tomb of the Unknown Soldier in Arlington National Cemetery near Washington, D.C. The tomb is also under continual guard. Before one guard's duty is over, another comes to take his place. As the replacement soldier comes, he receives these words of command: "Order remains unchanged." Day after day, all through the years, the command remains. Before Christ ascended to heaven, He gave the following command to His disciples, which is called the Great Commission: "Go and make disciples of all nations, baptizing them in the name of the Father and of the Son and of the Holy Spirit, teaching them to observe all things that I have commanded you; and surely I am with you always, even to the end of the age" (Mt. 28:18, 19).

As Christians we know that for 2,000 years this command remains unchanged, and is passed down from one generation of Christians to another, through our Church. It has not been altered. Our responsibility, as was that of the first century church, is to proclaim the Good News of the gospel through faith in Jesus Christ. Although we are not all evangelists in the formal sense, we have all been given gifts that we can use to help fulfill the Great Commission. As we obey, we have comfort in the knowledge that Christ is with us always.

Jesus Himself affirms the Trinity. He did not say to baptize them in the names (not plural), but in the name (singular) of the Father, Son and Holy Spirit. The verse properly describes the Three-in-One nature of Father, Son and Holy Spirit. How is Christ with us? Jesus was with the disciples physically until His ascension, and then spiritually through the Holy Spirit since the Day of Pentecost (Acts 1:4 & ch. 2). Christ continues to be with every faithful, even today, through His Spirit.

Like a pebble in a pond, with ever widening ripples, the gospel spread geographically; from Jerusalem into Judea and Samaria, and to the whole wide world, including Armenia. We are the first people to accept Christianity as our state religion (301 AD). Tradition tells us that the gospel was brought to us through Christ's disciples Thaddeus and Bartholomew, who evangelized that part of the world. The gospel is not limited to any race or nationality, but is for all people. God speaks to all of us through His Word and through His Holy Spirit. Are we listening?

Much has changed in the 2,000 years since Jesus chose His twelve disciples. But regarding the Great Commission, Christ's words have not changed. The Good News of the gospel is always the same, and can still be repeated: "ORDER REMAINS UNCHANGED."

*T*he story is told that a man attended a dinner meeting where the guest lecturer was long-winded. When a listener could stand it no longer, he got up and slipped out a side door. In the corridor he met a friend who asked, "Has he finished yet?" "Yes," the man replied, "he has been through for a long time, but he's not aware of it! He simply won't stop!"

Unfortunately we have all experienced at least once in our lives, where we were stiff in our chairs, hoping for the speaker to finish at any moment. This doesn't necessarily mean that the subject was boring. The speaker might have been repetitive, presented too many unnecessary details, or perhaps the presentation of the subject lacked creativity and imagination. Therefore, what we say and what we don't say are both important.

The idea of coming to the point and saying something worthwhile briefly is also good counsel for us as we talk with others each day. Proper speech is not only saying the right words at the right time, but controlling the length as well. We can pause a moment and think about what our conversation is like. Are we the only ones talking? Do we give an opportunity for others to speak? Are we repetitive? Is our speech profitable to others? The wisdom of God that helps us control our tongue can also help us control the subjects we choose. Accepting God's wisdom will affect our speech, and our attitude will convey humility and self-control.

The book of Proverbs is an excellent source for such learning. The wisest man who ever lived, Solomon, left us a legacy of written wisdom in three books – Proverbs, Ecclesiastes, and Song of Solomon. In these books, under the inspiration of God's Spirit, he gives practical insights and guidelines for life. In Proverbs 1:7 he writes, "The fear of the Lord is the beginning of knowledge, but fools despise wisdom and instruction." He then gives us hundreds of practical examples of how to live according to Godly wisdom. We can learn more about God and His wisdom by regularly attending church to worship Him, and applying it in our lives

Proverbs covers a wide range of topics, including youth and discipline, family life, self-control and resisting temptation. It also covers business matters, the tongue, wealth and poverty, immorality, and of course wisdom. Its 31 short chapters are an invitation to all of us to read a chapter a day for a month.

Why not listen to the thoughts and lessons from a truly wise man who was inspired by God, and apply these truths to our lives. No matter how wise or spiritual we may think we are, we all could control our speech more effectively. We must allow the Holy Spirit to fill us with new attitudes. Then our speech will be pleasing both to God and man. And no one will walk out when we speak.

$\mathcal{N}$otre Dame, the 12th century cathedral in Paris, France, and the 19th century Arc de Triomphe, have both had a new clean appearance. On a recent trip to Paris I was able to see and admire the beautiful clean white facades that the Parisians are so proud of. Years of pollution had darkened the surfaces, and the intricate architectural designs had turned almost black. Since only the facades were cleaned, one could easily see the difference. In time, I understand, the rest of the surfaces will be cleaned. Presently both famous historical monuments truly shine white and clean in the sunlight.

This experience reminded me of the story of a perfectly white plant that was growing by the side of the entrance to a coal mine. Visitors were astonished that the coal dust continually blew and settled everywhere, but this little white plant remained unaffected. A miner took some black coal dust and threw it on the plant to test it, but not a particle would cling. Nothing could stain the plant's snowy whiteness.

This illustrates what every Christian's life should be like. We live in a world surrounded by a multitude of ungodly influences. It is every Christian's mission to remain pure and "unspotted" by the world before God. That is the goal St. James sets out in his epistle (Js. 1:27). To keep ourselves from being polluted by the world we must commit ourselves to God's ethical and moral standards. We are not to adapt to the world's value system if it's against our Christian principles. True faith means nothing if we allow unethical actions to contaminate our principles.

The Apostle Paul also teaches us to become "blameless and innocent children of God without fault in the midst of a crooked and perverse generation, among whom we shine as light in the world" (Phil. 2:15). Our lives should be characterized by moral purity, patience and compassion, so that we will "shine as lights" in a dark, depraved world. A transformed life is an effective witness and an example of the power of God's Word.

In Prov. 4:20 – 27, Solomon also advises us to make wisdom our life's goal, guard our hearts against evil, never speak or act deceitfully, keep our eyes on what is good and pure, and keep our feet from evil ways. It is not easy for us and for our children to make our way through the maze of godlessness that often threatens our daily lives. Therefore, as Christians we need to ask God each day to guide our steps and guard our hearts. It is the only way to leave an exemplary mark on the world, rather than allow the world to leave its mark on us, as it did with the above two famous monuments.

If the Lord can keep a plant white as snow in the midst of clouds of black dust, can He not, by His grace, keep our hearts pure in the world we live in? Yes! Absolutely! God can clean even a spotted heart completely. When we put our faith in Christ, recognize our wrongful acts, and turn our lives around, we are not only forgiven, but God's Holy Spirit transforms us, making us pure. Then we can shine as lights in the world, unaffected and blameless. Only God can transform and whiten a spotted heart into a shining, joyous soul of grace!

*W*hile visiting the beautiful and picturesque city of San Antonio, Texas, last April, my husband and I took a city tour to see the prominent sights. We climbed onto the tour bus and sat in the first row so that we could see and hear everything. At one point of the tour our guide informed us that we would soon pass through the King William Historical District, with its architecturally beautiful old homes. He was quite articulate with the history and life of that era, and suggested that we pay close attention to the ceilings of each porch.

The houses were off white, but the ceilings of each porch were painted light blue. He stated that at the end of the tour he was going to ask us if we knew the reason why. I turned to my husband and whispered that perhaps the light blue color gives the illusion of depth, and therefore makes the ceilings look like sky. Being so close to the guide as we were, he heard me. He agreed, but there was more to the story. At the end of the tour we learned that since the blue color gives the illusion of depth, the birds thought it was sky and would not build their nests there.

Amazing discovery! Birds often instinctively have more sense than some people. Yes, the birds were deceived by the light blue color, thinking it was sky. They were cautious about where to build their nests. Not wanting to take any chances, they wanted to be certain that their nests were on a solid foundation.

This lesson brings to mind what we read in the gospels of Luke 6 and Matthew 7 about the wise and foolish builders. The Bible states that the wise man who listens and obeys the Word of God is like a man who builds his house on a strong foundation laid upon the rock. When rain waters rise and winds blow and beat against the house, it stands firm, for it is built on rock. For those who hear God's Word but don't put it into practice are like a foolish man who builds his house on sand. When rain comes and winds blow against the house, it crumbles into a heap of ruins.

Are we building our lives on perishable pursuits and shallow principles, or on the solid foundation of God's Word? Without Him as our foundation, we should realize that we are building castles on sand and nests in open sky.

When life is calm, our foundations may not seem to matter. But when crises come, our foundations are tested. We may seem secure as long as things are calm and the sun is shining. But when the storms of disappointment, illness or heartache come, we feel the need for a solid foundation to rest our souls. Christ is life's only solid foundation. He died for our sins. He empowers us with His Holy Spirit. His Word provides the needed wisdom to meet the great challenges of life.

Perhaps we are not fully aware of His love for us. It has no boundaries. Our human ability to measure His love falls short. We are each very special in His sight. His unconditional love should form the foundation of our trust in Him. Are we standing on His foundation with the joy of knowing Him personally? He is the foundation of yesterday, today and forever. Let us build our lives on Him. Let us build to last.

*W*e were on the freeway going to a social function. The traffic on the 405 was heavy. We came off the freeway and took surface streets. Anticipating this, we had left the house a bit early and arrived at our destination on time. When we came home, my husband Steve looked at a map and said that if this were to happen again, he now knew an even shorter way to the same location after coming off the freeway. It's good to have alternate ways to go anywhere or do anything. We often talk about Plan A, Plan B, and possibly Plan C.

There is one area of life, however, in which there can be no alternate plan. No Plan B. There is no other way to eternal life at the end of this life. There is only one plan, only one way, no other options. Jesus Himself said, "I am the Way, and the Truth, and the Life, no one comes to the Father but through Me" (Jn. 14:6).

Many people react negatively to the fact that there is no other way than through Jesus. Yet, this isn't our idea or something the Church decided. It is the way Jesus Himself taught. If God made it that clear in scripture, why should we question it? Who are we to argue? If God designated Jesus to be the Savior of the world, no one else can be His equal. We can't say it does not matter what we believe, as long as we are good and sincere individuals.

Christians are to be open-minded on many issues, but not on eternal life. No other religious teacher came to earth as God's only Son, died on the cross and rose from the dead. Our focus should be on Christ, Whom God offered as a perfect sacrifice as the way to heaven, and for an eternal relationship with Him.

Jesus further said to His disciples, "Truly, truly I say to you, he who believes in Me, the works that I do, he will do also; and greater works than these he will do; because I go to the Father" (Jn. 14:12). Jesus is not saying that His disciples would do more amazing miracles. Rather, the disciples, working in the power of the Holy Spirit, would carry the gospel of God's kingdom out of Palestine and into the whole world. They would perform greater works by preaching the gospel and spiritually redeeming multitudes of people throughout the world after the day of Pentecost.

Jesus was soon going to leave the disciples, but His Holy Spirit would soon come to care for and guide them. The regenerating power of the Holy Spirit came on the disciples just before Jesus' ascension (Jn. 20:22, 23), and the Holy Spirit was poured out on all faithful at Pentecost (Acts 2).

Through Christ's disciples and other faithful followers of Jesus, the scope of their work would be greater over time, multiplied through the growth of the Church! As the book of Acts describes, disciples of the early Church fulfilled the prediction that they would do greater things.

The same Holy Spirit is with all faithful, helping us to live God-pleasing lives and serving His Church on earth. By faith we can appropriate the Spirit's power each day. We can also proclaim that there is no other way than the One Who is the Way. There is no Plan B!

*E*ven after more than 90 years, people are still fascinated by the "Titanic," the "unsinkable" ship that sunk. On a recent trip to Halifax, Nova Scotia, Canada, our excursion included a visit to Fairlawn Cemetery. We were led to a section where some 121 bodies, passengers of the "Titanic," are buried. In fact, I noticed an Armenian among them. The tombstone read: "M. Der Zacarian, April 15, 1912 #304."

The "Titanic" sinking truly was one of the worst maritime disasters in history. The British luxury liner of the White Star line, a 46,000-ton ship, was on its maiden voyage from Liverpool, England, to New York City, when just before midnight on April 14, 1912, it struck an iceberg. Of the 2,231 persons aboard, about 1,513 lost their lives, including the American millionaires John Jacob Astor, age 48; Benjamin Guggenheim, 47; and Isador Straus, 67.

Although the ship had been proclaimed unsinkable, the "Titanic" sank in less than three hours! Why did the ship go down so quickly? Since the day the luxury liner sank, most researchers believed that an iceberg ripped a giant gash as long as a football field in the ship's hull. But recently an international team of scientists and engineers dove to the "Titanic's" remains, and using sound waves to penetrate through the mud, found the damage to be astonishingly small. The New York Times article reported six openings across the starboard hull 13 to 15 square feet each. Because each of the wounds was in a separate watertight compartment, the ship flooded quickly and sank in just over two hours with the loss of 1,513 lives.

Small damage in various key places caused great loss. There is a lesson for us from this worst maritime disaster of the modern era. Perhaps some of us knew a strong Christian who seemed to have changed almost overnight. One day the person was an outspoken, highly visible member in the community, the church and for Christ, and then all of a sudden that individual wants nothing to do with former Christian friends. How could this happen? More often, it's the result of several small harmful influences and events in key areas of life that resulted in the transformation.

Therefore, the Apostle Paul encouraged his young "spiritual son" Timothy to "Fight the good fight, holding on to faith and good conscience." But then he offered this word of warning: "Some have rejected these and so have shipwrecked their faith" (1 Tim. 1:18, 19). How can we hold on to good conscience? We must treasure and protect our faith in Christ with more dedication than anything else, and do what we know is right. Each time we deliberately ignore the voice of our conscience, we are hardening our hearts. If we continue this, over a period of time our judgment will get blurry, and eventually that precious voice will diminish, and then, silence.

No matter how serene our lives may be, it can end in "shipwreck" at any moment. Let's be thankful for a good conscience. And when it gives us a warning whistle, let's pay attention. St. Paul's message of **S.O.S.** in all his epistles is: To Surrender Our Souls to the Word and will of God. No big sinking ship for the Apostle and for us! Just a big heart for God!

*H*ow can one finance one's education? A few of the options are: scholarships, grants, financial aid, student loans, savings by planning ahead, paid by the parents, etc. But Mike did it in a most original way—by one penny at a time.

Back in 1987, Mike, who was a freshman studying chemistry at the University of Illinois, thought that anyone should be able to spare a penny to help him finance his education. So, he wrote to his friend, a Chicago Tribune columnist, and convinced the writer to ask each of his readers to send in a penny for Mike. The article asked the readers to send just a penny, which didn't mean anything to anyone, but it would help Mike. The article stated that everyone who reads this column and looks around the room, will find a penny somewhere—under the couch cushions, on the corner of a drawer, on the kitchen counter, etc. That's all Mike asks, the article suggested, a penny from each reader for Mike.

It is amusing. To mail a penny, one had to put a stamp on the envelope. But the amazing thing was that the readers loved the idea and the "penny fund" grew. Eventually Mike ended up with $28,000.00!

A penny isn't worth much unless it is added to a lot more pennies. Or, unless it is one's last one. And that is exactly what we see in Mk. 12:42 – 44, where a woman came into the temple and gave her offering. The Bible says, "A poor widow came and put in two very small copper coins, worth only a fraction of a penny." They were the smallest coins then in circulation in Palestine. Though her offering was meager, the widow brought all that she had.

This woman was more fit to be a recipient of charity than a donor. Calling His disciples to Him Jesus said, "I tell you the truth, this poor widow had put more into the treasury than all the others. They all gave out of their wealth; but she, out of her poverty, put in everything—all she had to live on." In the Lord's eyes this poor widow gave more than all the others, though her gift was by far the smallest. The value of a gift is not determined by its amount, but by the spirit in which it is given. A gift given grudgingly or for public recognition loses its value. When we give, we must remember that a gift of any size is pleasing to God when it is given out of gratitude to Him and in a spirit of generosity.

We are grateful that God blesses some people with wealth to benefit others. Their donations are not "just a penny." No! We all know truly generous benefactors who continue to give in mighty ways to help the less fortunate. But as Christians, we all know that we enjoy God's blessings in various ways. We must humbly acknowledge Him as the source of all that we have, never taking it for granted, and sharing willingly and generously with others in every way we can—our time, talents and treasures.

Since God measures our giving by the degree of our sacrifice, many who have little to give in this life will be immensely rewarded in the life to come. Our value is determined, not by what we have, but by what we do with what we have. Giving is a privilege, not a burden!

$\mathcal{R}$egardless of where we are in our lives or careers, constant reevaluation is vital. Perhaps for some of us, our work or other activities take up more and more of our valuable time, causing us to neglect our family, loving relationships and worthy activities. The man in Jesus' parable of the "Rich Fool" (Lk. 12:13 – 21) didn't take time to evaluate his life. He was too busy counting and measuring his silos, and building bigger barns to store all his crops. Spiritual issues and compassion for the needy didn't concern him. "Me, myself and mine" were his only focus. He said to himself, "You have plenty of goods laid up for many years. Take life easy; eat, drink and be merry." By the time he realized the real "bottom line," it was too late! God said to him, "Fool! This night, your soul will be required of you."

We are fortunate in that we can learn from his mistakes, which was Christ's lesson for us. The world around us may argue against the wisdom of this parable, but we know that man's life does not consist of the abundance of one's possessions. Spiritual riches are the most valuable. We all face uncertainties. We also have discovered by experience that the desire to have valuables is soon replaced by the fear of losing them. Eventually we come to realize, as King Solomon did toward the end of his life, that there is only one solid foundation to counter the uncertainties of life. "Fear God and keep His commandments, for this is the whole duty of man. For God will bring every deed into judgment, including every hidden thing, whether it is good or evil" (Ecc. 12:13, 14).

Solomon, the wisest man of his time, discovered that everything in this life—possessions, accomplishments, people—will eventually fade away. Only God's Will, Word and Work are permanent. We must stop grasping the temporary and focus our time, talents, treasures and energy on the permanent—the Word and eternal life through Christ.

Life is short and riches can't buy God's gifts. Death is not impressed with wealth. It keeps its appointments with people indiscriminately; young and old, rich and poor. The rich man in the parable lived as if he controlled everything, and that there was no God to Whom he would be accountable. He soon realized, however, that he could not overrule death's appointment. It is interesting that everything money can't control, God has fulfilled in Christ and brought under His rule.

Life is uncertain, but God's judgment is certain. Therefore, St. Paul says, "For it not those who hear the law who are righteous in God's sight, but it is those who obey the law who will be declared righteous…This will take place on the day when God will judge men's secrets through Jesus Christ" (Rom. 2:13 – 16).

Though much of life is futile, one must grasp its opportunities and use them to the fullest in serving God. There will be no such opportunities in the grave. We must often evaluate our direction, enjoy our life, live each day to its fullest, but always with eternity in mind. When we put spiritual priorities at the top of the list, we'll be able to handle all the rest. God measures us by what we are, not by what we have.

*C*ountless cars had filled the parking lot of a shopping mall. Surprised by the unexpected crowd, I wondered if it was a holiday I somehow had missed. As I parked, I looked for the number on the light post so I could find my car later. When I returned, there was an even bigger crowd. To make things worse, impatient drivers had caused a fender bender. Their patience wore thin and tempers flared. Several people stood around while witnesses were describing the incident to the curious.

As I pulled away, I thought, what if instead of a number on each light post, they placed a word such as "Patience" on one post, "Love" on another, "Understanding," "Kindness," "Graciousness," "Smile," "Friendliness," "Goodness," "Gentleness," etc. Would it help? This might be even more necessary in smaller parking lots, where getting in and out is even more difficult. Church parking lots might need it also. It's amazing how quickly the love we have for our brothers and sisters in Christ can disappear in a parking lot!

Jesus says, "Love one another as I have loved you" (John 15:12). Some people think the Bible is a book of do's and don't's. But Jesus neatly summarized all these rules in Matthew 22:37 – 39, when He said, "Love God with all your heart and love your neighbor as yourself." "Neighbor" would be anyone with whom we come in contact. He called these two the greatest commandments of all.

As Christians, our faith must transform our conduct as well as our thoughts. If our lives remain unchanged, that will mean we don't truly believe the truths we claim to believe. Keeping the commandment of love, as we know it from the Word of God, shows that our faith is vital and real.

Many have the idea that self-love is wrong. But if this were the case, it would be pointless to love our neighbors as ourselves. Loving others as ourselves means actively working to see that their needs are met. There will be days when some of us may have to face a hostile environment. We must constantly remind ourselves that genuine faith transforms lives. The world is watching for evidence of Christ in our lives. We must put our faith into action. Our walk must match our talk.

Why is love for others something we owe? We are forever in debt to Christ for the love He has lavishly poured out on us. The only way we can begin to repay this debt is by loving others in return. Because Christ's love will always be infinitely greater than ours, we will always have the obligation to love our "neighbors."

The testing of our faith is more likely to occur in a check-out line, while driving, in a parking lot, etc. That is where we can demonstrate our love for God and neighbor! The clear sign of our faith is not what we say, but what we do.

*T*housands of tourists throughout the centuries have visited the famous Parthenon, the ancient Greek Temple of Athena, on the Acropolis in Athens. And thousands of visitors from around the world have picked up a piece or two of marble to bring home as souvenirs. Why hasn't the supply of marble pieces been exhausted long ago?

The first time I went back to Greece with my family was in 1972. Naturally, we visited the Acropolis. I noticed a sign that read, "Don't remove anything from the premises." It was posted in several languages. Seeing a Greek security guard nearby, I asked if people were really taking anything home. After recovering from his surprise of a tourist speaking fluent Greek, he said, "My dear lady, every year truckloads of marble fragments are scattered around the whole Acropolis area. So tourists go home happy with what they think are authentic pieces of ancient history." I then asked if the marble fragments they bring are extracted from Mt. Pendeli, the famous marble from which the Parthenon is built. He smiled and said, "We get it from tombstone cutters and other marble cutting businesses."

We can easily be deceived by other kinds of imitations as well. We all take in a vast amount of information every day through radio and TV talk shows, popular books, magazines, etc. This can be very dangerous if, as Christians, we are not alert and watchful. What we do with all this input is vitally important. Living in a world system with mostly godless values, we are bound to encounter a lot of undesirable information contrary to our standards. We must be discerning, wise, avoiding all ungodly influences that we can, and rejecting what we can't avoid. Above all, compare everything with the Word and God's standards.

When we know the truth we can detect the untrue. We must know the authentic, the genuine, to recognize the imitation. Experts who recognize counterfeit money know and have studied the genuine so well that they can recognize the imitation. Not the other way around.

The Apostle Paul tells us in Phil. 4:8 to program our minds with thoughts that are true, noble, right, just, pure, lovely, of good report, virtuous and praiseworthy. If we ever have any problems with impure thoughts, we can begin to examine what we put into our minds through TV, movies, people we associate with, the Internet, etc. We can replace harmful input with wholesome material. It isn't enough to read God's Word, or even know it well. We must also put it into practice. How easy it is to listen to a sermon, but forget what was said. Or read the Bible, and not think of how to apply it to our lives. Knowing the truth of God's Word must lead to obedience. Believers of the Truth should act in harmony with God's divine standards. Let's be alert for imitations. What we put into our minds determines what comes out in our speech and actions.

*E*veryone knows or has heard of the leaning tower in the city of Pisa, Italy. No matter how many postcards, slides or videos one has seen of it, seeing it in reality is an overwhelming experience! It was intended as a bell tower for the cathedral which is nearby. Construction began in about 1173, but progress was suspended by problems with the foundation. Nevertheless, it was completed in 1350. It is known to the world as the Leaning Tower of Pisa.

What caused this white marble cylindrical tower to lean? The foundation of the tower was laid on soft, sandy soil, and only ten feet deep. This may explain why it leans. In recent years cement was injected into the soil at the base to prevent further leaning. How far does it lean? If we were to stand at the top and drop a stone to the ground, it would hit 16? feet away from the wall at the base. In the last 100 years, the tower has leaned an additional foot. According to some engineers, it should be called "The Falling Tower" because they believe it will eventually topple over. In recent years, visitors are not permitted to enter or climb its 300 stairs. Roped around its base a sign warns visitors to keep their distance.

Isn't it amazing that for a structure about 180 feet high, its foundation was laid on soft, sandy soil? Let us see what the Word of God teaches on the subject. In the gospel of Matthew 7:21 – 27, Jesus says that whoever hears His Words and obeys them is compared to a wise man who built his house on the rock. The rain fell, the floods came, the winds blew and beat on the house; but it did not fall, for it was built on the rock. But anyone who hears His Words, and does not act on them is like a foolish man who built his house on the sand. When the rain, floods and winds came and beat on that house, it fell completely.

Christ also adds, "Not everyone who says to Me, 'Lord, Lord' shall enter the Kingdom of Heaven, but he who does the will of My Father in heaven." Jesus is more concerned that we do right rather than just say the right words. He is more concerned about our walk than our talk. To build "on the rock" means to be a hearing, responding disciple, not a superficial one. When life is calm, our foundations don't seem to matter. But when crises come, our foundations are tested. Like a house of cards, the fool's life crumbles.

Why would people build their lives on sandy foundations? Perhaps because they are influenced by worldly values, or by friends who have already settled on "sandy areas." Perhaps they think disaster can't happen to them. Whatever their reason, those with shaky foundations are shortsighted. A building is only as solid as its foundation. The foundation of our lives is Jesus Christ. He is our Rock, our reason for being. Are we building our lives on the only real and lasting foundation? Faith in Christ is what counts. He is our Rock on which to build and lean at any time of life.

On a recent visit to Paris, France, I saw the replica of our Statue of Liberty. I was surprised to find myself unimpressed by it. I think the problem was that the statue, not only is rather small, but is erected close to Grenelle Bridge, on the banks of the Seine River. The viewer sees not only the statue, the beautiful bridge, the picturesque river with colorful boats in motion, but also several historical monuments in the background, all competing for one's attention. It was a very busy picture with many points of interest. Each in itself, however, was breathtaking. Although this was not my first visit to Paris, the experience of seeing all these was still overwhelming.

Our Statue of Liberty, on the other hand, is an overwhelming sight towering above New York Harbor. It is the work of the French sculptor Auguste Bartholdi. The statue was a gift from the French people to the United States to commemorate the 100th anniversary of American independence. The work was dedicated by President Cleveland on October 28, 1886. It rises 305 feet from the bottom of the pedestal to the tip of the torch. The Statue of Liberty is a lasting gesture of international friendship, and has become a world symbol of freedom, especially to thousands of immigrants arriving in the U.S.

How many people have arrived within this free and beautiful U.S.A. enjoying the freedom so dearly sought? On a plaque at the base of the famous statue, the words of the American poet Emma Lazarus cry out from Lady Liberty: "Give me your tired, your poor, your huddled masses yearning to breathe free." Millions have come and found political freedom, but still may feel bound by something else.

The cross of Christ stands not on a pedestal in a harbor, but in the heart of every Christian and in the pages of history as a monument of spiritual freedom! Christ calls out, "Come to Me, all you who are weary and burdened and I will give you rest" (Mt. 11:28). These are the dearest, the sweetest words ever heard by mortal ears. Christ frees people from all burdens. The rest that He promises is love, healing and peace with God, not the end of labor. A relationship with God changes meaningless, wearisome toil into spiritual productivity and purpose.

Christ also promises "If you abide in My word, you are My disciples indeed. And you shall know the truth, and the truth shall make you free" (Jn. 8:31, 32). Jesus Himself is the source of truth, the perfect standard of what is right. He liberates us from the consequences of sin and self-deception. His truth frees us to be all that God meant for us to be.

"Truth" here has reference not only to the facts surrounding Jesus as the Messiah, the "anointed one," and Son of God, but also to the teaching that He brought. A genuinely obedient follower of Christ knows divine truth, which comes not merely by intellectual consent, but by commitment to Him through faith. As Christians we celebrate a much more important liberty—freedom through Christ with the promise of eternal life. As impressive as the Statue of Liberty is, the cross is truly every Christian's everlasting symbol of freedom!

*W*hen we associate Jesus with a kiss, Judas Iscariot's kiss of betrayal comes to mind. There is, however, a most fascinating account in the gospel of Luke 7:36 – 50, where Jesus expected to be greeted with a kiss, but was not.

A Pharisee named Simon invited Jesus to dinner. Perhaps his motive was to entrap or accuse Him in some way. While Jesus sat at a low table for dinner, as was the custom in Biblical times, propping Himself up on one elbow, an uninvited woman who was a sinner, came in. Knowing that Jesus was a guest at the Pharisee's house, she brought an alabaster flask of an expensive fragrant oil. She knelt at Jesus' feet, weeping as she began to wash His feet with her tears, wiped them with her hair, kissed His feet and anointed them with her oil. Knowing her reputation, her act was shocking to all present. This took great courage, revealing her desperation for forgiveness. Her weeping was an expression of deep remorse and repentance.

Simon thought that if Jesus were truly a prophet, He would have known her character and would have sent her away. Jesus, knowing Simon's thoughts, said, "Simon, I have something to say to you." "Yes, teacher, tell me," replied Simon. Then Jesus tells this parable: There were two men who owed money to a moneylender. One owed 500 denarii and the other 50. Neither one could pay him back, so the lender canceled both debts. Which one will love him more? Simon said that the one who owed more, for being forgiven for more. "You are correct," said Jesus. Then He said to Simon, "Do you see this woman? I have come to your home. You did not give Me any water for My feet, but she has wet My feet with her tears and wiped them with her hair. You did not give Me a kiss, but this woman has not stopped kissing My feet. You did not put oil on My head, but she has poured perfume on My feet." Jesus used the woman's actions to make a point.

Simon had committed several social errors of hospitality. Was he so proud that he didn't treat Jesus at least as an equal? Providing water for guests' feet was an essential formality. Sandaled feet get dirty. A welcome kiss between two men was a gesture of warm hospitality and friendship. Anointing with aromatic oil was a sign of festivity in the ancient Near East. (Anointing with oil was also means of investing someone with divine appointment and authority of office, such as a king, or consecrating someone or something for holy purpose.) Here it was the grateful prostitute, and not the selfish Pharisee, whose sins were forgiven! Jesus knew the woman's reputation, but He was more interested who she could become through God's grace! God hates sin but loves the repentant sinner!

Only those who realize the depth of their sin can appreciate the complete forgiveness God offers. Jesus said to the woman, "Your faith has saved you. Go in peace." Although this unnamed woman doesn't say a word in the entire account, her actions speak volumes about her repentant heart. She was forgiven through her faith. She understood God's forgiveness, love, mercy and grace!

$\mathcal{T}$o perpetuate our precious heritage and culture, the late Catholicos Karekin Hovsepian proclaimed October as Armenian Cultural Month. This wonderful tradition focuses further attention throughout our Armenian American Community on how rich our cultural heritage is.

Throughout history we have seen that the path most worthwhile often is the most difficult. In our history we find that anything meaningful and precious involved overcoming difficulties and persecutions. One of the most basic characteristics common to us Armenians is that we are God-loving people. Our forefathers not only were the first to accept Christianity as our state religion, but continued to demonstrate their love of Christ as the cornerstone of their faith. Despite hard times they looked beyond their difficulties and put their trust in God's goodness in all circumstances.

Our sacred family values have been another strong, precious characteristic of our people. These most vital distinguishing qualities interlaced together have shaped and motivated us to live exemplary lives wherever we lived. Our Armenian churches, schools, community involvement and press have played most vital roles in our identity and commitment to unity as Armenians.

Today we are fortunate to be living in the United States of America. Armenians perhaps have never before enjoyed such blessings of liberty and freedom as we do now. How do we use this freedom? Freedom is never free! With freedom comes responsibility. We can enjoy this freedom by living the exemplary God-honoring lives of our forebears as we continue to remain law abiding citizens, and bring honor and justifiable pride to our name as Armenian Americans.

Christ teaches us, "Let your light so shine before men, that they may see your good works, and glorify your Father in heaven" (Matt. 5:16). Yes, let our light shine by dedicating ourselves to safeguard that which makes us the unique people that we are. Let us pass those treasures of our spiritual and cultural traditions and family values to our next generation. They in turn will be proud of their precious Armenian heritage!

*D*uring the social hour at a church banquet, I was talking to a couple while my granddaughter Haley, age 5, was standing by my side. At some point this couple commented how nicely Haley is growing and what a beautiful little girl she has become. After I thanked them for their kind words, I added that she goes to Armenian school and Sunday School as well. While our conversation was all in Armenian, I inserted the words "Sunday School" in English. At this point, Haley gently touched my hand and corrected me by repeating the words "Sunday School" in Armenian (Geeragnorya Tbrotz)! I laughed, put my arm around her shoulders and said, "You are right, Haley, you're right!" Needless to say, the couple was also amazed.

What an eye-opener that was for me! As minor an example as this is, we know that our children and grandchildren compare our actions with our words. In more serious matters, if what we say and what we do don't match up, they'll be confused by our mixed messages. When it comes to material things, such as heirlooms for example, we give plenty of thought about what we pass on to our children. Some people cherish crystal and chinaware that belonged to great grandmother. For others it might be handmade lace works, a rug, a quilt, an old family Bible, etc. Heirlooms are important to us. But the values we leave in our children are even more important than our valuables. Passing on an exemplary life to live by is even more important, such as an honorable character, a good reputation, our language, traditions, and the best gift of all, our Christian faith!

The Apostle Paul writes to young Timothy, about the spiritual heritage and the genuine faith he received from his both grandmother Lois and his mother Eunice (2 Tim. 1:3 – 5), and urged Timothy to continue in the things which he has learned and been assured of. Christians whose actions and words are consistent can influence generations of people for Christ.

The greatest legacy we can leave our children and grandchildren is a spiritual one that no amount of money can buy. It is an example of unwavering trust in God's love and wisdom. Children put a searchlight on our actions, and are more likely to do what we do, than to do what we say. Haley's correction in my Armenian was once again a good reminder. Our actions, lifestyle and values must reflect the principles we teach them. An ounce of example is worth more than a ton of advice.

A parent's work is vitally important. Teaching our children the Word of God at home and taking them to Sunday School is our responsibility. We often fuss about not having the Ten Commandments posted in the schools any more. Yes, that's true. But do we have them posted in our homes? Jesus summarized the Ten into Two, and called them the two Greatest Commandments: Love the Lord your God with all your heart, soul and mind, and love your neighbor as yourself (Mt. 22:37 – 40).

As ambassadors of Christ, when we practice these two commandments in our lives daily, we need not worry about our children. A life of faith and obedience to God's Word is the most precious inheritance we can leave to our children!

*W*eeks following the tragic events of September 11, 2001, a woman, very upset, called the Sean Hannity radio program and asked, "What's this hatred, all of a sudden, against the United States anyway?" I was surprised. "All of a sudden"? Obviously this woman was not aware of the emotional climate in some countries. Yes, most countries love American tourists and the money they spend in their land. It's the American government they have a problem with.

We began to travel with the children when they were still young. In 1972, we went to Greece. I noticed no antipathy toward America. But, in 1978 I was shocked to see huge banners in Athens in Greek saying, "U.S. Go Home With The Bases." Five American military bases were stationed in Greece at the time.   Visiting the ancient sites of Olympia, we saw an anti-American Communist youth rally. Later I asked a shopkeeper for his opinion. He said, "My dear lady, it's a very small percentage of our youth who make all that noise. Don't worry, enjoy yourself with your family." It resembled Berkley to me. I tried to minimize the situation for the children. They suggested that we converse only in Armenian. In 1984, we again had a similar experience on the island of Skiathos.

The U.S. military eventually moved their bases from Greece to Turkey. Now, the Greeks were more upset! There is no love lost between Greece and Turkey. While at a resort in Greece, a hotel/restaurant owner, who looked very much like William Saroyan, welcomed us. When he learned that we were Armenians, he hugged my husband Steve, kissed him enthusiastically on both cheeks, and said, "Ah, we have a common enemy—the Turks!" That was unexpected!

From our experiences, neither the French nor Germans were friendly to Americans. English, Scots, Welsh, Italians and Turks were very friendly. In Jordan, even Queen Noor spoke to us! In more recent years, our guide in Egypt was hostile toward our group of 52 Christians, just because we were Americans. She was a PhD history professor, dressed in traditional attire. We kept her only for one day. In Damascus, Syria, a local shopkeeper suggested that it was better to say we were Armenians than Americans. Here we go again, I thought. I was very pleased that Armenians were so well thought of. And why not? We are industrious, honest, trustworthy people with a strong commitment to our families and our church. As for antipathy of America, it didn't happen "all of a sudden," as the lady commented on the radio. Whatever agenda each country may have, one thing is clear: They all envy the U.S., and try to imitate the West—unless they are oppressed.

I often think of Ecclesiastes 3:1: "To every thing there is a season, a time for every purpose under heaven." God is in control. We must continue to pray for world leaders, but especially for leaders of our nation and our president. May God grant him wisdom and guidance in these difficult times. We must also pray for our men and women in uniform who protect our freedom. Facing the unknown may cause us some anxiety, but seeking God's presence in prayer strengths our relationship with Him. And that's the most important reason to pray.

*A*ll Greek calendars, even today, begin the week with Monday and end on Sunday. In the Greek language the word for "Sunday" is "Kyriakee," which translates as "Lord's Day." It comes from the root word "kyrios," which means "lord" or "master." These calendars follow God's creation. We read in Gen. 2:3, "Then God blessed the seventh day and sanctified it, because in it He rested from all His work which God had created and made." God blessed and set apart the seventh day for holy use. This act is picked up in the Ten Commandments (Ex. 20: 1 – 17) where God commanded observance of the Sabbath.

Our calendars in the United States begin with Sunday and end on Saturday. We follow the first century Christians of the early church who made it their custom to worship on the first day of the week, associating it with the day of Christ's resurrection. Each of the gospels emphasize that Jesus was indeed raised on the first day of the week (Mt. 28, Mk. 16, Lk. 24, Jn. 20). The promised Holy Spirit came on the day of Pentecost, which also was the first day of the week (Acts 2:1 – 4).

Whichever calendar one uses, as Christians we have much to celebrate, and not by ourselves or just a few times a year. We are to meet regularly on the Lord's Day with other faithful in Christ to encourage one another in love and good works. St. Paul writes, "We are no longer strangers and foreigners, but fellow citizens with the saints and members of the household of God, having been built on the foundation of the apostles and prophets, Jesus Christ Himself being the chief cornerstone..." (Eph. 2:19, 20).

A church building is often called the House of God. In reality, Christ's Church is not an architectural masterpiece (although such structures are needed for worship). Rather, Christ's Church is a masterpiece of human relations—believers from different backgrounds, being built together into a single, unified entity—a building without walls. We have a strong foundation composed of the apostles and prophets, but Christ Himself is the sturdy cornerstone that such a building needs. Through Him, we congregate to form a beautiful church, fit for God to dwell in.

The Church, the Body of Christ, is also made up of people with different gifts and abilities. God wants us to work together toward a common goal with Christ as our cornerstone and His Holy Spirit as our unifier. We all need each other. God has designed it so that the Church needs us and we need the Church. Every child of God is obliged to recognize his or her particular gifts or talents, and to use them in His service to fulfill His purpose and for His glory. God-given gifts to us must not be squandered, but fully used with joy and enthusiasm.

God began His church-building program about 2,000 years ago, and that program continues to this day. You and I are gifted craftsmen, and we are building the greatest masterpiece in the world—God's Church! Let's get together, not only on the Lord's Day to praise and worship our Creator, but also whenever necessary. Every believer is a Church builder. Are we using our gifts and abilities for His glory and for the blessing of others? Let's not waste our gifts. Use them!

*D*riving through the states of Idaho, Montana and Wyoming is quite an experience for Californians. For countless miles one sees nothing but cattle grazing land. Small farming towns, often with populations with less than one hundred, make these tranquil parts of the U.S. charming.

We were on one of our driving vacations. While in Wyoming, my husband Steve and I stopped at a restaurant for lunch. A mature couple that was seated at the adjacent table greeted us with a smile. I noticed the man's physique. He was tall, very muscular, robust and, despite his age, many young men would have been envious of his well-developed upper body. We started a pleasant conversation. They were local folks who lived there all their lives.

I asked the gentleman what he did before retirement. He said, "I have been milking cows all my life—the old fashioned way, using these hands!" I was amazed. His hands were enormous! But he quickly added that now everything is done automatically by machines. "Life has been good here—very good," he said.

As I glanced at the menu, I noticed they served nothing but beef prepared in various ways. It sure was cattle country! I asked one more question: "What would you say is the best social entertainment for local folks around here?" His answer was enthusiastically given in one word: "Rodeo!" His wife then added, "Picnics after church on Sundays." I admired and respected their happy disposition, but above all their attitude of contentment! Yes, life was good there!

Each generation, it seems, raises the "contentment bar" a little higher these days. With so many technological advancements, we seem to need more and more things to be satisfied, or have the latest model to take care of our needs – such as computers and their functions, or other things. But many people have had to learn that perhaps the greatest disappointment is wanting something badly, getting it, and then still feel that emptiness in their souls. How sad!

The Apostle Paul, on the other hand, teaches us how to be content: "I can do all things through Christ Who strengthens me," he says in Phil. 4:13. Can we really do all things? Does that mean that we can leap over tall buildings? No! The power we receive through Christ is sufficient to do His will and face the challenges that come our way. Contentment does not imply laziness or lack of motivation. It's simply an attitude to be thankful and joyful no matter how much or little we possess, or what peaks or valleys we face. We can enjoy profound peace, joy and thankful contentment, especially when we realize Who has given us what we have. I saw it in the attitude of the Wyoming couple.

To what are we drawn when we feel empty inside? The answer lies in our perspective, our priorities and our source of power. The secret of contentment is found in the power of Christ, not in man's inventions, comforts, techno-toys, wealth or amusement. It is accepting what God has given us, and by His strength, making the most of it. Then the message of Philippians will not be limited to a four-chapter book in the Bible, but be displayed in our everyday experience of life.

A twelve-year-old boy, who was a key witness in a lawsuit, understood the oath: To tell the truth—nothing but the truth. One of attorneys, after intense questioning, asked the boy, "Did your father tell you what to say?" "Yes," said the boy. "Tell us then," continued the attorney, "what were his instructions?" "My father told me that the lawyers would try to confuse me while giving my testimony, but if I tell the truth, I will be able to say the same thing every time."

That is certainly the truth. We read in Proverbs 19:5, "A false witness will not go unpunished, and he who speaks lies will not escape." Lying destroys truth and tears down relationships. Yet, statistics are often exaggerated, rumors and gossip are passed on, etc. As Christians, we must be committed to tell the truth. St. Paul teaches us to not lie to one another, since we have laid aside our old self with its evil practices, and we have put on our new self that is being renewed in knowledge in the image of its Creator (Col. 3:9). Laying aside the old self is like stripping off old clothes, or like pealing off a layer of that which was our old self—our old nature. Putting on the new self occurs when we receive Christ in our hearts, and change our ways because of Him. As Christians, our conduct should match our faith. Lying is the language of the ungodly.

This reminds me of our recent cruise to Alaska. On the last night, as my husband Steve and I were escorted to the Captain's Table, I was seated next to the hotel manager. This was a 37-year-old godly Greek man who had entered a monastery by permission for two days for prayer, fasting and meditation before taking on his new responsibility. As we were conversing in Greek, one of his guests across the table took a candid photo of us. When he turned to look, the woman said jokingly, "Now we can blackmail you!" The hotel manager responded with a victorious smile, "Hey, I don't care, I have nothing to hide!"

How wonderful to be able to say that, I thought, for any of us. An honest person has nothing to hide, but a dishonest one, sooner or later, pays an awful price. One lie leads to another to cover up the previous one, and eventually the liar is caught in a web of deceit. But when one tells the truth, as the 12-year old boy said in the above story, the answer will always be the same. For a follower of Christ, our most important consideration is that truthfulness should reflect our relationship with the Lord.

Every Christian is in a continuing educational program. The more we know of Christ and His ministry, the more we are being changed from the inside to resemble His image. Because this process is life-long, we must never stop learning and obeying His Word. There is no justification for drifting away. But there is an incentive to find the rich treasures of divine wisdom and spiritual growth. It takes practice, patience and perseverance to keep in line with His will.

Lying may seem like a convenient way out, but it's really a dead end. The right and sensible choice, therefore, is to always speak the truth—nothing but the truth!

*T*he recent tremors in Southern California reminded me of how powerless we are as people. As the smaller aftershocks continued, I remembered a conversation I had with a young woman in Albuquerque, New Mexico, a few years ago.

She was changing her outfit in a dressing room from casual to a business suit. As I walked in she asked me for some help. When she learned I was from California, Los Angeles area, she enthusiastically informed me that she was on her way to a job interview, and that the boss of the company was from L.A. As our conversation continued, I found out that there were many families from the L.A. area who had moved to Albuquerque in great numbers after the 1972 and 1994 earthquakes, and they are still coming sporadically. I also learned that they are families with children of all ages. Most of them live in a newly developed community, own a variety of businesses and even have a new school in that area for their children. I was amazed! Although many people come to California annually from everywhere, now I knew that many were leaving as well.

Whatever the intensity of the tremors, no one likes earthquakes. And yet, the reality is that they are with us, and we are reminded from time to time of how completely helpless we are. Wherever we live, and whatever natural disasters we face, one thing is certain—that God is in control. A verse, Psalm 127:1, comes to mind: "Unless the Lord builds the house, they labor in vain who build it; unless the Lord guards the city, the watchman stays awake in vain."

All of life's work—building a home, establishing a career and raising a family—must have God as the foundation. A family without God can never experience the spiritual bond God brings to a relationship. It is a mistake to leave God out of our lives. If we do, all our accomplishments will be in vain. As Christians we should make God our first and highest priority, and let Him guide our paths. We should build our families on the principles of God's Word, just as the wise man who builds his house on the "rock" which withstands all storms of life. Jesus says in Mt. 7:26, 27 that everyone who hears these words and does not put them into practice, is like a foolish man who built his house on the sand. As the winds of life blew, the house fell. Although the two houses may appear equally secure for a long time, when the storm comes, the destruction of the foolish one's house is total. So it is with the lives of those who ignore the words of Christ.

The house also represents devoted Christian life. The storms represent divine judgment. Only the one built on the foundation of Christian principles and obedience to God's Word stands. The key difference in the two houses is not their external appearance, but their foundations. The house built on the rock will stand the test of God's judgment, but the house on sand will fail the test. In the final analysis, wherever we move, wherever we build our family life, we cannot call ourselves Christians unless we practice the principles that Christ taught.

*W*hile on a Caribbean cruise we shared our dinner table with several couples. One of them was a gentleman in his eighties with a younger woman who introduced herself as his nurse caregiver. She had been hired by his daughter to care for him. Interestingly, the nurse said that she was registered with a hospital, and took jobs such as this throughout the U.S. On the third and fourth nights this couple didn't join us for dinner. My husband and I were concerned. We asked the maitre d' if he knew what had happened to them. "Oh," he said, "The gentleman died two days ago and his nurse got off the cruise ship at our last port and flew home!" We were caught by surprise! The man looked fine, robust, enthusiastic, walked with no cane, and yet he was gone! He had died in his sleep!

A verse from James 4:14 came to mind: "Whereas you do not know what will happen tomorrow. For what is your life? It is even a vapor that appears for a little time and then vanishes away." Yes, life is short no matter how long we live, but as Christians we can let God fill it with infinite meaning. If not, trivial pursuits will only bring empty results. God is our Creator and in control of every life. Yet we often resist His power and wander from His care. We forget that we desperately need a place of refuge. God's Word and His love, however, call us back to Him. The only way to find our way through the desert of life is through the trustworthy leading of our Lord. Those who know God intimately will be victorious in the end.

For what is a day? A twenty-four hour segment of time never lived before, and never to be repeated. We may never live to see another day just like this one, as the gentleman who died in his sleep. We may never be closer to a decision we need to make, a new step we may need to take, or forgiveness we may need to grant someone. Why not then do it today, before tomorrow's demands eclipse today's desires.

A wise person once said that the value of life is determined, not by its duration, but by its donation. Except for the obvious necessity of the cross, Jesus could have continued performing amazing deeds if He had lived longer. But that was not according to God's timing, and such deeds would not have enlarged His supreme donation—His ministry. His short life and painful death provided our salvation and eternal life. And the works that He completed are still bearing fruit through His Spirit. Equally important to remember is that one's harvest is not always reaped in this life. God's work through our lives will continue to bear fruit long after we are gone. That is a comforting and challenging thought. No matter what our life's duration, we have an opportunity to make a lasting donation—a lasting legacy to those around us or our next generation.

What is built on Christ lasts forever. We should treasure each hour of each day as a gift of great value from God, and use it wisely. And rather than counting our days, we can make our days count.

The story is told of a pastor who was invited to dinner in the home of a very wealthy man in Texas. After the meal, the host led the pastor to a place where they could get a good view of all the surrounding area. Pointing to the oil wells, he boasted, "Twenty five years ago I had nothing. Now, as far as you can see, it's all mine." Looking in the opposite direction at his fields of grain, he said, "That is also mine." Turning toward huge herds of cattle, be bragged, "They too are mine." Then, pointing to a beautiful forest, he exclaimed, "All that is mine as well."

The Texan then paused, expecting his guest to compliment him on his great success. The pastor, however, placing one hand on the man's shoulder and pointing heavenward with the other said, "My dear brother, how much do you have in that direction?" The man hung his head and confessed, "I never thought of that." Although the wealthy Texan had achieved financial success, he failed to acknowledge his Creator. Jesus says in Mk. 8:36, "What will it profit a man if he gains the whole world, and loses his own soul?" To have all that the world has to offer, yet not have Christ, is to be eternally and spiritually bankrupt.

There isn't a word in scripture against financial prosperity, as long as it is earned honestly and handled with integrity. Let's face it; the opposite of wealth is poverty, and we can't accomplish much in God's service and ministry while impoverished. The Bible teaches us that only the "love of money," when it comes before and above God, is "the root of all kinds of evil" (1 Tim. 6:10). How much we possess is not as important as our attitude toward our possessions. Money itself is not evil, since it is a gift from God (Deut. 8:18).

We must be happy that God blesses some people with wealth to benefit others. As Christians, we may enjoy God's blessings without feeling guilty, but we must also humbly acknowledge Him and praise Him as the source of all that we have. Then willingly and generously, we can share with those in need. What we have is meaningless unless it is used for something meaningful. In the spiritual realm, only that which we give away can we keep forever. Seed kept in the granary will mold and decay, but thrown into the ground, in due time will increase manifold. Whether we consider ourselves rich, poor or somewhere in between, our love for the Lord should be the reason we need to be generous in our giving. Boastful pride and a selfish attitude that ignore God's work, as demonstrated by the wealthy Texan, will weaken our faith and hinder His blessings.

Our attitude is more important than the amount we give. We don't have to be embarrassed if we can give only a small gift. God is concerned about how we give from the resources we have. St. Paul says in 2 Cor. 9:6, 7: "He who sows sparingly will also reap sparingly, and he who sows bountifully will also reap bountifully. So let each one give as he proposes in his heart...for God loves a cheerful giver." A wise investor lays up treasures in heaven. May we so live that we will reap eternal benefits.

*T*he story is told of a young Christian man who asked an elderly mature believer to pray for him, that God would grant him patience. The older man got down on his knees and prayed, "Oh Lord, send this young man tribulation in the morning, send this young man tribulation in the afternoon, send this young man..." At this point the young Christian interrupted, "No, no, stop! I didn't ask you to pray for tribulation. I wanted you to pray for patience." "Ah," responded the wise mature Christian, "It's through tribulation that we learn patience." How true!

The above wise advice echoes the Apostle James' words in 1: 13. He says, "My brothers, count it all joy when you fall into various trials, knowing that the testing of your faith produces patience." It doesn't say **if** we face trials, but **when** we face trials. It's a fact—we will have trials, and it is possible to learn from them. The point is to not pretend to be happy when we face pain, but to maintain a positive outlook because of what trials can produce in our lives. St. James tells us to turn our hardships into opportunities to learn. Tough times can teach us patience!

The Apostle Paul also has a similar message for us. In Romans 5: 3 he says, "We glory in tribulation, knowing that tribulation produces perseverance, and perseverance, character; and character, hope." Patience or perseverance often translates as "steadfastness," the ability to remain firm under difficulties without giving in. That was certainly true in St. Paul's life and ministry. He was beaten with rods, stoned, imprisoned, shipwrecked, yet he remained steadfast in his faith, and didn't shrink from his calling.

Some of us find our patience tested in some way every day. Can we look at difficulty as an opportunity for growth? We are asked to rejoice in suffering, not because we like it or deny its tragedy, but because we know God is using life's difficulties to build our character and teach us patience. I must admit I've often taken this scriptural advice myself. It is not a "joy" by any means. It was only after it all resolved itself that the lesson became clear.

When we face hardships, it is easy to lose sight of the big picture. But we aren't alone. Many have made it through life, enduring far more difficult circumstances than we have experienced. Suffering is the training ground for Christian maturity. The patience we develop will make our final victory sweet.

As we encounter trials in life, we are often tempted to sit at the base of that difficult hill, and remain there, convinced that the slope is too steep for us to continue. That is why we need the encouragement of God's Word in prayer. It will draw our attention away from our problems and toward our loving God, Who knows our every need. When we feel that life is crushing heavily on us, and we cannot go another step, let us remember that we can call upon God to renew our strength. God always gives enough strength for the next step.

As children of God, we are all under His wise control. All that is happening to us is designed to develop perseverance and patience. Some of life's greatest lessons are indeed learned in the school of affliction.

A young man wearing a three-piece wool suit walked into my adult watercolor class. The suit surprised me. After all, this was a three-hour evening art class. But that wasn't all that was curious about Andrew. As the art class progressed, I noticed his unusually clean, soft, well-cared-for hands. This man, I thought, has never changed a tire in his life. Andrew was from England, visiting the U.S. for a few months. He soon informed me that he was going to miss a class next week because he had an important job interview in Washington, D.C. And if all would go well, he was going to move to Canada.

When he returned he was very happy. He had the position. Then he thanked me because through this art class his eyes were opened to a world he was too busy to see previously. While in Washington, D.C., he had visited the National Art Museum, several art galleries, appreciating his new awareness in the arts. I saw the excitement in his eyes. Then I asked what position it was that would take him to Canada. "Chief of Surgery in one of the best hospitals in Montreal," he said quite pleased. I congratulated him. Andrew produced some very good art in class, and I suggested that he have some framed.

Human hands are amazing! There were many pairs of hands in my class. Some rough, others I noticed had permanently injured fingers, some were left-handed individuals, and all did their best in producing good work. God has created us to use our skills and use them for good works in His service. His work is done by ordinary people who are committed to Him. Some of us may feel inadequate at times and question our abilities. Yet, God used the hesitant, inarticulate Moses to lead the Israelites out of Egyptian bondage (Ex. 3:7; 4:10). He used men of herds and flocks, as well as fishermen to accomplish His work and record His Words. A simple carpenter and a peasant girl raised God's Son! That is still the way the Lord works. We read in 1 Cor. 1:27 that God chooses "the weak things of the world to put to shame the things which are mighty."

Since ascending to heaven, Christ no longer has a body on earth, except ours. He has no hands or feet on earth except for the members of His body, the Church. That's us! So, we must never underestimate the importance of being the body of Christ on earth, not only spiritually, but also physically. Therefore, He sends us out to be His body to one another and to the world, and to go about doing good.

Whatever kind of hands we have, soft or rough, let us not deny or belittle our God-given gifts; but thank and praise Him for them, and allow Him to use us in His service and for His glory. Let us determine to leave a lasting legacy of love and good works, and be an example to our next generation. Whatever our calling might be, let's keep in mind that Christ has no body on earth but ours. It is ordinary people who do God's extraordinary work. God has been using ordinary people like you and me for thousands of years. Why would He stop now?

FRIEDA THE FIGHTER

*T*he best way I can describe Frieda is tall, muscular and husky. I met her at the gym. Frieda was in her thirties, blond, with the most beautiful blue eyes. Her muscular body and physical strength caught my attention. She used very heavy weights in her workout. "You are very strong! I'm impressed! What are you involved in?" I asked. "I'm a fire fighter," she replied. That explained everything. Frieda, I'm sure, could easily climb a rope, carry heavy fire fighter's hoses and perform all that her job entails.

I commented on the honorable and dangerous service fire fighters provide to society. "Well," she said. "We have received a bit more recognition and appreciation after September 11." Frieda is married to a farmer, has two children, and they live on their ranch. She works four days a week as a fire fighter and sleeps in the fire station a few nights a month. I commented about her beautiful eyes. "That's the only thing I have going for me," she said with a twinkle in her eyes.

She finished her workout and came to say good-bye. I took the opportunity to ask her about her job experiences and the people she rescues from danger. I said, "What are people's reactions, and do they cry just before you get them to safety?" Her answer was immediate: "Help, dear God! Dear God, help!" Then she added, "Even the non-religious call upon God, Whom they previously ignored. I have rescued people from plane crashes, floods, fires, auto accidents, earthquakes, etc. In all tragic events, people seem to call on God as their last hope. We pull them to safety, and then we run back to rescue more. There is always that danger, however, that we won't make it out alive ourselves," she added.

Frieda's last sentence brought the following verse to mind: "Greater love has no one than this, than to lay down his life for his friends" (Jn. 15:13). God loved us so much that He gave His only begotten son, so that whoever believes in Him will not perish, but have eternal life. We may never be called upon to make the kind of sacrifice that Jesus made. We may never even be called upon to do what Frieda does on her job. Yet daily we have opportunities to practice sacrificial love; listening, helping, encouraging, calling, writing notes, etc. We have opportunities to set aside our comfort to demonstrate love to our neighbors.

It is sad that only tragedy and near-death experiences make some people call upon the Lord for help. God our Creator knows all the events of our lives, and sometimes allows events to occur for His purpose. Are we aware that the King of kings, Whose hands rule the universe, is always with us and holds our hand? From the womb to the tomb, our daily lives are known to God. The question is, are our lives intertwined with His? Let's not wait for a close call with death to call on God.

"I am the vine, you are the branches," Jesus says in Jn. 15:5. "He who abides in Me, and I in him, he bears much fruit." As Christians and as His ambassadors on earth, we have security and protection in the hands of God. Our time is also in His mighty hands. And one day in heaven, our hands will touch the nail-scarred hands of the Savior!

*W*e all know that pulling weeds can be a struggle, whether it's unearthing a string of ivy or digging up dandelions. We also know that when the ground is hard and dry, weeds are highly resistant to being uprooted. But when water softens the soil, they yield quite readily. Also we know that the youngest weeds are easier to remove, but older ones that are widely spread and established are more stubborn.

This example reminds me of our bad habits. The longer they remain with us, the more difficult they are to remove. Do we recall the last time we tried to change a bad habit? It wasn't easy. A bad habit is like a soft chair—easy to get into but hard to get out of. Because we were comfortable with the old way, the new felt awkward. That is why we often hesitate to make needed changes. For example, perhaps we speak words we shouldn't. Or we may be critical of others instead of helpful. We can fill in the blanks of our own wrong habits or actions—we all have them. It certainly takes a conscious effort on our part and God's help to change. If we uproot them early, when our heart is tender toward God's love, we will have the best chance for success.

Taming the tongue and eliminating undesirable habits have been with us since creation. Therefore, the Word of God has countless examples. God created us with the ability to choose and speak words that nourish others. St. Paul writes in Eph. 4:29, "Do not let any unwholesome talk come out of your mouths, but only what is helpful for building others up." But in reality, the words we speak are sometimes fired at high velocity with the intent to hurt. St. James puts it even more bluntly: "Out of the same mouth come praise and cursing. My brothers, this should not be" (3:10). In Proverbs we read, "Reckless words pierce like a sword, but the tongue of the wise brings healing" (12:18). As Christians, the above few verses should be our motto in all our relationships.

Jesus had plenty to say about the power and importance of every word we speak. He says in Mt. 12:36, "I tell you that men will have to give account on the day of judgment for every careless word they have spoken." According to our Lord, the need for change goes far deeper than taming the tongue. "Make a tree good," Jesus said, "and its fruit will be good...For a tree is recognized by its fruit. For out of the overflow of the heart the mouth speaks" (Mt. 12:33, 34). What we say reveals the contents of our heart.

The truth of God's Word and His abundant love for us can soften the soil of any hard heart. And when we remember that Christ died on the cross to free us from the penalty of sin, we will see the need to fight aggressively against sinful habits. "Pulling weeds" is often a painful process with failures to follow. But persistent effort can bring success! The most effective bad-habits-control takes place when we let Christ soften our thirsty hearts with streams of His "Living Waters" (Jn. 4:10). Then victory is certain!

THE BLACK SPOT

A pastor was the speaker at a men's fellowship breakfast. As he addressed his audience, he took a large piece of white paper and made a black spot in the center with a marking pen. Then he held the paper up before the men and asked them what they saw. One person quickly replied, "I see a black mark." "Right," replied the pastor. "What else do you see?" Complete silence prevailed. "Don't you see anything other than the black spot?" he asked. Only "no" answers came from the audience. "I'm surprise," the speaker commented. "You have overlooked the most important thing of all—the sheet of paper."

Most of us are often distracted by focusing our attention on small disappointments and forget the many blessings we receive from the Lord. Often, like the sheet of paper, the good things in life are overwhelmed by the adversities that monopolize our attention. The problem might be on the job, or a cherished relationship that has been broken, or the problem might be physical. In all trials it's hard to feel grateful.

When suffering invades our lives, we often wonder what we have done to deserve it. Yet even Jesus, our perfect Savior, suffered during His life on earth. Hebrews 5:8 says "He learned obedience by the things which He suffered." We also read in 2 Cor. 12:7 – 10 that St. Paul had a "thorn in his flesh." We don't know exactly what that "thorn" was, because he doesn't tell us. It was some chronic physical problem which at times was a hindrance to his ministry. He pleaded with the Lord three times that it might depart from him; but God refused.

Although God did not remove the "thorn" as Paul requested, He continually supplied him with grace to endure it. This kept Paul humble and reminded him of his need for constant contact with the Lord. It also benefited those around him as they saw God at work in his life. Often our trials not only help us develop Christian character, but also deepen our relationship with our Creator. Because by admitting our weaknesses, we affirm God's strength.

When we are strong in all areas of our lives, we are tempted to forget our Creator, and that can lead to pride. God does not intend for us to be weak, passive or ineffective. No! Life provides enough hindrances and setbacks without us creating them. But when those obstacles come, we must turn and trust the Lord, because only through His power can we be effective.

Our Heavenly Father, Who created the world and sustains everything that exists by His mighty hands, can gently touch the lives of His suffering children. Rather than concentrating on our trials of life—"the black spot"—we should focus our attention on our blessings. We have the privilege to say as the Apostle Paul does in Phil. 4:13, "I can do all things through Christ Who strengthens me!"

*T*here is an old expression that says, "If you want to make God laugh, tell Him your plans." Although this seems funny at first, God truly wants us to talk to Him about all that is going on in our lives, even though He already knows everything. So why pray?

Among many reasons for prayer are: Prayer is the means through which God can grant us grace and mercy and help us in time of need; prayer with thanksgiving is God's way for us to obtain freedom from anxiety and fear, and to receive His peace that surpasses all understanding; prayer is God's way for us to obtain what we ask from Him—an example is the Lord's Prayer (Mt. 6:11). We also pray for others by interceding for healing, comfort, justice, etc. God, of course, can accomplish all that without us, but He gives us the privilege to be involved with Him in prayer.

We should always pray "according to His divine will" (1 Jn. 5:14). When we do that, our attitude of prayer changes, and we are better prepared to accept whatever God's divine answer will be. Prayer is not a magic wand for satisfying our own wishes, but an opportunity to fellowship with the Lord to accomplish His purpose.

I saw a T-shirt recently with the word "GAP" in big letters. At first I thought it was the clothing store. Then I saw the rest. "GAP" was the acronym for "God Answers Prayers"! Yes, God always answers our prayers, but He answers them according to His divine will. Sometimes His answer is immediate. Sometimes it is delayed, which means, "Have patience—wait." And sometimes the answer is "No!" In any case, God always answers. It might not be what we wish, but "No" is also an answer. And He has a very good reason for not granting our request. We read in Isaiah 55:8, "For My thoughts are not your thoughts, neither are your ways My ways."

This reminds me of an amusing incident described in Acts 12:5 − 17 of prayers answered immediately. The Apostle Peter was in prison. The faithful of the early church prayed fervently for God to deliver Peter. The Lord did just that through an angel. Not only did Peter's chains fall from his hands, but the angel led him out through the iron gate, passing two guard posts. Then the angel disappeared. Peter, now free, went to the house where the faithful prayed. He knocked at the door. The servant girl recognized Peter's voice. But in the excitement, didn't open the door, but ran to tell the rest that Peter was outside. They didn't believe her, and told her she was beside herself. When they finally opened the door and saw him, the Bible says that they were astonished. They failed to believe that the Lord had done just what they had requested. Imagine!

Do we have plans to make? Let's make sure to include God in the process. His love and power are great, and His resources are endless! We should seek His divine wisdom through His Word, and consult Him for guidance in prayer. If we leave Him out, our best laid plans may leave Him laughing.

*M*ost of us in the United States know that in times of emergency, dialing the numbers 9-1-1 will get us prompt help. Even pre-school children have saved lives of family members by dialing those three numbers. Emergency help is as close as dialing those three numbers, providing that the phone is connected.

Situations we often face, however, cannot be remedied by human rescuers. Many times our lives' crises require divine assistance. When that occurs, we can call a different kind of 9-1-1. We read in Psalm 91:1, "He who dwells in the shelter of the Most High shall abide in the shadow of the Almighty." In this Psalm we find that the help and protection we need is even closer than running to the phone to dial 9-1-1. In this Psalm we don't have to be concerned about being electronically connected. In this Psalm our Almighty's line is always open and connected, day or night, for the prayer life of His beloved children. When we are in distress we must always remember that the distance between our problem and God is as close as the distance between our knees and the floor!

God is our "shelter," a "refuge," particularly when we are afraid. Our Almighty God is our Protector Who would carry us through all dangers and fears of life. His love and care is the refuge and fortress that He provides for His own. Have we taken notice of the names of God in this one little verse? Most High and Almighty! This should be a picture of our trust—trading all our fears for faith in Him—no matter how intense our fears or emergencies. To do this we must "dwell" and "abide" in Him. By entrusting ourselves to His protection, and pledging our daily devotion to Him, we will be kept safe.

In Luke 11:1 we read that the disciples did not ask Jesus to teach them how to preach or how to sing, but rather for what was most important. They said, "Lord, teach us to pray." More is accomplished by prayer than has ever been or will ever be accomplished by other means. Prayer is everyone's privilege. The gift of prayer is available to all, and all of us may call upon the power of our Almighty God.

Prayer, as P-mail is faster than E-mail, and with no wires needed. We have direct access to God Himself. No middle computers, no need for uplinks or satellites, no need for codes. Just God and us. Person to person, heart to heart. Those who draw near to God can have that instant peace through Him, however difficult their circumstances might be. God hears the cries of His people, and we can be certain that He'll answer according to His will and in His perfect timing.

Our Almighty Father is eagerly anticipating to hear from us, not only during crises or emergencies, but prayers at times of doxology, exhortation and thanksgiving. We must never forget that gratitude is an attitude, and it should be expressed at all times. Cheerleading for God is spelled P-R-A-I-S-E! Yes, prayer is every Christian's open line to heaven. And God takes each call personally.

*T*he British statesman and reformer, William Wilberforce (1759 – 1833), was a clever debater, a shrewd politician and a popular socialite. At age 21, he was elected a member of Parliament in England during a time of terrible moral and spiritual decline, where the poor were oppressed and the slave trade was booming.

For a time, Wilberforce went along with these evils, thinking only of his personal ambitions. But at age 25, he traveled to France with one of his former teachers, Isaac Milner. During this trip Wilberforce read and studied the Bible with Milner. Before long, he surrendered his life to Christ and was transformed into a merciful human being. The parties he once enjoyed now seemed indecent. The suffering of the poor now troubled him. The fight to abolish the slave trade attracted him, and he soon became the leader in the battle against slavery. And primarily due to his efforts, in 1833 slavery was abolished in England. Wilberforce was transformed because he studied and obeyed the Bible.

Among the many names given to our Lord in the Bible, one is especially dear to me. It is the name "Redeemer." The word "redeem" literally means to "buy back" or "pay off." For example, when a slave was redeemed, someone paid money to buy his or her freedom. For us Christians, the purchase price for our redemption was the sacrificial death of Jesus Christ, which met the demands of God's holiness. The Apostle Paul says in Rom. 3:23, "For all have sinned and fallen short of the glory of God." Everyone who accepts God's gift of forgiveness, love and grace is set free, and becomes a servant of Christ, the Redeemer. We read in 1 Pet. 1:19 that God redeemed us from the slavery of sin, not with silver or gold, but with the precious blood of His Son Jesus Christ.

The story is told that many years ago, a man visited a slave market. He watched for a while, and then bid on a slave until no one was able to go any higher. After paying the price, he gave the bill of sale to the slave and said, "I have purchased you to set you free." Overcome with gratitude, the slave refused to leave him, and became his devoted servant for life.

Jesus paid an enormous price for our freedom. As Christians our old nature was crucified with Him. The penalty of sin died with Christ on the cross. The good news is that through faith in Christ, we stand acquitted—"not guilty" before God. Christ now lives in us, guiding us through His Holy Spirit.

William Wilberforce was transformed because he studied and obeyed God's Word. If we want to have a closer personal relationship with God, and feel His boundless love and grace, then we would want to do His will and serve Him for life. That will bring radiance and victory into our lives, now and eternally. Christ gave His all for us. Are we giving our all for Him?

I never tasted a "Famous Amos" cookie, but I understand they are good. Catchy name, easy to remember, even by children—an excellent marketing plan! One thing seems sure; that the "Famous Amos" cookies made Amos famous.

In the Old Testament there is another Amos who was not so famous. He was a man of God—a person whose life was devoted to serving the Lord. He was a prophet who lived in the southern kingdom. Israel was a divided kingdom at the time. The southern part was called Judah and the northern Israel. Amos was called by God to go and prophesy to the northern kingdom.

Amos was a layperson. He was herding sheep and tending sycamore-fig trees in the Judean countryside. But God gave Amos a vision of the future and told him to go and announce His message of judgment to the north. The northerners enjoyed unprecedented economic and political prosperity. Not since the days of King Solomon had times been as good. Without any special preparation or upbringing, Amos obeyed God's call. Here we see again, that God doesn't always call the person who may seem to be qualified, but He qualifies the one He calls.

Amos was burdened over the sinful life led by his brethren for their self-indulgence and for their gross idolatry. He announced that God was going to judge His covenant-breaking people. His message was not popular, to say the least. Amos was told to leave the country. "Get out, you seer!" he was ordered (Am. 7:12). But Amos preached fearlessly. One of the visions he preached was God's "plumb line" –a symbol of judgment. The plumb line is a cord with weight tied to one end. Ancient builders used it to ensure a straight wall. If not straight, a wall will eventually collapse. Amos sees the Lord with a plumb line testing Israel, which didn't meet God's standards. Israel was crooked.

God permits evil to take place. Israel suffered the consequences of its actions. God allowed Assyria to carry a large number of the northern kingdom's population into captivity to Babylon. Their punishment was that they would be absorbed into a pagan world. They were indeed exiled in 722 B.C., and later Judah, the southern kingdom, including Jerusalem, met a similar fate in 586 B.C.

What do ancient visions mean to us today? Because the visions given to the Old and New Testament men of God were revelations from God, they can benefit us centuries after they are given. We can be inspired and challenged. Often God reveals principles that apply to many different situations, even though specific details may change.

Perhaps some of us have been in Amos' position. With genuine concern, we have delivered warnings to friends or family members about their poor choices and behavior. They didn't like it. They may even have told us to back off—it's none of our business—and to leave them alone. It's their life. Pointing to the truth, even lovingly, gently, out of heart-felt concern, never makes one famous. But we have done what's right according to God's standards, and that will make us famous as Amos in God's eyes!

Growing up, I remember the following story repeated by adults. Someone asked Narsadin Hodja what the protocol is at funerals. "Should the friends of the deceased walk ahead of the casket or behind?" Hodja replied, "It doesn't matter as long as you are not in it."

It seems, however, that a man in South Africa did just that. He staged his own funeral to find out what his friends would say about him. He wore his best suit, got into a casket, and with the help of a few family members, went through an unusual deception. During the funeral service, for nearly two hours, he carefully listened from his coffin how his friends eulogized him, expressing their grief and love with touching stories. When he had heard enough, the "dead" man got out of the coffin. Confident of his friends' love, he realized he was dead wrong about his doubts. Pleased with what he heard, he joyfully declared that his friends had passed the test.

What this man did was very unusual and strange; perhaps even illegal. The information he wanted, however, is something we should all be thinking about while there is still time. What will people say some day about us after we die? Will they say that our life and speech gave ample evidence that we had a close relationship with God?

When we go through a busy day, do we give time to things that have eternal value? Can we balance accomplishments and check items off our "to do" list, while also making time to serve God? We all can, and we should. Before Jesus departed earth He gave special instructions to Apostle Peter. Three times He communicated His desire to him: "Feed My sheep" (John 21:15 – 19).

God has special directions for all faithful. He is our Heavenly Father, and He knows our hearts to the last detail. As we go through our day; after class, after work, meeting inevitable deadlines, or being very busy at home, let us listen to His call on how He wishes us to balance our lives. We can ask ourselves a few simple questions and be confident that God will speak to our hearts: Is my faith in Christ obvious to others? How can I balance God's call with my personal, academic, business and family life?

The highest of relationships is our intimacy with God. Now, we certainly don't want to become preoccupied with death. Instead, let us think about how we can <u>LIVE</u> so that no matter when we die, people and God will say that we knew the Lord well. That is the best way to live!

*T*here are perhaps some people who feel that a Christian's life is a series of joyless tasks, a super-serious attitude and a gloomy, burdened life. If that is the idea that some have about us, they are profoundly mistaken.

Christians are to "Rejoice in the Lord always" is the Apostle Paul's message (Philip. 4:4). Our inner attitude should not be affected by our outward circumstances. No matter what happens, we know that Christ is with us. Yes, it is easy at times to get discouraged due to unpleasant events, or take rather unimportant circumstances too seriously. But if we have not been joyful lately, we may not be looking at life from the right perspective. Ultimate joy comes from Christ dwelling within us.

In light of that, we can laugh and be joyful, by the grace of God, and experience afresh His love daily. As strange as it might seem to many, the Bible is filled with humor and amusing parables. Sarah's laughter first comes to mind. When she was told at age 90 that she and her husband Abraham, age 100, were going to have a child, she laughed. The baby was named Isaac, which comes from the Hebrew word for "laughter" (Gen. 18:12 and 21:3).

We can also imagine the joy Jesus restored to the wedding at Cana, when He turned the water into wine, and festivities continued joyfully for family and guests (John 2:1 – 11). There is humor in Christ's teachings as well. The image of one blind person leading another, and both of them falling into a pit, was an appropriate humorous illustration of what the Pharisees were doing by refusing to see the truth of Christ's teachings (Luke 6:39).

Humor is also seen in the Words of Christ in the mental picture of a camel passing through the eye of a needle (Mark 10:25). In this case Christ was talking about the impossibility of a hardened heart to follow Him. And isn't it also humorous when Christ points out the irony of seeing a speck in a brother's eye while ignoring the log in one's own eye? (Matt. 7:3 – 5). A truly "judge not" lesson for all of us.

Let us determine to be joyful whenever we can. We should allow the joy of the Lord to bubble up like a spring within us. With an outlook of optimism and an attitude of joy, let us laugh a little—maybe a lot! It's in the Bible. I cannot imagine Christ not smiling and joyfully speaking to the little children when they came to him to be blessed. This scene is recorded in three Gospels.

When laughter finds its roots in the joy of the Lord, it makes life for us and those around us more relaxed, pleasurable and fun. Yes, we should laugh a little—maybe a lot! It's in the Bible. Rejoice in the Lord always!

*I*t is not God's intention to give gifts to members of His family so that we become spectators in the work of the church. His plan is not structured like an athletic event with only a few involved in the game, while the majority sit in the stands watching. The spiritual gifts and abilities God has given us are to be used on the playing fields of churches and its youth groups, schools and campus organizations, at work and other worthy community involvements.

When we compare the number of church members who simply attend to those who actively participate, we often see a very sad picture. It is usually a small group of diligent Christian workers who joyfully struggle to get the team going, and often fill many positions. The rest act like spectators, sitting on the sidelines. That small group of people could gladly use some rest if those from the sidelines were willing to join in and get involved.

Christian life is not a spectator sport. We are called to be participants. St. Paul writes to the Corinthian faithful that "The manifestation of the Spirit is given to each one for the profit of all" (1 Cor. 12:7). Gifts, natural or spiritual, come from God. These gifts are like tools that accomplish the purpose of building up God's Church. Our main goal should be that united, we use our abilities to strengthen the Church. All gifts, talents and abilities can be further developed and improved through practice. Often new gifts can surface in us suddenly and extraordinarily, by God's grace. That is the most exciting experience!

Are we spiritually mature, exercising the gifts God has given us? We must not only use them, but dedicate them to God's service, and not for our personal success. If we know what our gifts are, we must look for opportunities to serve. If we don't know, we can pray and ask God to show us, perhaps with the help of Christian friends. If we say we have no gifts or abilities, we are truly insulting our Creator. God has blessed each one of us, often with more than a single gift.

Christians should be on the front lines, not the sidelines. Every believer has his or her own position and role to play on the team. So, what is our position now? Let's go for it, and play for the glory of God and "for the profit of all." We are all needed down on the field of play. How exciting it would be if we were all involved in the game, with no one sitting in the grandstands!

*A*n acquaintance invited me into her office during her lunch hour. I was amused by her mannerism. She had the printer on at one side of her office, while a microwave oven was warming her lunch in an adjacent room. She would impatiently glance at both and order them to hurry. Neither seemed to be going fast enough for her. I made a teasing comment, and we both laughed.

We live in a rush-rush world. The more conveniences we have, the more impatient we become. We often face delays while taking care of daily errands, or have to stand in line and wait. No one likes that, yet to get things done in an orderly manner requires that we "queue up" and wait. Waiting in line, however, or any delay could be a productive time. Although waiting may seem inactive and wasteful, it actually gives us an opportunity to think about God and our relationship with Him.

Many Christians use these delays to pray. We can praise God for our blessings. All of us have a praise list, even if we are not aware of it. We can also pray to God about our concerns, pray for our loved ones, or we could ask God to teach us patience for all life's delays. Prayer is a key weapon in a Christian's daily battle. We are encouraged in 1 Thess., "Be joyful always; pray continually, give thanks in all circumstances, for this is God's will." (5:16 – 18) Being in constant communication with our Creator can be done anywhere, any time, at any place. Waiting therefore, should not be an empty, pointless time for us Christians. While waiting we could be making our most important decisions, or we may receive our most creative inspirations. Our feet don't have to be moving to get things done. The ceaseless communication of our heart, mind, soul and spirit with our Heavenly Father will bring us peace, renewal and victory in all circumstances.

Why not then, use every waiting opportunity to pray, even if we are waiting at a red light. When God's spirit is in us, His strength brings us triumphant victory. We read in Isaiah 4:31, "But those who wait in the Lord, shall renew their strength; they shall mount up with wings like eagles, they shall run and not be weary, they shall walk and not faint." Now *that* is victory! This is God's promise!

A beautiful and valuable silk scarf was ruined by a permanent ink stain. The owner sadly showed it to a friend who was an art critic and painter. The artist took the scarf, and with remarkable skill, transformed the ugly ink stain so that it became the center of a beautiful design. The silk scarf was now far more valuable than before!

God, our Creator, faced a situation somewhat similar to that of the artist, except that the problem was immeasurably greater. Adam and Eve were God's supreme creation, but they ruined their purity by sinning. With their original perfection lost, they were justly and eternally stained. But by the amazing divine plan of the cross, our gracious God and Creator, the supreme Artist of the universe, took stained sinners of the world and gave them the opportunity for a new birth, a renewed self, to reflect the beauty of His Son, Jesus Christ.

With this in mind, St. Peter says, "Praise be to God and the Father of our Lord Jesus Christ! In His great mercy He has given us new birth into a living hope through the resurrection of Jesus Christ from the dead, and into an inheritance that can never perish, spoil or fade—kept in heaven for you" (1 Pet. 1:3). St. Peter's words offer joy and hope in time of trouble, and he bases his confidence on what God has done for us through Christ. Our hope is not only for the future; eternal life begins when we invite Christ into our hearts and put our trust in Him, and join His divine family.

The Apostle Paul says in 2 Cor. 5:17, "Therefore, if anyone is in Christ, he is a new creation; old things have passed away; behold, all things have become new." This restoration is the fulfillment of God's plan and purpose since Adam and Eve. As children of God, we are brand new people on the inside through the Holy Spirit.

In Creation (Gen. 1:3), God said, "Let there be light." And there was light, and the light was good. God separated light from darkness. As Christians, we are illuminated with the light of Christ and the knowledge of His Word.

God formed us, sin deformed us, but Christ can transform each one of us. When we put our faith in Christ, we are not only completely forgiven, but God's Holy Spirit transforms us, making us our Creator's prized possessions. Only God can transform a stained soul into a masterpiece of Grace!

*W*hen our three children were young, my husband and I carefully planned an itinerary for a six week vacation in Europe. We flew to Frankfort, Germany, bought a VW Minibus, and drove through six beautiful countries. While in Greece we saw a few long-time friends. Then we took several of them with us and went to a small village in the mountains to visit some more friends who were vacationing there.

My husband is a great navigator, and he drove during the entire vacation. When we arrived in this charming village to find our friends, we were advised to ask some local people who knew everyone. On the winding road ahead we saw a couple with a goat walking in the same direction we were going. We stopped to ask. The man offered to show us the house. He climbed into the car while his wife continued on her way with the goat. Naturally, we made room for him to sit. Not only would he not sit, but he carried a heavy bag containing a big watermelon that he wouldn't rest on the floor. When I asked him to sit, he replied, "I'm fine, ma'am, I don't want to trouble you." He soon pointed out the house. We thanked him and he went to his home nearby.

We often do the same as the man who wouldn't put down his heavy bag as we carry life's heavy burdens in our hearts. We worry and fret and hold onto them tightly instead of turning them over to God. It might be something in our past that weighs heavily on our conscience. Perhaps it was something we might have said or done that we now regret. No wonder we become so weary and lose courage. And like the man in the car, we hang onto our "heavy bags."

What can we do to free ourselves? In Matt. 11:28 Jesus says, "Come to Me, all you who are weary and burdened, and I will give you rest." Christ offers to free us from all weariness and grant us forgiveness. Those who turn to seek Him can find renewal, freedom from all baggage through fellowship with Him. Through the ages, the above verse has been one of the most beloved in the New Testament. A relationship with Christ changes meaningless, wearisome toil into spiritual productivity and purpose. Jesus crossed national, racial and economic barriers to spread His "Good News." His message of love, faith and forgiveness is for the whole world. God's grace is available to everyone. He died on the cross and rose from the grave to set us free—to give us true liberty and freedom from all baggage. What a gift from God! What grace!

As we look to the future, are we cautiously guiding our thoughts and deeds? Are our actions and speech God-honoring, or are we in danger of creating a new set of baggage? Obedience to God brings abundant blessings. Only with the help of God's Holy Spirit and prayer can we continue to keep ourselves free from needless baggage forever. We can all use a much needed rest. What joy!

*H*urts from our past and unresolved conflicts resurface from time to time. What can we do to repair its lingering effects? Answers don't come easily, but the Bible gives us some principles.

One example is Joseph, related in Genesis chapters 37 to 50, who was given a colorful robe by his father Jacob. This "coat of many colors" indicated favoritism and possibly the birthright. Although Joseph was Jacob's eleventh son, he was Rachel's first born. Rachel was Jacob's favorite wife. Also Joseph's reported dreams of his future ascendance aggravated the situation. This was unbearable to his older brothers, who conspired against him.

Adversities are often blessings in disguise. Joseph's brothers stripped him of his colorful coat, threw him into a pit, and then sold him as a slave to some passing merchants. They told their father that he was killed by animals. The merchants sold Joseph to Potiphar in Egypt. Although his brothers stripped Joseph of his coat, they could not strip his God-given vision. His faith was greater than his circumstances.

Joseph was 17 years old. By diligent work, he soon became the head of Potiphar's household. All was well until he was falsely accused of trying to seduce his master's wife, and was thrown into prison. In reality, the opposite occurred. As Joseph fled from her presence, she grasped his coat and kept it as evidence. This was the second coat that Joseph had lost. We can imagine the sense of betrayal he felt in prison.

But God can turn obstacles into opportunities, and was about to transform Joseph's trials into triumphs. Because of his God-given vision, Joseph was finally brought to interpret a dream of the Pharaoh himself. Amazed, Pharaoh was won over. He recognized Joseph as a man in tune with God's spirit and made him governor of Egypt and administrator of grain reserves. Joseph had predicted a future famine by interpreting Pharaoh's dream. Pharaoh put his signet ring on Joseph's finger, clothed him in garments of fine linen, etc. What a blessing. Joseph finally stopped losing coats and received new ones of honor!

Famine forced Joseph's brothers to come to Egypt to buy grain. They stood at Joseph's mercy, whom they didn't recognize, but who recognized them. After two trying accounts, Joseph finally revealed his true identity. He said, "I am your brother Joseph, the one you sold into Egypt! And now, do not be distressed...for selling me here, for it was to save lives that God sent me ahead of you." (Gen. 45:4, 5). "You intended to harm me, but God intended it for good..." (Gen.: 50:20)

Joseph became a model of courage. Under God's providence he became the "savior" of his family, including those very brothers who had treated him so cruelly. And when he finally had the opportunity for revenge, he forgave them! When some day we see Joseph in heaven, he will be wearing his final heavenly robe of righteousness!

The same God Whose grace and power took Joseph to the top can also help us overcome our worst obstacles. When pain from the past surfaces, we can go to the Great Physician. We can call on Him for His forgiveness and reconcile our past. We can overcome a painful start with a blessed ending!

*Y*ears ago we had a peach tree that produced sweet, delicious fruit. Unfortunately the birds had also discovered that, and they ate most of it before we did. I made a scarecrow one year, which I thought was quite creatively convincing, but it didn't help. Wise birds know that a scarecrow is simply an advertisement. It really announces that some very juicy and delicious fruit is there for the picking! They aren't afraid nor do they see it as an obstacle hindering the way to their goal. They know that there are scarecrows in all the best gardens. I admired their perseverance.

Nature often teaches us valuable lessons. What are some of our difficult circumstances? Uncertainty? Personal inadequacy? Fear of failure? What is our scarecrow today that hinders our way to success? Perhaps that which we see as an obstacle, our scarecrow, is simply an invitation. It could be announcing that a very desirable blessing with our name on it is there waiting to be picked! Our own fears and uncertainties often may have prevented us from walking in fruitful paths more times than we could number.

As Christians however, we too can treat our scarecrow as though it were an invitation. Every giant, every difficulty in our way which makes us feel like a grasshopper, is only a scarecrow trying to prevent us from receiving God's richest blessings. And most often, trials and troubles could be but blessings in disguise. We must believe therefore, that when we fix our eyes on God, our fears will vanish.

The Apostle Paul says in Rom. 8:31, "If God is for us, who can be against us?" The condition makes it clear that there is no doubt about it. If God gave the supreme gift of His Son to save us, He will certainly also give whatever is necessary to bring to fulfillment the work begun at the cross! Our part is to have faith and trust God at all times. We must trust God as if everything depended on Him, while working toward our goal as if everything depended on us.

In the gospel of John 14:6, Jesus says, "I am the Way, the Truth and the Life. No one comes to the Father except through Me." Some may argue that this is too narrow a way. But in reality, it is wide enough for the whole world, if the world chooses to accept it. As the Way, Jesus is our path to the Father. As the Truth, He is the reality of all God's promises. And as the Life, He joins His divine life to ours, both now and eternally. Jesus is the visible, tangible image of the invisible God.

Christ came to set us free and to let us soar and glide away from all worldly weights. Our faith makes us like a bird which loves to perch on scarecrows. Therefore, let us perch on our scarecrows by faith and start singing, and expect an abundant feast.

*M*ost of us remember the slide rule. It may seem like an ancient relic today, but not long ago engineers and scientists found the slide rule to be indispensable. Only a generation ago, engineering students could be identified on campus because they all carried one. In fact they wouldn't leave home without it. Then, what happened? Almost overnight, the slide rule virtually disappeared. In mid-1970's, the pocket calculator changed everything!

Various things that we consider indispensable today may quickly become obsolete and be discarded as relics. For generations, as the dominant instrument of scientific calculation, slide rule manufacturers felt completely secure. Then it hit them from an angle they did not expect!

As Christians, what is our greatest strength? In what area of our lives does Christ have no competition for our loyalty? The Apostle Paul warns the Corinthian faithful (and us as well), "If you think you are standing firm, be careful that you don't fall!" (1 Cor. 10:12) As ambassadors of Christ we must always be alert, but not afraid. God promises that with every temptation, He will also provide a way out. There is a choice. Satan tried to tempt Jesus three times; right after He had fasted forty days and nights following His baptism. But Jesus had scriptural answers for each temptation (Matt. 4:1 – 11). Being tempted is not a sin. Yielding to temptation is.

St. Peter felt very secure in his faith. He told Jesus, "Lord, I am ready to go with you to prison and to death" (Luke 22:33). But Jesus, knowing the future, answered, "I tell you, Peter, before the rooster crows today, you will deny three times that you know me." We all know what happened. Peter then remembered Jesus' words and wept bitterly. Jesus assured Peter that his faith would be renewed, and he would become a powerful leader. Yes, Simon Peter later repented and was commissioned by Christ to feed His lambs. After Christ's ascension, the Apostle became a true ambassador for Christ. He devoted his life to Him and His Church, and died as a martyr in Rome.

Unguarded strength can be a hidden weakness. It is no wonder we are warned to be careful that we don't fall. Divine strength comes to us only through the Word of God and prayer. Have the centuries been kind to the Bible? Yes!! That is one precious thing from the ancient past that has endured, and will always be needed, treasured, cherished, used daily and will never become obsolete. Yes, the Bible, God's Holy Word.

No matter how much technological scientific changes and progress take place, we can be secure in knowing that the Bible remains the one sure means for getting right answers to complex questions of life; our purpose, our behavior, and our ultimate destination. It is a treasure house where we can always find daily guidance for our hearts, our souls and our minds.

*F*ires started by arsonists are senseless crimes. We have seen more than a few here in California and around the country. Woodlands vanished, homes reduced to ashes, and wherever the blazing flames burned, they left their ugly scars.

The Bible says that slander is verbal arson. Untruths about a person's character or actions are extremely destructive. They consume reputations and destroy relationships. We read in Proverbs 26:20, "Where there is no wood, the fire goes out; and where there is no talebearer, strife ceases." How true! This refers to extinguishing something much more devastating than the burning of physical elements. It's the fire of an irresponsible tongue and the pain that burns in the hearts of those who have been scarred by its heat. What deep and lasting wounds the tongue can inflict on others!

St. James, in the third chapter of his epistle, compares the damage the tongue can do to a raging fire and the devastation it can bring. He says that words spoken carelessly and irresponsibly can destroy a relationship that took years to build. He continues; animals, birds, reptiles and creatures of the sea are being tamed and have been tamed by man, but no one has been able to tame the tongue. "Out of the same mouth come praise and cursing. My brothers, this should not be" (3:10).

Most of us are not guilty of generating those kinds of sparks. But as Christians we need the help of the Holy Spirit to have discernment so that only words of wisdom and edification will come out of our mouths. Even if we may not achieve perfect control of our tongue, we can still learn enough to reduce the damage our words might cause. St. James admits that we all stumble in many ways because we are not perfect. Therefore we must remember that we are not fighting this alone. When we lean on God, divine power is available to control our speech.

As Christians we know the Bible teaches us not to let any unwholesome talk come out of our mouths, but only what is helpful for building others up. Truth and honesty are always timely; it applies today and will apply in the future because it is connected to God's changeless character.

God is truth. We can trust His Word to guide us and change us from the inside out. As we lean on Him the Holy Spirit purifies our hearts and gives us self control to speak God pleasing words. Someone has said:

Of all the fires that swept the land and left an ugly scar,
Of all the blazing flames that burn, the tongue's the worst by far.

A study published in the Journal of Scientific Study of Religion surveyed students at the University of Western Ontario. The following questions were part of that survey. Are you healthy? Are you happy? Are you free from undue stress? If your answers to these questions are yes, chances are you are an active, involved Christian.

The study proved that students who were involved in Christian campus activities expressed greater satisfaction in such areas as friendships, family, educational achievements, and financial circumstances than those who were not. These individuals not only believed in Christ, but were putting their faith into action. The results were a healthier and more satisfied, fruitful life.

Yes, everyone has stressful moments. God's Word never promised us a trouble-free life. We read in Matt. 5:45, "God makes His sun rise on the evil and on the good, and sends rain on the just and on the unjust." This plainly teaches that God's love extends even to those who have not yet turned to seek Him. This universal love of God bestows blessings on all indiscriminately. This is known as God's grace; the unmerited favor of God. It must be distinguished, however, from the everlasting love God has for His beloved children.

Satisfaction for the faithful does not come from avoiding problems; rather it results from overcoming them through God's power. Life has its share of difficulties for people of all ages everywhere. But when we let God enlighten our path through His Word, we receive divine wisdom through His Holy Spirit, and mature spiritually. Bad consequences are the results of bad choices. Bad choices are the product of wrong thinking. A moment's bad choice can bring a lifetime of regret. God did not call us to a life of failure, but to a life of success.

We read in Prov. 3:5 – 6, "Trust in the Lord with all your heart and lean not on your own understanding; in all your ways acknowledge Him, and He will make your paths straight." It's that simple. When we fail to study God's Word, we stop growing in His ways. When we cease to grow spiritually, we begin to deteriorate. We can never arrive spiritually in this life—there is always a higher plateau to be reached.

A Christian lady, I was told, was recently challenged by this question: "How can you believe in God when the world has so many problems?" She replied, "With all those problems, how can you make it without God?" Now that is a wise and health-generating response!

A well-known magazine reported in an article a few years ago that pollsters tried to find a definite answer to the following question: "Which is the happiest nation in the world?"

Although there were claims to the contrary, one survey pronounced France as "one of the unhappiest societies on the continent." The same survey in Germany found that "less than one-third admitted to being very happy." Still another survey disclosed that among the population of Great Britain, "Fifty-four percent felt that their country is a bit snobbish, class-ridden society." When asked if they would like to leave the country, 47 percent said, "they would pack their bags before tea time." We don't truly know how accurate or serious the surveys were.

Genuine happiness, contentment, joy and hope don't depend on the country in which one lives. For Christians, it depends on a right relationship with God. In the Old Testament we read in Psalms 144:15, "Happy are the people whose God is the Lord!"

In the New Testament, all joy is associated with Jesus Christ. This dominant theme is strong in St. Luke's Gospel where the birth of Jesus points to the outpouring of human and heavenly joy. His ministry and resurrection evoke the same response. Even more characteristic of this is St. John's Gospel. All joy is associated with the person of Jesus and the perfect joy of those who are secure in their fellowship with Him (John, chapters 15 to 17). Further, St. Paul's letters are filled with the theme of rejoicing which is closely linked to the Holy Spirit.

Joy can be experienced even in the midst of great difficulties. Apostle Paul's letters to the Philippians were written under circumstances of severe suffering, yet they are the most joyous of all his letters. True joy is far deeper than happiness. We can feel joy in spite of our deepest afflictions. Happiness is temporary because it is based on external circumstances, but joy is lasting because it is based on God's presence within us. As we contemplate His daily presence, we will find contentment. As we trust our future to Him, we will experience joy.

Geography and race don't determine happiness or membership in God's family. Faith in Jesus Christ determines that. Let's not base our lives on circumstances, but on God. Let's rejoice that as citizens of our Lord's Kingdom, we, by His grace, can experience true joy and happiness, which come only from knowing God.

*W*e all know people who try very hard to get as much out of life as possible. Whether it is pleasure or financial success they desperately seek, they want to get all they can before it's too late.

We also know people who think more deeply, however, and who live by faith in Christ and look at life from a different perspective. These individuals are more interested in what they can put into life than what they can get out of it. For them, life's enrichment and joy come more through giving than through getting. The quality of their lives is measured by output—by what they can contribute to the lives of others.

Whether we are at the beginning of the year or its end, the time is not important, but our thoughts are. How can we, for example, think of ways to bring blessings to others? How can we follow Jesus' example when He said, "It is more blessed to give than to receive." St. Luke is quoting Jesus in Acts 20:35.

If we want to lead others to know God better, serve Him, and teach them the art of giving in any way possible, we cannot overemphasize the importance and the power of example. Leadership by example is contagious. That's how Christ and His disciples communicated the message of giving—by giving of themselves.

Giving is a natural response to love. When we love someone, we want to give that person our time and attention, and provide for their needs. At other times we want to shower the individual with gifts. If we refuse to help or to give, especially when there is need, our love is not really genuine. The Apostle Paul says something very important to the Corinthian faithful: "For you know the grace of our Lord Jesus Christ, that though He was rich, yet for your sakes He became poor, so that you through His poverty might become rich" (2 Cor. 8:9). In response to the Father's will, the eternal Son, in His incarnation and atoning death on the cross, emptied Himself of His riches, so that through His poverty, we might become rich!

God demonstrated His unlimited love for us by offering His precious Son so that we might have eternal life. Today the risen Christ brings us a new life of love, joy and peace to all those who receive Him in their hearts by faith. The love produced by God's Spirit is the only way to meaningful existence. This was the greatest and most precious gift ever given.

What can we give in return, now that we are rich? The word "Serve" and "Love" are each written about 300 times in the Bible. God has given us gifts so that we can share them with others. Even when we feel inadequate, our limited ability accents God's unlimited power. God wants our availability and He provides the ability, just when we need it. God also doesn't always call the person who is qualified, but He qualifies the one whom He calls.

As we look forward to the days ahead, let us open our hearts to God's calling and look for ways to enrich the lives of others. Every day is an opportunity to praise God and give generously any way we can. Every day is a good day to focus on God from Whom all blessings flow! And let's remember—God GAVE!

*T*he story is told that a group of botanists were exploring remote regions of the Alps in search of new species of flower. One day they noticed through their binoculars a flower of such rarity and beauty that it promised great value to the study of botany. It lay in a very deep ravine with cliffs on both sides. To get the flower with its root someone had to be lowered over the cliff on a rope.

A curious young boy was watching nearby. The scientists told him they would pay him well if he would agree to be lowered over the cliff to bring up the flower from below. The boy looked down the depth of the gorge and said, "I'll be back in a minute." In a short time he returned with a gray-haired man and said to the botanists, "I'll go down the cliff and get you that flower if this man holds the rope. He's my father."

Have we learned to have faith in our heavenly Father just as much as the boy trusted his father? Do we have the confidence in God's eternal love? When we are certain in our hearts that God holds our rope, we will not fear. God's Word says in Heb. 13:5, "I will never leave you nor forsake you. So we may boldly say, ' The Lord is my helper, I will not fear.'"

God's love is unchanging for His faithful children in the midst of a changing world. Pilots put confidence in their planes, commuters place confidence in trains, cars, buses, etc. Each day we put our confidence in something or someone. If we are willing to trust a plane or a car to get us to a destination, are we willing to trust God to guide us here on earth and to our eternal destination? How futile it can be to trust anything or anyone more than God.

Even when surrounded by impossible circumstances, the faithful in Christ can proclaim, "The Lord is my shepherd; I shall not want" (Ps. 23:1). If our trust is in the Lord's strength and guidance, we need not fear. Although relying on other people or things is part of living, our ultimate trust should only be placed in our heavenly Father. He is in control. He holds the rope however steep the slope. We can do our best, pray for guidance and trust Him with the rest.

Even in our most critical trials, God cares. When we are discouraged thinking no one understands us, we can be assured that God knows our every problem and sees our every tear. Jesus reminds us in Mt. 10:30 of how much God understands us. He says that even the very hairs of our head are all numbered! The same God Who created life in us can certainly be trusted with the details of our lives.

Our acceptance by God comes by believing in His Son Jesus Christ. When we believe in His birth, His ministry, His death and resurrection, we become members of His divine family. By trusting in Him our mind will open through His Holy Spirit to understand His Word and fulfill His purpose in our lives. Someone once said, "Since I accepted Christ into my heart, it seems that scripture was rewritten— now I understand it."

*P*redictions about the future usually are not good guesses, and often are amusing when remembered years later. When we consider what some well-known people said years ago about the future, we realize that their predictions were completely wrong! For instance, what if people had believed the following statements:

"Everything that can be invented has been already been invented." Charles H. Duell, Director of U.S. Patent Office, 1899.

"Who on earth wants to hear actors talk?" Harry M. Warner, President, Warner Bros., 1927.

"Sensible and responsible women do not want to vote." Grover Cleveland, 1905.

"There is no likelihood man can ever tap the power of the atom." Robert Millikan, Nobel Prize in Physics, 1923.

"Heavier-than-air flying machines are impossible." Lord Kelvin, President, Royal Society, 1895.

What knowledge might have appeared sensible at the time became ludicrous later. One source of knowledge that is never wrong is God's Word—the Bible. "For prophecy never came by the will of man, but holy men of God spoke as they were moved by the Holy Spirit" (2 Pet. 1:21). The Bible is the living Word of God. It is the Book of books, and the world's bestseller, because it was inspired by God and reveals His truth to us. The forefathers of this nation also recognized the value of the Bible. Here is what some of them said:

"It is impossible to rightly govern the world without the Bible." George Washington.

"The Bible is a book worth all other books that were ever written." Patrick Henry.

"It is impossible to mentally or emotionally enslave a Bible-reading people." Horace Greeley.

"A thorough knowledge of the Bible is worth more than a college education." Theodore Roosevelt. Regarding this last one, I would encourage all young people to do both—chosen field of education and studying the Bible.

God's Word is true, precious and most valuable, whether presidents or other wise individuals acknowledge it. But because they do, it gives us an added affirmation and reason to be encouraged. Just 40 or 50 years on earth can change the human body (as some of us know all too well), but the Word of God still stands as an ageless instrument of the Holy Spirit in bringing life and encouragement to all who read it and believe.

The Bible also has reassuring words for all who believe that Jesus died on the cross for each one of us, and rose again (1 Thes. 4:14). The Apostle Paul gives us the comforting words, that all believers who have placed their faith in Christ will one day be with the Lord eternally. No one knows what's ahead of us, but as children of God, we can be certain of this: We can trust our all-knowing God, even when we don't know the future.

A Frenchman was a guest on Bill O'Reilly's T.V. talk show a few months ago, expressing his dissatisfaction because American fast food restaurants in France were changing the French people's eating habits. According to this Frenchman, hamburgers, fries and milk shakes were what the new generation in France preferred to eat, rather than their traditional croissants. I found the conversation rather amusing. Then I thought that at least the fries are called "French fries." That should count for something.

Some time later, on a trip to Paris, France, while my husband and I were on the famous Champs Elysees Boulevard, facing the Arc de Triomphe, our guide informed us that everything sold on the right side of the street was more expensive than the left side. The reason, she explained, is because the right side of the street is sunny, bright and warmer throughout the day, while the left side is always shady, damp and cold. And although the Parisians know this, they still prefer to shop on the sunny side and pay more! As I observed the beautiful boutiques and cafes, could you guess what caught my attention? The Golden Arches of McDonald's! And yes, on the sunny side of the Champs Elysees, of course! I could see now why the Frenchman was so upset. The place was full of people.

The two sides of this boulevard can be applied in the spiritual realm as well. In scripture, light and darkness are very familiar symbols. Light represents what is good, pure, true, holy and reliable. Darkness represents what is sinful and evil. "...God is light and in Him is no darkness" (1 Jn. 1:5). That means that God is perfectly holy and true, and that He alone can guide us out of darkness. Light is also related to truth, because light exposes everything, good and bad.

Jesus says, "I am the Light of the world. He who follows Me shall not walk in darkness, but have the light of life" (Jn. 8:12). What does it mean to follow Christ? As a soldier follows his captain, so should we follow Christ, our commander. As we follow the advice of a trusted counselor, so should we follow Jesus' commands to us in scripture. As we follow the laws of our nation, so should we follow the laws of God. Most people don't wish to walk in darkness. Others perhaps, don't want their lives exposed to God's light for fear of what might be revealed. As we study God's Word, we will come to see that it is better to walk in the light. When we let Christ guide our lives, we will never stumble in darkness.

Christ is the true Light. His life brings light to mankind. In His light, we see ourselves as we truly are. Jesus also told His disciples, "You are the light of the world...Let your light so shine before men, that they may see your good works and glorify your Father in heaven" (Mt. 5:14 – 16). As Christians, we must shine brightly as beacons of truth, even if we find ourselves on the shady and damp side of the road of life. God has placed His love and light in our hearts through His Holy Spirit. Even a little light reflecting Christ can make a big difference in the dark. As Christians, how do we brighten a room – by entering it, or leaving it?

*L*arry Elder, a radio talk show host, often likes to begin his program with an unbelievably true story. Not long ago, very upset, he told the following story.

A young man and a woman went to a party together. After having several drinks, the two spent some intimate time together at the party. A few months later, the woman discovered that she was pregnant. The couple blamed their host for the alcoholic drinks that were available at the party. They claimed that if it weren't for the alcohol, she would not have conceived the baby. Sounds crazy? The story doesn't end there. The couple sued their host for some outrageous amount of money, and they won the case!

Whatever happened to individual responsibility and self-control? The Bible has plenty to say about it. As Christians, we must live and act according to God's standards and principles, and flee from tempting situations. We are also to accept the consequences of our own wrongful acts. We are not helpless victims of Adam and Eve's mistakes. In the garden, Eve blamed the serpent, Adam blamed Eve, and said to God, "The woman whom You gave to be with me, she gave me of the tree, and I ate" (Gen. 3:12). Does Adam blame God also for giving him Eve? Whatever happened to true confessions and taking responsibility for one's actions?

The truth is, we all have a bit of Adam and Eve in us. That is why so many people today shift the blame for their bad behavior from themselves to environmental factors, or the faulty upbringing they often claim they received from their parents. And the list goes on.

The good news is, however, there is hope. Jesus says in Jn. 3:16, "For God so loved the world that He gave His only begotten Son, that whoever believes in Him should not perish but have everlasting life." The Apostle Paul persecuted the Church and Christians in ignorance and unbelief. Yet later, he accepted full responsibility, referring to himself as, "formerly a blasphemer, persecutor, and an insolent man" (1 Tim. 1:13). Although he saw himself as the "chief" of sinners, he was not bound by the guilt of his past actions. His primary emphasis was on the Lord's marvelous grace that freed him from a debilitating sense of unworthiness.

It is true that we often deserve God's condemnation, but it is also true that Jesus came into the world to save sinners. That's good news for all of us. As long as we are still on this earth, the possibilities of God's grace remain, just like the thief on the cross who acknowledged his own sinfulness, put his trust in Christ and asked for His help. And that thief, who was considered unfit for society, was made fit for paradise! We can all become new creations through Christ. "All things have passed away; behold, all things have become new" (2 Cor. 5:17).

If God were to execute justice without mercy and grace, we would all be lost. In His mercy, He does not give us what we deserve, and by His grace, He gives what we don't deserve. Even though God demands perfection, He doesn't leave us without hope. Believers in Christ are not victims, but victors! God hates sin, but loves the repentant sinner.

*A*dversities are often blessings in disguise. For most of us, when suffering invades our lives, we ask ourselves, "Why did this happen to me? Why this pain now?" But let's, for a moment, consider the origin of a pearl and the lesson we can learn from an oyster.

A pearl is formed by an oyster's internal response to a wound that is caused by an irritant, such as a grain of sand. The oyster doesn't like this one bit, but since he can't get rid of it, he uses the irritation to do the loveliest thing an oyster ever has an opportunity to do—create a pearl. Since he can't remove it, he improves it. The final result is a lustrous pearl!

In the book of Genesis, we see Joseph in Egypt in a position of influence; a position God soon used to feed surrounding nations, including Joseph's own family, during a famine. But how did he become influential? It all began with a terrible "wound." Joseph was sold into slavery by his ten envious brothers (Gen. 39), which eventually produced a "pearl" of usefulness. God was preparing Joseph for His own purpose. Joseph trusted God through all his suffering and humiliation, and as a result he became better, not bitter. "You meant evil against me; but God meant it for good!" he told his brothers later (Gen. 50:20).

Do we trust God enough to wait patiently for Him to bring good out of a bad situation? Can we trust God, as Joseph did, to transform any evil act in order to bring about His intended results? It is true that success often rises out of the ashes of pain and failure.

If there is an irritation in our lives, there is only one thing to do: trust God and let's make a pearl. It may have to be a pearl of prayer and patience, but in any case, we are taught to make a pearl. If the oyster could have gotten rid of the irritant, the glorious opportunity that followed would have been lost. Therefore, let us remember: No wound—no pearl!

*G*rowing up, I remember a story often repeated among adults that has helped me through problems of daily living. I would like to share it with you, since no one gets through life without some personal burdens and difficulties.

A young man was at the end of his rope. Seeing no way out, he dropped to his knees in prayer, "Lord, I can't go on. I have too heavy a cross to bear." The Lord replied, "My son, if you can't bear its weight, just place your cross inside this room. Then walk around and pick out any cross you wish." The man was filled with relief. "Thank you, Lord," he sighed, and did as he was told. As he searched for a while he saw many crosses, some so large that the tops were not visible. Then he spotted a tiny cross leaning against a far wall. "I'd like that one, Lord," he whispered, almost afraid that his wish might not be granted. The Lord replied, "My son, that is the cross you just brought in."

When life's problems seem overwhelming, let us look around and see how others are coping. We might find ourselves fortunate. The most comforting thoughts and wisest advice, however, come to us from the Word of God. If our cross is too heavy to bear, Jesus calls all those who are burdened and He assures us rest. (Matthew 11:28) His promises are love, forgiveness, healing, joy and peace.

God's power and blessings are available to all of us today. What wonderful uplifting promises! The more we read His Word, the more wisdom we receive. The Bible is the inspired Word of God. The treasures of the Bible seldom lie like pebbles on the surface. If we wish to mine gold, we have to dig. It will change our lives from wearisome toil into spiritual joy, productivity and purpose. Someone has said of the Bible: "Read it to be wise, believe it to be safe, and practice it to be right."

*I*n recent years medical reports encourage us to drink plenty of water daily. As a result many people carry water in bottles everywhere they go. But let us examine another kind of fine water offered in the Word of God.

In John Ch. 4 Jesus offers another kind of water to a Samaritan woman. Jesus and His disciples left Judea to go to Galilee, taking the shortest route through Samaria. Ignoring the antipathy between Jews and Samaritans, Jesus came to Jacob's Well. He sat by the well while His disciples went into town to buy food. Some history is necessary to clarify this prejudice that separated Jews and Samaritans.

After King Solomon's rule, the nation of Israel divided politically in two. The northern kingdom, with Samaria its capital, fell captive to the Assyrians in 722 B.C. (2 Kings 17:5, 6). Assyria exiled most of the ten northern tribes into Babylon. However, they left some Jews in Samaria. The Assyrians then transported many non-Jews into that region. Intermarriage between these foreigners and the remaining Jews resulted in a mixed race, "impure," in the opinion of Jews in the southern kingdom. The "pure" Jews disowned this mixed race called Samaritans. But Jesus disregarded this tension. Besides, He had an appointment with divine destiny in meeting the Samaritan woman to whom He would reveal His Messiahship.

Wells were generally located outside the city. Women came to draw water in the morning and evening to avoid the heat. A Samaritan woman came to Jacob's Well at noon, perhaps to avoid meeting people who knew her reputation. Jesus said to her, "Will you give Me a drink?" Surprised, she said, "You are a Jew and I am a Samaritan woman. How can you ask me for a drink?" This violated all social and religious customs. A Jew would become ceremonially "unclean" if he used a vessel handled by a Samaritan. Further, a rabbi never spoke with a woman of ill repute. But Jesus did. The gospel is for everyone. He crossed all racial and social barriers and past sins to share the gospel.

Jesus spoke to her about "Living Water." He said, "Everyone who drinks this water will be thirsty again, but whoever drinks the water I give him will never thirst." Jesus spoke to her of eternal life. Oh, she wanted that water, but she failed to understand the nature of Living Water. Jesus then referred to her husband. She confessed she had no husband. Jesus agreed. He told her of her past five husbands and of the man she now lived with. "You are a prophet!" she exclaimed. The woman then spoke of the coming messiah. Jesus declared, "I Who spoke to you am He." The Samaritan woman, after meeting her Savior, enthusiastically ran back and told the whole town, and her testimony led many Samaritans to Christ.

Most of us made a similar discovery. Before meeting Christ, we drank from the finest earthly fountains and achieved a measure of success, pleasure and fulfillment. Yet, if we multiply these triumphs, and even add them together, they can't compare to the Living Water offered by Christ to a spiritually thirsty person! Are we drinking from earthly fountains and still feel thirsty? Only Christ's Living Water can satisfy a thirsty soul, the best "thirst aid" of all!

*T*en year old Jay went to spend Easter vacation with his grandparents who lived on a farm. One day his grandfather, wishing to teach Jay the principles of farming and the basic law of cause and effect, asked Jay if he wanted to be a farmer for a day. Jay accepted the challenge enthusiastically. Then grandpa took him out to the side of the house, showed him a small area of land, and told Jay that this was to be his small farm. He then gave him a bag of corn. The soil was ready. After giving some sowing instructions, grandpa went into the house.

A while later, Nick, a neighbor boy, asked Jay if he wanted to go fishing. Delighted, Jay accepted the invitation. He quickly made a big hole in the ground, poured all the remaining seeds into it, and covered it up. Then he watered his little farm and ran into the house announcing that he was all finished and was going fishing with Nick.

Vacation was over. Jay went back home, but returned during his summer vacation. "How's my little farmer?" grandpa exclaimed with a smile when he saw him. Jay was anxious to see his little farm. Together they went to the side of the house. The corn was growing beautifully, row after row, except at one end where there was a huge corn bush growing uncontrollably! Jay looked at his grandfather, rather surprised at first, and then lowered his head in embarrassment looking guilty. He apologized, remembering what he had done. Grandpa loved him just the same, but Jay learned by this that he could not fool Mother Nature!

The law of the harvest is referred to repeatedly in scripture. The Apostle Paul writes in 2 Cor. 9:6, 7: "He who sows sparingly will also reap sparingly, and he who sows bountifully will also reap bountifully. So let each one give as he purposes in his heart...for God loves a cheerful giver." Giving in any way is like sowing seed. The amount of harvest is determined by the amount of seed sown.

Our attitude is more important than what we give. The resources God gives us are not to be hidden or foolishly squandered. Instead, they should be cultivated in order to produce more. When we invest what God has given us in His service, He will provide with even more to give. Every person has at least one talent along certain lines, but so many people have long buried their talents. We must put to work every talent we have, great or small, so that they may grow day by day. The world is filled with people who want something for nothing, who never realize that one of the basic laws of life is that we should first give before we can receive.

The law of cause and effect simply means that whatever we do in life will come back to us in due course, returned with interest. We reap whatever we sow. When we give freely of our time, God will stretch our time to have more to give away. When we set no limit on our love, we'll have more love for others than before. God blesses those who give, and the generous giver will never be in need. We will then find out, as it says in Acts 20:35, "It is more blessed to give than to receive."

*A*ccording to a legend, a king once placed a heavy rock in a roadway. Then he hid and waited to see who would remove it. Many who passed by it loudly blamed the government for not keeping the roads clear. But no one stopped to push the obstacle out of the way. At last a poor peasant stopped and rolled the rock into the gutter. To his surprise he found a bag full of gold beneath the rock with a note that said, "This is the king's reward for anyone who would remove the troublesome object!"

There are certain lessons that can only be learned in the valley of pain and distress. In the same manner, God our King has hidden a blessing under every trial we might be facing. The obstacles in our path are placed there for a purpose. By them God tests our faithfulness, perseverance and our willingness to turn our attention toward heaven, with added opportunities for spiritual rewards.

Christians who have suffered much and deepened their dependence on God have become even more sensitive individuals. They seem to have souls full of compassion for others and deeper love for their Creator. Someone confessed to me recently that the greatest sermons he had ever heard were not preached from pulpits, but from sickbeds. The precious truths of God's Word have often been expressed by those humble souls who have gone through the school of affliction.

No difficulty is without God's blessings. Some of the most grateful people I have known are not those who had traveled an easy road all their lives, but those who were confined to their beds for some time, a wheelchair, or had to be hospitalized because of illness. They learned to depend on God and praised Him daily and cheerfully for their blessings!

We read in Proverbs 3:5, 6: "Trust in the Lord with all your heart, and lean not on your own understanding; in all your ways acknowledge Him and He shall direct your paths." To receive God's guidance we should acknowledge Him in all areas of our lives. About a thousand years after the wisdom expressed in Proverbs was written, Jesus emphasized this same truth in Matthew 6:33 by saying, "Seek first the kingdom of God and His righteousness and all these things shall be added unto you." In whatever state we are in, we should turn to God and fill our thoughts with His desires, serve and obey Him.

The Bible tells us that if we respond with patience to the trials of life, we will develop godly maturity. As St. James writes, "The testing of your faith produces patience" (Js. 1:3). These same tested individuals can often be a blessing to others who might be going through similar trials. It is comforting when others understand us—they've been they—they know.

Does it seem that some of us are buried under a "rock of trials"? Are we discouraged and feeling low? Perhaps we should change our perspective. Why not roll our burdens onto God, and in time we will find divine favor. When we trust God in our trials, we might discover that most often our trials are blessings in disguise!

𝒫eople often look for advice when decision-making becomes difficult. "Dear Abby" and "Ann Landers" have stayed busy for decades giving advice and suggesting solutions to life's dilemmas. There is nothing wrong with asking for a second opinion, especially from someone who might have had a similar experience, or has "been there and done that." Professionals in the field of counseling can also be very helpful.

But some people turn to a different kind of "guidance counselor." They call a psychic advisor, and through astrology and other means, these "psychics" make their clients depend on them. And slowly but surely the clients become dependant on their counseling for many decisions. For some, even their travel plans are made around certain dates that the astrologer sets for them! They eventually become slaves to fear, and pay plenty to those who claim to know the future.

As Christians, however, we know that God is the only One Who knows the future. And in His own wisdom He has chosen to keep certain things hidden from us. The Lord says, "I know the plans I have for you, … plans to prosper you and not to harm you, plans to give you hope and a future" (Jer. 29:11). Isn't that a comforting promise?

We are all encouraged by a leader who inspires us to move ahead, someone who believes we can do the task he has given us, and who will be with us all the way. For us Christians, God is that leader. He knows the future, and His plans for us are good and full of hope. As long as He guides us daily we can have boundless hope. This doesn't mean that we will be spared pain, suffering or hardship, but God will see us through to a glorious conclusion.

In time of deep distress, it may appear as though God has forgotten us. But He may be preparing us for a new beginning, with Him at the center. We must make every effort to strengthen our faith and trust in our Creator as we walk with Him daily on the road of life.

Trust doesn't come easily. It was not easy for David to believe that he would become king, even after he was anointed. Yes, he was crowned king after years of adventure in the school of life as he matured in the process. In the meantime, he trusted God. It was not easy for Moses to believe that he and his people would ever escape from Egypt, even after God spoke to him from the burning bush. But he trusted God. And also, it may not be easy for us to believe that God will fulfill His promises, but we must trust Him. We read in Heb. 13:5, "I will never leave you nor forsake you." One tiny verse, yet it delivers such comfort and hope into our hearts! God worked in the lives of biblical heroes, and He will certainly work in our lives as well, if we let Him.

So, instead of following the stars, why not follow the eternal God, the One who made the stars? God most certainly knows the future and He is in control of everything! No unreliable, inaccurate or vague fortune telling is needed. Our future is in God's loving hands, and that's all we need to know.

*I*t was in 1975 when I first saw one; a mood ring! It was a clever concept for a fad. They were inexpensive rings with a plastic stone containing heat sensitive liquid crystals. Shortly after the ring was slipped on one's finger, the crystals would change color because of body temperature, and it was believed to reveal one's mood. Americans bought more than 15 million mood rings! Amazingly, they were so popular, especially among the youth that they came back in 1995.

Whether we are happy, sad, depressed or upbeat, those close to us don't need to look at our mood ring to know how we feel. Most of us don't hide our feelings that well, and we all have difficulty at times lifting ourselves out of a gloomy state of mind. And no one is immune to it.

The psalmists revealed their constant struggles with discouragement and anxiety. "Why are you downcast, O my soul? Why so disturbed with me? Hope in God, for I shall again praise Him for the help of His presence" (Ps. 42:5). One antidote to depression is to meditate on God's goodness, and the miraculous works He has done for us in the past. This will take our mind off the present situation and give us hope to focus on God's divine ability to help us, rather than our inability to help ourselves.

The Bible isn't a psychology textbook, but it gives us the wisest counsel for experiencing happiness. We read in Proverbs 17:22, "A merry heart does good, like medicine, but a broken spirit dries the bones." That simple statement was recently proven by the extensive research of Dr. David Mark, a heart specialist at Duke University. The New York Times article that reported his findings carried this headline: "Optimism Can Mean Life For Heart Patients and Pessimism Death." The article began with these words: "A healthy outlook helps heal the heart."

But another heart specialist, Dr. Nancy Frasure-Smith, who studied the effects of depression, anxiety and anger, admitted, "We don't know how to change negative emotions." But we as Christians know that faith in God and prayer can produce that change. People who look beyond their present difficulty and put their trust in God's goodness and mercy cannot help but be joyful. Happiness is a result of happenings in our lives, but our joy comes from the Lord.

Mood rings were a passing fad, but mood swings are a reality for many of us. The experience isn't new, and neither is the answer. In addition to God's Word, as Christians we can also help and encourage each other. All of us, young and old, need a word of encouragement from time to time, especially when facing a new challenge. We also need words of appreciation as we carry out our daily responsibilities, whether at home or at work.

It is not always what we accomplish in life that matters, but what we overcome. And some of us have more to overcome than others. Isn't it significant that Christ, our Lord, fully aware of life's many crises, said on several occasions, "Be of good cheer! I have overcome the world" (Jn. 16:33). No matter what happens, we can be joyful in the Lord.

*C*hristians are called to be people of integrity. They are to be honest, choosing a good name above all in a world that often seeks quite the opposite.

The story is told that a newspaper reported an unusual incident that occurred at a fast-food restaurant. The manager had put the day's cash receipts in a paper bag for deposit that night. But an employee mistook it for a food order and gave it to a couple at the drive-through window. A short time later, when the couple opened the bag in a nearby park, they were shocked by its contents. They immediately drove back to return the money.

The manager, not knowing quite what happened to the bag with the cash, reported it as a robbery. Police cars and TV crews were on the scene. How relieved the manager was to get the money back! He said to the couple, "You should be featured on the evening news for your honesty!" "Oh, please, no publicity!" replied the man nervously, "She's not my wife!"

It is not consistent to be honest with someone else's money, but dishonest with someone else's spouse. The measure of moral depth and honesty in one's whole character is called integrity. God expects us to do what is right. Therefore, Jesus says in Mt. 7:12, "Whatever you want men to do to you, do also to them, for this is the law and the prophets." Christ repeated the commonly known "Golden Rule," well known even from Old Testament times. The teachings of Christ demand our integrity, responsibility and accountability. When they are practiced, we all become more dependable and fulfilled individuals.

The University of Santa Clara, California, conducted a research of 1,500 business managers. They were to ask their employees the question: "What do you value the most in a boss?" The research revealed that employees respected a leader who shows competence, has ability to inspire workers and is skillful in providing clear directions. But there was a fourth quality they admired even more – integrity! Above all else, workers wanted a manager whose word was good, one who was known for his honesty, and one whom they could trust. Integrity should characterize all Christians, no matter what their position. Honesty is the very heart of every godly person who is known as one who does what he says.

It is often tempting to neglect our "word" in favor of personal advantage or financial gain. When we give our word we must keep it. Jesus says in Mt. 5:37, "Let your 'Yes' be 'Yes' and your 'No' be 'No'." If we make a commitment, we must honor it. If we take on an obligation, we must fulfill it. If non-Christians can trust us in business matters, they will be more likely to believe us when we speak of our faith. As ambassadors of Christ, our behavior must be above reproach. And integrity may well be the key that opens the door to spiritual effectiveness.

Do we have the kind of rock-solid integrity that can stand the test of living honestly day-to-day? Do those around us admire our integrity? In a society that often treats honesty like an artifact from an ancient world, followers of Christ are surely a delight to our heavenly Father! A person of integrity has nothing to hide!

*C*hildren were playing a soccer game at the ballpark. I went to meet my friend whose sons were in the game. We sat on the benches, and before we even began to discuss the subject for which I met her, she opened a bag and offered me food. "Let's have a picnic before anything else," she said happily. I admired her attitude. "You certainly came prepared," I added, seeing the variety! "Eat, eat," she insisted, "There is plenty for the kids as well." She reminded me of my mother, always planning ahead!

The more than 5,000 people who came from nearby towns to hear Jesus by the Sea of Galilee apparently didn't plan ahead. Had they forgotten all about food in their excitement to be with Jesus? We don't know. But as evening approached, the disciples asked Jesus to send the crowds away so they could go to the villages and buy some food. Jesus replied, "They do not need to go away. You give them something to eat" (Mt. 14:13 – 21).

It was beyond the disciples' power to do that, and Jesus knew it. But it was not beyond His power, and He included His disciples in the miraculous solution. As it turned out, one wise mother had packed some bread and fish for her son. It wasn't much, but what she had prepared for her son became enough to feed thousands when blessed by the Lord!

The disciples reported that they only had five loaves of bread and two fish—the boy's meal. Jesus said, "Bring them here to me." He directed the people to sit down. Taking the five loaves and two fish, and looking up to heaven, He gave thanks and broke the loaves. He then gave them to the disciples, and the disciples distributed them to the multitude. The Bible says that they all ate and were satisfied, with twelve basketfuls left over! The number of those who ate was about 5,000 men, besides women and children. Although what was originally given to Jesus was insufficient, in His hands they became more that enough.

We often feel that our contribution to God's ministry is meager, but He can use and multiply whatever we give Him, whether it is our talent, time, treasure, or all of the above. It is when we give that our resources are multiplied. Jesus could have fed those people in some way even without the boy's bread and fish. But it is for us to know that we must give to God's ministry to see it multiply a thousand fold. The total number of people that Jesus fed could have been 10 to 15 thousand. The men are listed separately because in the Jewish culture of the day, men and women ate separately when in public. And the children ate with the women.

We can trust that God will always meet our needs, including the courage to face our difficulties. Problems are often opportunities to discover God's awesome solutions. What seemingly insurmountable needs are we facing today? It is at those times that we can rely on our Lord's willingness and ability to meet our every need. St. Paul says in Phil. 4:19, "My God shall supply all your needs according to His riches in glory by Christ Jesus." True faith is not just believing that God can, it is trusting that He will.

*I*n poverty-stricken countries everything is used and reused until there is nothing left. One of those reusable commodities, I was told, is old tires. Truck and car tires are cut up and fitted to make sandals and sold very inexpensively. Interestingly, this creative shoe manufacture that began by Christians is called "Jesus' feet," because they look like the sandals depicted in paintings of Jesus.

Jesus left tracks from His sandals on the dusty roads of Palestine. Wherever He went, He brought love, peace, freedom, hope. He healed the blind, liberated the emotionally and mentally disturbed, helped the lame to walk and the deaf to hear. He healed the lepers and raised His good friend Lazarus to life again. In fact, the Bible says, "Jesus did many other miraculous signs in the presence of His disciples, which are not recorded in this book. But these are written that you may believe that Jesus is Christ, the Son of God, and that by believing you may have life in His name" (Jn. 20:30).

The natural question to ask ourselves would be: If someone were to follow our shoe or sandal tracks, would he find people consoled and helped? Would he find people who might have been discouraged, but who now are lifted up? People whose hearts had been troubled but who now are at peace with God because of our words of comfort, encouragement, enlightenment and help. The Apostle Paul repeats several times in His epistles, "Imitate me, just as I also imitate Christ" (1 Cor. 11:1). St. Paul was not being boastful. He had in fact stated earlier that he was not perfect. But he was quite confident of his "sandal tracks." We must keep in mind that at this time, the faithful of Corinth and Philippi didn't know much about the life and ministry of Christ. St. Paul could not tell them to imitate Jesus, because the gospels had not yet been written, so they didn't know what Jesus was like. The best way to point these new Christians to Christ was to point them to a Christian whom they trusted. Paul had been with them long enough to build a relationship of trust with many of these new faithful. Therefore, that's why he said, "Imitate me, just as I imitate Christ." In other words, "Follow my tracks"!

The fact that St. Paul could tell others to follow his example is a testimony to his character! Can we say the same? What kind of follower would a new or young Christian become if he or she were to imitate us? What tracks are we leaving behind for our children and grandchildren? A Christian has no greater calling or purpose than that of following the Word of God while serving Him on earth. Jesus Himself says, "You shall be perfect, just as your Father in heaven is perfect" (Mt. 5:48).

Christian growth and maturity is a process that will continue throughout our lives. Although Christ set an unattainable goal, and His "sandal tracks" are an impossible standard for us to meet, the marvelous truth of the gospel is that Christ has met this standard on our behalf! His great love for us led to His sacrificial death on the cross so that we might live. When we walk with Him, our love for others can be of the same kind—a life of exemplary service, self-sacrifice and devotion.

*L*ittle is known of Moses' childhood. An Egyptian decree to kill all newborn Hebrew males led his mother to hide him for the first three months. Then by faith, she cast him adrift on the Nile in a watertight basket. As his sister Miriam, about age eight, watched from a distance, Pharaoh's daughter came with her maids to bathe in the river. Delighted, they found the child. Miriam discretely offered to find a nurse for the child—his own mother. Not only was Moses' life saved, but his mother was even paid for his care! God's plan had begun to rescue His people from Egypt.

Our challenges often may appear humanly impossible. But concentrating on God's power with faith will help us see the way out. "The child grew and she brought him to Pharaoh's daughter, and he became her son. So she named him Moses" (Ex. 2:10). No detail is given of the child's growth to adulthood in Egyptian court society. We know from Acts 7:22, however, that Moses was learned in all the wisdom of the Egyptians and was mighty in words and deeds. As the adopted son of Pharaoh's daughter, Moses enjoyed all privileges of a prince. But there was this little matter of his being a Hebrew, and his powerful sense of justice.

When he was about forty, he reemerged as a man who identified himself with his people, the enslaved Israelites. One day he saw an Egyptian taskmaster unjustly beating a defenseless Hebrew. Angered, Moses killed the Egyptian and hid him in the sand (Ex. 2:12). Moses supposed that his brethren would understand that God was granting them deliverance through him (Acts 7:25). He knew that what he did was wrong. He looked this way and that way before striking the Egyptian down, but he did not look up to God. Moses' timing as a "deliverer" was also wrong. He was forty years ahead of God's plan to lead his people out of Egypt. The following day, seeing two Hebrews fighting, Moses tried to stop them. One of them said to him, "Who made you a prince and judge over us? Do you intend to kill me as the Egyptian?" Moses realized he had to flee the country. Despite his privileged position, Pharaoh sought to kill him. He had committed a capital crime. So he fled Egypt into the land of Midian.

Sooner or later wrongful acts catch up with us. Moses became a stranger in a strange land. It took another forty years for him to be used by God. When we feel that God has forgotten us in our troubles, we must remember that He has His own timetable, which is always perfect. In Midian, Moses was humbled and broken by God. He became a shepherd, a nomad, a job he had been taught to despise. As a shepherd in the desert Moses also learned about survival in the wilderness. All this time, God was preparing him for leadership!

At this time in his life Moses was walking by sight, not by faith. One day he was a prince, then a shepherd for the next forty years! Moses at forty thought he could do no wrong. Moses at eighty thought he could do no right. He was mistaken again, because now God had other plans for him. When we focus on God we are always on course. At age eighty God used Moses in a mighty way, and He can use each one of us, whatever our age.

*M*any people who stood on the threshold of greatness caught a glimpse of the enormous challenges ahead and backed away. Unaware of his prophetic mission, Moses' attention was first caught by a burning bush on Mt. Horeb (Sinai) that was not consumed. Slowly, his reaction changed from curiosity to awe as he realized that he was in God's presence (Ex. 3:1 – 22). God may use unexpected sources when communicating to us also, whether through people, thoughts or experiences. Are we willing to be open to God's surprises?

Moses had been just told by God that Israel had suffered long enough under the Egyptians. It was time to send a deliverer. "I will send you to Pharaoh that you may bring My people, the Israelites, out of Egypt." Moses was skeptical. He had tried that act of deliverance 40 years earlier, and what did it get him? He had killed an Egyptian to defend a fellow Hebrew. He was wrong. God administers justice in His own time. As a result he became a runaway, a stranger in the desert of Midian.

"Who am I that I should go to Pharaoh," said Moses. On a smaller scale, we can identify with Moses. We often find ourselves overwhelmed by a challenge we are asked to do for God, and we look harder for excuses than for ways to make it work. Besides, why should the Israelites believe that Moses was their chosen leader? We can do what Moses eventually did. We can commit what we have to the Lord, do all we can and leave the rest to God.

What do we have that should be committed to God? Our lifestyle, study habits, our tongue, our heart, our will? When we face an "impossible" assignment, we can depend on God's strength and say, "Yes, Lord, guide me," instead of "Who me?" Moses at 40 thought he could do anything by himself. He was proud and arrogant. Moses at 80 said, "Who am I?" Perhaps it was an expression of guilt before God for the murder he committed years ago. We see a humble man now who had learned how weak he was alone.

Despite all, God revealed His plan to Moses, and His timing is always perfect. In the wilderness Moses had become an experienced desert survivor with a fine education in "desertology"! He knew every reptile and possible difficulty the desert presents. That was the school God sent him to. After series of excuses, and with the assurance that God Himself, the great "I AM," will surely be with him, Moses obeyed the call. As a prophet, Moses stands above all others. We read in Deut. 34:10, "Since then, no prophet has risen in Israel like Moses, whom the Lord knew face to face."

As Christians we must know that we will never be left without the resources we need. God qualifies the one whom He calls. And often He molds us through various means. He did it for Moses – He'll do it for us. There need be no "buts" or "what ifs" in our relationship to God's will. When the Lord says, "I will send thee," every provision has been made for the appointed task. When the Lord says, "I will not fail thee," we must know that He Who gives the command will also provide. In every desert of trial God has an oasis of comfort.

*A*fter the death of Sarah, Abraham took another wife whose name was Ketura who bore him six sons (Gen. 25:1, 2). The fourth son's name was Midian. These six tribes and their descendants settled to the east and south of the Hebrews, in a land that is now Jordan and Saudi Arabia. So, when Moses left Egypt as a fugitive, he went south to Arabia to the land of the Midianites. Moses at age 80 was commissioned by God and had finally agreed to lead the Israelites out of bondage. But he was still apprehensive about how the Egyptians and even his own countrymen would react.

We also often build up events and walls in our minds, and then panic over what might go wrong. God does not ask us to go where He hasn't provided the means to help. We must go where He leads, trusting Him to supply courage, confidence and resources at the right moment.

While Moses was still reluctant, the Lord said to him, "What is that in your hand?" "A rod," answered Moses (Ex. 4:2). Great miracles were accomplished with that rod when Moses obeyed God. The rod was insignificant in itself, but it became a powerful instrument when it was committed to the Lord. God used the simple shepherd's rod Moses carried as a means to teach him important lessons. God often uses ordinary things for extraordinary purposes.

What are some of the ordinary things in our life—our voice, a musical instrument, a computer, a hammer, a broom, etc.? While we might be thinking that God can use only special skills, we must not hinder His use of the everyday contributions we could make. Young David had only a sling in his hand, but it was enough to go against the giant, and the great Goliath fell before the shepherd boy!

"What is that in your hand?" God asks us daily. However insignificant it may seem, it's enough when it is dedicated to God. Out time, talents, treasures; all can be used by God for things that will live while the world endures. It is somewhat amusing that one the excuses that Moses gave was, "Oh Lord, I have never been eloquent, neither in the past nor since You have spoken to Your servant. I am slow of speech and of tongue" (Ex. 4:10). So, the Lord said to him, "Who has made man's mouth? Or who makes the mute, the deaf, the seeing, or the blind? Have not I, the Lord? Now therefore, go, and I will be with your mouth and teach you what you shall say." Moses still implored, "Oh Lord, please send someone else to do it." Does that sound familiar to some of us?

The Bible says that the Lord's anger burned against Moses and said, "What about your brother Aaron?" Moses made a mistake having Aaron for his spokesman. God allowed it, but Moses later would see that Aaron would cause him problems. God did not really want a divided command.

Let us not sell ourselves short. If God has called us to a task, He'll equip us for it. He merely asks, "What is that in your hand?" Let's use what He has given us for His glory, and we'll see what He can do with little or big things.

*W*hat qualities do women find attractive in a man? A recent study at the University of Kentucky revealed that women generally look for men who are kind, dependable and honest. Money, they thought was a plus, but only if the man was a nice guy.

In 1 Samuel 25:2 – 43, we meet two unlikely marriage partners—an odd couple, as it were. Nabal was a crude, rude, very wealthy drunkard who was married to an intelligent, beautiful woman named Abigail.

While David was hiding from King Saul, he and his 600 men protected Nabal's flocks at Carmel. Hearing that Nabal was shearing his sheep (a customary time for festivities) David sent ten of his men saying: Peace be to you and your household. My men and I have protected your herds for some time. Therefore, let us find favor in your eyes, for it is a feast day. Please give whatever comes to your hand to your servants and to your son David.

Nabal rudely refused David's request, even though his prosperity was due to David's protection. The knowledge was widespread that David was the king-elect, anointed by the prophet Samuel. When Nabal's answer reached David, he was furious and swore that he would kill every male in that household by daybreak.

One of Nabal's servants ran and told Abigail of his master's behavior. He told her of David's protection, kindness and loyalty to Nabal. Abigail lost no time. She took 200 loaves of bread, wine, roasted meat, raisin cakes and pressed figs, loaded them on donkeys, and followed her servants. She said nothing to her husband.

When she met David at a mountain ravine, he was on his way to attack. Nevertheless, he stopped to listen to Abigail. Her masterful, humble speech is worth reading. She fell at his feet and said, "My lord, let the blame be on me alone. I, your servant, did not see your men." Abigail was certain that David would be the next king of Israel after Saul's death. She didn't want him to jeopardize his throne or violate God's will by seeking vengeance. And she told him so.

Abigail's wisdom, humility and beauty impressed David. He said, "Praise be to the Lord... May you be blessed for keeping me from bloodshed. Go home in peace. I have granted your request." When Abigail went home, Nabal was drunk. When he became sober the following day, she told him what she had done. The Bible says Nabal became "like a stone" and died ten days later. When David heard of Nabal's death, he praised God again from keeping him from doing wrong. Then he sent word to Abigail asking her to become his wife.

Life's tough situations often bring out the best in people. Abigail saw the big picture. She saved her household and David from doing wrong. She used good judgment, was a quick thinker and persuasive communicator. Do we use our skills to promote peace? We don't need a prestigious title to play a significant role. What challenges do we face today that may need the help of a godly person? Abigail became David's wife and bore him a son.

The story is told that Socrates, the Greek philosopher, had just finished building his new house. The building was as small as a closet. This naturally surprised his neighbors. When they asked why he built it so small, he said, "I will consider myself a very fortunate man if I could fill my home with true friends."

We all need a few close friends—someone we can turn to, talk to, and even cling to if necessary. When we have a close friend or two, we have a warm spot in our hearts, knowing of the mutual love and trust we share with each other. And this gives us comfort and makes our days seem brighter. But while listening to Dr. Toni Grant, the radio psychologist, I heard her say this on the subject of friendship: "If you were to tell me you have one true friend, I would say you are very fortunate. If you were to tell me you have two true friends, I would be a bit skeptical. And if you were to tell me you have three true friends, then I'd say you are naïve!"

Not everyone has a friend. Many people go through life with the sinking feeling that they really have no one close to their heart—that trusted true friend. It is, I'm sure, a lonely feeling. To anyone like that—in fact for all of us—the ultimate friend is the Lord our God, the One Who, far more than any human friend can meet our deepest companionship needs. In John 15:15, Jesus says, "No longer do I call you servants...but I have called you friends." How comforting and reassuring to be chosen as Christ's friends.

Some "friends" can be fickle. In Proverbs 19:4, Solomon wrote, "Wealth brings many friends, but a poor man's friend deserts him." A true friend, however, cares at all times. It has been said, "A friend is the first person to come in when the whole world goes out." To have a friend who remains devoted under all circumstances is a blessing. But the support, encouragement and love that only an intimate friend can offer is always available from our Lord Jesus Christ, the One Who laid down His life for His friends (John 15:13).

Christians especially have an inside track on making and being friends because we are part of one family. Perhaps some of us felt a special connection while talking with a stranger, only to discover that we had Christ in common. For example, I had an experience recently while waiting at JFK Airport in New York. I started to have a warm conversation with a woman sitting next to me on the bench. At one point she got up to ask a question at the counter. When she returned she saw me reading a Christian booklet and said, "Oh my goodness!" She opened her purse and showed me the same booklet! "We are sisters in Christ," she added. My goodness indeed!

Although God can fill the emptiness in the human heart, friendships with our fellow man are important too, and it must begin with us. The Word of God says in Proverbs 18:24, "A man who has friends must himself be friendly." Friendships are seldom found. They are made and cultivated over many years. We must take the initiative to develop relationships with others. Let us be to others what we desire for ourselves. To have a friend, we must be a friend. To have one, we must be one.

*W*alking through a department store, I noticed many sweaters stacked up on low benches. The display was set near the central aisle to catch attention. But something else caught my attention. A child of about age 3 or so had found a new pastime. He was playing with the small round adhesive tags that identified each sweater as small, medium and large. He was busy removing and rearranging the tags back and forth, switching the sizes around. Someone is having fun, I thought. A young lady was busy paying her bill nearby. I assumed the child was hers.

As I left the department store, I thought of the sweaters and the rearranged sizes. How confusing and puzzling it will be for the women who try on the sweaters in the dressing room, guided by the sizes attached to the garments. Confused and misled, they would have to double check the size shown inside the sweater to see the truth.

The Bible says that during the prophet Isaiah's day, the people of Israel had rejected God's law. They were misled by idolatrous influences. They devalued virtue and routinely subverted justice, and everyone did what they felt was right in their own eyes. Does this sound up to date? Some people in our society are doing pretty much the same as the Israelites did centuries ago.

It's sad to see so many people today confused, searching for meaning in life while rejecting God's Word—the direction book of life. Others rearrange the words of His standards to suit their life style. Some even say, "No one can decide for anyone else what is really right or wrong!" What a poor example to the world, and especially for children. When we make excuses for our wrongful actions, we break down the distinctions between right and wrong. When we don't take God's Word as our standard, soon all moral choices appear fuzzy. And without Godly values we are headed for disaster and much suffering.

Yet, modern society longs for peace of mind. If we love God and obey His laws, we will have His peace. "You will seek Me and find Me, when you search for Me with all your heart," declared Jeremiah (29:13). And Jesus said, "Seek, and you will find" (Matt. 7:7). In times of trouble, it may appear as though God has forgotten us. But God may be preparing us for a new beginning with Him in the center of our lives. Therefore, we must never be discouraged. May we who know Christ be the examples of goodness, justice, wisdom and purity. God's standards should be our compass that keeps us on course.

God's message of truth and grace is for everyone. Its facts never need updating, rearranging or revision to suit our lives. It is the truest source of wisdom and understanding known to man for all generations. Do we treasure God's Word and recognize its superiority as the ultimate guide for our lives? Blessed are those who seek truth and walk in the law of the Lord!

DRESS FOR SUCCESS

*W*e all like to dress appropriately for every occasion. Some of us even update our wardrobe every season to have suitable clothes for all occasions. We have clothes for work, clothes to relax in, to exercise, clothes for church, weddings, parties, etc. We do our best to be prepared to wear just the right thing at the appropriate time. The Bible, however, teaches of a different kind of wardrobe, one that most Christians usually overlook. Yet this garment is far more important than any current style we can imagine. The occasion for which we never think to dress is war – the daily struggles which each of us faces as Christians.

If we take a moment to think, would a soldier go into battle without first being equipped and armed properly for it? Not if that soldier wishes to return unharmed or alive. Yet every day of our lives, we as Christians enter the battlefield unprepared. It is with this in mind that Apostle Paul says in Ephesians Ch. 6, "Put on the full armor of God so that you can take your stand against the devil's schemes." He is not talking about one piece, but the "Full Armor." Paul names the different parts of a Christian's armor—breastplate (righteousness), belt (truth), footwear (readiness in knowing Him), helmet and sword (God's Word). But when he comes to the shield, he emphasizes its importance. For with the shield of FAITH, he assures us that no evil can hurt us, because we are all conquerors through God who loves us. Don't you love the vivid pictures Paul draws symbolically? No one could ever accuse Apostle Paul of being "Mr. Dull." His teachings demonstrate pure enthusiasm.

Paul was very much aware of the worldly battle in which every Christian is constantly engaged. Attacks often come in the form of insults, setbacks, temptations of various kinds, discouragement, lack of self-worth, and in short, the world wants us to doubt God and ourselves. The shield of Faith, however, protects us from the fiery darts.

In actual war situations, soldiers recognize their enemy by the uniforms they wear. In our daily lives our enemy wears no uniform. The enemy is invisible, but quite real, and often friendly. Faith and God's Word are our only defenses against fear, insecurity, anxiety, doubt and anything that would keep us apart from trusting God. It is not self-confidence that Paul is teaching us, but "Christ-confidence" – confidence in His power through us.

Therefore, for whatever occasion we appropriately dress daily, why not symbolically put on the full armor of God piece by piece, and above all, let us not forget the shield of Faith; a vital part of every Christian's armor. It's the only way to dress! Dress for success!

*A*bout the year 221 B.C., a great emperor united various parts of China into an empire. His name was Shish Huang Ti, the first emperor of the Ch'in dynasty. It is from this dynasty that the name "China" is derived. To protect his country from the barbaric hordes of the northern lands, he ordered that a wall be built. This wall would be built so long and so high that all the northern provinces of China would be protected. So they erected the Great Wall of China.

The massive wall is the longest in the world. With all its windings, it stretches more than 1,500 miles. Because it was built as a defense system, it follows mountain crests and takes advantage of narrow gorges. The wall is built of earth, stone and brick. Its height ranges from 15 to 30 feet from the base, with watch towers rising at regular intervals 40 feet above it. Along the top runs a 13 foot wide roadway. The wall was too high for the enemy to climb, too thick to tear down, and too long to go around. This Great Wall was truly a tremendous project at enormous cost of wealth and human life. Did the emperor accomplish his goal with the Great Wall? Unfortunately no!

During the first 100 years of the wall's existence, China was invaded three times. How was the security breached? The enemies simply bribed a gatekeeper, and then marched easily through a gate! The fatal flaw in China's defense lay in spending its wealth to build a great wall, but paying no attention to building the character of their gatekeepers. Yes, a defense system is necessary to protect any nation. But its citizens must contribute to the country's security.

St. Paul says in Philip. 2:15, "Be blameless children of God without fault in the midst of a crooked and perverse generation, among whom you shine as lights in the world..." "Blameless and without fault" describes a life that cannot be criticized for wrongful acts. It can also be translated as above reproach. St. Paul describes the quality of life required of the Christian. To "shine as lights" is a metaphorical reference to spiritual character. The faithful's character must shine in the midst of a dark culture as the sun, moon and stars shine in an otherwise dark sky; a marked contrast to their "crooked and perverse" contemporaries.

Since that time, the Great Wall has been extended, repaired and rebuilt many times. But despite all that, much of it still stands. The Great Wall did serve, and still serves today, as a kind of boundary between Chinese and Mongol cultures, and between a way of life based on agriculture and one of nomadic herding.

We see again the wisdom of Prov.13:34, that a nation is only as strong as the character of its citizens! "Righteousness exalts a nation, but sin is a reproach to any people."

*W*e have all heard the expression, "The grass is greener on the other side." This saying must have originated by observing cows in the fields.

When I was about age 10, our family spent a summer at a mountainside village in Greece. From the road most houses looked like one story buildings, but from the back, one could see that they were two or three stories high because they were built on a slope. There was a large field near the house we stayed in that was divided into four sections. The cows were moved from section to section weekly for fresh pasture. Although there was plenty of green grass for the cows to feed, for some, no grass seemed quite as green and tasty as patches outside their own pasture. They would stretch their necks through the fence to reach the other side, while right behind them was everything they needed—excellent grazing land, beautiful shade trees, cool refreshing mountain spring water, and even a big chunk of salt. What more could they want?

But this one cow, as she stretched through the fence, somehow caught her head in the fence and was unable to pull back. The downhill slope was also a disadvantage, and she was stuck there for some time, mooing until she was rescued. This became the talk of the village for days.

Some people are like that cow. They think the "grass is greener on the other side." They constantly reach out, seeking something or other, thinking it might be better than what they have. To enjoy all earthly gifts and benefits without knowing the Heavenly Giver is a tragedy of titanic proportions. God's Word clearly teaches that if we don't respond to His gracious gifts by acknowledging our Heavenly Benefactor, our ungratefulness will only ensure our final doom and misery (Rom. 2:4 − 10).

For us Christians, the greatest blessings in life are already ours. God is our Heavenly Father. He has promised never to leave us and will supply our every need. As Thanksgiving Day approaches, let us be thankful for all that God has given us. When we have an attitude of gratitude, we will not only learn to appreciate the "green grass" on our side, but will also discover that God dwells in a thankful heart through His Holy Spirit. We should be thankful for our family and friends and the good health we enjoy; thankful that we live in a country such as this where we are free to worship Him and read His Word. How truly rich and blessed we are!

*A*re we often burdened with a load of care? Does the cross seem heavy we are called to bear? Do we question, "Why me, God?" or "Why is God allowing this to happen?"

In one sense, it's good that we do ask, "Why me, God?" It indicates that we know and believe God is truly in control of our lives. Yet, why is it that when good and wonderful things happen to us, we never ask, "Why me, God?" Could it be that we have forgotten that only by God's grace and mercy do we enjoy all of life's blessings?

If we ask God that question about our troubles, we would have to ask Him the same about our blessings. Even in suffering, we must not forget the mercies God pours into our lives. "Why me, God? Why this undeserved favor! What is the reason?" We usually don't think in those terms.

Growing up, I remember that my grandmother and mother often reminded me that if I had truly thanked the Lord for every blessing sent, then I'd have very little time to complain or be discontented. We often don't realize that in the spirit of dissatisfaction we overlook the gifts God is constantly showering upon us.

If this is true with any of us, we can determine that with God's help we could rid ourselves of this habit. So, whenever we begin to complain, we can stop and thank God for the many blessings we have that money can't buy. Why not center our attention on praising rather than pouting.

As Christians, we have so much for which to praise the Lord. We also know that genuine happiness and prosperity begin in the heart. Thankfulness and an attitude of gratitude ought to be characteristic of every child of God. The Apostle Paul writes to the Ephesians, "Always give thanks to God the Father for everything, in the name of our Lord Jesus Christ." (Eph. 5:20)

Life takes a different meaning when we spend our time counting our blessings. Let's be grateful! Let's follow St. Paul's advice and give thanks to God always. In both good and bad times, we need to remember what Job said when he went from being the most prosperous man of his generation to a pauper in no time. He observed, "The Lord gave and the Lord has taken away. May the name of the Lord be praised" (Job 1:21). Yes, may the name of the Lord be praised!

*C*an anyone disagree with the Apostle Paul that nature bears witness to the wisdom and power of God the Creator? (Rom. 1:20) To know God is to observe His creation. As we look outside, what do we see? Majestic thunderclouds? A dazzling sunrise? A tranquil sunset? Who makes the leaves turn to all those beautiful colors in autumn? Who splashes rain in shining puddles? Who makes the stars shimmer in the night? Such questions make us thank God the Creator and stimulate our own grateful meditation.

God reveals His divine nature through creation. It is God who controls the sun to rise at its appointed time every morning. It is God who keeps the earth steadily rotating at tremendous speed. It is God who feeds the sparrows and dresses the lilies in their splendor. It is God who guides the feathered flocks southward in autumn and then brings them north again in spring.

All these phenomena in nature leave us without an excuse for disbelief. As Christians we are saddened by some people's inability to see evidence of God's creations everywhere in the universe. Many do not believe that God has revealed Himself in His Son Jesus Christ. They also disagree with Christ's positive declaration: "He who has seen Me has seen the Father" (John 14:9)

If the Lord has opened our eyes and hearts so that we believe in Him, we can only humbly thank Him for His grace. We have done nothing to merit God's mercy. We must keep praying that the Almighty Designer will do for unbelieving skeptics what He has done for us; to open our eyes, in order to turn from darkness to light. We are designed and created by our Master Designer Who has a plan and purpose for our lives. He is God of all. He can quiet the raging storms and calm the crashing seas.

Reserve a few minutes today for quiet observation. Listen to the harmonies that are sounded by a harp of branches strummed by the wind. Notice the tiny details of design in the petal of a flower or a blade of grass. Why all this? Because we need the stability of knowing who controls our existence. We need to be reassured that God has not only filled His universe with life's exquisite and delightful extras, but has also promised to protect us with His loving hand. When we depend on His help, we can have even more confidence as we serve Him.

We don't know what each day may bring. We do know, however, that God will amaze us with His unfailing compassion. The design of creation points to our Master Designer. Therefore, let us give honor, praise and thanksgiving to our Heavenly Father—our Mighty Creator!

*T*he month of November, more than any other time of the year, gives us an opportunity to reexamine our many blessings and humbly thank God for the privilege of living in this great nation, the United States of America. Several generations arrived on these shores, worked hard and contributed to make America what it is today.

Our people, the Armenians, also struggled to maintain their ideals, making us proud to be called Armenian-Americans. For those who are not citizens by birth, America has made citizenship available to all. In this free and prosperous land, Armenians, past and present generations, have excelled in their chosen fields, and in doing so, continue to be a source of pride and inspiration.

The most delightful moments in life seem to catch us by surprise! A few years ago, while visiting Epcot Center in Florida, I read the following words on the wall of the American Pavilion:

> YOU WHO HAVE BEEN BORN IN AMERICA,
> I WISH I COULD MAKE YOU UNDERSTAND
> WHAT IT IS LIKE NOT TO BE AN AMERICAN—
> NOT TO HAVE BEEN AN AMERICAN ALL YOUR LIFE—
> AND THEN SUDDENLY WITH THE WORDS
> OF A MAN IN FLOWING ROBES TO BE ONE,
> FOR THAT MOMENT AND FOREVER AFTER.
> ONE MOMENT YOU BELONG WITH YOUR FATHERS
> TO A MILLION DEAD YESTERDAYS—
> THE NEXT YOU BELONG WITH AMERICA
> TO A MILLION UNBORN TOMORROWS.

George Magar Mardikian

I became very emotional as I recalled the day I became an American citizen many years ago. Deeply touched, I photographed it.

The abundant blessings we enjoy in this country are endless. As Armenian men and women let us be inspired and continue our duty to preserve our ideals. Thanksgiving should be a part of our everyday lives, not a once-a-year holiday. The hymn of Rev. Oatman comes to mind:

> Count your blessings, name them one by one;
> Count your many blessings, see what God hath done!

$\mathcal{P}$lymouth, England was a location I visited recently. My husband and I went to the site from which the Pilgrim Fathers sailed to America. It all looked familiar—we had visited that location before—but where was the Mayflower Stone? The huge rock was not where I had first seen it a few years earlier. I asked a local man who informed me that the rock is now built into the sidewalk memorial. Sure enough, near the ocean and under a beautiful arch, the famous rock was now smooth and was embraced in the company of concrete blocks. The inscription read, "September 1620." From that point the Mayflower had sailed from Plymouth, England to America.

The colonists landed at Plymouth Rock in Massachusetts Bay. After enduring the hardships of settlement in the new land, they set a day apart for thanksgiving to Almighty God for the blessings which He had bestowed upon them. Their heads were bowed in reverence and humility; their hearts were lifted up to God in gratitude. That was the first Thanksgiving Day in America. It was not, however, until President Lincoln's administration that a proclamation for a national Thanksgiving Day was issued in 1863. Since then, every president of the U.S. has proclaimed a day for national Thanksgiving.

A recurring theme in Apostle Paul's epistles stresses thankfulness in every circumstance of life. "In everything give thanks; for this is the will of God in Christ Jesus for you" (1 Thes. 5:18). We also read, "Be anxious for nothing, but in everything by prayer and supplication, with thanksgiving, let your request be made known to God" (Phil. 4:6). All these may sound unrealistic, but healing begins when we count our blessings. Gratitude is a God-honoring attitude. If we pause to think, we'll have reasons to thank Him. Are we thankful that the best things in life—God's forgiveness, joy, assurance of His love, and our citizenship in His kingdom—are still free?

When the pilgrims first settled in America, not only did they suffer many hardships, but because a group of London investors had financed their voyage in exchange for most of their produce from America during their first six years, some even had debts to worry about as well. But they were still grateful because their harvests were becoming more abundant, the streams and ocean were full of fish, the forests provided plenty, and most importantly, they had religious freedom! In their hardship, they chose an attitude of thanksgiving, and they practiced the art of thanksliving!

How fortunate we are to be living in the United States of America! Freedom is not free. We must pray for this free land we live in and thank God for all the material and spiritual blessings He has given us!

$\mathcal{T}$he emotional and psychological trauma we all experienced on September 11, 2001, added a new chapter in the history of America. As our hearts and prayers go out to the families of the victims, we know that this Thanksgiving Day will be a lonely and painful one for them. But as for the rest of us, we mourn the loss of security and peace that we always felt and enjoyed living in this great country, the U.S.A. Whether in times of war or peace, however, God never promised us freedom from adversity. Tragedies and disastrous events of this world will always occur. In fact, His Word guarantees us troubles. But God exists above and outside this world. He is our Creator, and therefore, we should put our trust in Him and not on the temporary things of this world.

From the dawn of time, since the Garden of Eden, God gave men and women the freedom to make their own choices. Unfortunately, that freedom has resulted in countless disastrous events over the centuries. Jesus spoke to His disciples about troubled times and said, "These things I have spoken to you, that in Me you may have peace. In the world you will have tribulation; but be of good cheer, I have overcome the world" (Jn. 16:33). With these words Jesus encouraged His disciples that in spite of the inevitable struggles they would face, they'd never be alone. And He will never abandon us either.

Difficulties don't pause for a Thanksgiving break. We can claim the peace of Christ anytime, and especially in troubled times. This peace is the result of the power of His Holy Spirit. Unlike worldly peace, which is usually defined as the absence of conflict, this peace is confident assurance in all circumstances. With Christ's peace, we need to fear neither the present nor the future.

This year, as we sit around our Thanksgiving table with family and friends, let us think and humbly thank God for His goodness and the many material and spiritual blessings He has given us. Thank Him also that we live in a country where we are free to worship Him and read His Word. But most of all, thank Him for His Son, Jesus Christ, Who is the light of the world. Each day is an opportunity to praise God. Gratitude is a learned attitude. For each of us, reasons for thanks may differ, and yet the gesture of gratitude is the same. Thanksgiving reveals humility.

Yes, it is difficult to give thanks in every situation; the loss of one's job, the breakup of a precious relationship, or illness in the family. But we can learn to thank God because He gives us the strength to bear it all, knowing that He is accomplishing what is best for us—even through suffering. How can we best express our gratitude to God? First by maintaining a thankful spirit in all that we do—<u>Thanks Living</u>. Then, by giving generously and cheerfully of our time, talents and treasure in His service—<u>Thanks Giving</u>. And finally, always keep in mind that circumstances may change, but God remains the same! That's always a cause for praise.

A blessed Thanksgiving Day to all!

*R*esearchers at a university in England gave both current students and former graduates a camera. Their assignment was to take a variety of photos that best describe their school. It seems the two groups viewed the university quite differently. The current students returned with pictures of buildings, while the former graduates brought back photographs of people. It was all a matter of perspective.

If we were given a camera and asked to take pictures of our church, what would we bring back? Would they be pictures of the sanctuary or pictures of people? In 1 Cor. 12:27 and Eph. 2:20 – 22, we read that as Christians we are the "body of Christ," with Christ Himself being the "chief cornerstone." St. Paul compares the body of Christ , the Church, to a human body. Each part has its specific function that is necessary to the body as a whole. The parts are different for a purpose, and in their differences they must function as one according to the will of God, with Christ always as the Head.

Members of the Body of Christ are composed of many people with spiritual gifts who come from a variety of backgrounds with a multitude of blessings and abilities. God's gifts must not be wasted, but fully used. What gifts has the Lord given to each of us? Are we using these precious God-given spiritual gifts for His glory and for the blessing of others?

Using the analogy of the human body, The Apostle Paul emphasizes the importance of each church member. If a seemingly insignificant part is taken away, the whole body becomes less effective. Therefore, it is important that we faithfully and obediently use all our various gifts and abilities. By doing so we will find our richest personal fulfillment as we offer our time, energy and resources to God's purpose. By performing our God-given tasks unselfishly, to the best of our abilities, not only do we bring honor and glory to His name, but we also demonstrate to others the difference Christ can make in our lives. His Holy Spirit is the unifier Who binds us to work together as one.

Christ's Church is a masterpiece of human relationships. We are built together into a single, unified entity. We are truly a Church without walls, with Christ Himself as our precious, life-giving cornerstone. We are part of Him, and through Him we come together to form a beautiful church, fit for God to dwell in. Therefore, let us use that camera and take a group picture. We are His Church.

A beautiful plant was presented to a dear sweet lady I know for perfect attendance at a weekly Bible study for seven continuous years. Even more amazing is the fact that this exemplary lady does not even drive. She has several friends who attend the same Bible study who provided transportation for her over the years. When I congratulated her, she modestly told me of an 81 year old lady she knows, Mrs. A, who had perfect attendance in Sunday School for 20 years. That's 1,040 Sundays! Amazing!

The natural question comes to mind. Doesn't Mrs. A ever have colds, the flu or feel tired at times? Doesn't Mrs. A ever have company on Sundays to keep her away from church? Doesn't she ever take a weekend trip or sleep late on Sunday morning? Does it ever rain or snow on Sunday mornings where Mrs. A lives? And finally, doesn't she ever get her feelings hurt by someone in the church? One is tempted to ask what is the matter with Mrs. A? The answer: Nothing at all! But if we are not in church when we should be, and we can be, there is something wrong with us! We can certainly take a lesson from both these ladies.

Church attendance is a privilege. It is understandable that perhaps some people cannot go because of physical limitations or other legitimate reasons. But those who can be in church should be. Prayer, praising God, singing, learning God's Word and enjoying Christian fellowship are just what we need for the week ahead.

Jesus announced, "As long as I am in the world, I am the light of the world" (John 9:5). But before He physically left this earth, Christ told His disciples, "You are the light of the world…Let your light so shine before men, that they may see your good works and glorify your Father in heaven" (Matt. 5:14 – 16). His light continues to shine through His followers; His disciples. That's us!

Today we are to be the light of the world, reflecting His light in a dark world where people often wander aimlessly. To keep our light shining we first need to prepare ourselves. Studying God's Word and attending church is a privilege. We should look forward to Sundays with joy. We should attend church and consider it our spiritual civic duty to ourselves and to our community.

If we are truly ambassadors of Christ, we will glow like lights. Whether we are a candle in a corner or a beacon on a hill, let us allow our light to shine. Our week should not be complete till we make it our goal to honor the Lord's Day and nourish our soul.

LET
US
SING HIS
PRAISES

A man and his wife were considering buying a piano and donating it to their church. Wishing to know and appreciate the various steps of its construction, they made arrangements to visit a piano manufacturing plant.

The guide took them first to a large workroom where the workers were cutting and shaping wood and steel. Nothing there suggested the resemblance to a piano. Then they were escorted to several workrooms where parts were being smoothed, painted, polished and assembled, but still there were no strings or keys—no music.

Finally, the guide took the guests to the showroom, where someone skillfully was playing music of the masters on a beautiful piano. The visitors, now more informed of the various steps involved in the development of this marvelous musical instrument, were able to see the finished product and fully appreciate its beauty.

The Word of God comes to us through St. John, "Beloved, we are children of God, and it has not yet been revealed what we shall be." (I John 3:2) If our spiritual progress or maturity seems slow at times, let us not be discouraged. "God, who began a good work in us, will bring it to completion..." (Phil. 1:6) The scriptures portray Christian life as a process of growth in which we advance from one stage to the next; from spiritual infancy to maturity, from being rooted in faith to being firmly established. When we sincerely open our hearts and minds to God, and wish to know Him more intimately, He brings us to wondrous maturity one step at a time.

When one day His work will be completed in us, the results in His showroom will be worth all the time spent being formed, shaped and polished in His workroom! God is at work, and He is not finished with us yet!

On a recent cruise, my husband and I had the opportunity to get acquainted with the ship's officers, who were all Greek, beginning with the captain. Since I speak the language, we were once again treated as special guests. As I was chatting with the captain one day, he invited us to meet him on the ship's bridge. The following day arrangements were made, and we were escorted there. The panoramic view from the bridge was incredible! Visibility was excellent, and the weather conditions great! It was the best spot on the entire cruise ship.

As the many panels, controls, etc., were explained to us, one thing became clear. When one sails on the high seas, one needs to know three important facts; one's location, destination and course. By referring to the map and compass, one can reach the desired destination. With all the modern technology, it sounded so simple.

As I thought of the events of that day, the following question came to mind. How does a follower of Christ stay on course and avoid spiritual "shipwreck"? The Apostle Paul wrote in 1 Tim. 1:19, "…having faith and a good conscience, which some had rejected, concerning the faith have suffered shipwreck…" As Christians, how do we hold onto a "good conscience"? As God's children, we must treasure our faith in Christ more than anything else, and do what we know is right.

A "good conscience" serves as the rudder that steers the Christian through the rocks and reefs of error. Those who ignore the truth of their conscience, as a result, suffer shipwreck of their Christian faith, which is spiritual catastrophe. God created man with a conscience as his self-judging faculty. Because God wrote His law on man's heart (Rom. 2:15), man knows the basic standards of right and wrong. When we violate those standards, our conscience produces guilt, which acts as the mind's security system and generates fear, shame and doubt as a warning to the soul's well-being. On the other hand, when we do God's will, we enjoy the affirmation, assurance, peace and joy of a "good conscience."

In order to work as God designed it, the conscience must be informed and cultivated to the highest moral and spiritual level. That means submitting it to the Holy Spirit for guidance, and through the study of God's Word. St. Paul's fully enlightened conscience exonerated him completely. But ultimately, only God can accurately judge man's motives.

There is evidence of God's moral law in every society and culture. For example, all cultures prohibit murder, and yet in all societies that law is broken. We know what is right, but we insist on doing what is wrong. It is not enough to know what is right, we must also do it. No one must ever violate their own conscience—their warning system—when it is activated. Repeatedly ignoring the conscience's warning desensitizes it, and eventually silences it. That is what St. Paul refers to as "spiritual shipwreck."

How are we doing? Are we on course? As we live in faith and act on those inner tugs, which are the divine guidance of the Holy Spirit, what we do will be right. To stay on course, we must trust the unfailing compass of God's Word.

*W*hile I was chatting with a friend, she said jokingly, "I felt neglected, like the last tree on the lot on Christmas Eve!" I smiled and confessed that I had never heard that expression before. "You know," she added, "it is like when people pass you by because you are the wrong size, or have twisted branches, or your needles are shedding."

An interesting expression! Perhaps some of us may at times feel like the neglected last tree on the lot, as though we don't quite measure up to people's expectations. But there is good news. God doesn't look at us as people do. He looks at our hearts. In 1 Samuel, chapter 16, we see that although Saul was king of Israel, God was displeased with his ungodliness. The Lord assigned the prophet Samuel to go to Jesse's house, for God Himself had chosen a king among Jesse's sons. Samuel was to anoint the next king who one day was to succeed Saul.

Obediently, Samuel went to Jesse's house, not knowing which of his sons he would anoint. The Bible describes King Saul as "an impressive young man without equal among the Israelites—a head taller than any of the others" (1 Sam. 9:2). Samuel looked at Jesse's seven tall handsome sons, wondering which would be the chosen one. But God promptly warned Samuel to look not at their appearance alone, because He had refused all of them! The Bible says, "For man looks at the outward appearance but the Lord looks at the heart."

Then Samuel asked Jesse, "Are these all the sons you have?" Jesse replied, "There is still the youngest, but he is tending the sheep." Jesse hadn't even considered his youngest son. When Samuel saw young David (about age 16), the Lord spoke to him, "Arise and anoint him; for this is the one!" Samuel did, and the Bible says, "The Spirit of the Lord came upon David from that day forward." God saw in David, "A man after His own heart, who will do His will" (Acts 13:22).

David was anointed king, but it was done in secret; he was not publicly anointed until much later (2 Sam. 2:4 and 5:3). Saul was legally the king, but God was preparing David for his future responsibilities. Although God rejected Saul's kingship by not allowing any of his descendants to sit on Israel's throne, Saul remained king until his death in battle.

When people judge by outward appearance, they may overlook capable individuals who lack particular physical qualities that society admires. Fortunately, God judges by faith and character, not appearance. And because only He can see what is inside, only He can accurately judge. Most of us spend time maintaining our outward appearance. We should do even more to develop our inner character. Jesus says, "For what is highly esteemed among men is an abomination in the sight of God" (Luke 16:5).

Even if people pass us by, like the neglected Christmas tree, it is comforting to know that our Lord still looks for hearts that are ready to serve Him, just as He did in David's time.

*T*hough at times we may think we are at the end of our rope, we are never at the end of hope! The story is told of an elderly widow who became physically restricted from performing her normal activities. Still eager to serve God, she felt she could bring blessings to others by playing the piano. She soon placed this small ad in her church's newsletter, and also informed several homes for the aging: "Pianist will play hymns by phone daily for those who are depressed and despondent—the service is free."

Within a few months her music had brought not only cheer to several hundred people, but she was also able to encourage, and prayed with many. As a result, a unique ministry had begun. She soon discovered that her situation was much better than most, and that God still had work for her to do. She also discovered the secret of victorious living!

The power of right-thinking is the power of faith and willingness to serve others in spite of limitations. St. Paul compares the body of Christ, the Church, to a human body. Each part of the body has a specific function that is necessary to the body as a whole. The parts are different for a purpose, but they work together in harmony as one (Romans 12:4 – 8).

Our churches are composed of many individuals from a variety of backgrounds, with a multitude of gifts and abilities given by the grace of God. Our various backgrounds and abilities complement our efforts. In addition, despite our diverse backgrounds, we as Christians have one thing in common—our faith in Christ. On this essential truth our churches find strength and unity.

If a seemingly insignificant part is taken away, the whole body becomes less effective. Therefore, we must always be ready to serve God any way we can throughout our lives, as one body with oneness in Christ. By doing so, we will soon discover that whatever we give will be returned to us many times over!

Let us learn from this sweet Godly woman's example. The power of right-thinking is the power of faith. Our weak bodies are subject to error and suffering, but God never abandons us. Our trials are opportunities for God to demonstrate His power and presence in us! Our responsibility is to let people see Christ through us. Then we too will discover the secret of victorious living.

A young life dedicated to God can be the beginning of many years of God-honoring service. The Bible gives us several examples of young people whom God used to bring glory to His name.

A young boy sharing his lunch of five small barley loaves and two small fish became the occasion for Jesus to show His miraculous power by feeding the 5,000. (John 6:1 – 13)

Samuel, while still a boy, became a valuable instrument in His service. He was called to fill many different roles; judge, priest, prophet, counselor, and God's man at a turning point in Israel's history. Samuel anointed Kings Saul and David, and was the last and most effective judge of that land. God worked through Samuel because Samuel was willing to be God's servant. (1 Sam. 3)

Young David, a shepherd boy, depending on God's divine power, fought and killed Goliath with only a sling shot. This was the beginning of his adventurous life of faith. Later David became the greatest king of Israel, and was described as "a man after God's own heart." (1 Sam. 13:14)

Esther's beauty and character won the heart of Persian King Ahasuerus. Although she became his queen, her life was still in danger because of her faith. Prayerfully, she risked her life to save her people from Haman's plot against the Jews. Queen Esther's faith proved that God was the source of her strength and security (book of Esther).

Daniel, although young when deported from Judah to Babylon, remained true to his faith. God delivered him from prison, a den of lions and from enemies who hated him. Daniel possessed the gift of prophecy and served many years in a country hostile to God. He was persistent in prayer and disinterested in power for personal glory (Dan. Chapters 1 – 3).

The Apostle Paul advises young Timothy, "Let no one despise your youth, but be an example to the believers in word, in conduct, in love, in spirit, in faith, in purity." (1 Tim. 4:12) Timothy was a young pastor. He had to earn the respect of his elders by his exemplary life.

Regardless of our age, God can use us for His glory. He knows our true potential. Whatever our age, we should never make it an obstacle. God can bring us through any difficulty we might face, when we ask in faith for His wisdom and guidance. When we also take Apostle Paul's advice to Timothy and live the exemplary life of a Christian, others will see Christ in us.

The story is told of a man who went to see his pastor and told him he was soon going to the Holy Land. It was his intention to climb Mount Sinai, and from its top, loudly read the Ten Commandments. Thinking this would please his pastor, the church member was surprised to hear him say, "I can think of something even better than that. Instead of traveling thousands of miles to read the Ten Commandments on Mount Sinai, why not stay right here and keep them?" God wants us to read His Word, of course, but more importantly, He wants us to obey it.

St. James says in his epistle (1:22), "But be doers of the Word, and not hearers only, deceiving yourselves." Professing Christians must not be content with only hearing the Word. It must be put into action.

There is an element about the Word of God which makes it different from any other book. There are many books which provide information, knowledge, or entertainment. But the Word of God is different; it demands action. "Be doers of the Word, and not hearers only." We can read history, but it asks nothing of us. We can read a cookbook, study a recipe, but it does not say we have to cook. There is no demand. But the Word of God is a command. It is a call to action.

St. James continues saying that if a person just listens and doesn't obey, he is like a person looking at his face in a mirror, but as soon as he walks away, he forgets what he saw. But the person who looks steadily into God's Law, will not only remember it, but will also do what it says, and God will greatly bless him in everything he does.

First century mirrors were not glass, but metallic, made of bronze, silver, or for the wealthy, gold. The metals were beaten flat and polished to a high gloss, and the image they reflected was adequate, but not perfect. With that analogy, St. James says, unless Christians act promptly after they hear the Word, they will forget the changes and what improvements they need to make.

The Bible is not a popular book in today's world because it shows us who we are in a true light. It is the best seller, but the least read book. Still, it is our mirror showing us exactly who we are and what we look like in God's eyes. The unbelieving world today may not be reading the Bible, but they are carefully reading Christians like you and me. Our actions are written, not with ink for the world to read, but by the Holy Spirit of the Living God. Our behavior is written, not on tablets of stone as the Ten Commandments, but on tablets of flesh—that of our hearts. Let us continue to be "doers of the Word!" For many, we might be the only gospel they read!

*A*lthough there is e-mail communication available, we still need the use of regular mail, for which we depend on the Postal Service. Whenever we mail anything anywhere, and put the appropriate stamp on the envelope, do we realize that it is truly an exercise of trust? When we write a letter to a distant friend, for example, we know that we need the help of the Postal Service. We drop our letter in the mailbox, and then we trust the mail service to take over, until our letter is delivered to its destination. Although we can't see exactly what happens and how many people are involved, our trust and confidence in the Postal Service assures us that our letter is as good as delivered.

On the other hand, when we are faced with a serious problem and have not been successful in solving it, our faith is challenged. When we finally realize that it's impossible to resolve the problem through our own efforts, we recognize our need for God's help through prayer. Until that moment, we are still holding onto our problem, as an unmailed letter with the stamp on it. We know the situation will not get resolved until we let go of our problem and send it into our God's loving hands. Once we do that, we must then trust God to take over until the problem is resolved in His own way and in His own time. Although we can't see what He's doing, the Bible says, "Faith is the substance of things hoped for, the evidence of things not seen" (Heb. 11:1). As we continue to pray for divine wisdom and guidance, we receive the assurance that His work is as good as done, according to His will.

Jesus prayed constantly and He told us "Pray always and not lose heart" (Lk. 18:1). Prayer is our open line of communication with our Creator. We must remember, however, that God's thoughts are not our thoughts, nor are His ways our ways (Is. 55:8). Even when His answer is "no," He has a very good reason. What we prayed for might be contrary to His plan. And His refusal can be very good indeed; meaning that He has a better plan! Nevertheless, we must hang in there in faith.

Heb. 11:6 says, "But without faith it is impossible to please Him, for he who comes to God must believe that He is, and that He is a rewarder of those who diligently seek Him." Now that is good news! God wants a personal, dynamic relationship with each one of us that will transform our lives.

Is someone's faith challenged perhaps? Some people need to doubt before they truly believe. If doubt will lead to questions, and questions would lead to answers, and answers are accepted, then doubt has done good work. But when doubt becomes stubbornness, and stubbornness becomes a lifestyle, that doubt harms faith. When we doubt we must continue to search for answers. The Bible says, "Faith comes from hearing, and by hearing the Word of God" (Rom. 10:17).

Let's grow in His Word and remember that no burden is too great or too small to bring to God. His stamp is already on our burden. Let's drop it in His mailbox. When we trust God, He turns our problems into opportunities!

A gift certificate for gourmet coffees was given to me a few weeks ago. Rather than spend it for just coffee, I bought two spill-proof cups. The cashier put a coupon in each cup, and told me with a smile that whenever I would come back with these cups and coupons, the first cup of coffee would be on the house. I thanked him, and left.

A few days later, my husband and I took our cups and went for that cup of coffee I was promised. I approached the lady behind the counter, and enthusiastically said that we had come to claim what was promised to me. "Certainly," she said, and waited for our order with a smile. "What kind of coffee can we have?" I asked somewhat hesitantly. "Any flavor you two wish is yours," was her answer! It sounded wonderful. We both had a cup of their special blend coffees, and it was delicious!

If people can stand firm behind their promises, how much more would our Heavenly Father. Jesus says, "Ask and it will be given to you; seek and you will find; knock and the door will be open to you. For everyone who asks receives; he who seeks finds; and to him who knocks the door will be opened" (Matt. 7:7, 8). The first letters of Ask, Seek and Knock spell "ASK." It is God's will that we ask with confidence, humility and faith. Knowing God takes faith and patient, persistent, persevering prayer.

Further, Jesus says, "Which of you, if his son asks for bread, will give him a stone? Or if he asks for fish, will give him a serpent?" (Matt. 7:9, 10). On the other hand, if a child asks for a poisonous serpent, would a wise father grant his request? Often we don't know what is best for us, but our Almighty God, having a panoramic view of our lives, knows that we often pray for "serpents" and therefore, doesn't grant our wishes. But let us not give up on our efforts to seek Him. We must continue to ask God for more patience, wisdom, love, discerning spirit, and He will give them to us. As the Holy Spirit directs our hearts, we will desire those things that will benefit us spiritually.

God is our loving Heavenly Father Who cares and knows what is best for us. If humans can be kind, gracious, and keep their promises as did the people at the gourmet coffee shop, how much more can our God, the Creator of kindness be! Let us trust Him and Ask, Seek and Knock. A.S.K.

*M*ost of us have experienced the following: We call a business establishment, expecting to speak to someone who can help us. "Can you hold, please?" a cheerful voice asks, and we immediately hear music. A taped message often assures us that our call will be answered soon. We wait and wait. We feel forgotten—neglected.

As Christians we sometimes feel that God also has put us "on hold," or He does not hear us. We pray fervently about a certain matter of extreme importance to us, but nothing happens. Nothing! Nothing?

As God's children we must know that God does hear each one of our prayers—along with millions of other faithfuls around the world, each in his or her own native language. For some of us who find it difficult to understand two children talking to us at the same time, it is indeed a miracle that God can hear so many of His children simultaneously.

How can we then reconcile God's apparent silence to our repeated prayers? By remembering that God's wisdom surpasses ours. We cannot see the whole picture. Our Heavenly Father does, and knows what's best for us. Often times I have come to thank the Lord for not granting some of my prayers. For in the light of future events, often years later, I could see God's wisdom and love in denying me that very thing for which I had so fervently pleaded.

In Isaiah 55:8 we read, "For my thoughts are not your thoughts, neither are your ways my ways." When God is silent He has a very good, loving and caring reason. When God puts us "on hold," let us not get impatient. It is a privilege to humbly and honestly open our hearts and pray to God. This brings us into a closer personal fellowship with Him as we admit our need and dependence on our Creator. We can bring to God our most cherished longings and wishes, then patiently wait for Him to answer us lovingly in His own way, in His own time. Millions of faithful throughout the world pray to God daily. Let us rejoice in knowing that we can always "get through." God hears our prayers!

*G*rowing up in Greece, I attended both Greek and Armenian schools. Religious studies in Greek schools was part of the curriculum. The first five books of the Old Testament, the Pentateuch, were combined into one text, and the four gospels, Matthew, Mark, Luke and John, into another. It was written in simple Greek language, and I had great fun studying my religious studies textbooks.

These studies often led me to ponder deep theological questions. The source of pain in our world created by a perfectly Holy God, was one. For example, my father died at age 42 when I was 8 years old. Also, was the calendar used in Old Testament days the same as ours today? How could people live to be several hundred years old? And what about God as the unity of three persons: Father, Son and Holy Spirit?

Since I was only a child, I expected that by the time I reached a mature age I would know all the answers. Today I feel that I know only a tiny bit more than I did then. Over the years, I came to realize that I don't have the mental capacity to grasp fully what is infinite and eternal. I also came to realize that what matters most is not gaining more knowledge about life's mysteries (although I continue to have a curious mind), but putting into practice what God has allowed me to learn so far through His Holy Spirit.

The Apostle James teaches us to "Be doers of the Word, and not hearers only..." (Jas. 1:22). Believers who hear the Word of God must receive it with a teachable mind and spirit, and apply it to their daily lives. Yes, it is important first to know what God's Word says, but it's even more important to obey.

For many centuries the Bible circulated in scrolls and hand written manuscripts. But since Johannes Gutenberg devised the printing press around 1455, scripture has been reproduced in countless editions. This makes us appreciate our forefathers' strong faith and love for God even more. They survived trials, persecutions, and many even gave their lives for their Christian faith! How did they do it without a family Bible or their own copy, as we do?

May God bless our spiritual leaders and the Church that helped our people keep their Armenian Christian faith alive in their hearts. Those of us in the United States are blessed when compared to the suffering of our forefathers. In this land of comfort, God's Church needs our support. We are the Church, with Jesus Christ Himself as the chief cornerstone and head of the Church. Let's be "doers of the Word." Many books can inform, but only the Bible can transform lives! A transformed life enjoys coming into God's presence. We must attend church regularly—joyfully, thankfully, reverently. Christians are like coals of fire—together they glow; apart they grow cold. What gifts has God given us? We are accountable for them. God's gifts to us must not be squandered. Let's use those gifts with our time, talents and our treasures in His service and for His glory.

*W*ho has not been accused wrongly at least once? Blame or criticism is always difficult to accept, especially when we are innocent. It's equally difficult when we've had no opportunity to justify ourselves. I'll share a simple personal story with you.

On my morning walk not long ago, a huge, very friendly beautiful dog followed me with an affectionate attitude. He jumped happily all around me so that it was getting difficult to walk, and was very annoying. I told him to go home several times, but he didn't get the message. We came to an intersection about a mile away from home. As intelligent as dogs are, this one had no sense of danger. He began to cross the street in heavy traffic. I was terrified. I covered my face—I didn't want to see this dog get hit by a car. In the meantime, furious motorists were shouting at me, "Get a leash" and "Control your dog," and a lot worse. Fortunately the dog made it to the other side unharmed. What a relief!

After I crossed the street, he continued to follow me until a woman came out of her house with a cute, tiny poodle on a leash. The big dog forgot all about me and off he ran to meet the tiny dog. This time the woman looked at me angrily. But before she said anything, I finally had the opportunity to say, "It's not my dog!" It felt so good to say that! Without a word, the woman went back into the house, and the big dog left me at last.

As simple and innocent as these accusations were, criticism is always difficult to accept, whether a person is guilty or not. If innocent, the truth will eventually be exposed; no serious harm done. Although there is a beautiful verse in Prov. 18:13 that says, "He who answers a matter before he hears it, it is folly and shame on him." Judging before getting the facts can bring embarrassing results. DNA could also stand for "Do Not Assume." But if criticism contains any truth, we must first examine the source and listen carefully to what is being said. If correct, we should receive it with humility and a desire to improve. We must learn from it, even if it is not given in the right spirit. We must also remember that we are not infallible, and need God's grace and wisdom to keep on the straight path – the path to wisdom.

We read in Prov. 9:8, "...Rebuke a wise man, and he will love you." Wisdom begins with knowing God. He gives us insight in living because he created life. But what do we do when, as a result, we feel burnt out spiritually? We can learn a lesson from Ben Franklin. During the Revolutionary War, a pessimistic friend wrote him this note: "The sun of liberty has set." Ben's response was, "Then light the candles." When we feel discouraged and our "light" is fading, and we feel spiritually down, we can let God lift us up. He is our divine power source.

Do we want to be wise? We must know our Creator better through His Word. Let God recharge our spiritual batteries. When we are criticized, let's accept what is true and act upon it. As a result we'll become stronger individuals. He who profits from rebuke is wise. We must never fear criticism when we are right, and never ignore it when we are wrong.

Our ability to love is often shaped by our experience of love. We usually love others as we have been loved.

During the years that Jesus walked on earth, He had a special friend. That friend was John, one of His disciples. For most of us, the thought that Jesus might have needed a good friend seems a little strange. But because He shared our humanity, Jesus also had the need for a close friend. Why was John the chosen one? We know that some of the greatest statements about Christ's loving nature were written by John, who experienced Christ's love in a unique way. John not only devoted his life to Him, but was also so committed that he put the spotlight on Christ by not even using his own name in the gospel. He referred to himself only as "the disciple whom Jesus loved" (13:23). Although Jesus' love is clearly communicated in all the gospels, in John's gospel it is a central theme.

John was one of the twelve disciples, and with his brother James and fellow disciple Peter, were the closest to Jesus. John wrote five New Testament books; the gospel of John, the letters John 1, 2 and 3, and the book of Revelation. Before following Jesus, he was a fisherman, an unlearned man, though while with Jesus, he carried in his mind the whole truth of what he saw and experienced. Fellowship with the Father and His Son Jesus Christ granted him blessings, revelation and wisdom!

Jesus trusted John to write about Him. John had a lot of inside information that Jesus knew John could accurately communicate. He also trusted John with His precious mother, Mary. Even on the cross, in His dying hour, Christ was concerned about His beloved mother's welfare. From the cross, Jesus saw His cherished mother Mary with the other women and the "disciple whom He loved" standing near. Jesus said to His mother, "Dear woman, here is your son," and to His disciple, "Here is your mother." We read that from that moment on, John took her into his house (John 19:25, 26). Jesus entrusted His mother to that special disciple, His best friend, who stayed with Him until the end on the cross. That disciple was John!

The Apostle John is the only disciple who died a natural death at an advanced age. It is believed that it was from Ephesus that St. John wrote the gospel and the epistles John 1, 2 and 3. Then, for his faithful preaching of the gospel, St. John was exiled by the Roman authorities to the island of Patmos where he wrote the book of Revelation.

John had been an eye witness and participant in Jesus' earthly ministry and saw the incarnate Christ. Through the guidance of the Holy Spirit, the beloved apostle's goal and purpose for writing was to reveal the full identity of Christ as the Son of God, the Light of the world, and to give warning and hope to all believers. In John 13:34, he quotes Christ, "Love one another as I have loved you, by this all men will know that you are My disciples." If we all practice this sacrificial love modeled after Christ's love for us, nothing more is needed.

$\mathcal{D}$iligence should be a way of life. God has given us abilities and opportunities to work so that we can use our time well and be productive. He expects us to be industrious and do our best in whatever He gives us to do.

The story is told of a student who went to see his pastor, asking him how to obtain an easy job with good pay and convenient hours. His pastor replied without hesitation: "If that is your attitude, son, you will amount to nothing. You cannot be an editor or a lawyer, or even think of entering the ministry. None of these professions is easy. You must forget the fields of engineering, science, merchandising, the practice of politics, and certainly not medicine. To be a farmer or a good soldier, you must study and think. My son, you have entered a hard world. I know of only one easy place in it—the grave."

Those who refuse to be industrious will eventually be disappointed. The Apostle Paul, in his epistle to the Thessalonian faithful, says this about diligence: "For you yourselves know that you ought to follow us, for we were not disorderly among you; nor did we eat anyone's bread free of charge, but worked with labor and toil night and day, that we might not be a burden to any of you" (2 Thess. 3:7, 8). St. Paul is not saying that he never accepted hospitality, but that he had not depended on others for his living.

There is a difference between leisure and laziness. Relaxation and recreation provide a necessary and much needed balance to our lives. But when it is time to work, Christians should jump right in. We must make the most of our talent and time, doing all we can to provide for ourselves and our dependents. Every day has 24 hours filled with opportunities to grow, serve, be productive and work purposefully. Yet it is easy to waste time, letting precious days slip from our grasp.

Why not see time as God's gift, and seize our opportunities to live diligently for Him. When we choose God's way, He grants us wisdom. His Word, the Bible, leads us to live right and make right decisions. Then we will carry out our work with diligence and discipline.

*I*n 1983 a teenage girl in England began an 11 year difficult journey around the world on foot. When she was asked why she did it, she said, "I had to discover myself." That's a lot of walking for self discovery! On the other hand, a podiatrist recently stated that the average person's feet travel more than four times the earth's circumference in a lifetime! That's also a lot of walking! But where do our feet take us, and why? The Apostle Paul writes to the Roman faithful, quoting from the book of Isaiah 52:7, "How beautiful are the feet of those who preach the gospel of peace, who bring glad tidings of good things!" (Rom. 10:15).

The imagery of messengers who bring good tidings is taken from 2 Samuel 18:26. During wars in biblical times, messengers would run from the scene of battle, across hills and mountains to the city that was waiting to hear the news. The glorious message of this messenger that St. Paul is writing about is redemption and forgiveness of our sins through Jesus Christ; a victorious deliverance for all of us.

Are our feet beautiful? St. Paul is not talking, of course, about whether the shoes we wear are beautiful, or if our toes and feet are properly cared for. He's talking about the feet of those who carry the Good News of the gospel wherever they go. He says that unless someone goes and tells others about Christ, how will they hear? How will they know? "So then, faith comes by hearing, and hearing by the Word of God" (Rom. 10:17). It is a privilege to share God's Good News with others.

In biblical times everyone walked everywhere. Today we don't even have to step out of our homes to carry the Good News of the Bible and be a blessing to others. So let's bring ourselves up to date. Let us appreciate all the modern means of communication we have; the U.S. mail, the telephone, E-mail, etc. We can have a beautiful ministry by being available to others with a loving note, an encouraging phone call, or an E-mail message. If we wished to step out, we can let our automobiles do the walking for us. Are our feet "beautiful"? With that in mind, we can walk with a cause—not to discover ourselves, but to help others discover Christ.   As Christians, we carry Christ's name. What does the world see by watching us? Do our actions bring honor to His name? Does our behavior reflect His presence? The story is told that after retiring, a man went back to live in the small village where he was born. Wishing to share God's Word with others, he began passing Christian literature to the village people. As he gave one to a young boy, the youth said, "Sorry, I don't know how to read, but I'll be watching you."

A heart dedicated to God will overflow with selfless goodness for others. One way we can help others is to be there for them. "Rejoice with those who rejoice, and weep with those who weep" (Rom. 12:15). To rejoice in the blessings, honor and welfare of others, and show sensitivity and compassion to the hardships and sorrows of our fellow man, is every Christian's privilege and responsibility. The best kind of giving comes from the depths of the heart.

So, wherever our feet will be going today, let's make sure they are "beautiful"!

*I*t has been said that the opposite of love is not hate—it is self! The story is told that an officer was directing repairs of a military building during the American Revolution. He was harshly ordering the soldiers under his command who were trying to raise a heavy wooden beam. As the men struggled in vain, a man who was passing by stopped to ask the one in charge why he wasn't helping his men. With an emperor's flair, the soldier responded, "Sir, I am a corporal!"

"Oh, you are, are you?" replied the passer-by. Then taking off his hat and bowing, he said, "I ask your pardon, Corporal." Then the stranger walked over and strained with the soldiers to lift the heavy beam. After the job was finished, he turned and said, "Mr. Corporal, when you have another such job and don't have enough men, send for your Commander-in-Chief, and I will come and help you a second time." The corporal was shocked. The person speaking to him was General Washington!

True greatness is not attained by ruling over others, but by humble service. Jesus said, "…Whoever wishes to become great among you shall be your servant, and whoever wishes to be first among you shall be your slave; just as the Son of Man did not come to be served, but to serve, and to give His life a ransom for many" (Mt. 20:26 – 28). Jesus certainly described leadership from a new perspective. A true leader has a servant's heart. Humble leaders appreciate the worth of others, and realize that they are not above any job.

The Bible says in at least three separate passages, "God is opposed to the proud, but gives grace to the humble" (1 Pet. 5:5). We often wonder about our position and status, hoping to receive proper recognition for what we do. But we also know that God's recognition counts more than human praise. Therefore, we can humbly obey Him regardless of our present circumstances, and God will bless us in His proper time and will lift us up. When the Holy Spirit fills us, we'll see that this world's seductive attractions are only poor substitutes for what God truly has to offer.

God measures greatness by service. When Christ washed the feet of His disciples, He gave us an example to follow (Jn. 13:14 – 16). The Lord Jesus, though He was God and worthy of all honor, served all throughout His ministry. We too are to do the same selflessly. That was the attitude General Washington demonstrated in the above story, in sharp contrast to the corporal who was a self-saturated man.

No one is ever going to be perfect here on earth, so we must accept and love others in spite of their shortcomings. Besides, are we that perfect? We should be patient, gentle, and with humility, demonstrate flexibility and tolerance for one another with love. Rather than dwell on the individual's weakness or look at their faults, we can focus on that person's strengths and pray for their weaknesses. To be great in God's sight, we must serve. The acronym **J.O.Y.** stands for putting **J**esus first, **O**thers second, and **Y**ourself last. That will bring joy and approval in the eyes of our Creator.

*T*he Bible is not a written record of perfect people, except for Jesus Christ. God's Word, from beginning to end, points out the painful mistakes made by its characters. From the beginning God designed man to live forever in the beautiful Garden of Eden. The one condition was that they be obedient to Him. But man failed. Someone said, "It was not the apple on the tree that brought sin into the world, but the pair on the ground." Adam and Eve's disobedience was transference of control of their lives from God to themselves. By their disobedience they made themselves their own masters. Is not that the essence of human sin?

Disobedience inexorably means being cut off from our Creator, which leads to spiritual death. Adam and Eve learned by painful experience the consequences of rebellion. Their fall from God's gracious presence affected all creation. Our first ancestors were the highlight of God's creation—the very reason God created the world. In rapid succession, we see how evil began weaving its destructive web. The first couple's first son became a murderer, and evil bred evil. The Bible recounts painful stories of lives ruined as a result of disobedience.

Since the fall of man, God began His plan of redemption. The entire Bible is the story of how that plan unfolds, ultimately to God's own visit to earth through His Son Jesus Christ. We are descendants of Adam and Eve. The Bible says, "For all have sinned and fall short of the glory of God..." (Rom. 3:23). We read in John 1:14, "And the world became flesh and dwelled among us..." This emphasizes Jesus taking on human form. We are not to minimize His humanity or His divinity. Jesus is both fully God and fully man. He is God's only begotten unique Son.

The invisible became visible. The supernatural One reduced Himself to natural. By dwelling among us, Christ became the perfect teacher, the perfect example, the sinless perfect model of what we should strive to become. By His death on the cross and resurrection, He became the perfect sacrifice and redeemed humanity from all transgression (Col. 1:15 – 20). Christ gives us the opportunity to bridge the gap between man and our Creator.

Disobedience is toxic to our well-being. It takes away our joy and peace, contaminates our lives and separates us from God. Life is short. We must learn by the mistakes of those biblical personalities. We can't possibly live long enough to make all those mistakes in order to learn. Christ opens the door for us to renew our fellowship with God. His unconditional love is available to all those who turn to Him in repentance. When we do that, His Holy Spirit takes residence in our hearts and gives us power to live victoriously. "I am the way, the truth and the life. No one comes to the Father except through Me." says Christ in John 14:6.

There is hope in God's Word. No matter how dark the world seems, God has a plan. No matter how insignificant we may feel, God loves us and wants to use us in His plan. No matter how separated from God we may feel, His plan of redemption is available. The good news is, there is hope—always—when we choose life!

A group picture was to be taken at a social function. The person who was about to take the photo said that he had a panoramic view camera. While he focused on his subject, his camera's eye included much more detail than he expected. So he took a moment to rearrange some stack-up chairs that happened to be nearby, brought in some flower pots, and took away some empty plates from a table. The camera's eye took in the entire panoramic scene.

That is often similar to our lives. We concentrate only on what is happening at the moment and fail to realize that God has a panoramic view of our entire lives. This panoramic divine surveillance has been going on since creation. We read in Proverbs 5:21, "For a man's ways are in full view of the Lord and He examines all his paths." Knowing that our Heavenly Father sees everything we do should motivate us to live a life that pleases Him. And what a comfort it is to us, for our God, to Whom all is revealed, still cares for His own.

Small children think that if they close their eyes and can't see us, then we can't see them either. Many adults today may have wished that hiding from God were as simple as closing their eyes. Although they may close their eyes to their wrongful ways, their acts certainly are not hidden from God. Even our unfair or wrongful attitude is noticed by God. Job says in 31:6, "Let me be weighed on honest scales, that God might know my integrity."

At times it seems that God has let evil run rampant in the world, and we wonder if He even notices. But He sees both the evil actions and the evil intentions. He is not an indifferent observer. He cares and is active in our world. His work may often be unseen and unfelt, but one day He will wipe out evil, He will establish the good, and reward those who do His will.

As Christians we must keep up our courage. We cannot always choose what happens to us, but we can choose our attitude toward each situation. The secret to a merry heart is in Philippians 4:8, "Finally, brothers, whatever is true, whatever is noble, whatever is right, whatever is pure, whatever is lovely, whatever is admirable—if anything is excellent or praiseworthy—think about such things."

Do we sometimes question God? Perhaps someone has been laid off from a job, or one had to drop out of college for financial reasons. Someone may have just broken up a relationship with a special person. We may be seeing only a part of the big picture. Although our eyes zoom in on today, God sees the entire picture. His love for us is unconditional. We are never out of His sight. We can trust Him with our plans, our dreams, and our entire life. He has the panoramic view!

$\mathcal{N}$ot long ago on a warm sunny day, four high school students couldn't resist the temptation to skip classes and go to the beach. The next day they told the teacher that they missed his class because the auto in which they car pool to school had a flat tire. The teacher smiled and said they missed a quiz the other students took. He asked them to take their seats, and get paper and pencil ready for the quiz. Then he said, "First question: Which tire was flat?"

Truth is one of God's distinguishing qualities. As common or amusing the above story might seem, it is still dishonest. Why not tell the truth? As Christians, we offend God when we lie. An ethics theorist wrote, "Most evil acts are committed, not by villains, but rather by decent human beings—in desperation, momentary weakness, or an inability to discern what is morally right or wrong among confusing circumstances." Often, one thing leads to another, and before long, the lie is out of control.

But God expects us to do what is right. There are countless verses in God's Word on truth and honesty in both the Old and New Testaments. Jesus says in Matthew 5:8, "Blessed are the pure in heart, for they shall see God." In this case, "heart" means the center of one's being, including the mind, will, and emotions. Christian living often contradicts the world's standards. If we want to live exemplary lives, we must be ready to say and do what seems strange to the world around us. We must be willing to give when others take, to love when others hate, to help when others abuse.

Psalm 24:3, 4 also talks about clean hands and pure hearts: Guiltless actions with righteous attitudes and motives. God values honesty. Dishonesty might often come easily, especially when complete truthfulness could cost us something, make us uncomfortable, or put us in an unfavorable light, such as the students in the above story. Without honesty, however, a relationship with God is impossible. If we lie to others, we really deceive ourselves. God cannot hear us nor can His Holy Spirit talk to our hearts if we build walls of self deception.

Jesus continues in Matthew 7:12, "Whatever you want men to do to you, do also to them, for this is the Law and the Prophets." This verse is commonly known as the "Golden Rule." This principle was stated by a number of ancient thinkers as, "Do not do to others what you do not want done to you." Jesus made it a positive obligation. It is not hard to want to get even with others. It is much more difficult to take the initiative to do something good for them.

The "Golden Rule" as Jesus formulated it is the foundation of active goodness and mercy; the kind of love God shows us every day. As Christians we are blessed to have God's Word as our guide. The opinion of man is no substitute for the Word of God!

*U*nquestionably, the favorite of all Christmas carols is "Silent Night." Yet, when the hymn was first written in 1818 by two humble church leaders, little did they realize the universal popularity it would eventually receive.

It was a few days before Christmas when Franz Gruber, a church organist in the little town of Oberndorf, Bavaria, discovered that the church organ would not function. Knowing that there was no repairman in town, and they had been snowbound for days, he was afraid that there would be no music for Christmas. He hurried to Father Joseph Mohr to inform him of the problem. Not wishing to disappoint his faithful flock, Father Mohr decided to write his own Christmas hymn, one that could be sung without an organ. He began reading of Christ's birth from his Bible. Among many other verses, he read, "Behold I bring you good tidings of great joy, which shall be to all people. For unto you is born this day in the city of David a Savior, who is Christ the Lord." (Luke 2:10, 11)

As he meditated on the words, the full meaning grasped his soul, and he completed a poem about the wondrous birth. The organist took the newly written words and composed the melody. The carol was completed in time for Christmas, and the two sang their new hymn, accompanied by Gruber's guitar.

The carol made a deep impact upon the parishioners, and before long, "Silent Night" was sung throughout Germany and Austria. It was first heard in the United States in 1839. Today the hymn is sung in all major languages of the world.

As we sing this much loved carol of Christ's humble birth once again this year, may the true meaning of Christmas grasp our souls. Let us allow its peaceful melody inspire us to worship in awe as did the shepherds on that silent night over two thousand years ago.

*A*mazing as it may seem, the countdown to Christmas has already begun. One of the many things we do in preparation for the Holy Season is to select our Christmas cards. What message do we wish to extend to friends and loved ones? Illustrations of reindeer, poinsettias or Santa on a sled? Some cards have even omitted the word "Christmas." As beautiful as these cards can be, they do not affect the hearts or lives of those who might not know Christ. Only the Word of God has the power to reach and touch searching hearts and bring hope. With that in mind, why not consider what printed message we will send this Christmas; a message about Christ the Savior or a scene in which He is nowhere to be seen?

We must also reflect on whose birth we prepare to celebrate. Although the message and promise of the Holy Season are the same since the very first Christmas, we must always renew our faith, knowing that the birth of Christ is God's most precious gift to mankind. God made His entrance into history and into our own lives in the form of a child! Shepherds in the fields of Bethlehem keeping watch over their flocks at night were the first to hear the divine news from the angel. "Do not be afraid, for behold, I bring you good tidings of great joy which shall be to all people. For there is born to you this day in the city of David a Savior, who is Christ the Lord" (Luke 2:10, 11).

The shepherds gathered their flowing garments to hurry to Him. The Magi passed deserts and mountains to find Him. Wise men and women still seek Him; for through Christ we find forgiveness, inward peace, joy and the promise of eternal life.

An unknown author wrote: "He became a man that we might become children of God. In infancy He troubled a king. In boyhood He puzzled the teachers. In manhood He ruled the course of nature. He healed the multitudes without medicine. He never wrote a book, yet the libraries of the world are filled with volumes written about Him. He never penned a musical note, yet He is the theme of more songs than any other subject. Great men have come and gone, yet He lives on."

While it is true that wise men and women still seek Him, it is even more amazingly true that He seeks us whoever we are. As Christians let us renew ourselves spiritually by reopening our hearts to Christ. As we prepare our homes during this Holy Season, may we be even more aware of God's marvelous gift of His love. May Christ's birth be evident in all that we do, including the message we choose to send to friends and loved ones.

Over two thousand years ago, quietly and unannounced, Joseph and Mary entered the little town of Bethlehem and searched for a place to spend the night. Although it was a busy time in the Judean village, the excitement and unusual activities were not earthly plans for the celebration of the birth of Jesus. It was because, in those days, Caesar Augustus had issued a decree that a census should be taken. Everyone went to his own town to register. Joseph and Mary also went from Nazareth to the city of David, which is called Bethlehem. Joseph was of the lineage of King David and went to register with his betrothed wife. The people had no idea that Mary was about to deliver Christ the Savior.

What a contrast with the Christmas celebrations of today! It is almost as if people want to make up for missing the first Christmas, the birth of Christ. Yet, a proper preparation for Christians is not a matter of decorations and lights, but rather the preparation of one's heart. Even we Christians can miss the point of Christmas if we are not careful. Christmas is not only about the birth of Jesus, but about the Person He grew to be, and the One Who alone can redeem the world from its sins.

When the angel of the Lord appeared to Joseph, he said, "Joseph, son of David, do not be afraid to take Mary as your wife, for that which is conceived in her is of the Holy Spirit. And she will bring forth a Son, and you shall call His name Jesus, for He will save His people from their sins" (Mt. 1:20-21). The conception and birth of Jesus Christ are supernatural events beyond human logic or reasoning. Therefore, God sent angels to help certain people understand the significance of what was happening (Mt. 2:13, 19; Lk. 1:11, 26; Lk. 2:9).

Why is the virgin birth important to the Christian faith? Jesus Christ, the Son of God, had to be free from the sinful nature passed onto all human beings by Adam. Because Jesus was born of a woman, Mary, through the Holy Spirit, He is both fully human and fully divine. Because of this, Jesus completely understands our experiences and struggles, and because He is divine, He has the power and authority to deliver us from sin. We can bring to Jesus all our thoughts and needs. He has the divine power to help.

St. Matthew in 1:22, 23 quotes the prophet Isaiah, saying, "Behold the virgin shall be with child, and bear a Son, and they shall call His name Immanuel, which translates 'God with us'" (Is. 7:14). Jesus was God in the flesh, and was literally among us; "with us." Christ is present today in the lives and hearts of every faithful through His spirit. Perhaps not even Isaiah understood how far reaching the meaning of "Immanuel" would be.

It is only as we see the birth of Christ, in light of His crucifixion and resurrection, that we are able to grasp the full meaning of His coming. The mission of the cross is hidden in the message of the cradle! The greatest story ever told!

*T*he angel who announced the birth of Christ to the shepherds nearly 2,000 years ago, had a special blessing in the Christmas message that is frequently missed. The birth of Christ is not simply an interesting fact of history unrelated to our present life. Rather, it has a direct and important bearing upon each one of us. The angel said: "Fear not, for, behold, I bring <u>you</u> good tidings of great joy, which shall be to <u>all peo-ple</u>. For unto <u>you</u> is born this day in the city of David a Savior, which is Christ the Lord." (Luke 2:10, 11) Yes, it was for us that Jesus came. Our names were in God's mind when He sent His Son into the world to share our humanity and become one with us, so that we might live forever with Him.

It was only a few years ago when, through personal experience, I became more aware of this verse's true meaning. My husband and I went to the Holy Land with some 50 faithful. While in Jerusalem we visited a location believed to be the site of the Upper Room. While in the room, I was overwhelmed by the spiritual signifi-cance of this very location; the Last Supper, Jesus washing the disciples' feet. I then noticed a young couple coming up the stairs who were from some part of Africa. They were colorfully dressed, with scarves wrapped around their heads. As they walked around, they started to sing a hymn familiar to all of us; "Nearer My God to Thee." We all joined them, singing the same hymn. They sang in their language, some of us sang in Armenian and some in English.

Suddenly I felt so connected to these people; a couple I had never seen before. We were singing the universal language of Christianity. It was an awesome experience. At the end of the hymn they said, "Amen, Jesus, amen." They did not have to say more. We had communicated as fellow Christians. That day, like never before, I experienced the powerful meaning of the words "good tidings of great joy ... to <u>all</u> people." We were all one in Christ!

Yes, Christmas has a very personal message for all of us—especially to us Armenians. We are the first nation to embrace Christianity. We were the first to accept God's love and grace with our personal response. Christ is God's gift to <u>all</u> people. "For God so loved the world, that He gave His only begotten Son, that <u>whosoever</u> believeth in Him should not perish, but have everlasting life." (John 3:16) Christ was born not only to Mary and Joseph, but for all who would humbly receive Him into their hearts.

The real meaning of Christmas is indeed "good tidings of great joy ... to <u>all</u> <u>people</u>."

*H*ow do we define the Christmas spirit? Would it be the sound of familiar carols, a tree with twinkling lights, brightly wrapped packages, or just that good feeling we get at this time of year? Christmas is not about festive dishes, bells or Santa Claus. It is possible to have a perfectly happy Christmas without any of these. Christmas is not even about shepherds, angels and wise men. These lovely ingredients are but the "wrapping paper" in which God sent His amazing gift. I'm sure we all agree that it wouldn't be right to make more of a fuss over the wrapping paper than over its contents. Christmas is about God's precious gift to us of His Son Jesus Christ. Without Christ we can have all the mid-winter festivities and celebrations, but it won't be—and it can't be—CHRISTmas.

We give gifts to loved ones at Christmas, and most of us struggle in the decision-making process. What shall I give her? What does he like or need, etc.? God had no such problem when He gave us His Christmas gift. He knew exactly what we didn't have, and what we desperately needed. He gave us what we could never have on our own unless He gave us that gift.

Without a Savior we could not make ourselves acceptable to a Holy God. Morally, we can change our life-style and behavior, but spiritually, it is not possible. Therefore, God gave us what we needed—His Son Jesus Christ. Unfortunately many people choose not to receive the "Gift." These same individuals love the "wrappings" of the Christmas story, but reject the precious Gift—the Savior.

It is wonderful to celebrate all the season's festivities if Christ is kept uppermost in our lives. He is, after all, the reason for the season. We can celebrate His birth, sing carols, gather with family and friends, and even make shopping an occasion for thankfulness, remembering God's goodness. This Christmas, whether we give a simple hand-made gift or something more extravagant to our loved ones, the key is to give of ourselves with the gift. If we begin the spirit of Christmas with love, it will make a difference in the lives of all those we come into contact with. That is one ingredient of the spirit of Christmas.

In Phil. 2:4 – 11, St. Paul describes how the God of heaven and earth lay aside His divine glory and entered our planet, becoming our servant. He urges us to duplicate that same attitude and humble ourselves in service to others. That also is the spirit of Christmas. And it should not end with the season, but practiced throughout the year in all that we do.

But the true meaning of Christmas is CHRIST. It is the best news and the best gift ever given to us. God became one of us that we might live spiritually forever with Him. Christ is the reason for the joyous season.

*T*he joy and blessings of Christmas depend on how we respond to the Christ child born in Bethlehem over 2,000 years ago. As we read about Christ's birth in the Gospels of Matthew and Luke, we see at least three ways individuals responded to Him.

One response was given by the innkeeper when Mary and Joseph were looking for a room. The innkeeper was not angry or opposed to them—he was just very busy with a crowded inn. He was apathetic and preoccupied. There was no room in his inn. No vacancy!

This is the response that so many give today. Just like the innkeeper in Bethlehem, they simply have no room for Christ. All the accommodations in their hearts are reserved by many other overwhelming interests. This kind of response is not atheism. It is simply indifference; a belief that they can do just as well without Christianity.

Another response was given by King Herod. His reaction was one of hostility and opposition. Since his royal title was not genuine, Herod constantly worried about losing his position. When he heard from the wise men about their search for the "new king," he planned to locate and kill the child before He could become a threat to his throne (Mt. 2:1, 2).

In many parts of the world, this attitude still exists. The world objects to a reigning, life-changing Christ. Perhaps He is a threat to their way of life.

But another response was totally different from the previous two. It came from an elderly, devout man in the temple whose name was Simeon. He had been promised by God's Spirit that he would see the Messiah before he died. Simeon immediately recognized the infant as the promised Messiah when Mary and Joseph presented Jesus at the temple. He held the infant in his arms, and praised God saying: "Sovereign Lord, as You have promised, You now dismiss Your servant in peace. For my eyes have seen Your salvation, which You have prepared in the sight of all people." (Luke 2:29, 30)

Simeon's response was one of devotion and deep faith. This is the response of all faithful. Over the centuries, millions have found a new life of forgiveness and peace with God, through faith in Jesus Christ. They have found room in their hearts for Him.

Yes, true joy and blessings of Christmas are tied to our response to Christ. We read in John 1:12, "To all who received Him, to those who believed in His name, He gave the right to become children of God." Membership in Christ's family! Citizenship in His Kingdom! What a precious gift!

*W*hen the angel proclaimed the birth of Christ to the shepherds, the importance of His coming was emphasized. "Fear not, for behold, I bring you good tidings of great joy which shall be to all people" (Luke 2:10). Most of us hear about "great joy" and relish the season as we decorate our homes, shop in cheerful malls, attend festive parties and exchange gifts with loved ones. In our busyness however, we often miss the wonder of what Christmas is all about.

Christmas begins with Christ; a gift given to humanity over 2000 years ago. A child was born in a stable in Bethlehem and laid in a manger. His birth was announced by wise men from the east guided by a very special star. It was a gift we needed most; a Savior, the Holy Son of God.

Christmas is a vivid demonstration of God's love for us. Jesus Christ was God's love gift to the world, that we might live through Him. Why was God's gift of a Savior so important? There was an urgent need for the Messiah. God's creation, mankind, had become estranged from its Creator. Therefore, "when the fullness of time had come, God sent forth His Son..." (Gal. 4:4). Not only was the need great, but the gift was also great! In the manger in Bethlehem hope was born into the world, for the Son of God "became flesh and dwelt among us" (John 1:14).

More than twenty centuries have come and gone, and today the risen Christ is still the central figure of the human race. His birth divides history into two eras. One day of every week is set aside in remembrance of Him. And the two most important holidays we celebrate are His birth and His resurrection. On church steeples around the world His cross has become the symbol of victory over death. This one man's life has provided the theme for more songs, books, poems and paintings than any other person or event in history. All the armies that ever marched, all the navies that ever sailed, all the governments that ever governed, all the kings that ever reigned, have not changed the course of history as much as this one single life.

Over the centuries millions have found a new life of forgiveness, love and peace with God, through faith in Jesus Christ. He came for each one of us. He gave His life to bridge the gap between a Holy God and imperfect man!

During this Christmas season let us refocus our attention on the true meaning of His birth. The most important part of the word Christmas, is the first six letters—CHRIST!

A Blessed Christmas and a Happy New Year to you all!

*I*f we were to go to the corner of Hollywood and Vine and randomly ask ten individuals, "How many wise men visited Jesus?" Most of them would probably say three. Yet, the Bible doesn't give us a number. How then, have we been led to believe that there were three Magi? Tradition has portrayed them as three because of the three gifts they presented to Jesus; gold, frankincense and myrrh. It is also believed that the wise men didn't travel alone, as we see them depicted in Christmas cards, but with an entourage of servants and others for protection from desert bandits. They were from the East, which could mean Arabia, Mesopotamia or elsewhere, and were learned men who had studied the stars and planets. They were probably Gentiles, since they didn't know scriptural prophesy concerning the location of the Messiah's birth (Micah 5:2). They came guided by the bright Star to Jerusalem, capital of Judea, and asked King Herod about the newborn King of the Jews.

King Herod was disturbed. He was a non-Jew (Idumaean) who was appointed king over Judea by the Romans. He was also hated by the Jews. Not knowing what the Magi were talking about, Herod called all the Jewish chief priests, asking them where the Messiah would be born. "According to scripture prophesy, in the town of Bethlehem, in Judea," they answered. This troubled Herod even more. He called the Magi back and gave them the information. Bethlehem was five miles south. He then instructed them, that when they find the child, to let him know so that he could also go and worship Him. The Jewish priests were indifferent.

As the Magi parted, happily they saw the Star once again leading them to where Jesus was. Entering the house, they saw the child with His mother Mary, and bowed down and worshiped Him, and presented their valuable gifts to Him. Also, having been warned in a dream not to go back to Herod, the Magi returned home by another route. The wise men found Jesus with Mary, not in the manger, but in a house (Matt. 2:11). It is believed that the child was about a year old or so by now.

The three gifts presented to Jesus have symbolic meaning: gold, a gift worthy of a king; frankincense, a gift for deity; and myrrh, an aromatic spice used for embalming or anointing the deceased (Mark 16:1 and John 19:40). From the cradle to the cross, Christ's purpose on earth was to minister and to die; God's gift to us all for eternal life!

The greatest story ever written is the birth of Christ. Today, over 2,000 years later, we can still learn from these past events. It is truly sad that some people today still look for Jesus in the wrong places. They need the illuminating light and guidance of His Star found in His timeless Word. After finding Christ, our lives must take a different direction, one that is responsive to God's will and obedient to His Word. One thing is certain, that wise men and women still seek Him. Wise men and women still go the extra mile to meet Jesus. Wise men and women still worship Him because He is the perfect, just, and Almighty Creator of the universe. And wise men and women still give Him their very best!

*W*e don't often read that Jesus had "marveled." Yet, the Bible says He marveled at a centurion's faith. A centurion was a career military officer in the Roman army in charge of 100 soldiers. At that time Palestine had been under Roman control for about a hundred years. Roman officers were generally cruel, and despised by Jews. But some of them, influenced by Jewish religion, were good men. This centurion identified in Mt. 8:5 – 13, who is also mentioned in Lk. 7, was a kind person. He liked the Jewish nation and was personally responsible for building the local synagogue (Lk. 7:5) in which Jesus often talked and healed infirmities.

As Jesus entered Capernaum, this centurion came pleading to Him, saying, "Lord, my servant is lying at home paralyzed, dreadfully tormented." This centurion's tender concern for a lowly servant was contrary to the reputation of Roman officers in Israel.

It is interesting that the centurion's plea to Jesus was not to heal a member of his family, but his servant, who most likely was a Jew. Servants didn't count for much in those days, and besides, this centurion had many. What difference would it have made if he had one less? But NO! He came begging to Jesus for help. Also, the centurion could have let many obstacles stand between him and Jesus, such as pride, doubt, language, race, power and time. But he didn't. He humbly came to Jesus.

Jesus said to him, "I will come and heal him." The centurion answered, "Lord, I am not worthy that You should come under my roof. But only speak a word, and my servant will be healed. For I also am a man under authority, having soldiers under me. And I say to this one 'Go,' and he goes, and to another, 'Come,' and he comes…" When Jesus heard it, He marveled at the faith of this centurion—a Gentile, a foreigner—and said to those following Him, "Assuredly, I say to you, I have not found such great faith, not even in Israel!" Then Jesus turned to the centurion and said, "Go your way; and as you have believed, so let it be done for you." And his servant was healed that same hour!

Jesus didn't need to be present to heal. This hated Gentile officer's faith put to shame the Jews—His own people. The centurion was familiar with authority exercised at a distance. If a lesser officer can give orders, certainly Christ, Who possesses all divine authority, could. Jesus' message is for everyone. It is universal. Each individual has to choose to accept or reject the gospel. No one can become part of God's kingdom on the basis of heritage. Having a Christian family is a blessing, but it won't guarantee us eternal life. We must each believe and have faith in Christ. The Bible says, "Without faith it is impossible to please God" (Heb. 11:6).

Christ says, "I am the Way, the Truth, and the Life. No one comes to the Father except through Me" (Jn. 14:16). As the Way, He is our path to the Father. As the Truth, He is the reality of all God's promises. As the Life, He joins His divine life to ours through His Holy Spirit, both now and eternally. The centurion by faith recognized God's message for mankind. That same message is for each of us today.

*W*hich day of the year do children wake up early? Christmas morning, of course, to open their presents. As they go to bed on Christmas Eve, they wait with anticipation the excitement of the following day, knowing that their parents would give them something special.

Perhaps our childhood was similar to that. But how did we wake up this morning? What would our attitude be if we viewed each day as a gift from our loving Heavenly Father? Perhaps that is what the psalmist had in mind when he wrote, "This is the day the Lord has made; we will rejoice and be glad in it" (Psalm 118:24).

There are days, however, when the last thing we want to do is rejoice. We feel gloomy, our circumstances might seem out of hand, and our sorrow overwhelming. Then we can relate to the writers of some of the sad psalms. But no matter how sad the psalmists felt, they were always honest with God. As they talked to Him, their prayers ended with praise.

When we don't feel like rejoicing, we can do the same. We will then find out that God will give us a reason to rejoice. He has given us this day to serve Him—let us then be glad in it. Each new day is sacred; a rare and precious gift from God. A new day brings with it another opportunity to start all over with a joyful attitude and a glad heart. We must not take it for granted that we are alive, and that the earth still turns on its axis, and that a new day arrives every 24 hours! Celebrating each new day helps us develop the ability to be grateful for all new moments, with God in each one of them.

What is our alternative? If we are not thankful, we become bitter. If we are not content, we become rebellious. By this we indicate that God is not trustworthy, and that He doesn't desire our well-being. But if we were to compare these conclusions with Scripture, we would discover how wrong we are! God's Word instructs us that He is majestically in control of all our circumstances. "And we know that in all things God works for the good for those who love Him, who have been called according to His purpose" (Rom. 8:28).

The same God Who formed the world in six days knows every hair on our heads. The same God sent His only Son to this earth to die on the cross to redeem each one of us! God's love for His children is not determined by the circumstances in our lives. His love is steadfast. If we truly believe that each day is a special gift from God, we would be like children on Christmas every morning of the year! So let us then make every effort to repeat the following beautiful verse during each day in the new year: "This is the day the Lord has made; we will rejoice and be glad in it!"

*T*housands of immigrants nationwide are expected to become American citizens again this year. Here in Los Angeles, the candidates take the oath of citizenship, usually during a mass swearing-in ceremony in the Convention Center. A few years ago I had seen a photo in the L.A. Times taken immediately after the ceremony of some 14,000 people. The new citizens were from more than 100 nations worldwide, a diverse gathering, even by today's Los Angeles standards. Many were euphoric, some teary eyed, others solemn. Most held a small American flag provided for the occasion. Someone had made the statement that they felt more American than those who were born here. "We are Americans by choice—by conviction!" one added with pride. The joy of accomplishment was truly evident on their faces.

I felt their joy and pride remembering my personal experience many years ago. Not having any prior citizenship (all Armenians born in or emigrated to Greece were considered "neutral"), I felt so overwhelmed to be accepted and adopted by the best and greatest country in the world, with all the rights and privileges of an American born citizen (except to be president). Even after 44 years, I still find it incredible, and the subject always brings tears to my eyes.

As Christians, however, we have a dual citizenship. We are citizens of this world, no matter what nation we live in, and as followers of Christ, we are also citizens of heaven. We have all the rights and privileges, as well as responsibilities that accompany being a child of God. The Apostle Paul writes in Eph. 2:19, 20: "Now, therefore, you are no longer strangers and foreigners, but fellow citizens with the saints and members of the household of God, having been built on the foundation of the apostles and prophets, Jesus Christ Himself being the chief cornerstone..."

What a comforting thought for Christians! Built on the foundations of the apostles and prophets means that the Church is not built on modern ideas, but rather on the spiritual heritage given to us by the early apostles and prophets of the Christian church.

Although born in Tarsus in Asia Minor, St. Paul had the same rights and privileges as the citizens of Rome because he was a Roman citizen. Likewise as Christians, we will one day experience all the special privileges of our heavenly citizenship because we belong to Christ. The Kingdom of God is international. This citizenship is not associated with any nation on earth. Its identity does not display any skin color, race or nationality. We are citizens of God's Kingdom, and Christ is our King!

Sometimes our dual citizenship might present us with a crucial choice. With whose "flag" will we identify? If as Christians we continue to give allegiance to our Heavenly Father and live a life that brings honor and glory to His Name, we won't have to be concerned about anything. When the watching world sees that we are marching under the "flag" of the King of kings and Lord of lords, our dual citizenship will remain spotless!

*A*lthough some farmers may be shoveling snow in parts of the country during winter months, others may be enjoying the warmth of a fireplace, and those in California may even be playing some golf. But regardless of their leisure time now, they all think ahead, anticipating spring planting. They know that if they want to plant, the soil must first be broken. Even the most productive land needs to be turned over, tilled, and the right fertilizers spread to get the earth ready for seed. Farmers know that the better they prepare in the spring, the better their harvest will be.

Jesus used that kind of word picture in the parable of the sower, which is repeated in three gospels. The sower represents the pastor, or those who teach and preach the Word of God. The seed is the Word, and the soil is the human heart.

In those days, seeds were spread by hand, which by its nature resulted in some of it being scattered on unproductive ground. Jesus identifies four kinds of soil in this parable. Some seeds fell along the path, landed on hard soil, were eaten by birds and lost. That represents the hard heart. Other seeds fell on rocky soil and took no root. That represents the shallow heart. Some other seeds fell on thorny soil that choked the seeds, and they bore no fruit. That represents the worldly heart—fertile but possessed by other interests. And finally, some seeds fell on good soil that received the seeds, grew and produced a crop, multiplying hundreds of times (Matthew 13:23). This is the receptive, understanding heart

It is amazing that only one fourth of the soil in the parable was ready for the seed, and brought forth fruit! Only one fourth of the hearts were ready to receive the Word of God and be productive! The rest of the hearts had no room in their lives for God.

What kind of "soil" are we? What is the condition of our hearts? Has God's Word taken root in our lives? Are our hearts prepared, cultivated to receive the seeds of God's Word, or are there hindrances that keep us from maturing and bearing fruit in His service? We must give our best to God. He gave His best to us—His only begotten Son (Jn. 3:16). Christ's presence demands decision. The test of a true child of God is perseverance. As we follow Christ, our values, morals, goals and purpose in life perhaps may set us apart from certain groups. But our commitment to God should come first.

The parable of the sower teaches us that the gospel won't be received with equal effect by everyone. But when it takes root, God's Word will produce fruit in the lives of the faithful in His service. Faith in God can't be made to follow a mathematical formula. Rather, it is a miracle of God's Holy Spirit, which through His Word, leads others into His family.

Spiritual growth occurs when faith is cultivated. "Faith comes by hearing, and hearing by the Word of God" (Rom. 10:17). Attending church each Sunday cultivates our faith. How much fruit we'll harvest depends on how well we prepare and cultivate the soil.

*T*he Christmas holidays have come and gone. Now that the decorations have come down and ornaments and lights are packed away in boxes, let us not store away our Christmas spirit along with them. "Silent Night" will be silent for another year, but our personal relationship with Christ knows no season. He is our Lord, the same yesterday, today and forever. His plan for us never changes.

When we take a moment to think of the happiness or satisfaction a few material gifts have brought into our lives during the past Christmas season, we realize how transitory and temporary that happiness can be. We soon realize, perhaps to our surprise, that the happiness often fades away even before the Christmas lights and decorations are down.

In this coming new year, let us celebrate the excitement of His presence in our lives daily. Christ says in John 8:12, "I am the light of the world. He who follows Me shall not walk in darkness, but have the light of life." Christ is the spiritual light of the world, our eternal gift from God. He is the creator of life, and spiritual light for mankind.

In His light we see ourselves just as we really are. When we follow Christ, the true light, we don't walk blindly, falling into darkness. He lights the path ahead of us and removes all darkness of sin from our lives so we can live God-honoring, God-pleasing lives. All spiritual illumination comes from Christ. As Christians and as His representatives on earth, we are to be Christ's light bearers, letting His light shine through us. Darkness or evil never has and never will extinguish the light of Christ.

All Christmas lights, small or large, are taken down and stored away for another year. The light of the world, Jesus Christ, will shine forever in the hearts of all faithful. As we allow the glowing light of Christ to shine into our lives, others will see Christ in our actions. He is the light of the world, the one who promises wonderful hope for all mankind. Therefore, Christ instructs us, "Let you light so shine before men that they may see your good works and glorify your Father which is in heaven" (Matt. 5:16). This is the purpose of all good works among men—to glorify our Heavenly Father.